Interpreting Christian Art

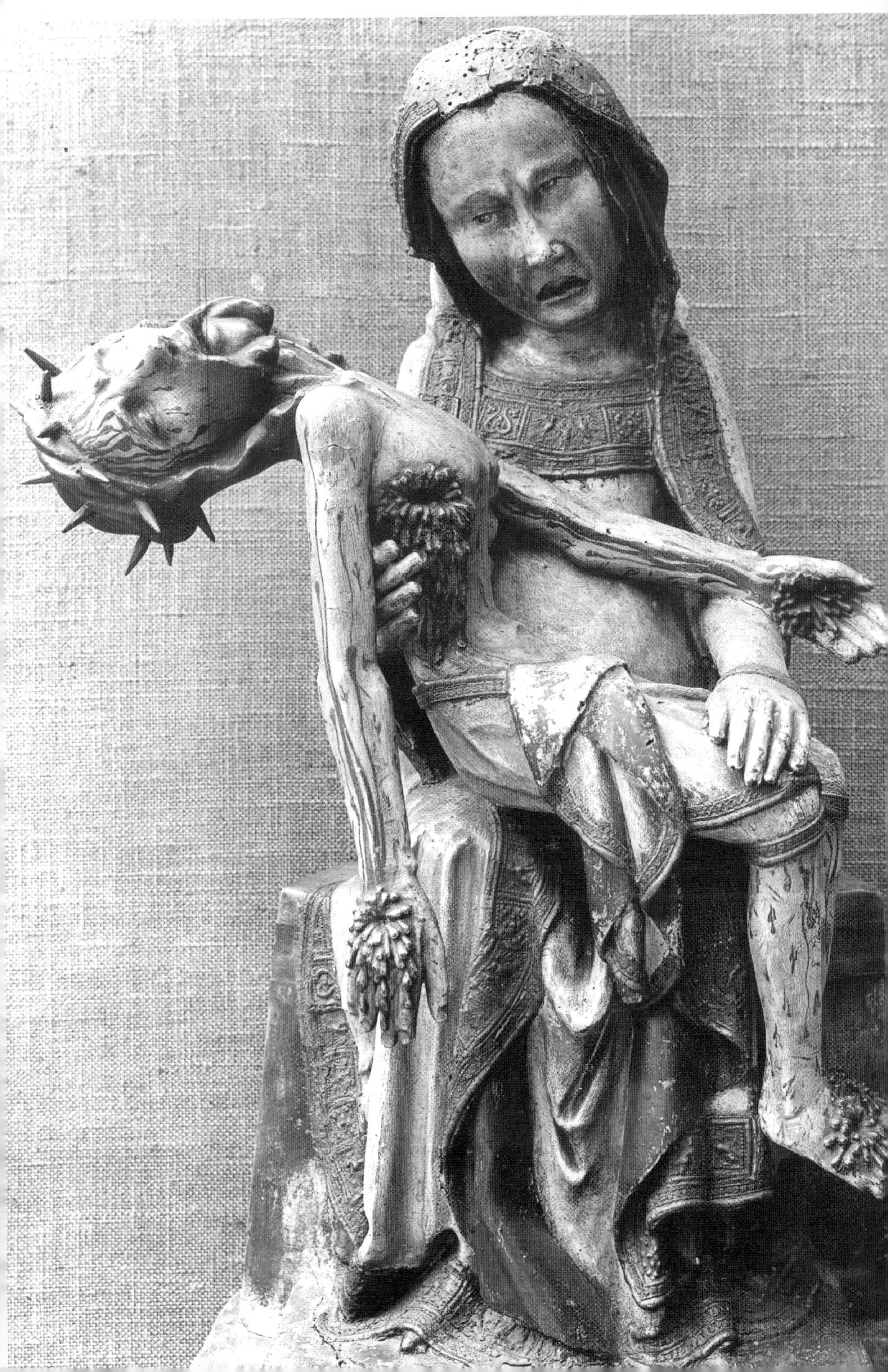

Interpreting Christian Art

REFLECTIONS ON CHRISTIAN ART

Heidi J. Hornik and Mikeal C. Parsons, Editors

MERCER UNIVERSITY PRESS • MACON, GEORGIA • 2003

ISBN 0-86554-850-1
MUP/H641

First Edition.

Book design by Burt & Burt Studio

Library of Congress Cataloging-in-Publication Data

Interpreting Christian art / edited by Heidi J. Hornik and Mikeal C. Parsons.— 1st ed.
p. cm.
Includes bibliographical references and index.
ISBN 0-86554-850-1 (alk. paper)
1. Christian art and symbolism. I. Hornik, Heidi J., 1962- II. Parsons, Mikeal Carl, 1957-
BV150.I58 2003
246—dc22

2003016021

Contents

Preface

Baylor University sponsored a conference on the general theme of "Interpreting Christian Art," under the auspices of the Pruit Memorial Symposium on 26–28 October 2000. The symposium was co-directed by Dr. Heidi J. Hornik, associate professor of art history, and Dr. Michael Beaty, professor of philosophy and director of the Institute for Faith and Learning. The Pruit Memorial Symposium Endowment Fund was established in 1996 by Lev H. and Ella Wall Prichard of Corpus Christi, Texas. The symposium is intended to be an annual event that will bring the perspectives of the Christian intellectual community to bear on issues of common concern. The symposium is charged to deal with "issues of the day from both a Christian and a Baptist perspective and shall contribute to a world view that distinctly represents the free church traditions of Protestantism." The vast majority of the essays collected in this volume were presented at the symposium.

Art and church historians, theologians, and biblical scholars—all with deep interests in the visual aspects of the Christian tradition—were brought together to engage in the task of identifying and interpreting Christian art. Two presentations, by Margaret Miles and John Cook, were intended to frame the discussion by providing historical overviews of the issues involved in appropriating the visual arts in contemporary communities of faith. The other presentations aimed at close analyses of specific examples of art from particular historical periods: early Christian (R. Jensen, Snyder), Byzantine (Cutler, Barber), Renaissance (W. Jensen, Hornik and Parsons), and Baroque (Berdini). Such textured analyses represent a viable and fruitful alternative to the kind of vague generalizations about art that often characterize interdisciplinary efforts to join religion and the arts.

Recovering the visual aspect of the Christian tradition for Protestants, and especially for heirs of the radical Reformation (Baptists, for example), was an important sub-theme of the conference and also this volume. While not all of the authors explicitly address this issue, the cumulative effect of the papers is to draw attention to the rich, but often neglected, resources that Christian art has to offer to contemporary reflection.

We would like to take this opportunity to thank several individuals who helped bring these papers to press. Those associated with the Pruit Symposium—especially Mr. and Mrs. Prichard, Dr. Donald Schmeltekopf, and Dr. Michael Beaty—are due a special thanks. Thanks also to the Lilly-funded Horizons Grant Program, administered by Baylor's Institute for Faith and Learning, for a generous grant that helped defray the expenses associated with the production and copyrights of the images included in the volume. Dr. Wallace Daniel, dean of the College of Arts and Sciences, provided timely assistance in terms of release time and research funds necessary to complete this volume. We also wish to acknowledge the support of the College of Arts and Sciences Sabbatical, University Research, and Allbritton Grant for Faculty Scholarship committees of Baylor University. Finally, gratitude is expressed to our respective chairs, Professor John McClanahan, chair of the art department, Dr. Randall O'Brien, chair of the religion department, our president, Dr. Robert B. Sloan, and provost, David Lyle Jeffrey, for their tireless and enthusiastic support of our research.

Heidi J. Hornik
Mikeal C. Parsons
Baylor University
Waco, Texas

1.

Achieving the Christian Body: Visual Incentives to Imitation of Christ in the Christian West

Margaret R. Miles

Graduate Theological Union, professor emerita

"And the Word was made flesh, and dwelt among us…
full of grace and truth." (1 John 1:14)

My 1988 book, *Practicing Christianity*, explores the instructions in living the Christian life to which most historical Christians had access.[1] My primary sources were the popular devotional manuals of the history of Christianity from the earliest extant catechetical instructions to early modern printed bestsellers like John Bunyan's *Pilgrim's Progress* and Thomas à Kempis's *The Imitation of Christ*. Theological texts, preferentially studied by modern historical theologians, were not often read by (or to) popular audiences and thus cannot tell us much about most people's Christianity.

[1] Margaret R. Miles, *Practicing Christianity: Critical Perspectives for an Embodied Spirituality* (New York: Crossroad, 1989); see also my article, "Image," *Critical Terms in Religious Studies*, ed. Mark C. Taylor (Chicago: University of Chicago, 1998) 160–72.

[2] Michel de Certeau, *The Practice of Everyday Life*, trans. Steven Rendall (Berkeley: University of California, 1984).

Religious paintings do not offer an exact parallel to the distinction between popular devotional manuals and theological treatises. Until the Renaissance there was usually no clear distinction between art works known only (or primarily) to an educated elite and those that were publicly accessible. Religious paintings were seen *in situ*, that is, in the churches that commissioned them and placed them in the liturgical context that directed their interpretation.

My question, however, remains the same when I explore images from the Christian West as when I examined devotional manuals: How were most people—whole communities—instructed in the practice of Christianity? What were the primary metaphors that guided them? To these questions, both texts and religious images answer unequivocally: The Christian life is to be practiced by imitating Christ.

Physical participation has always been an explicit priority in Christian communities. It has been recognized from the earliest Christian movement that the religion of the incarnation cannot be practiced as isolated contemplation. Presence at ritual gatherings, catechetical exercises involving fasting and abstinence from sex, naked baptism, and eating the communal eucharistic foods—these practices defined Christians perhaps even more than their beliefs. Beliefs that are not embodied in images and practices remain abstract, un*realized*.[2] Theological texts may instruct, but they cannot concretely depict imitation of Christ. And for purposes of devotion, the issue is always how to make vivid, to translate into practices, to weave into lifestyle, and to freshen traditional instructions. Moreover, we need to look beyond theological texts if we seek to understand the historical appropriation of the doctrine of incarnation. In texts from Paul forward, "the flesh" has been used as a synecdoche for sin's agenda. Quite the opposite is found in Christian art, which consistently and insistently made the point that Christianity is the religion of the Word made flesh.

More than 1,000 years separate the first textual advocacy of imitation of Christ and detailed articulation, in devotional manuals and paintings, of how this could be done. In late antiquity, in order to participate in a scriptural event, a pilgrim had to undergo arduous travel to a holy site or a holy person.[3] Until religious paintings articulated and fleshed out what it might look and feel like to imitate Christ, imitation of Christ was accessible primarily to pilgrims and monks. By the fourteenth century, however, Christian pictures represented bodies whose postures, gestures, size, physical characteristics, and weight are directed by religious values. Moreover, the effectiveness of devotional practices requires an integration of the familiar and the spiritual. For this purpose, images have been considered critical to devotional life by generations of Christians.

In the fourteenth and fifteenth centuries, thanks to new materials, styles, and subjects of painting, imitation of Christ became a vivid popular topic. This essay will explore this theme as it was described verbally and visually in late medieval and early modern popular devotion. I will first sketch its theological origins, the essential background for its new visual representation at the end of medieval Christianity.[4] Then it will be necessary to ask how Christians who used images thought about the role of images in religious life. Finally, my interest in the resources of historical Christianity is not purely historical; I will conclude by asking if the concept of imitation of Christ is still a useful one for Christians, and whether American culture provides adequate symbolic resources for the present-day practice of Christianity.

THEOLOGY

Theology deals with concepts, not experiences. But concepts direct experience. Thus it is important to consider not merely the images that accompanied worship in the fourteenth and fifteenth centuries, but also to reconstruct what people thought they were doing when they contemplated an image in the context of worship.

The theology surrounding imitation of Christ rests on two bases: first, belief in the incarnation of God as a human being, and second, the scripturally-based belief that humans are made in God's image. One of the earliest Christian controversies, between gnostics and incarnationist Christians, argued over whether Christian "spirituality" could simply ignore human bodies as unredeemable and biodegradable. In the second century, Irenaeus, who has been called the first systematic theologian, marshaled the doctrines of Christian faith to refute gnostic claims that Jesus had come to earth solely as a spirit in

---

[3] Georgia Frank, *The Memory of the Eyes: Pilgrims to Living Saints in Christian Late Antiquity* (Berkeley: University of California, 2000).

[4] Historical religious images representing imitation of Christ predate the Protestant reformations of the sixteenth century. Yet these images belong to the history of Christianity to which both Protestants and Roman Catholics are heirs. When Protestants insist that their origins lie in the sixteenth century and that nothing prior to that time can be considered useful, it is, I believe, a sad rejection of valuable and needed resources. All Christian traditions begin with the incarnation of the founder and exemplar Jesus of Nazareth.

[5]Irenaeus, *Against the Heresies* 5.14.2.

[6]Athanasius, *On the Incarnation of the Word*, in *Christology of the Later Fathers*, ed. Edward Hardy, Library of Christian Classics series (Philadelphia: Westminster Press, 1954) 68.

[7]Gregory of Nyssa distinguished between attributes of Christ that can be imitated and those that must simply be worshiped: "The marks of the true Christian are all those we know in connection with Christ. Those that we have capacity for we imitate, and those which our nature does not approximate by imitation, we reverence and worship. Thus, it is necessary for the Christian life to illustrate all the interpretive terms signifying Christ, some through imitation, others through worship." *On Perfection*, vol. 58 of Fathers of the Church series, trans. Virginia Woods Callahan (Washington, DC: Catholic University of America, 1967) 99.

order to save the human spirit. He wrote: "For if the flesh were not in a position to be saved, the Word of God would in no way have become flesh…. But now…the Word has saved that which really was created: humanity which had perished…but the thing which had perished possessed flesh and blood; he had himself, therefore, flesh and blood."[5] The result of the conflict has been called the triumph of the incarnation. By the third century, Christian orthodoxy came to be measured by affirmation of the real body—the real human birth, life, suffering, and death of Jesus Christ.

The second theological basis for imitation of Christ is the claim that human beings are created in God's image and likeness (Gen 1:26). God's image is built-in, indestructible, a lifelong characteristic of human beings, theologians said. Likeness to God, however, was lost in the sin of Adam and Eve. Although the image of God cannot be completely lost, neither can it be developed without divine help due to the image's badly warped condition, the result of human sin. To illustrate, Athanasius used the metaphor of a damaged and defaced painting:

> For as, when a likeness painted on a panel has been effaced by stains from without, he whose likeness it is must needs come once more to enable the portrait to be renewed on the same wood, for, for the sake of the picture, even the mere wood on which it is painted is not thrown away, but the outline is renewed upon it; in the same way also the most holy Son of the Father, being the image of the Father, came to our region to renew man, once made in his likeness, and find him, as one lost, by the remission of sins.[6]

If humanity was made in God's image, then the actualization of human nature lies in developing this similarity to the divine.

It is by imitation of Christ, the perfect reflection of God, that Christians can become an "image of the image." Theology takes us this far, but some important questions remain. How, precisely, is this to be accomplished? Paul's injunctions to imitation of Christ are remarkably unspecific: "Be ye therefore followers of God as dear children" (Eph 5:1), and "Be ye followers of me even as I also am of Christ" (1 Cor 11:1).[7] To answer these questions we will need to examine the visual images that, together with devotional manuals, interpreted the theology of imitation. First, however, we must consider some important historical understandings of the role of images in the practice of Christianity.

IMAGE

Because North Americans' experience of images in a media culture is so different from that of historical Christians, we must note an ancient distinction between two kinds of images. The first kind can be illustrated by a painting. When the painting has been completed, the painted scene or model need not any longer be present for viewers to see the image. In fact, the painting often functions to inform or remind its viewer of the absence of the model. The second kind of image is exemplified by the image reflected in a mirror or a pool of water. For the image to be visible, the original's continuous presence is mandatory. The image fades instantly when the original disappears. Human beings, as image of God, are the second kind of image. However, in the case of human beings, even in the ongoing presence of the original—God—the pool may be clouded by dirt. Or the mirror may, like ancient mirrors, be nothing more than a polished piece of metal, which yields a nearly indecipherable reflection.[8]

In addition, an ancient assumption about the act of seeing is important for an accurate understanding of the relationship between seeing and imitating. Plato described the act of seeing as performed by a visual ray projected by the fire that warms and animates the body and is at its most intense in the eyes. The ray, initiated by the viewer, creates vision when it touches its object. Unlike modern theories of vision, which emphasize a necessary distance between viewer and object, visual ray theory emphasized direct contact of viewer and object through the touch of the visual ray. Moreover, the visual ray is a two-way street along which the object travels back to the viewer and is imprinted and stored in memory. This theory of vision emphasizes the activity of the viewer. The object does not "catch the eye," as in modern theories of vision; rather, the eye catches the object. What is significant for my argument is the quasiphysical contact of viewer and object posited by visual ray theory. Augustine, who accepted visual ray

[8]Carol Harrison, *Beauty and Revelation in the Thought of St. Augustine* (London: Oxford University Press, 1992) 1.

[9] Augustine *De doctrina christiana* 1.20.19.

[10] Richard Kiekhefer, "Major Currents in Late Medieval Devotion," *Christian Spirituality: High Middle Ages and Reformation*, ed. Jill Raitt (New York: Crossroad, 1987) 75–108.

[11] Ibid., 75. See also David Nirenberg, "The Historical Body of Christ," *The Body of Christ in the Art of Europe and New Spain 1150–1800*, ed. James Clifton (New York: Prestel, 1998).

[12] Quoted in E. Duffy, *The Stripping of the Altars: Traditional Religion in England 1400–1580* (New Haven CT: Yale, 1992) 237.

[13] Durandus of Mende, *Rationale divinorum officiorum* 3.4.

theory, said that the soul takes the shape of (*incipit configuari*) the objects of its attention and affection.[9]

If people think that in the act of intentional looking an irreversible bond is formed between viewer and object, they will have a different attitude toward the visual objects with which they engage than will people who are used to seeing images they think of as "entertainment." These theories of image and vision are critical to understanding the cultures in which imitation of Christ was pictured and presented to vision.

WESTERN LATE MEDIEVAL CHRISTIAN CULTURE

Historian Richard Kiekhefer has discussed the dramatic escalation of popular devotionalism in late medieval Christianity. The new interest, he writes, was based on "literary expression, artistic depiction," and new devotional practices.[10] It was also accompanied and inspired by new religious "paraphernalia"—paintings, statues, scented rosaries, and illustrated books of hours. New themes also appeared: the pieta, devotions to the sacred heart, the man of sorrows, and Corpus Christi. Kiekhefer writes: "This explosion of devotional forms unmistakably changed the tenor of Christian life."[11] In this new culture of devotion, paintings played a critical role. The fourteenth-century Carthusian monk, Ludolf of Saxony, wrote: "I know not for sure…how it is that you are sweeter in the heart of one who loves you in the form of flesh than as the Word.… It is sweeter to view you as dying…on a tree, than as holding sway over the angels in heaven, to see you as a man bearing every aspect of human nature to the end, than as God manifesting divine nature, to see you as the dying Redeemer than as the invisible Creator."[12]

Similarly, a fourteenth-century French theologian, Bishop Durandus of Mende, described the connection between images and devotion. Images, he said, "move the mind more than descriptions; for deeds are placed before the eyes in paintings and thus appear to be actually carrying on. But in description, the deed is done as it were by hearsay, which affects the mind less when recalled to memory. Hence, also, it is that in churches we pay less reverence to books than to images and to pictures."[13]

For both Durandus and Ludolf, the value of paintings lies in their ability to rouse feelings. Art historian David Freedberg has recently made the same point: "Imitation cannot take place without empathy; and empathy…can most effectively be aroused by real images."[14] Texts lack the immediate presence of images. But for the historian, texts are necessary too. Without their testimony she cannot claim, for example, that images incited to imitation.[15] Fortunately for my argument, fourteenth- and fifteenth-century texts are full of such claims.[16]

THE ART OF IMITATION

Consider now the questions that inform the art of imitation: First, who should be imitated? Sometimes readers of paintings and devotional texts are urged to imitate more contemporary exemplars who act as mediators or interpreters for imitation of Christ. Paul said, "Follow me as I follow Christ." We will find that fourteenth- and fifteenth-century exemplars were either Christ's first followers or more recent saints.

Theological texts also often leave unexamined the question of what features of Christ's life should be imitated. In devotional manuals and paintings, answers range widely. The most common features presented for imitation in the late medieval Christian West were Christ's suffering and passion. But at the same time that the West recognized the stigmata as the undeniable mark of sainthood (Figure 1), the Eastern churches believed that sainthood was exhibited by transfiguration (Figure 2). Saintly human beings, like Christ, were seen as bathed in light, thus "sharing the experience of Christ's glory."[17] Gregory Palamas wrote: "If the body is to partake with the soul in the ineffable benefits of the world to come, it is certain that it must participate in them as far as possible now…. For the body also has an experience of divine things when the passionate forces of the soul are not put to death but transformed and sanctified."[18]

These are wildly different interpretations of imitation of Christ. Common to them is the assumption that imitation of Christ will be somehow rendered visible in the imitator's body, the image of Christ's body. Christ's humanity, as evidenced by his human flesh, is a major theme of fourteenth- and fifteenth-century religious paintings. The

[14]David Freedberg, *The Power of Images: Studies in the History and Theory of Response*, (Chicago: University of Chicago, 1989) 174.

[15]The interdisciplinary study of religious images is relatively new to the disciplines of art history and religion. Until recently, art historians have focused their attention on the formal characteristics of an artwork and its place in a history of style, while scholars of religion have largely ignored religious images, using them occasionally only to illustrate a theological point. Most scholars, like myself, who examine religious images as historical evidence, were trained primarily in religion. At present, however, there are a number of scholars trained in art history who teach and publish both in art history and in religion. Working together to articulate and refine the burgeoning field of religion and art history, these scholars are achieving remarkable increments of precision and sophistication. My focus here is on the central role images played in creating and informing European religious cultures, that is, on images as historical evidence for the religious interests of late medieval people.

[16]The primary texts are Ludolph of Saxony's (d. 1378) *Life of Christ*; the anonymous fourteenth-century *Meditations on the Life of Christ*; Thomas à Kempis's (d. 1471) *Imitation of Christ*; and, as the terminus ad quem, Ignatius Loyola's sixteenth-century *Spiritual Exercises*.

[17]George Mantzaridis, "Spiritual Life in Palamism," *Christian Spirituality: High Middle Ages and Reformation*, ed. Jill Raitt (New York: Crossroad, 1987) 212.

[18]Gregory Palamas, *Homilies*, n.c.

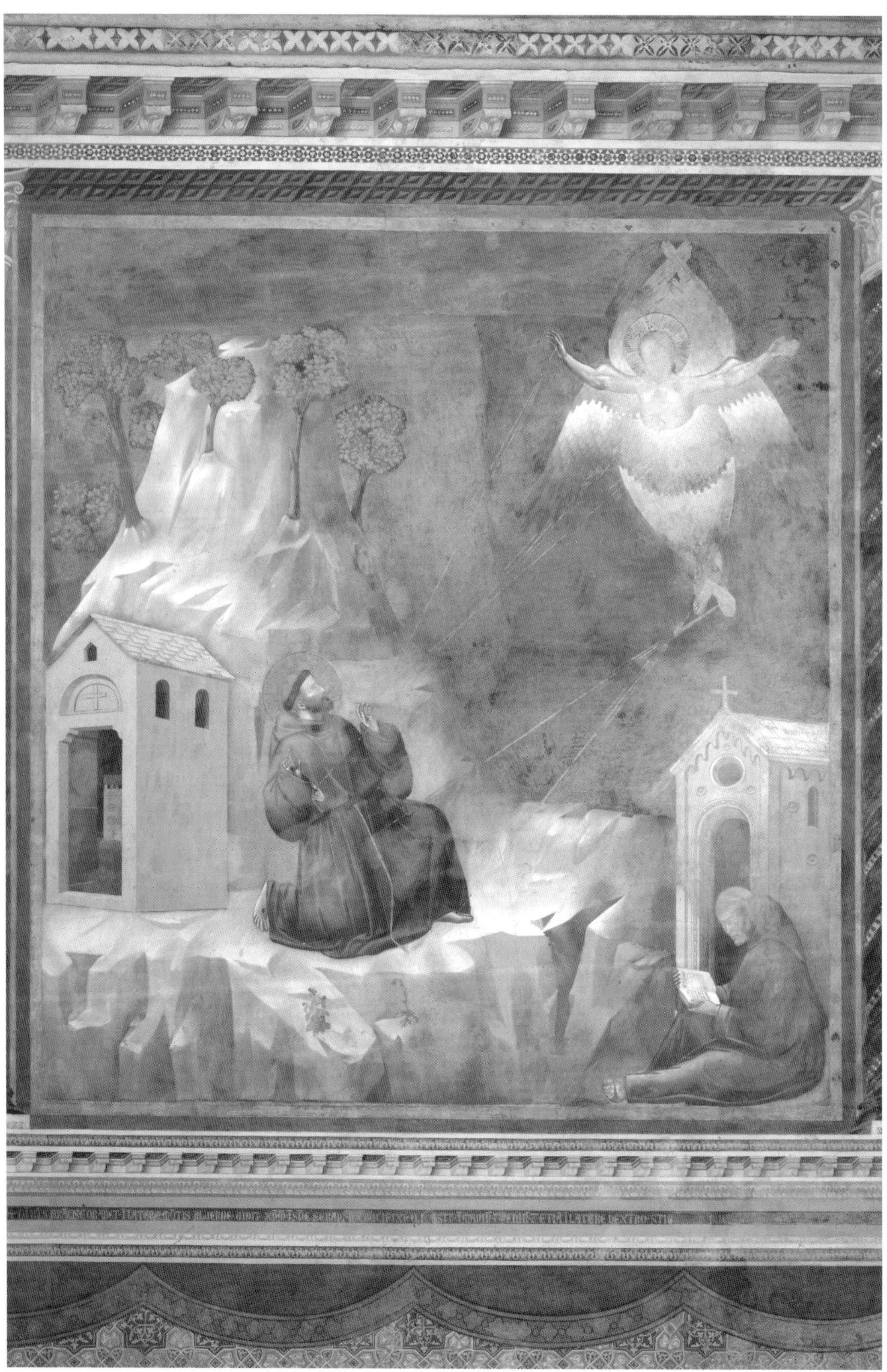

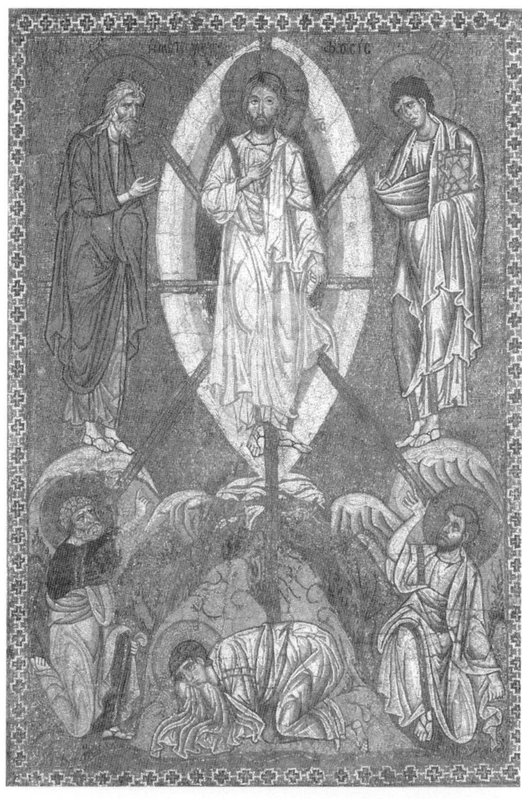

FIG 1. (Facing page) Giotto di Bondone, *St. Francis Receiving the Stigmata*, ca. 1292. Fresco. *in situ* (Upper basilica, San Francesco, Assisi.

FIG 2. (this page) *Transfiguration,* late twelfth century. Mosaic (guilded bronze, marble, lapis lazuli, glass, and wax on wood support. 52 X 36 cm (Louvre, Paris).

weakness and helplessness of the infant Christ, together with Christ's suffering vulnerability in crucifixion, deposition, and Man of Sorrows scenes show insistent visual fixation with Christ's human flesh.

Curiously, visual incentives to imitation of Christ largely neglect Christ's ministry years. The raising of Lazarus and the marriage of Cana are the two scenes most frequently depicted, but these scenes are far outnumbered, at the Scrovegni Chapel, Padua, for example, by apocryphal scenes depicting Mary's betrothal, Christ's birth and infancy, and the events of his passion.

Christ's interior life is depicted in scenes derived from scriptural accounts of his soul-searching in the garden of Gethsemane. Features of his life that do not focus on his flesh—his teaching, preaching, and even his healing miracles—are also less frequently imaged in the West. By contrast, Eastern Orthodox feast cycles offer communal and liturgical imitations of Christ. By participating in the events of Christ's life through the cycle of the liturgical year, Eastern Christians act out imitation of Christ.

FIG 4.
Cimabue, *Madonna Enthroned,* ca. 1280.
egg tempura on panel, 460 X 263 cm
(Uffizi, Florence).

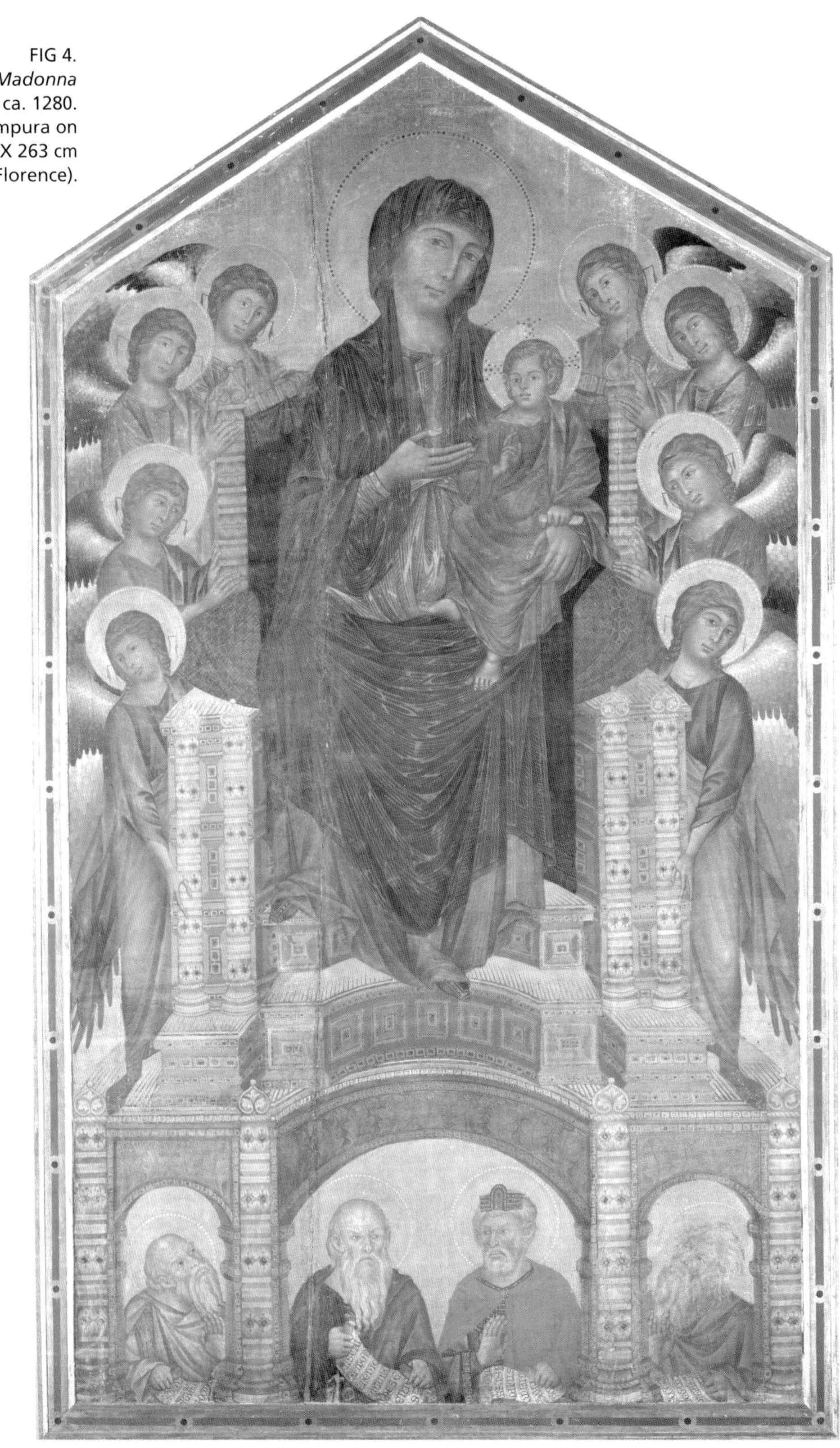

How did religious painting facilitate imitation of Christ? In her book, *Moving Pictures*, art historian Ann Hollander makes a useful distinction between painted narrative sequences and posed scenes. She brilliantly demonstrates that, beginning in the fourteenth century, many paintings exhibited "proto-cinematic" qualities and effects. In other words, they were meant to be seen as "moving pictures." Narrative sequences, she writes, are snapshots of an unfolding event. The viewer understands that the depicted action was different seconds before the picture was taken, and that it will move on to other actions immediately after. In order to "see" a moving picture, the viewer must imagine it as momentarily arrested in the process of movement.

"The story is not explained to an audience but revealed to a participant," according to Hollander.[19] Essentially a private viewing experience, "moving pictures" address the individual, inviting the eye to "keep on grasping what keeps on happening."[20] Furthermore, "proto-cinematic imagery sets the viewer's psyche in motion, reveals arbitrarily rather than describes thoroughly, disturbs more than it satisfies, and strongly suggests the impossibility of seeing everything at once."[21]

Posed scenes, on the other hand, depict a tableau, eternally presented to the viewer for contemplation. Tableaus present a "cleverly created artificial space populated by ravishingly believable" figures that can be read by their visual conventionality.[22]

Viewers were expected to respond differently to moving pictures than to posed scenes; moving pictures elicited emotional participation; posed scenes evoked contemplation. Both types of representation were used to engage the viewer in an intense devotional experience. Both used the viewer's concentrated gaze, or visual ray, as the medium by which the painted events and sacred characters were bonded on the viewer's psyche, forming and articulating her religious life.[23] I will give examples of each.

First, an anonymous fourteenth-century illustrated devotional manual (Figure 5), *Meditations on the Life of Christ*, will serve to exemplify "moving pictures," pictures, that is, that both occur within a narrative sequence and that move the viewer emotionally. *Meditations*

[19] Anne Hollander, *Moving Pictures* (Cambridge MA: Harvard University Press, 1991) 29.

[20] Ibid., 58.

[21] Ibid., 7.

[22] Ibid., 17.

[23] I adapt, rather than adopt, Hollander's distinction between "moving pictures" and posed scenes. Hollander identifies moving pictures with Northern European use of light, depiction of domestic interiors, and ordinary people—"uneventful scenes full of vivid objects." She identifies posed scenes with Italian Renaissance art. I find, however, that while Hollander's distinction is useful in terms of the *religious* purposes of the two kinds of painting, both types occur in both Northern and Southern European art, sometimes even in the same painters.

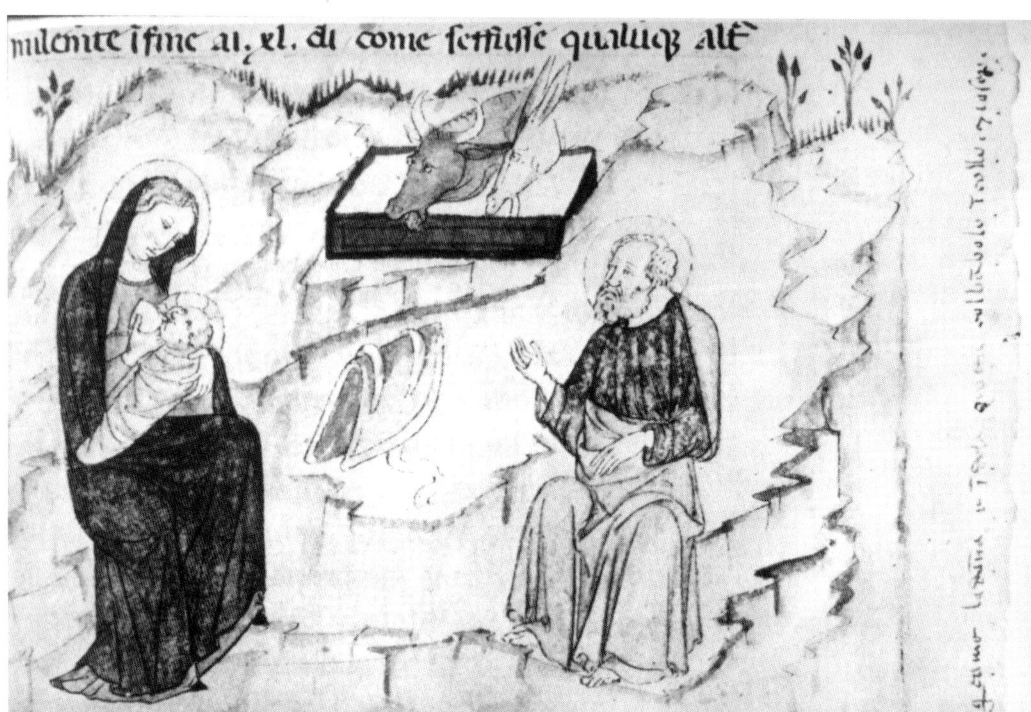

FIG 5.
Meditations on the Life of Christ, Nursing Madonna, fourteenth century manuscript (Ms. ital. 115, Fol. 19ro). Pen drawing on paper (Bibliotheque Nationale, Paris).

instructs the reader/viewer to "meditate on the humanity of Christ, which is given you in this little book," and to imagine herself an eyewitness and participant in the events described and depicted.[24] To do so is to realize that "on every side is material for compassion."[25] Instructions are sprinkled through the text, along with "snapshot" illustrations:

> "Be present at this event and be attentive to everything for, as I have said before, herein lies the whole strength of these contemplations."[26]

> "Accompany them and help to carry the Child and serve them in every way."[27]

> "Look at him well, then, as He goes along bowed down by the cross and gasping aloud. Feel as much compassion for Him as you can."[28]

[24] *Meditations on the Life of Christ: An Illustrated Manuscript of the Fourteenth Century*, ed. Isa Ragusa and Rosalie B. Green (Princeton NJ: Princeton University Press, 1961) 268.

[25] Ibid., 76.

[26] Ibid., 50.

[27] Ibid., 68.

[28] Ibid., 331.

Only about a third of the illustrations were completed. The picture sequence ends in the middle of Jesus' public life. The whole passion sequence is missing, but frames for additional illustrations and marginal instructions continue throughout the manuscript. In *Meditations*, images are used to further the book's intent to engage the reader in affective piety by visually stimulating her imaginative presence in the events of Christ's life.

Meditations is characteristic of Franciscan devotion in its interest in visual details. The viewer's *activity* of seeing was the preferred method for connecting her/his own subjectivity or spiritual life to that of trusted exemplars, the people who surrounded Christ. Moreover, texts of the time sometimes attempted to mimic paintings by providing detailed visual information. Thomas of Celano, St. Francis's friend and biographer, gives a remarkable description of St. Francis, similar in its attention to detail to that provided by the author of *Meditations*: "He was of middle height, inclining to shortness; his head was of moderate size and round; his face somewhat long and prominent; his forehead smooth and small; his eyes were black, of moderate size, and with a candid look; his hair was dark, his eyebrows straight, his nose symmetrical, thin, and straight; his ears upright but small; his temples smooth."[29] The description continues. This is enough to give a sense of its precision and its concern to provide a portrait that can be visualized. Consider: Scripture contains no such vivid description of Christ. Not until the discovery that pictures and visualization effectively inspired imitation of Christ did texts endeavor to emulate pictures in providing this visual detail.

Giotto di Bondone's cycle at the Scrovegni Chapel, Padua, painted in about 1305 (Figure 6), offers a second Italian, early Renaissance example of "moving pictures." The Scrovegni Chapel, a noble family's small private chapel, is next door to a large austere Cistercian abbey-church. Apparently the townspeople were not excluded from the chapel, however, for shortly after Giotto painted the chapel, a letter from the abbot of the Cistercian church complained that the abbey-church was deserted, while people flocked to the small chapel with its colorful, almost life-sized sacred figures placed at viewers' eye level.

[29]Thomas of Celano, *Vita primo*, 83. trans. A. G. Ferrers Howell, London, 1908, p. 81; quoted by Paul Hills, *The Light of Early Italian Painting* (New Haven CT: Yale University Press, 1987) 12.

[30]G. Boccaccio, *Decameron*, 6.5, trans. F. Winwar (New York: Modern Library, 1955) 365.

These are not posed photographs, but snapshots, moving pictures. To contemporary eyes, they were arresting in their realism. Boccaccio, Giotto's contemporary, remarked, "Giotto was able to paint all natural and artificial subjects in a completely lifelike manner, so that many persons considered them to be real."[30] It is safe to suggest that it was not Giotto's realism as such that engaged his first viewers, but rather the increment of devotional attachment enabled by it.

Meditations' instructions in cultivating deep empathy with the scriptural figures occurred within the same religious culture as Giotto's frescos in the Scrovegni Chapel. Giotto similarly focused on the affective content of scriptural events for the people who first experienced them. Paintings depict scenes from the life of Mary, from Christ's birth and infancy, from Mary's presence at the crucifixion, and from events after Christ's death. These are moving pictures. Each

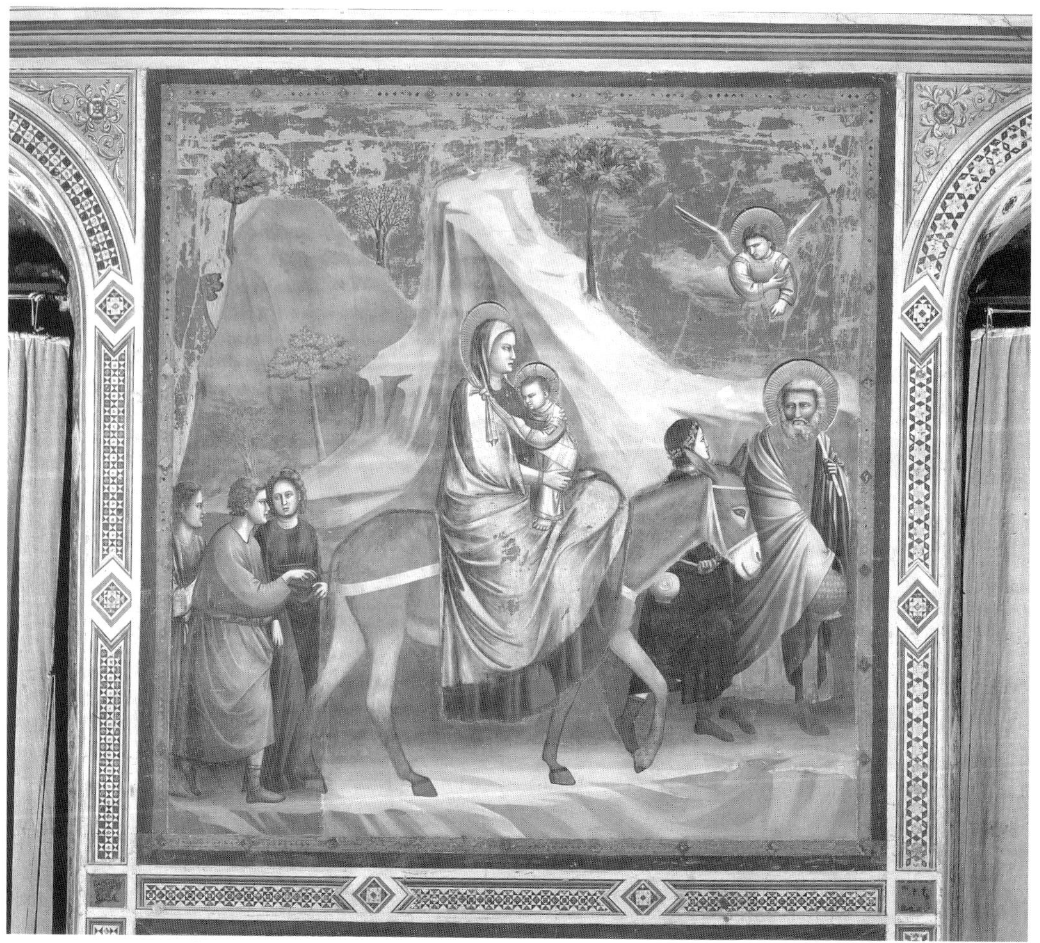

FIG 6.
Giotto, *Flight into Egypt*, ca. 1305. Fresco *in situ* (Scrovegni Chapel, Padua).

depicted moment assumes viewers' knowledge of prior and later moments. A twenty-first century person can almost imagine Giotto's paintings scanned, digitized, and animated.

In Northern Europe, a particular emphasis on imitation of Christ came from a new movement, the *devotio moderna*. The *devotio* inspired the most popular book of the fifteenth century, a bestseller also in subsequent centuries, Thomas à Kempis's *The Imitation of Christ*. Thomas à Kempis defined imitation of Christ as meditation on the life of Jesus in order to "make one's whole life conform to the pattern of Christ's life."[31]

What was new about the *devotio* was the claim that the piety could be as effectively practiced by laypeople as by monks. Followers practiced what they called "inner devotion," but the term is misleading, for devotions were neither mental nor individual. The literature of the new devotion instructed readers in clearly prescribed responses, both "an internal imitation of appropriate attitudes, emotions, and self-awareness, and an external imitation of acts and gestures."[32] Attention was paid to shaping the religious *body* in community by poverty and service. Actions and gestures, devotees believed, can both reveal and *produce* inner dispositions. The founder, Geert Groot (d. 1384), wrote, "Our bowing at the gospel and the bodily posture of reverence are symbols of the reverence of our minds. Moreover, the outward observance *is a means to induce inward reverence*. A bent posture does admirably befit devotion of mind, for *the motions of the spirit do bear a relation to the posture of the body*."[33] Awareness of the importance of postures and gestures for inciting devotion was not unique to the religious culture of the *devotio moderna*.

A new visual interest in everyday events, ordinary people, and domestic interiors accompanied the *devotio moderna*. This interest was aided by the creation of a new medium—oil paints. In the thirteenth and fourteenth centuries, tempera paint, made by mixing ground pigments with egg yoke, was used. But in Flanders in the early fifteenth century, oil-based paints permitted the use of glazes, which allowed artists to achieve subtle variations of tone, luminous highlights, and richer shades than had previously been possible. The *Merode Altarpiece*, painted in 1425 by the so-called "Master of Flemalle"

[31] For further description of the goals and practices of the *devotio moderna*, see Margaret R. Miles, chapter 2, "An Image of the Image," *Practicing Christianity* (New York: Crossroad, 1987).

[32] Otto Grundler, "Devotio Moderna," *Christian Spirituality: High Middle Ages and Reformation*, ed. Jill Raitt (New York: Crossroad, 1987) 189.

[33] Emphasis mine. Quoted by Grundler, "Devotio Moderna," 181.

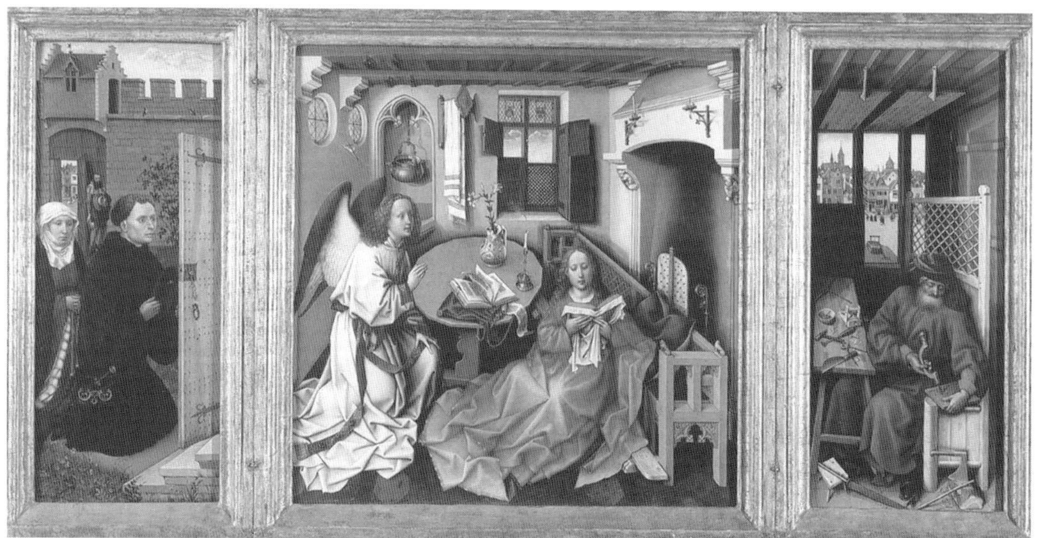

(probably Robert Campin), exhibited the new capability of oil paints to reproduce and heighten visual reality (Figure 7).

Presence—the viewer's and the donors'—at a scriptural event occurring in a Flemish domestic interior is the point of this altarpiece. Viewers are invited to participate in the integration of the spiritual and familiar in an everyday, spatial world in which a supernatural event is about to occur. Mary is not yet aware of Gabriel's presence; she is poised at the second just before the annunciation will occur, though a candle has already been extinguished by Gabriel's breezy entrance. A tiny infant Christ carrying a cross on his shoulder descends toward the Virgin.

In the left wing, the donors of the altarpiece wait in the wings. The arms of the city of Malines, their home, appears on the badge of the messenger who waits, hat in hand, just behind them. In the right wing, Joseph, surrounded by the tools of his trade, prepares a mousetrap with which to trap the devil. The miracle of Christ's incarnation appears in the midst of an ordinary (if rather well-appointed) room, viewed by ordinary people, surrounded by objects of daily life. Everything is as it was, except that you, the viewer, are there. Contemporaries praised both the piety and the realism of the Flemish painters.

In designing a devotional life that could be lived in the midst of ordinary secular life, the *devotio moderna* reacted against a centuries-old consensus that it takes full time to create and exercise a religious life. The monastery was thought of as the privileged place for cultivating the spiritual senses. In the managed environment of the monastery, full-time attention could be placed on the spiritual life even while routine duties were performed. Within this tradition, frescos painted by Fra Angelico (Giovanni da Friesole) in monastic cells at the Dominican monastery of San Marco in Florence emphasize an explicitly embodied imitation of Christ. These scenes are not "moving pictures," however, but posed scenes, and their purpose is to incite and assist contemplation.

The primary responsibility of the Dominican priest was preaching. Art historian William Hood argues that "the witnesses to biblical and apocryphal scenes in the San Marco frescos were the starting point for a mnemonic process in which the priors' meditation helped them to study sacred texts in preparation for preaching."[34] Preaching was not done by words alone, according to Dominican teaching, but by a life transformed by prayer and meditation. A mid-thirteenth-century Dominican novice manual from Bologna, *De modo orandi,* instructs in the use of precisely specified physical gestures and postures, many of which are found in the Dominican figures in Fra Angelico's paintings. The manual states the assumption that "specific states of mystical consciousness can be stimulated by deliberately assuming bodily postures."[35] The Dominican meditator was to imitate the figure in the painting and thus reproduce the figure's experience. The motto, *docere verbo et exemplo,* states the principle that by imitating the founder of the order, who himself imitated Christ, the Dominican novice could begin to preach with his life even before he was permitted to preach with words.

The inclusion of Dominican figures within sacred scenes was a striking innovation. In these cell frescos, the response expected of the viewer is modeled by the Dominican figure. For example, in a scene of the presentation of Jesus in the temple, Dominic is shown kneeling, with one hand raised and the other placed on his breast. *De modo orandi* states that this posture and gesture excites a sense of adoration. In the "Coronation of the Virgin," six Dominicans hold up their hands

[34]William Hood, *Fra Angelico at San Marco* (New Haven CT: Yale University Press, 1993) 205.

[35]Ibid., 201.

[36] Art historian David Morgan has traced the commodification of one such image, Warner Sallman's "Head of Christ," *Icons of American Protestantism: The Art of Warner Sallman*, ed. David Morgan (New Haven CT: Yale University Press, 1996).

according to instructions in *De modo orandi*: "And when thou speakest of any holy matter or devotion, hold up thy hands."

Fra Angelico's painting of the "Mocking of Christ" is unlike any other treatment of the scene (Figure 8). The monk is directed to identify with the blindfolded Christ as the scene takes place from Christ's perspective. The Dominican viewer sees only what Christ feels. No human being inflicts the blows Christ suffers. Only the body parts that strike, that spit, are shown. Christ holds the bat and ball his mockers have required in mockery of a scepter and globe. One mocker raises his hat in mock imitation of a gesture of respect as he spits. The monastic onlooker, Dominic, has closed eyes and a peaceful, even relaxed body, showing no visible emotion, while the Virgin exhibits a quiet sadness. They are not engaged in the emotions of the event, but in meditation on it.

The scenes, painted in the cells and meant to be lived with by their Dominican viewers, are often slenderly related to biblical events. They are not focused on narrating the original event but on the Dominican participants who contemplate the event in order to gather insight and energy for preaching. By contrast with the emotionally charged narrative provided by Franciscans for laypeople, the cell frescos at San Marco adopted a contemplative and intellectual approach to paintings and developed an art that directed viewers to the order's specific mandate and goal.

ACHIEVING THE CHRISTIAN BODY

I have discussed some examples of a newly visual devotion that, in the fourteenth and fifteenth centuries, articulated and brought to life centuries-old textual instructions to Christians to imitate Christ. Gestures, postures, even the clothing, positions, and size of the figures in relation to one another, all specify how to imitate Christ. Devotional goals clearly took precedence over historical accuracy.

Is imitation of Christ an outmoded concept, something that caught Christians' imaginations for centuries but now has no resonance for Christians in our society of consumerism and commodification?[36] Certainly, mass production and media images create a public unaccustomed to thinking of images as communicating

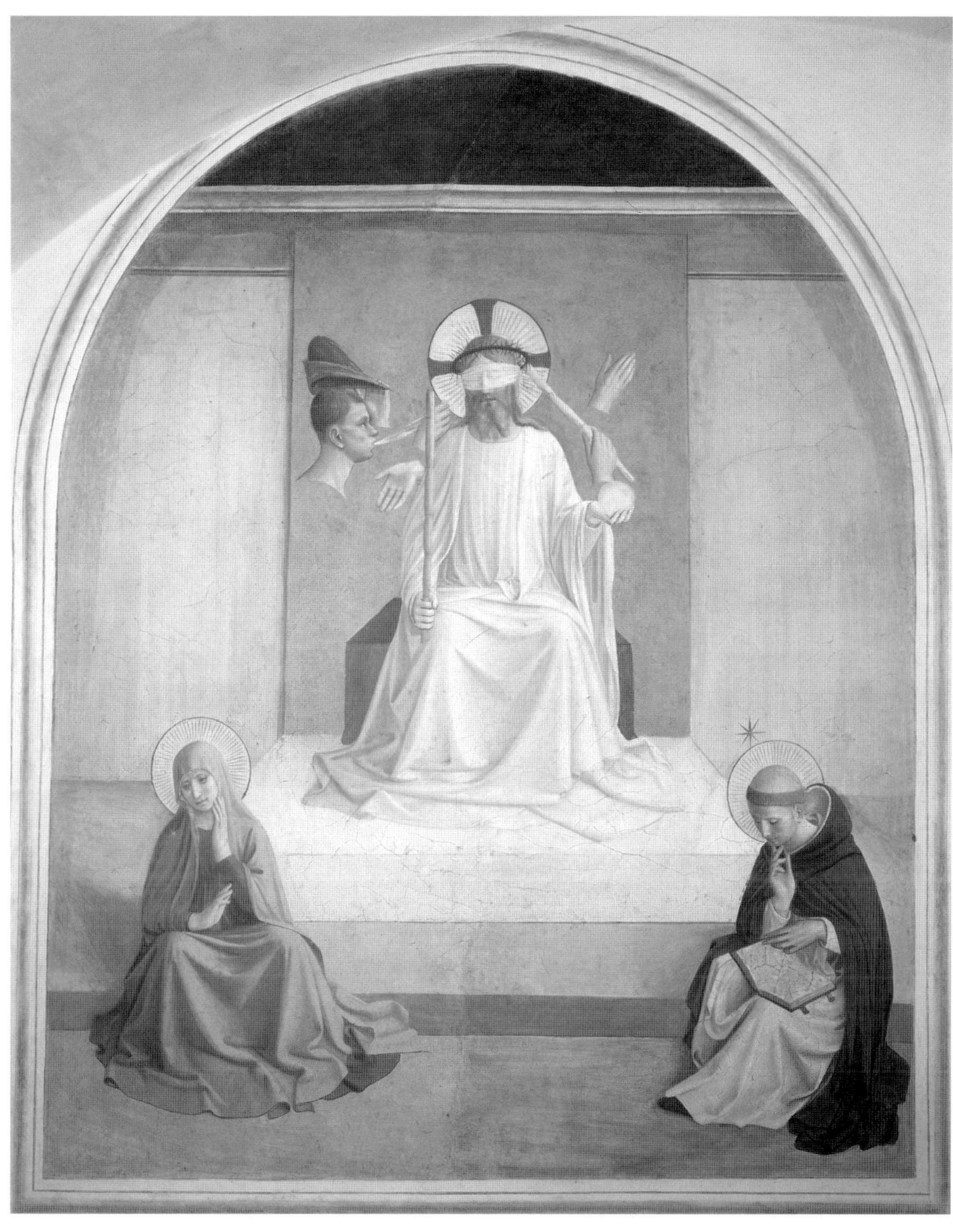

FIG 8.
Fra Angelico, *The Mocking of Christ,* ca. 1450. Cell #7 fresco, *in situ* (San Marco, Florence).

spiritual guidance. While musicals like *Jesus Christ Superstar* and movies like the *Last Temptation of Christ* and *Jesus of Montreal* invite viewers to re*think* the figure of Christ, I have argued in *Seeing and Believing: Religion and Values in the Movies* that they do not attract to imitation. In a nation still dominantly Christian, however, it is worth considering whether Americans' well-documented spiritual hunger

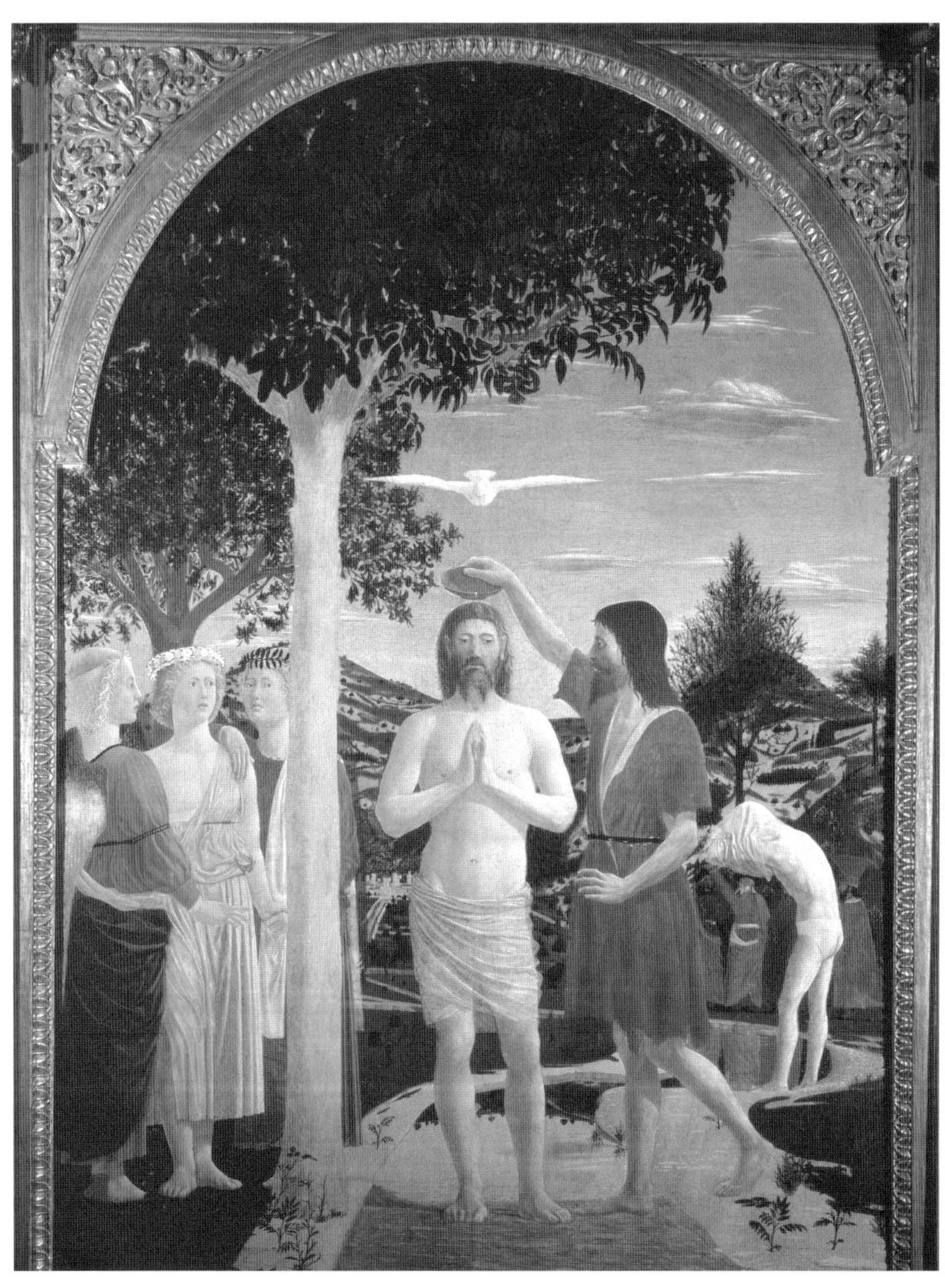

may relate to a lack of religious images capable of attracting to imitation.

What might imitation of Christ look like, feel like, now? What features of Christ's life might contemporary Americans select for imitation? I expect that the aspects of Christ's life that challenge Christians today would be different from those of earlier societies.

20   *Interpreting Christian Art*

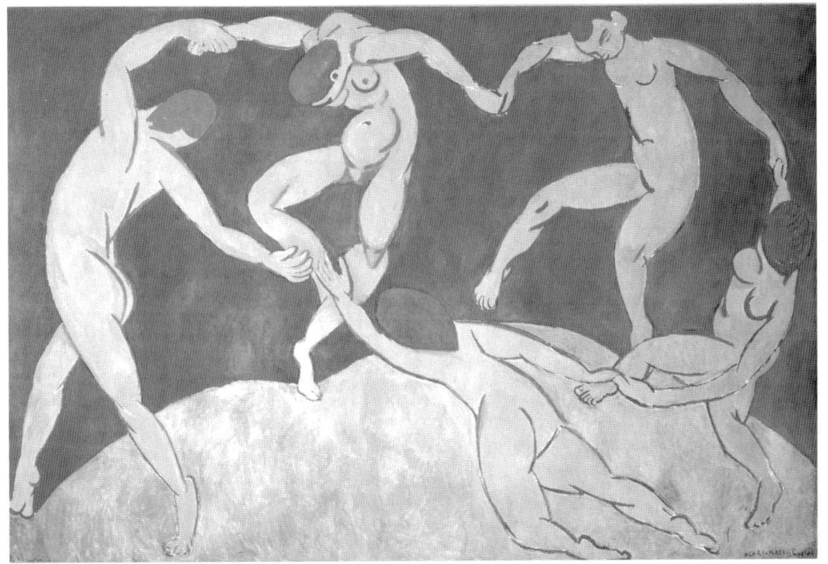

FIG 10.
Henri Matisse,
The Dance, 1910.
Casein on canvas,
102 1/2" X 154"
(The Hermitage,
Leningrad).

Twenty-first-century Christians might, for example, be less interested in depictions of Christ's suffering since our society has more capacity to relieve suffering, or at least to keep suffering out of sight, than did historical societies. But what about the ministry episodes of Christ's life (Figure 9)? Meditating on these might recall Christ's integrity, his commitment to the poor and needy, and his intelligent, thoughtful analysis of the sins of his society. Ministry episodes might remind contemporary Christians of Christ's passionate commitment to living lovingly and to figuring out what that meant, not in the abstract, but "on location." They might inspire imitation of his attention to bodies, to feeding and healing (Figure 11). In our culture of consumption, we might be reminded of other values by the scene in which Christ overturned the moneychangers' tables in the temple.

These are surely images that are conspicuously missing from the media images Americans consume daily. Indeed, they are fundamentally counter-cultural, challenging the greed and individualism that characterizes American life at the beginning of the twenty-first century.

Do contemporary Christians have a range of images that can effectively remind them of their calling? In our diverse society, Christians need to picture Christ as Asian, as African American, as Hispanic, as Native American, as Jewish. They need images of Christ's

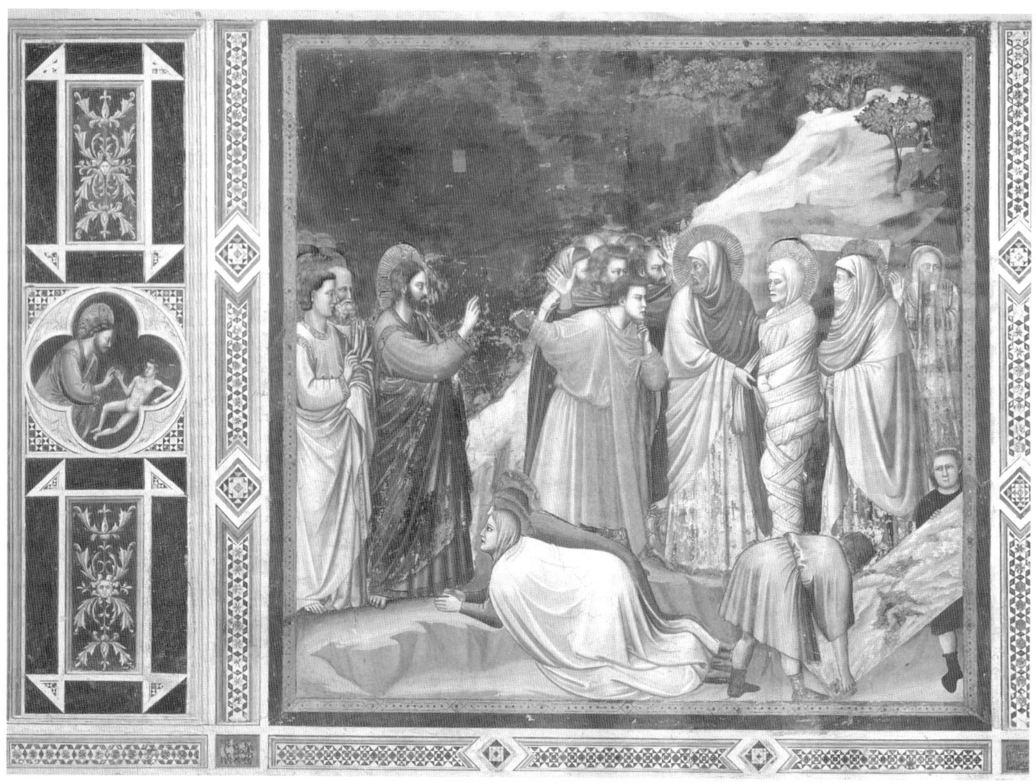

contemporary representatives as female, for example, Dorothy Day, Barbara Harris (the first woman bishop of the Episcopal Church), and Mother Teresa of Calcutta.

Do twenty-first-century Christians have images that suggest, inspire, attract? Churches are no longer major patrons of art. The very word "art" conjures in our minds museums and galleries that remove religious images from the life of religious communities (Figure 10). Secular images dominate American culture, and these are not reluctant to tell us what kind of bodies are desirable. Frequently using religious language and images, advertisements model the consumer body, the thin, rich, white body valued in our society.

Yet to Christians the doctrine of Christ's incarnation means that in some peculiarly intimate and absolute way, "bodies are us." Whatever can be known of the spiritual universe is present and immediate to human beings in bodies—our own, other people's, and those of all living beings. Even our best and richest ideas do not "transcend" the world we see and smell and touch and hear and taste, but come to us

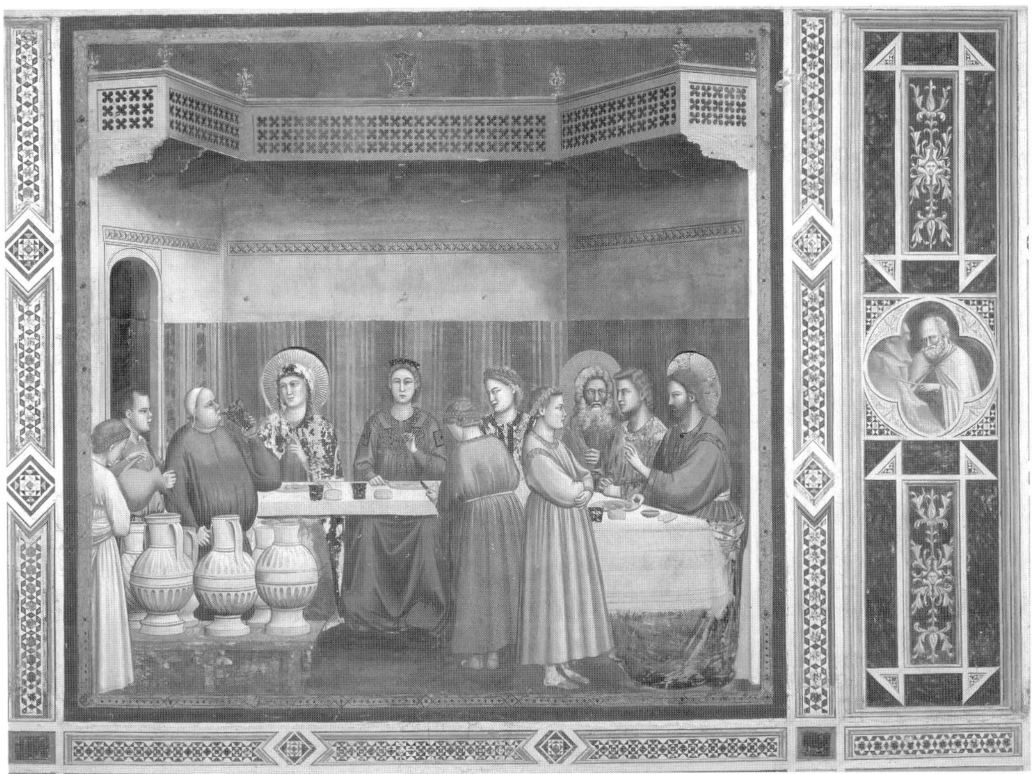

courtesy of our senses, our communities, and the neighborhoods we inhabit and that inhabit us (Figure 12).

For the goal of achieving the Christian body, contemporary Christians are, I believe, in need of the freshening and reviving of our visual repertoire. We need to see again, as late medieval people saw, that "the Word became flesh" and provided an exemplar for imitation.

FIG 12.
Giotto, *Marriage Feast at Cana,* ca. 1305. Fresco *in situ* (Scrovegni Chapel, Padua).

2.

The Fall and Rise of Adam and Eve in Early Christian Art and Literature

Robin M. Jensen
Vanderbilt Divinity School

The story of Adam and Eve, recounted in Genesis, comes just after God's creation of the cosmos. This timing is important, for as with most myths, this legend takes place out of ordinary (human) time and space, occurring in the primordial world, long ago and far away. The synopsis of events has less to do with history than with destiny. The place (paradise) exists not in a geographic sense, but rather as an ideal to be sought or hoped for. Thus the narrative tells more about the formation of a community and its values than about a series of events. And because its form is symbolic, it has no single meaning or message, and so may be shaped, changed, and challenged through time, and by different traditions. And this—its multivalence and adaptability—is precisely the reason for its success and survival. This is as true for its presentation in visual form as in literature.

The story has parallels in many foundational legends. Like the epic of Odysseus or the myth of Pandora, this is an account of promising beginnings and the consequences of mistakes. The characters learn to accept their flaws and failures and find ways to live on after tragedy. Lovers become estranged and separated, but through knowledge and struggle they eventually overcome death and find the way back home. Love, deception, jealousy, desire, and shame are motivating emotions and key to the plot. It is at once both a morality tale and a journey saga of both descent and ascent, loss and return. And instead of a single action hero, this tale has at least two (arguably four) main actors who alternately play roles in the creation and solution to the essential crisis. The solution, as in almost all such stories, lies in understanding the original mistake and summoning enough good to overcome its evil consequences. And so the story can have a happy ending, but only after travail, disgrace, and death—because salvation comes only after sacrifice.

Although this particular legend is briefly told in the second and third chapters of Genesis, the number of its versions and interpretations is probably beyond counting, not only in literature but also in visual art. And while its significance for the formation or justification of a number of key theological doctrines or social institutions is both complex and manifold, Adam and Eve's appearance in visual art often is interpreted primarily as a reference to sin and "the fall" as if this was the main point of the image and its essential message or meaning.[1] However, in Christian tradition, Adam and Eve's fall is only part of the story—a part that comes somewhere in the middle of the narrative. Early commentaries refer to the creation, the fall, and the restoration of Adam and Eve—to their eventual reinstatement as well as their expulsion. Similarly, the first human pair shows up in Christian art, in the places where human lives end and begin again.

For example, the fresco in the arch over Dura-Europos' ancient baptismal font (ca. 245) shows an image of the Good Shepherd with a group of sheep at his feet. In the lower left-hand corner of that painting, two relatively tiny figures representing Adam and Eve stand with a sketchy tree between them. A snake slithers along the ground below (Figure 1). Art historians have interpreted the image as representing "the fall" or even the "dogma of original sin," sometimes asserting that it occurs in this context because, according to Christian tradition, Adam and Eve's fall was the source of human sin, and baptism removes sin. Adam and Eve thus symbolize the sinful "old selves" of those who came to the cleansing waters of baptism.[2] Moreover, the small size and lower-left placement seem to suggest that the first couple's state must be overcome or repudiated. Initiates entering the font from the left move up and away from that image to the large welcoming Good Shepherd with his flock. They progress from old to new, from past to future, sin to salvation.

Such a reconstruction presumes that third-century Christians explicitly connected Adam and Eve's disobedience with their own need for forgiveness from sin. In other words, it assumes that they entered the font eager to remove the stain of some ancestral and inherited sin as well as their own. If we accept this, then Adam, Eve, and the snake symbolize this sin, while the shepherd represents the redeemer of that sin, Jesus Christ (the new Adam, following Rom 5). The visual composition then follows the literary one; the sin of the first Adam (and Eve)

[2] As a case in point, consider R. L. P. Milburn's description of the image over the font at Dura, *Early Christian Art and Architecture* (Berkeley: University of California Press, 1988) 12: "Then, on the west wall, two subjects appear; There are the diminutive figures of Adam and Eve, standing one on each side of the fatal tree, while pillars indicate the walls of the earthly Paradise they have forfeited. Above them, painted on a larger scale, stands the Good Shepherd.... The candidates for baptism might well reflect that Adam's transgression calls for the Saviour's arrival to seek and save that which was lost." A similar interpretation was offered by Grabar, *Christian Iconography*, 20, in which he asserts that the image of Adam and Eve in the Dura Baptistery represents the dogma of original sin, while the Good Shepherd represents the doctrine of redemption.

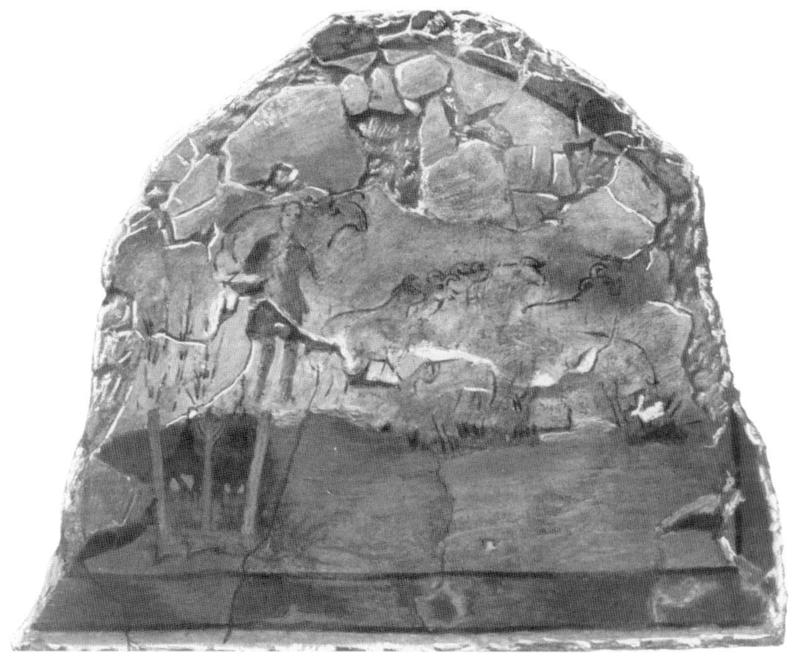

FIG 1.
Good Shepherd, fresco over the font, house church at Dura-Europos, ca. 245.

brought condemnation and punishment (death), while the righteousness of the second Adam brings acquittal and life.

As I will argue, however, the Adam and Eve story has a wider range of meanings in the early Christian tradition than merely a simple or direct equation of "bad" Adam (and Eve) with the Good Shepherd. And so we cannot so simply interpret the image, particularly in a baptismal context. Although the basic idea of "original sin" may have been implied in Paul's theology, the so-called "doctrine" was only just being formulated in the third century, among the Latin writers of Roman Africa (rather far removed from Dura-Europos on the empire's eastern border).[3] Furthermore, Paul's construction of Adam as the originator of sin is augmented by his presentation of Christ as the new (and improved) Adam. Thus Adam as a character is both positive and negative.

Early Christian writers from different parts of the empire (and in different languages) elaborated on the two Adams, and often with respect to the meaning of Christian baptism. The old Adam carried the potential for the new one, just as the first creation bore seeds for the new creation—and baptism was both the occasion and the sign of this renewal. For instance, Tertullian's treatise on baptism speaks of the rite as restoring the likeness of the one who originally had been formed in the image of God. Thus each candidate becomes a "new Adam" through the sacrament that destroys death "by the washing away of sins." Furthermore, "as the guilt is removed, the penalty also is taken away. In this way a person is restored to God, to the likeness of the one who had originally been in God's image—the image that had its reality in the one that God formed, but now the likeness becomes eternal."[4] Ephraem, writing from Syria more than a century after Tertullian, spoke of baptism as replacing the image of the "former Adam" with the beauty of the true likeness (Christ).[5] Likewise, Gregory of Nyssa's sermon for Epiphany on the baptism of Christ speaks of the rite as a total reversal of the consequences of Adam's disobedience and the renewal of the original creation:

> You did hate, and were reconciled; you did curse, and did
> bless; you did banish us from Paradise and did recall us;

you did strip off the fig-tree leaves, and unseemly covering, and put upon us a costly garment; you did open the prison and release the condemned; you did sprinkle us with clean water, and cleanse us from our filthiness. No longer shall Adam be confounded when called by you, nor hide himself, convicted by his conscience, cowering in the thicket of Paradise. Nor shall the flaming sword encircle Paradise around, and make the entrance inaccessible to those that draw near; but all is turned to joy for us that were the heirs of sin: Paradise, yes, heaven itself, may be trodden by humanity; and the creation, in the world and above the world, that once was at variance with itself, is knit together in friendship.[6]

The nudity of the candidates in the font was an especially powerful reminder of their status as new Adam or Eve. Early catechetical teachers often cited this physical state as signifying the renewal of the first man and woman through baptism. John Chysostom delivered instructions to the catechumens during Lent, probably in the last days of Holy Week, in which he explained the symbolism:

> After the anointing it remains to go into the bath of sacred waters. After stripping you of your robe, the priest leads you down into the flowing waters. But why naked? He reminds you of your former nakedness. For the holy writing says: Adam and Eve *were naked and were not ashamed,* until they took up the garment of sin, a garment heavy with abundant shame. Do not, then, feel shame here, for the bath is much better than the garden of Paradise. There can be no serpent here, but Christ is here initiating you into the regeneration that comes from the water and the Spirit.[7]

Thus the figures of Adam and Eve in Dura's baptistery are perhaps not there *only* as reminders of the ancestral sin about to be washed off in the font. They also may represent the renewal of original innocence and the rehabitation of paradise, restored through the rite of baptism.

[6] Gregory of Nyssa, *On the Baptism of Christ: A Homily for the Feast of Lights,* concluding prayer. Ernest Gebhardt, text ed. "In diem luminum," in *Gregorii Nysseni Opera,* vol. 9, Sermones/Pars I, ed. Gònter Heil, et al. (Leiden: Brill, 1967), trans. adapted from H. A. Wilson, NPNF (second series) 5, 518–24.

[7] John Chrysostom, *Baptismal Instructions* 11.28–29. *St. John Chysostom: Baptismal Instructions,* trans. and ed. Paul W. Harkins, ACW 31 (New York: Paulist Press, 1963) 170. For other references to nakedness in baptism as symbolizing the status of Adam and Eve in paradise see Cyril, *Mystagogical Catacheses,* 2.2; John the Deacon, *Epistle to Senarius* 6; and Theodore of Mopsuestia, *Baptismal Homily* 3.8.

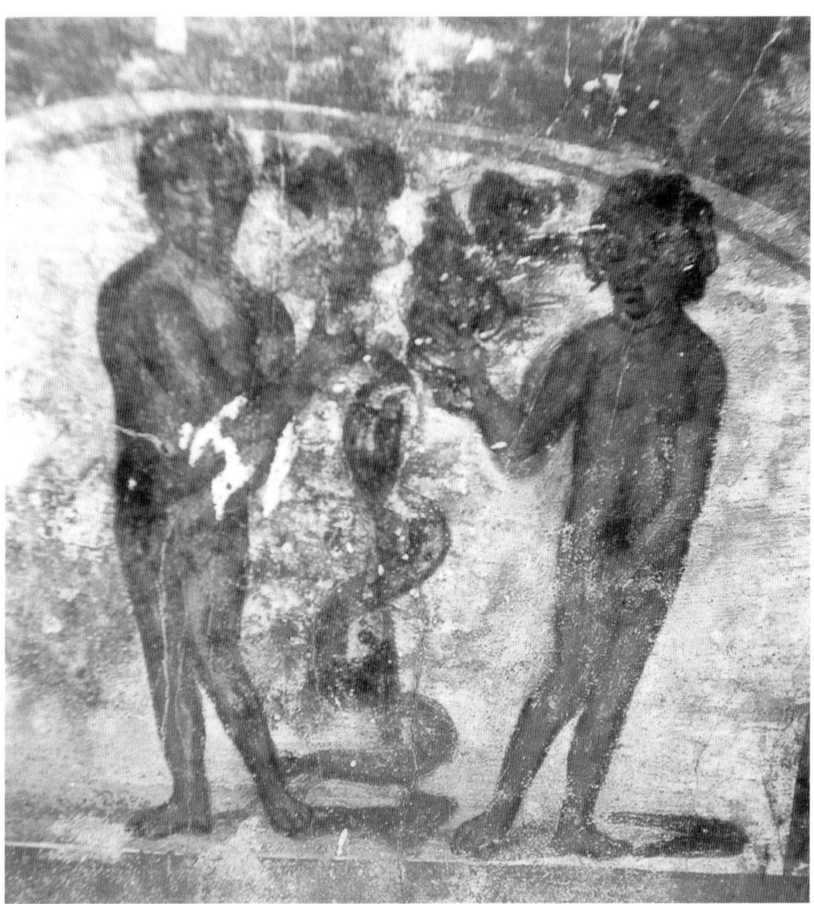

The iconography points both to their reconciliation and restoration as well as fall and expulsion. Moreover, their presentation as small and nude may refer to the naked state of the newly baptized Christians. With paradise regained, the nudity of the two may not signify their self-conscious shame so much as point to their recovered innocence.

The frescoes of Dura-Europos are unique. The only comparable artistic evidence for these house-church frescoes comes from the Christian catacombs in and around Rome, and those underground tunnels and chambers where Christians were buried in the third and fourth centuries provide many examples of Adam and Eve images (Figures 2 and 3). The most common presentation shows Adam and Eve standing on either side of the tree, trying to cover their nudity with hands or fig leaves. The snake usually, but not always, appears. Sometimes the two humans look a little sheepish; sometimes they look rather self-satisfied. Eve may point at the tree or at the serpent ("The serpent beguiled me, and I ate," Gen 3:13). Occasionally Adam points to Eve ("The woman whom you gave to be with me, she gave me the fruit of the tree, and I ate," Gen 3:12).

In addition to wall paintings, Adam and Eve are a regular motif among the relief carvings on Christian sarcophagi (large marble coffins), dating from the late-third to the mid-fourth century, as well

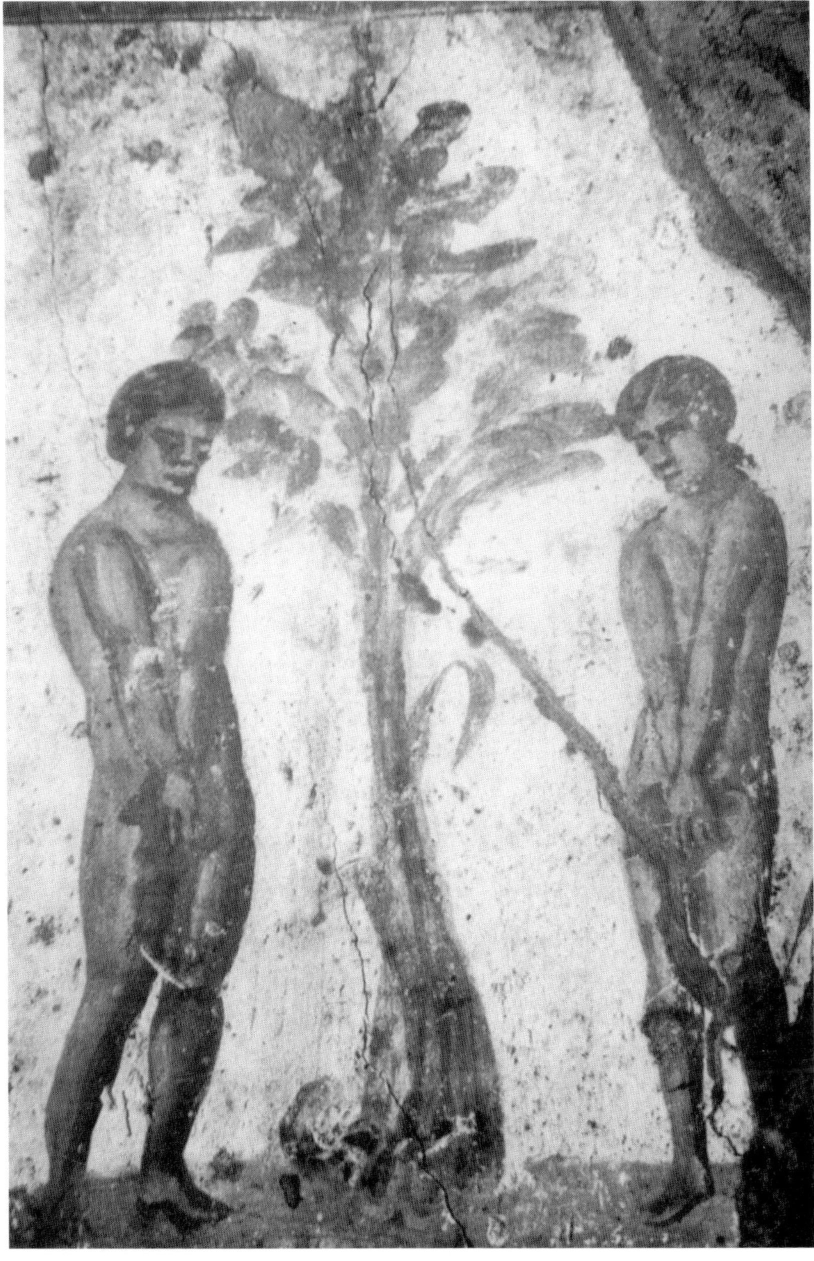

FIG 3.
Adam and Eve, catacomb of Figure 4. Sarcophagus lid, Pio Cristiano

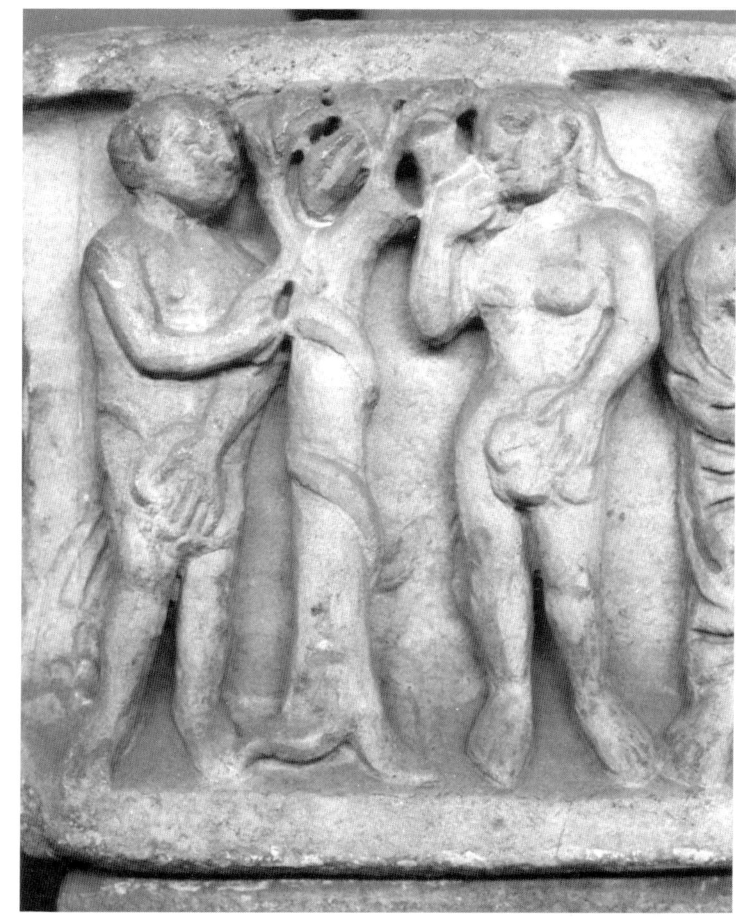

FIG 4. (top right)
Peter and
Marcellinus, early
fourth century.
Museo (Rome), late
third century.

FIG 5. (below)
*Adam and Eve with
miracle at Cana and
Jesus raising the
dead*. Sarcophagus
from Museo Pio
Cristiano (Rome),
mid-fourth century.

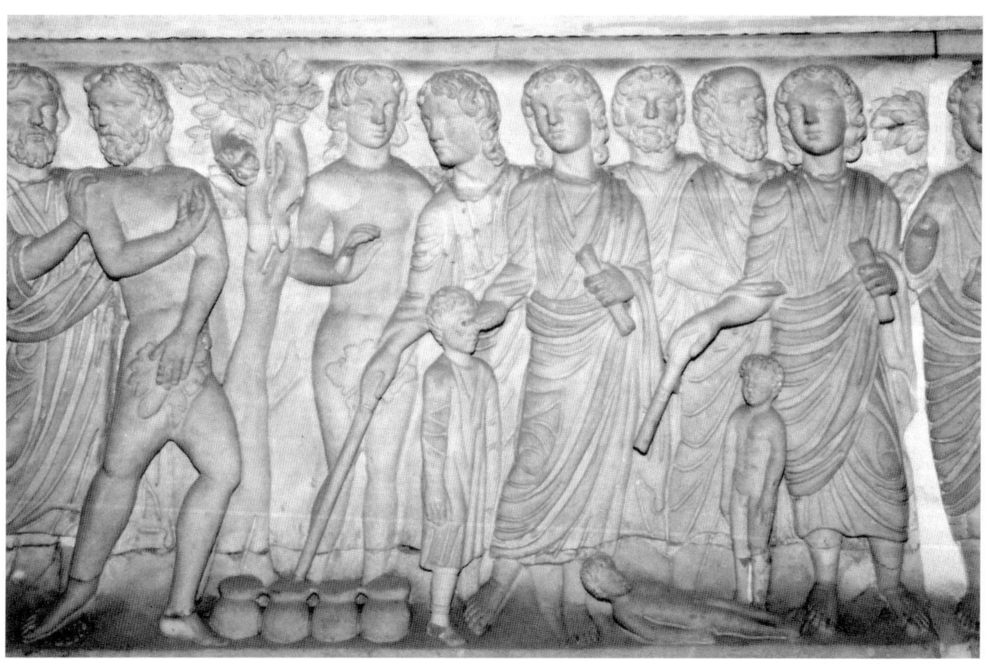

as on more minor arts—glass, pottery, gems, and tiles. In all of these, the standard composition reappears—Adam and Eve, the tree and the snake (Figure 4). The woman sometimes holds the fruit in her right hand, covering herself with leaves held in her left. However, several of the sarcophagus reliefs show interesting and significant variations. In some instances, another figure, identified by his facial features as either Jesus or the Divine Logos (or both), steps into the scene and looks over Adam's shoulder (Figure 5) as if he is catching the couple in their fateful act. In several early fourth-century compositions, the tree either disappears or moves off to one side, and Christ stands between the two, apportioning the symbols of the labor they will do in the world outside of Eden (Figures 6 and 7). The lamb (or hare as in Figure 7) and the sheaf represent the work of herding (or hunting) and domesticated agriculture.[8] Representations of the expulsion itself (the Logos sends Adam and Eve, dressed in animal skins, out through the gate of paradise) also occur in both fresco and relief sculpture.[9]

A rather different scene shows the creation of the original humans. Two small naked people stand (or lie) at the feet of a seated male who most likely represents God. This older figure makes a gesture of speech

[8] In Roman art, these symbols of agriculture and hunting may also represent spring and autumn.

[9] See the two Via Latina images in Antonio Ferrua, *The Unknown Catacomb: A Unique Discovery of Early Christian Art* (New Lanark: Geddes and Grosset, 1991) plates 29, 53; as well as on the so-called Sarcophagus of Lot in the Catacomb of S. Sebastiano.

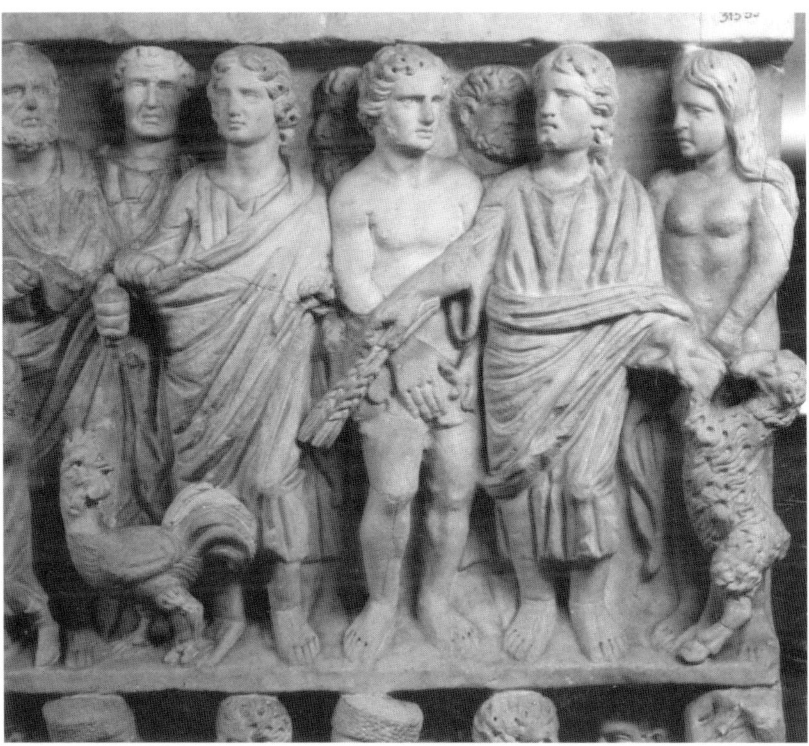

FIG 6.
Apportioning work, sarcophagus from Museo Pio Cristiano, mid-fourth century.

or blessing with his right hand. To his left and behind his chair are two other figures, probably intended to correspond to the Son (Logos) and the Holy Spirit (Figures 7 and 8). The three bearded faces are nearly identical in one of the images (Figure 7) but not in the other (Figure 8).[10] The standing male (Logos) to the Father's left has a special relationship to the two small nudes; in one example he places his right hand on the woman's head. Scholars have reasonably concluded that this image presents the Trinity creating Adam and Eve (compare Figure 9, which shows Cain and Abel bringing their offerings to a similar "Trinity" group). In this same composition, the adult-sized pair stands just to the right of the "creation" scene. Jesus (identified by his similarity to Jesus in other scenes on the same sarcophagus) is shown standing between them holding the symbols of their labor, while the snake coils around the tree to Eve's left. The faces on the adult Adam and Eve almost exactly match the faces of the small figures just being enlivened by the Trinity.

The other creation image is placed next to a scene of Jesus healing the paralytic. In this instance, Jesus' facial type is identical to that of the Son/Logos in the Trinity group, a logical way to visually present Christ as the image of the invisible God, the "first born of creation"

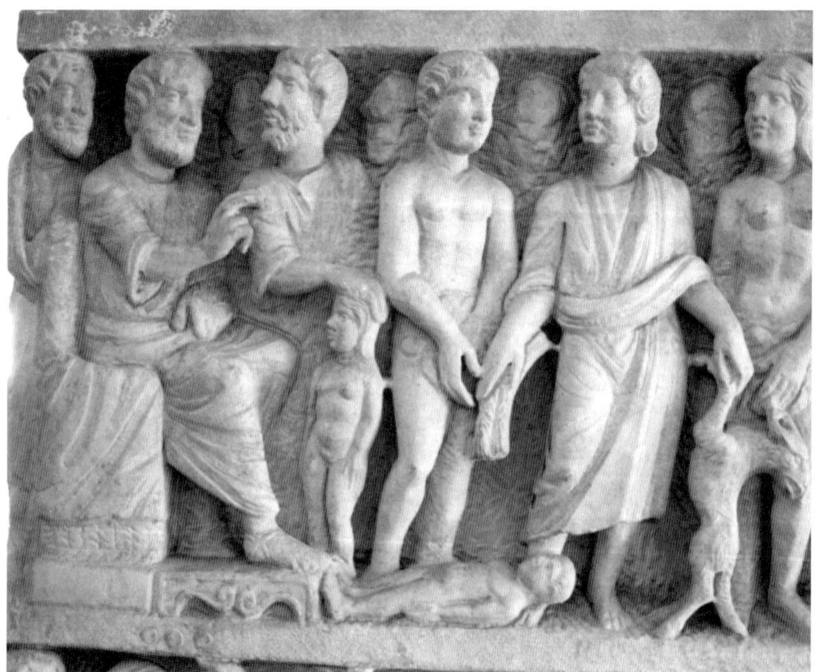

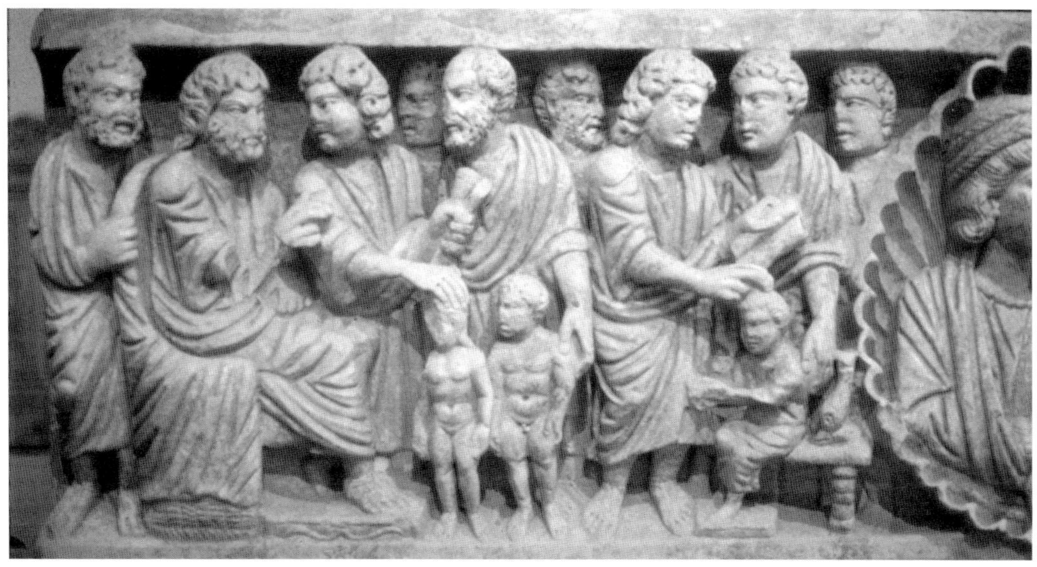

(Col 1:15-20—Figure 8). In some other instances, the Logos is distinguished from Christ by giving the Logos a beard, which allows him to appear ancient, even preexistent (see Figure 5, which has both types and in which the bearded Logos looks like Adam).

From this we can see that the wider context or composition of the artwork also contributes to the overall meaning of any individual scene. The story cannot be understood if one only views a small segment of it in isolation. The placement of the creation next to a scene of Jesus apportioning work or of the Logos/Christ healing is not accidental. For example, several of these images are placed near or next to representations of Jesus entering Jerusalem, healing the paralytic, or raising the dead (Figures 9 and 10). The first image speaks of the coming of salvation, while the other represents the hope of resurrection. The small figures being raised in the second image also bear a similarity to the small figures being enlivened in the creation scenes.

While the prominence of the Adam and Eve motif in early Christian art demonstrates its *general* popularity, its placement on the walls of burial chambers as well as sarcophagi also suggests that it had a *particular* suitability for funeral (as well as baptismal) contexts. The repeated appearance of certain artistic motifs in these contexts suggests a theological significance that is underscored both by their selection and their style. The work of discerning that significance, however, can be aided by reference to other contemporary data, including biblical, theological, homiletic, and liturgical texts. Visual art is a mode of theological reflection and, in this case, a type of biblical exegesis. Like any other form of interpretation and communication, art is firmly planted within a culture. Thus, it expresses ideas and values that parallel, reinforce, amplify, or react to (and with) other aspects of the surrounding religious culture—including available literary remains.

At the same time, modern interpreters must also allow art objects the same degree of primacy, authority, and autonomy as they do written documents. Visual images are not merely illustrations of narrative texts, nor are they simply aids for non-readers. Art communicates differently than expository prose and, in fact, is more like poetry than narrative. Initially, a visual image might appear to be simple and its message direct and obvious. The reference to a particular episode of a well-known story may be the first thing one sees about the image. But like any story (or myth) the image offers many different possible meanings and operates symbolically rather than discursively. Its particular message can offer insight into the beliefs and values of the Christian community that made and used it.

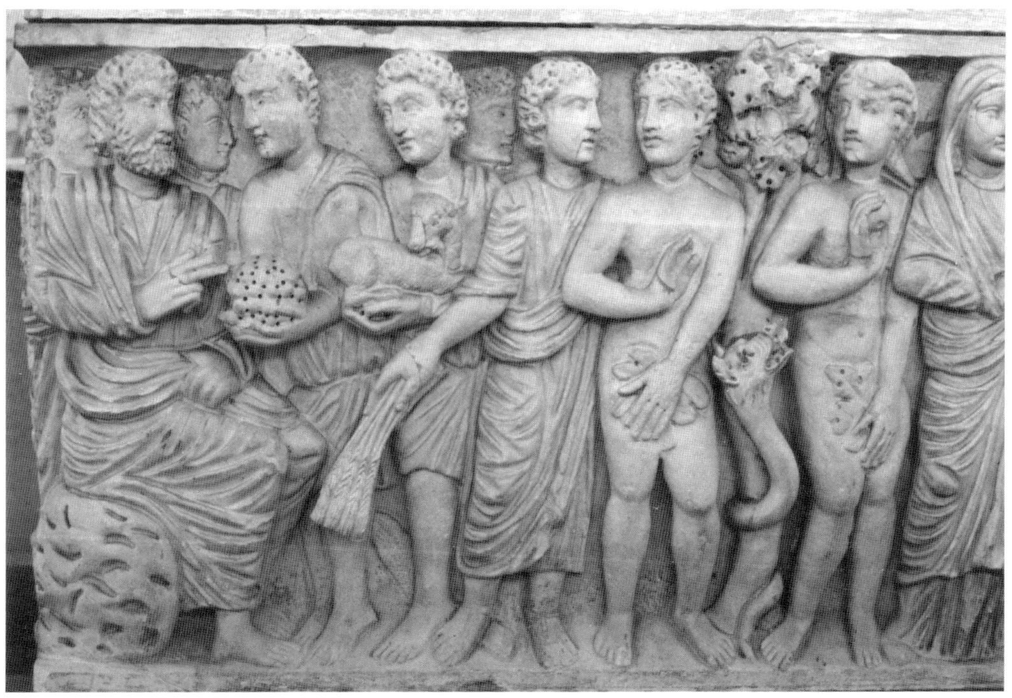

FIG 9.
Cain and Abel sarcophagus from Museo Pio Cristiano, fourth century.

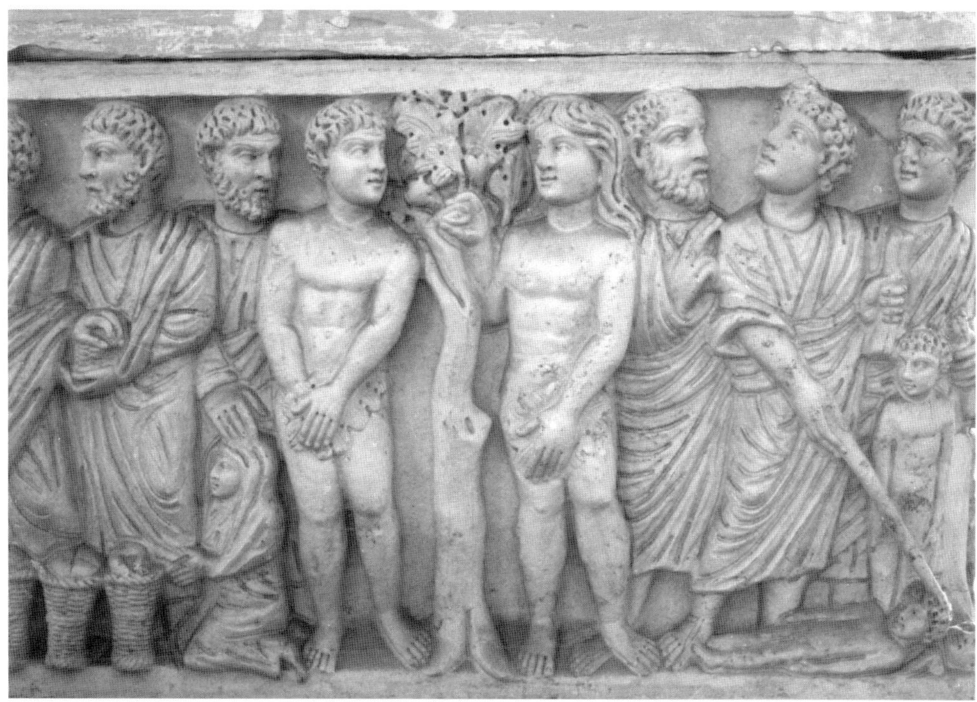

As with the Dura-Europos image, labeling or identifying most of these catacomb frescoes or relief carvings of Adam and Eve scenes simply as presentations of "the fall" reduces them to a single idea and suggests that they refer only to the story of sin and punishment. Such reduction misses much of the point as well as the richness of the symbolism implied by the image, especially considering the particular physical context of the artwork. A visual metaphor for failure and condemnation (to death) superficially seems inappropriate for tomb decoration. One wants, rather, to find some other meaning, perhaps a message of hope, in the iconography. If the imagery pointed to some aspect of the deceased's life, suggested something about the meaning of death, or pointed to expectation for the afterlife, viewers would have a different reaction to the artwork.

For instance, Adam and Eve do not always look ashamed of their act. One might then suspect that the two appear as a kind of standard "sign," indicating some meaning other than fall or failure. On the other hand, when Jesus enters the composition, either as the one who discovers their act or who apportions their work, the viewer must decide whether he is fierce or friendly. By virtue of familiarity with ideas circulating in the biblical, theological, or exegetical writings, an interpreter could conclude that the image portrays Christ as New Adam, already reconciling the two to God through his own future life and death: "For as by a man came death, by a man has come also the resurrection of the dead. For as in Adam all die, so also in Christ shall all be made alive…. The first man, Adam, became a living being; the last Adam became a life-giving Spirit" (1 Cor 15:21-22, 45). By noting that certain other images are placed right next to these Adam and Eve scenes, including the creation, healing, entry to Jerusalem, and the raising of the dead, the tomb iconography could suggest the hope of eternal life and new creation—an understandable choice. Death and sin are only the very first part of the iconographic message. The overcoming of sin and death is its conclusion.

Such an interpretation is supported by and paralleled in (but not derivative from) textual evidence. Extant writings from the early church contain various examples of how homilists, apologists, and catechetical teachers interpreted the Genesis 3 narrative and its role in Christian salvation history. The documents provide an independent witness as well as an analogous tradition that gives insight into the role the Adam and Eve story played in preaching, liturgy, and the construction of orthodox theology. A study of these documents shows that their authors go far beyond the simplistic reduction of Adam and Eve to the inventors of sin or those responsible for death. So, presuming written and visual data do not oppose one another in their message or intention, a set of possibilities for interpretation of the images emerges. Based on a general overview of both the available art as well as the extant and contemporaneous documents, three broad and interconnected themes can be discerned with respect to the Adam and Eve iconography.

ADAM AND EVE AS CREATED BY THE LOGOS

In early Christian writings, Adam and Eve are presented as having been created by the Divine Logos, the principle architect and primary assistant to God in the action of creation. Exegetes understood that this teaching was implied by the first person plural in Genesis 1:26: "Let *us* make humankind after *our* image and likeness," an assertion reflected and reinforced by John 1:3, "and all things came into being through him," and Colossians 1:15, "for in him all things were created, things visible and invisible."[11] The artistic representations of the creation of Adam and Eve by the Trinity apparently drew upon this teaching, especially as the Son appears to have a special creative activity as shown in the iconography. The creation of Adam and Eve "after the image" may have been visually presented in art by showing Christ, Adam, and Eve with similar facial features (see discussion below).

In some of the early writings, the creation was described as perfect but yet still evolving. Adam and Eve were considered to be immature and naïve forms of humanity. Part of God's plan was their gradual maturation. Two late second-century Christian writers, the apologist Theophilus of Antioch and the polemicist Irenaeus of Lyons both develop this idea of the "infancy" of the first couple at their creation, an idea that may be reflected in the artistic presentation of Adam and Eve as little children at their creation (Figures 7 and 8). This idea perhaps served a polemical purpose. Irenaeus, in his defense against gnostic theories of an incompetent demiurge, needed to account for the apparently flawed first creation (as demonstrated by the fall). According to him Adam and Eve were created innocent, but childlike. Through a kind of progressive or evolutionary development, in which the fall was a relatively minor event, humans are gradually perfected and finally brought to completion through Christ (the New Adam).

According to this theory, God had intended the fall in the first place and therefore had no reason to prevent it or to make a creation that was flawless. In his treatise *Proof of the Apostolic Preaching*, Irenaeus describes this original innocence: "And Adam and Eve 'were naked and not ashamed' for their thoughts were innocent and child-like, and they had no conception or imagination of the sort that is engendered in the soul by evil, through concupiscence, and by lust. For they were then in their integrity, preserving their natural state…as they kissed each other and embraced with the innocence of child-hood."[12] In his better-known treatise, *Against Heresies,* Irenaeus expands on this idea, even suggesting that the only way Adam and Eve could achieve perfection was through an initial weakness or failure; sin

[11] See Justin Martyr, *1 Apology* 6; and idem, *Dialogue with Trypho,* 61-62; Tatian, *Oration* 4; Theophilus, *To Autolycus,* 2.10; and Irenaeus, *Against Heresies* 2.2.4–5; 5.6.1; 1.10.1–3. On the creation of Eve in gnostic tradition, see *The Secret Book According to John 21-23.*

[12] Irenaeus, *Proof of the Apostolic Preaching,* 14. *St. Irenaeus, Proof of the Apostolic Preching,* trans. and ed. J. Smith, ACW 16 (New York: Newman Press, 1952) 56.

or its consequent suffering is an integral part of the divine plan: "Now it was necessary that man should in the first instance be created; and having been created, should receive growth; and having received growth, should be strengthened; and having been strengthened, should abound; and having been abounded should recover [from the disease of sin]; and having recovered should be glorified."[13]

Theophilus argues a very similar line, but his work adds a few ideas, including that Adam and Eve were neither mortal nor immortal in paradise. His purpose seems to be less polemical than pedagogical. He explains that the tree of knowledge was withheld from the pair in the garden because they were not yet mature enough for its effects. Depicting the two as children in need of limits leads to Theophilus's claim that being cast out of paradise, although a punishment, was yet a great benefit to humanity, in the way the discipline of a parent is of benefit to a child. God wanted to teach Adam to obey or test his obedience in the way a parent might train a child. After a time, the punishment was lifted and the two returned to the garden:

> Furthermore, it is shameful for infant children to have thoughts beyond their years; for as one grows in age in an orderly fashion, so one grows in ability to think.... For a father sometimes orders his own child to abstain from certain things, and when the child does not obey the paternal commands he is beaten and receives chastisement because of his disobedience.... So also the first formed man, his disobedience resulted in his expulsion from Paradise.... For this reason, when man was formed in this world it is described mysteriously in Genesis as if he had been placed in paradise twice; the first description was fulfilled when he was placed there, and the second is going to be fulfilled after the resurrection and judgment.... And in the resurrection he may be found sound, I mean spotless and righteous, and immortal...[God] gave him an occasion for repentance and confession.[14]

Theophilus's exegesis corresponds to aspects of the visual imagery—particularly of the scenes in which Jesus apportions work and where

---

[13] *Against Heresies* 4.38.3 (522)

[14] Theophilus, *To Autolycus* 2.25. *Theophilus of Antioch: Ad Autolycum*, text and trans. Robert McQueen Grant (Oxford: Clarendon Press, 1970) 66–67. Compare John Chrysostom's *Baptismal Homily* 2.4, where God is equated to a loving father with a disobedient son. Like the father who punishes with moderation for the good of the child, God expelled Adam from the garden as a kind of training exercise, hoping to strengthen humanity for the future.

the tree of knowledge has either been removed altogether or simply sidelined. Adam and Eve may be understood to be outside of the garden and beginning the long process of recovery or maturation, leading to their eventual return. Moreover, compositions that show Adam and Eve pointing to the tree may not indicate shame or blame so much as the significance of the tree itself (Figure 2). According to Theophilus, "the tree was good and its fruit was good. The tree did not contain death, as some suppose; this was the result of disobedience. For there was nothing in the fruit but knowledge, and knowledge is good if one uses it properly."[15]

In addition to serving as a symbol of knowledge gained through maturity, the tree of Eden also becomes an antetype of the cross at Calvary. Jesus' placement between Adam and Eve in the imagery suggests the cross/tree equation, as well as the resurrected Christ as a replacement for the tree of knowledge (Figures 6 and 7). Justin Martyr made this connection early on, claiming that Jesus' crucifixion on the cross was initially symbolized by the tree of life that was planted in paradise.[16] Irenaeus speaks of the sin done in connection with a tree reversed by the obedience on the tree of the Lord, and Cyril of Jerusalem compares the two trees in his baptismal catecheses and notes the verisimilitude: "In Paradise was the fall and in a garden our salvation. From the tree came sin, and until the Tree sin lasted."[17]

ADAM AND EVE AS PROTOTYPES OF CHRIST AND THE VIRGIN

While the tree of knowledge prefigures the cross, the cross itself is thought to have been erected over the grave of Adam. According to tradition, Golgotha (or Calvary, a Latin translation of Luke 23:33), "the Place of the Skull," takes its name from the skull of Adam lying at the base of the cross. The belief that Christ's crucifixion took place at the site of Adam's burial depends on the tradition of the two Adams— one redeeming the other and undoing the consequences of disobedience—and gives a geographical dimension to it. In a letter to Marcella, Jerome describes several locations in the Holy Land, including Calvary, the site where the blood of the Second Adam washed away the sins of the buried first Adam. According to Jerome, this fulfilled the prophecy "awake, sleepers and arise from the dead,

15 Ibid.

16 Justin Martyr, *Dialogue with Trypho*, 86; Prudentius, *Hymn* 10.620–25. Ignatius, *Epistle to the Smyrnaeans* 1.1 hints at the connection.

17 Irenaeus, *Against Heresies*, 5.19 and Cyril, *Catechesis* 13.1-19. *The Works of Saint Cyril of Jerusalem*, vol. 2, trans. and ed. Leo McCauley and Anthony A. Stephenson, FOC 64 (Washington, DC: Catholic University Press, 1970) 16–17. Note also later works of art (especially medieval illuminations) that show the tree/crucifix as set between Adam and Eve.

and Christ will give you light" (Eph 5:14).[18] The proximity of their skeletons (perhaps theirs were the tombs that were opened at the moment Christ died, according to Matt 27:52) may explain why the "harrowing of Hell" on Holy Saturday develops into the teaching that Adam and Eve, along with the prophets and patriarchs, are liberated through Christ's passion, a scene popular in Orthodox iconography.[19]

Adam thus prefigures Christ, and Eve becomes the type of Mary. This typology sets up a system in which the two paradoxically participate in humanity's salvation; type needs antitype. The original created image, lost through disobedience, is renewed through his mother's obedience as well as through Christ's, and thus the characters of both Adam and Eve are ironically essential for the working out of the divine economy. A variation on Irenaeus's understanding that only through their sin and consequent mortality could Adam and Eve achieve perfection (maturity), this theory asserts that the very act of disobedience was a kind of inverse blessing, a "happy fault" (*felix culpa*). If Adam and Eve had not misbehaved, there would have been no need for the redeeming gift of the incarnation.

As described above, Romans 5:14 provides the basis for the use of Adam as a figure of Christ, by calling him the "type of the one who was to come." In 1 Corinthians 15:47-49 the idea is extended to the creation in the image, an image that Adam lost and was restored in Christ: "The first man was from the earth, a man of dust; the second man is from heaven.... Just as we have borne the image of dust, we shall also bear the image of the man of heaven."[20] According to subsequent commentators, however, the image was not lost so much as obscured or distorted. Christ's coming allowed the image to be restored in large part simply by renewing the visible model. That model then could be individually and initially reclaimed in baptism and strengthened through the teachings and sacraments of the church. The baptized person is then like Adam and Eve when they were first created, the divine image new and fresh upon them.[21]

This idea, the restoration of Adam's image through the coming of Christ, is central for second- and third-century writers. Irenaeus, for instance, speaks of the incarnation as a "recreation" of Adam (again) after the image and likeness of God, just as later writers could speak of

---

[18] *Letter* 46.3. See also H. Leclercq, "Calvaire (Le Mont)," *DACL* 2/2 (1925): 1755–56. The skull at the base of the cross is standard in later iconography of crucifixion. Occasionally the whole figure of Adam appears as well.

[19] The tradition that Christ descended into hell between his crucifixion and resurrection stems partly from the need to explain what happened on the day between Friday and Sunday. See, for example, Tertullian, *On the Soul* 55; Prudentius, *Hymn* 9, 90–96; or the later apocryphal *Gospel of Nicodemus*. For a discussion of this in Christian iconography see Anna D. Kartsonis, *Anastasis: The Making of An Image* (Princeton NJ: Princeton University Press, 1986) esp. 156–58.

[20] Secondary literature on this topic is significant and includes Robin Scroggs, *The Last Adam: A Study in Pauline Anthropology* (Philadelphia PA: Fortress Press, 1966).

[21] See Athanasius, *On the Incarnation* 14, where the author compares the restoration of the image to the renewal of a painting.

the baptism of the candidate as a restoration of the image.[22] Tertullian perceives a kind of recapitulation of the creation and fall in the incarnation of Christ. Jesus may be called "Adam" because he had real human flesh and an earthly origin (Mary). In the incarnation the act of creation was repeated, but the pattern was inverted so as to reverse the results. Whereas in the first creation humanity was formed in the image of God, in the incarnation divinity came in the image of humanity. What was lost (or stolen) was thus recovered.[23] In some of the examples the facial features of Adam and Christ are strikingly similar, as if they were twin brothers. Of course, Adam also is named as Jesus' original ancestor in Luke's patronymic list (3:23) and so would share some genetic identity.[24]

The textual tradition avoids explicitly asserting that Christ renews Eve's image, perhaps because the lack of gender parallelism makes it seem awkward or because Adam was intended to represent the whole of humanity. Christ is not described as renewing *Eve's* image, but only Adam's, arguably because Christ as "New Eve" would sound odd in writing. "Adam" carries the linguistic sense of referring to humanity generically. Surprisingly, however, in some of the iconography Eve also looks a bit like both Christ and Adam, as if the artwork wants to show that she too shares the original divine image and its renewal (see Figures 5, 7, and 9). In this case the iconographic practice then diverges from the textual tradition, at least in the specific inclusion of Eve in the restoration as well as the creation in the image, allowing the visual imagery to make a point not easily stated in written text.

Even though Eve was not explicitly identified by the tradition as a pattern for restored humanity, she was certainly included when blame for the fall was assigned. Despite rare instances in which writers apparently forgot that she was there in the garden at all, the more common approach made her the primary agent of sin.[25] Eve is portrayed as such in 1 Timothy 2:11-15 where Adam is excused (he was not deceived) and Eve's disobedience is given as cause for women's silence and submission to men. Eve is only mentioned one other time in the New Testament (2 Cor 11:3), where she is held up as the bad example (having been led astray by the serpent) for a Christian "betrothed to Christ." Theophilus relies on this text and similarly depicts Eve as a

---

[22] *Against Heresies* 5.1.3.

[23] *On the flesh of Christ*, 17.

[24] Irenaeus mentions this in *Against Heresies* 3.22.3.

[25] For example, see Irenaeus, *Proof of the Apostolic Preaching* 16. Here, Irenaeus ignores Eve and blames the sin on Adam, who was tempted by a jealous Satan and his serpent-agent. As a result, Irenaeus keeps the woman out of his presentation of the fall, and shows God as rebuking the serpent and the angel and punishing the man.

dupe of the cunning snake: "The maleficent demon, also called Satan, who then spoke to Eve through the serpent and is still at work in those men who are possessed by him, addressed her as Eve because she was at first deceived by the serpent and became the pioneer of sin."26

Tertullian asserted that women are Eve's particular descendents and thus as a whole group follow her as being "the devil's gateway" and the one who destroyed the human image of God. Tertullian's statement is a notorious instance of blaming Eve in particular, not only for the fall but for its necessary redemptive remedy—the voluntary sacrifice of the Son of God.27 Here again, however, the iconography seems to take a different view of the matter. While some of the images show the snake in particular relationship to Eve, either turning toward her or holding the fruit out to her (Figures 9 and 10), there is no obvious blaming of Eve in most of the artworks, and in at least one case, the serpent's face may be the product of much later restoration (Figure 9). Eve and Adam look approximately the same, usually a little surprised or perhaps even a little resigned. Eve is no more shamed than Adam, nor is she presented as either especially weak or seductive.28

While Christ was not called "New Eve" in the literary tradition, Mary certainly was. Eve's role as the counterpoint to the obedient Virgin Mary may be hinted at in New Testament documents, if only in the parallels in the dialogues between the snake and Eve in the garden and Gabriel and Mary at the annunciation, or the description of the struggle between the woman and the serpent in Revelation 12 and the text of Genesis 3:15. And even though it seems like a logical extension of the Adam/Christ structure (with appropriate gender parallels), the full development of the Mary/Eve typology comes from Irenaeus in the second century: "For what the virgin Eve had bound fast through unbelief, this did the Virgin Mary set free through faith."29

Justin Martyr drew parallels between the "conceptions" of two female virgins, seeing the creation of Adam from the virginal earth as prefiguring the conception of Jesus by a virgin woman and the disobedience of Eve as a kind of conception in itself: "And he became man by the Virgin, in order that the disobedience which proceeded from the serpent might receive its destruction in the same manner in which it derived its origin. For Eve, an undefiled virgin, conceived the word of the serpent and brought forth disobedience and death. But the Virgin Mary, filled with faith and joy, answered 'Be it done unto me according to thy word' when the angel Gabriel announced to her the good tidings."[30] Tertullian also parallels Adam and Christ in a rather complicated excursus on the incarnation in which he refers to Adam's and Christ's virginal conceptions. Again, these were "aural" conceptions that took place through the organ of the ear. Whereas Eve received temptation through her ear and disobeyed, Mary received the word of Gabriel through *her* ear and obeyed. Eve believed the serpent, but Mary listened to the angel.[31]

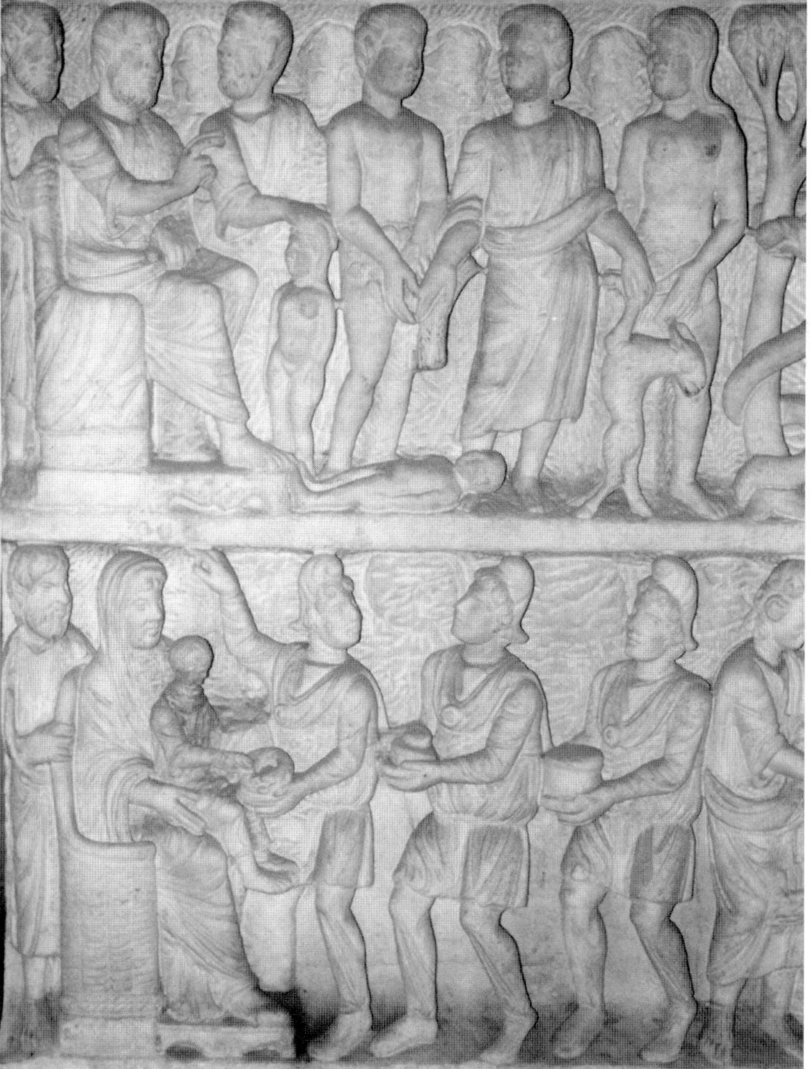

FIG 11.
Trinity Sarcophagus (cf. Figure 7) with adoration of magi (below), Museo Pio Cristiano. Roman sarcophagus, British Museum.

[30] *Dialogue with Trypho*, 100. *Saint Justin Martyr*, trans. and ed. Thomas B. Falls, FOC (New York: Christian Heritage, 1948) 305. Elsewhere (*Dial.* 84), Justin sees the creation of Eve from Adam's rib as a prefiguring of the virgin birth.

[31] *On the flesh of Christ 17.* See medieval and renaissance presentations of the annunciation, in which the small image of the incarnate Christ seems to be flying into Mary's ear as a visual presentation of this idea in later art works.

This typological system of birth, conception, fall, and incarnation visually appears on the two fourth-century sarcophagi that portray the creation of Adam and Eve (Figures 7 and 8). The left-hand side of the upper register presents the image of the Trinity creating Adam and Eve, while directly below (in the lower register) is a scene of the three magi presenting gifts to the Christ child, who is seated on his mother's lap (Figure 11). Mary sits in the same type of chair as God, while Joseph stands behind her in the same fashion as the figure corresponding to the Holy Spirit. Such compositional parallelism clearly suggests a relationship between the two scenes, one of the creation of humanity and the other of the nativity of Christ. And although a viewer might reasonably conclude that the artist intended to parallel Mary with God rather than with Eve, the meaning seems visually apparent if read from left to right and top to bottom. Creation is completed in incarnation. The "fall" of Adam and Eve is truly a part of the whole story of redemption. The first of the three magi hands a gift to the child and points with his right index finger to the star, but also to the upper register of the relief—as if to suggest that the beginning should be recalled in the moment of its perfection.

The prominence of this typological tradition in art as well as in literature suggests that Adam and Eve were understood to serve an important role in the economy of salvation. Once established, moreover, the imagery never fades.[32] Even the serpent, who never entirely drops out of the imagery, may have a key role in the working out of the solution and perhaps should not be understood as only an antagonist (a "snake in the grass"). The tradition of the snake as a positive symbol appears in gnostic mythology; or, at least according to Irenaeus, certain folks claimed that Wisdom herself (Sophia) became the snake and introduced humanity to wisdom and knowledge. For this reason, "the snake was thought to be more prudent than all other creatures."[33]

The wages of this original sin was death. Early exegetes argued that death was, in a sense, preventative of further fall—a kind of floor or safety net so that the slide into sin should not be infinite (at death, sin ceases).[34] Thus, in a funeral context Adam and Eve are the symbols both of death and its undoing, since the two ultimately are saved and restored to Eden at the end.[35] Irenaeus explained how it was that death had a positive value:

> Wherefore he drove him [Adam] out of Paradise, and removed him far from the tree of life, not because he envied him the tree of life, as some venture to assert, but because he pitied him [and did not desire] that he should continue a sinner for ever, nor that the sin which surrounded him should be immortal, and evil interminable and irremediable. But he set a bound to his [state of] sin, by interposing death, and thus causing sin to cease, putting an end to it by the dissolution of the flesh, which should take place in the earth, so that man, ceasing at length to live to sin, and dying to it, might begin to live to God.[36]

And so the iconography also continues to include the serpent, perhaps not only as a sign of sin but also as a reminder of sin's cessation and final destruction (the Virgin will tread on the head of the serpent).[37] The enmity between the seed of the serpent and the seed (offspring) of the woman was interpreted to be a prophecy of Christ's destruction of Satan.[38] A kind of cosmic (and final) destruction of the serpent was also understood as an allegory of humanity's achieving a kind of control over unruly human desires for self-gratification. The serpent is also associated with fertility and thus concupiscence and sexual knowledge. Clement of Alexandria (like Irenaeus and Theophilus) portrayed Adam and Eve as children at the beginning of creation, but especially as children who were seduced by pleasure and led astray by lusts, which were symbolized by the serpent. By the time the two achieved adulthood, the bonds of sin were holding them so fast that the Lord had to take on the "clothing of flesh" and subdue the serpent (and "tyrant death"). Thus, the one who had fallen through seeking pleasure was made free again.[39]

ADAM AND EVE AS SYMBOLS OF CONJUGAL DEVOTION AND HARMONY

The only Gospel allusion to Adam and Eve comes in Jesus' teaching on divorce. According to the text (Matt 19:4; Mark 10:1-12),

[35] Tatian's denial that Adam ultimately would be saved, was part of his heretical teachings in Irenaeus's eyes, *Against Heresies* 1.28.1: "they deny the salvation of him who was first created—a certain man named Tatian seems to have invented this blasphemy…an opinion due entirely to himself." And again in *Against Heresies* 3.23.8: "All therefore speak falsely who disallow his (Adam's) salvation, shutting themselves out from life for ever, I that they do not believe that the sheep which had perished has been found."

[36] *Against Heresies* 3.26.6. See also 3.23.7: "the last enemy, death was destroyed."

[37] Compare Prudentius's *Hymn* 3, 140–55, where the poet speaks of the "spotless maiden subduing the venom of the serpent; with *Hymn* 9, 85–94, in which blood from the cross is the antidote for the serpent's venom. Note that the serpent in early Christian iconography has the face of a monster, but not of a woman. In later art from the Middle Ages and Renaissance, the serpent often bears a likeness to Eve. For example, see Masolino's painting of Adam and Eve in the Brancacci Chapel, Florence. Also see the iconography of Mary as Queen of Heaven crushing the serpent.

[38] See Irenaeus, *Against Heresies* 5.21.1-3.

[39] *Exhortation to the Greeks*, 11.

[40] See Peter Brown, *The Body and Society: Men, Women, and Sexual Renunciation in Early Christianity* (New York: Columbia University Press, 1988) 57. For a general study of Roman values regarding marriage as well as the legislation that sought to encourage "strong families," see Judith Evans Grubbs, *Law and Family in Late Antiquity: The Emperor Constantine's Marriage Legislation* (Oxford: Oxford University Press, 1995). Jane F. Gardner, *Family and Familia in Roman Law and Life* (Oxford: Oxford University Press, 1998).

[41] Clement, *First Epistle*, 6.

Jesus reminds his audience that the original two were created male and female so that they might become joined together as one flesh and not separated by human agency. Readers can understand Jesus to emphasize not only the permanency of the conjugal bond, but also its symbolism. Roman Christians probably would understand that Adam and Eve's marriage was a divinely instituted and sanctioned model for human society—one that epitomized domestic concord and stability, as well as mutual obligation and affection. Such an understanding would not have contradicted traditional Roman (pagan) "family values." Spouses (wives in particular) who were devoted, faithful, patient, and tolerant represented an ideal in a society that generally believed a patriarchal system of dominant (but loving) fathers, submissive wives, and obedient children provided the best structure for a stable family and thriving community. Christians might interpret their own sources to support these widely held cultural values and thus could argue that domestic concord reflected a divine ideal, even showing forth the type of bond that existed between Christ and the church (see Eph 5:21-33). Adam and Eve thus became the paradigm of the happily married couple, whose devoted affection for one another could then symbolize God's care for human souls.[40]

The writer of Ephesians also cited the marriage narrative of Genesis when urging wives to be subject to husbands and husbands to love their wives as Christ loved the church and tenderly care for her as if for his own body: "For this reason a man will leave his father and mother and be joined to his wife" (5:31). In a different tone, however, the writer of 1 Timothy (2:11-15) accounted for women's submissive state by citing Eve's disobedience, and then offered a kind of consolation—the woman gains the possibility of salvation through childbearing, provided she continues in "faith and love and holiness, with modesty."

Domestic harmony was endorsed by first- and second-century Christian moralists, who also cited the relationship between Adam and Eve. Clement of Rome's first epistle refers to Adam's exclamation after the creation of Eve from his rib: "this is at last bone of my bones and flesh of my flesh" in his admonitions against destructive jealousy or rivalry between husbands and wives.[41] Likewise, Theophilus of

Antioch stressed the importance of marital love, especially in times of trial:

42 Theophilus, *To Autolycus*, 28.

43 *Against Marcion*, 2.4

> Moreover he [God] formed only man from the earth so that thus the mystery of the divine unity might be demonstrated. At the same time, God made woman by taking her from his side so that man's love for her might be greater. Adam said to Eve, "This is now bone from my bones and flesh from my flesh," and in addition he prophesies saying, "For this reason a man will leave his father and mother and cleave to his wife and the two shall be one flesh." This is actually fulfilled among us. For what man who marries lawfully does not disregard his mother and father and his whole family and all his relatives, while he cleaves to his own wife and unites with her, loving her more than them? For this reason, husbands have often suffered even death for the sake of their wives.[42]

Even Tertullian, refuting the gnostic denunciation of the married state, argued that marriage was a blessed state—at least for the men whom God gave women to be their companions and helpers: "Goodness also imposed a help meet for him, that there might be nothing in his lot that was not good. For, said God, that a man be alone is not good. God knew full well what a blessing to him would be the sex of Mary, and also of the Church." [43]

Thus early Christian moralists exhorted married couples to remain together and to live their lives in harmony and faithfulness. At the beginning of the fifth century (ca. 405), Paulinus of Nola delivered a poem written for the celebration of a marriage (*enthalmium*) between Julian of Eclanum and Titia, both the children of bishops and from aristocratic families. Typical pagan examples of marriage poems invoked the goddess of love and made frequent erotic allusions. Paulinus, on the other hand, banishes Juno, Cupid, and Venus, "those symbols of lust," and instead urges the young couple to make a "harmonious marriage alliance" both holy and honorable. The poem goes on to assure the couple that God's own command established

44 Paulinus, *Hymn* 25.13–27. *The Poems of St. Paulinus of Nola*, trans. P. G. Walsh, ACW 40 (New York: Newman Press, 1975) 245–46.

45 Ambrose, *On Paradise*, 6.33-34. *Saint Ambrose Hexameron, Paradise, and Cain and Abel*, trans. and ed. John J. Savage, FOC 42 (Washington DC: Catholic University Press, 1961) 310–13.

46 *City of God*, 14.11.

47 Brown, *Body and Society*, 401. Brown asserts, "On Roman sarcophagi of that time, Adam and Eve were freqently shown with their right hands joined in the *dextrarum iunctio* that rendered visible the concord of a Roman marriage." While this is essentially the point this paper would like to make, Brown is incorrect to say that the image appears *frequently*. To the contrary, the image of Adam and Eve joining right hands is very rare.

marriage by making the two (Adam and Eve) abide in one flesh in order "to confer a love more indivisible."44

Ambrose, in his treatise on paradise, explained Eve's act of eating the apple as one of simple disobedience. Her subsequent act, to give Adam the fruit, was differently motivated, however. Once she ate of the fruit of knowledge she understood what she had done. She *knew* that eating it was sinful and, having that insight, should not have lured Adam (whom she loved) to do likewise. Her newly acquired knowledge made her responsible for protecting her husband from her own mistake, and not doing so only compounded her sin. Ambrose goes on, however, to explain her actions as being motivated by her fear of being alone. She realized that she would be expelled from the garden. But he was also aware of others who gave her a different motive—love. According to Ambrose, some commentators argued that "she should be excused for the reason that, because she loved her husband, she was afraid that she would be separated from him."45 In his treatise *City of God*, Augustine argues a similar point, but from a different angle. According to him, no one could believe that Adam was led astray because he believed Eve told the truth, but because as a married pair they were so tightly bonded in their partnership that Adam refused to be separated from his only companion, even if it meant becoming involved in her sin.46

Marriage scenes frequently appear on pagan and christian funerary monuments in the first centuries of the common era. They show the couple extending their right hands in the legal gesture of marriage (*dextrarum iunctio*), often with Juno presiding as the goddess who blesses marriage with harmony and concord (Figure 12). The image parallels the common epitaphs of the era that were dedicated by one spouse to another and describe the deceased as dearest, or (in the case of wives) most sweet or most obedient (*carissima/us, dulcissima,* or *obsequentissima*). The Christian iconography of Adam and Eve occasionally employs this same gesture, perhaps as a way of adapting the pagan custom to a Christian context (Figure 13).47 Adam and Eve also appear on the left end of a Roman sarcophagus whose front frieze is crowded with images of Jesus' miracles. The lid of the sarcophagus has a portrait of the deceased with a central plaque bearing this inscription: *SABINO CO[n]IUGI QUI VIXIT ANN[os] XLIII M[enses] X D[ies] XIII B[ene] M[erenti] IN PACE* ("To Sabinus, husband, who lived forty-four years, ten months, thirteen days, a man of merit, in peace").[48]

Thus the beginning of the story comes around to the end. Adam and Eve appear in funeral art, perhaps because they are a touching symbol of a marriage partnership, one that has been blessed and, even after the expulsion from the garden, goes on to be fruitful and eventually the basis for (if not the source of) human redemption. Irenaeus's

[48] For an illustration, see Kurt Weitzmann, ed., *The Age of Spirituality: A catalogue of the exhibition at the Metropolitan Museum of Art* (Princeton NJ: Princeton University Press, 1979) entries 374, 417–18.

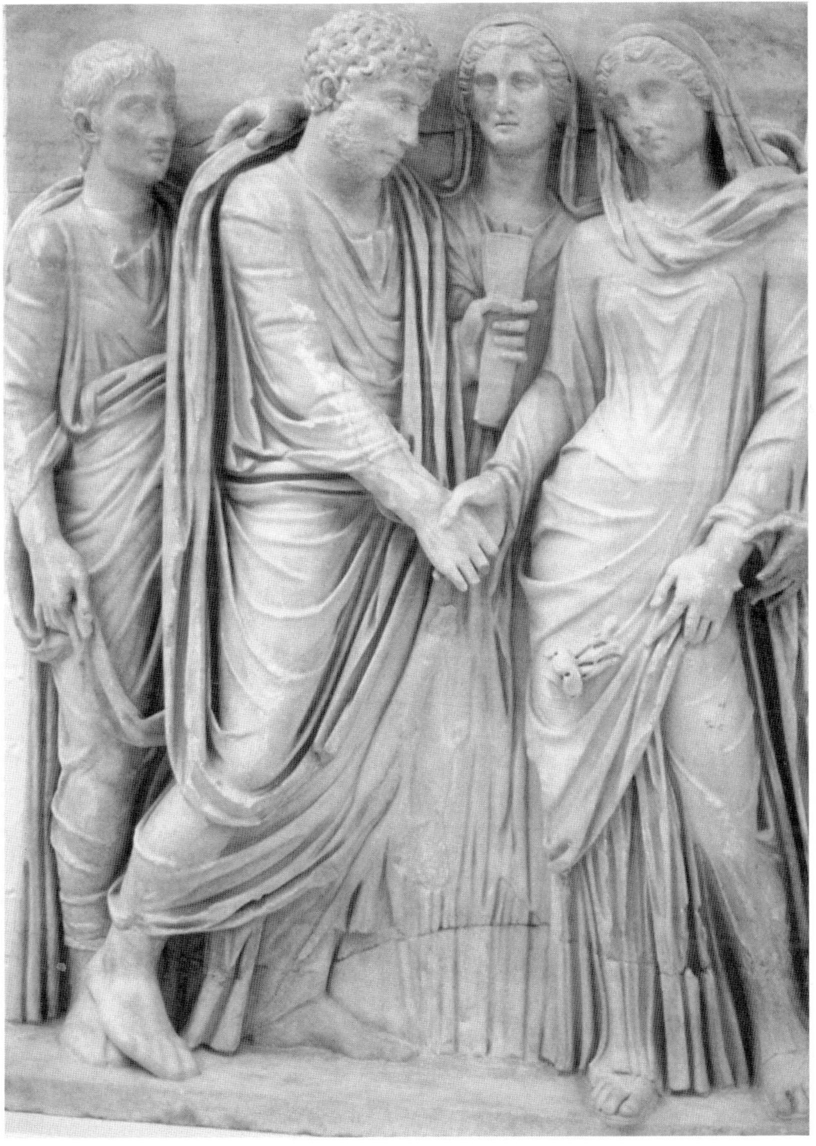

FIG 12.
Marriage Scene.
Second-century.
Roman sarcophagus.
British Museum.
Photo: Author.

[49] Ibid., entries 378 and 422. The *Age of Spirituality* catalogue here translates the inscription as "Rejoice in God, drink, live," probably based on the translation and interpretation of the inscription on a similar glass bowl ("VIVAS CUM TUIS PIE Z"), which is arguably a combination of Latin and Greek (in Roman characters); the first three words mean "Life to you and yours," and the last two are a form of two Greek words, meaning "Drink and be of good health." See D.B. Harden, "The Wint Hill Hunting Bowl and Related Glasses," *Journal of Glass Studies* 2 (1960): 45–80.

teaching included that a good and omniscient (not evil or incompetent) God created Adam and Eve as childlike and yet free to fail, able to be deceived but not utterly destroyed, and eventually to be restored and perfected through the completion of the original plan of salvation. Christ becomes a new Adam and restores the image. Eve's disobedience is countered by Mary's compliance, and both women are saved through their offspring. The human race learns through the consequences of the fall and finally grows up and realizes its potential for perfection. Thus, God offers the creation a second chance to obey, and this time unites the divine nature with human frailty so that it cannot fail.

And so the representation of Adam and Eve, whether in written documents or in artistic remains, is complex, multi-layered, and as filled with hope as it is with shame. There may be no other way to explain the fourth-century glass bowl found in a Roman tomb in Cologne that shows the naked Adam and Eve standing in front of the tree of knowledge. Around the tree's trunk coils the snake, and Adam raises his right hand in the traditional gesture of speech. Around the rim of the bowl is, perhaps, what the owner of the bowl is supposed to understand Adam to say: *GAUDIAS IN DEO PIE Z* ("Rejoice in God, drink, live").[49]

FIG 13. Velletri plaque, ca. 310 (Museo Civico, Velletri).

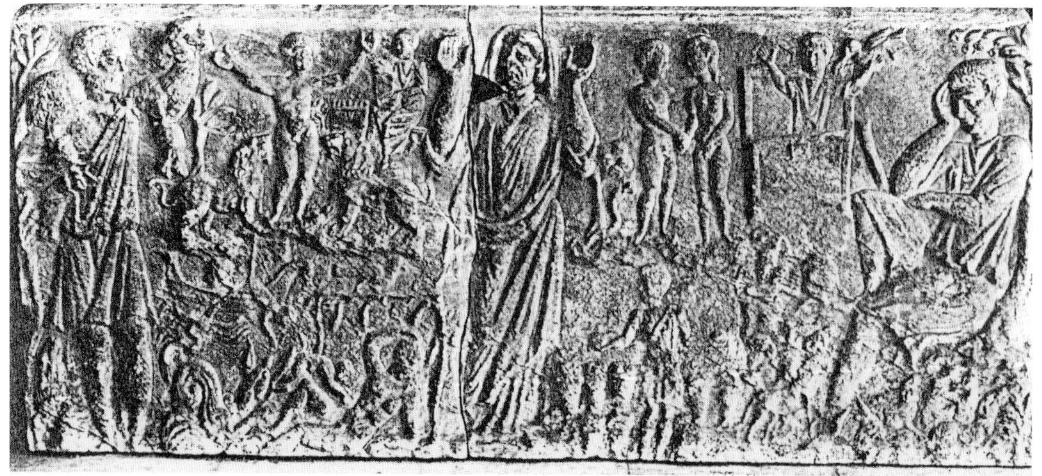

3.

Agape, Eucharist and Sacrifice in Early Christian Art

Graydon F. Snyder
Chicago Theological Seminary

Any interpretation of historical data, texts, art, inscriptions, or architecture deeply involves the perspective of the interpreter. Rather than hide under the pretense of objectivity, it would be better to state at the outset one's method and presuppositions. First, I come to the early church and the New Testament from an Anabaptist/Baptist perspective. That means I look for signifiers of the community of faith more than for ecclesiastical traditions. Secondly, as a corollary, my method is heavily sociological. I try to understand art more in terms of its social context than its aesthetics and liturgical or theological development. I seldom use parallel writings because I assume, perhaps overly much, that the sentiments of the religious actor usually differ from those of the religious writer. Furthermore, I assume we will normally find the sentiments of the religious actor in the visual field.[1]

[1] Margaret R. Miles, *Image as Insight: Visual Understanding in Western Christianity and Secular Culture* (Boston: Beacon Press, 1985) 15–39.

[2] Hans Lietzmann, *Messe und Herrenmahl—Eine Studie zur Geschichte der Liturgie* (Berlin: Verlag Walter de Gruyter, 1926) 249-52. Translated by Dorothea H.G. Reeve, *Mass and the Lord's Supper: A Study in the History of the Liturgy* (Leiden: E.J. Brill, 1979) 204–208.

Few problems are more indecipherable for the analyst than the origins of the agape and Eucharist. The researcher has to juggle the Jewish fellowship meal, the Jewish Passover, the Last Supper, the Christian fellowship meal, the Eucharist with or without a sacrifice, and the feeding of the 5,000. Up to this moment no analyst has managed a satisfactory explanation for the origin and development of the Eucharist. The intention here is not to propose a solution to the problem but to examine how early Christian art informs the issues.

The pivotal study on the Eucharist was published by Hans Lietzmann in 1926.[2] Whether one agrees with Lietzmann or not, his incomparable research cannot be overlooked. Put very simply Lietzmann sees two meals in the New Testament. Both can be found in Paul's letter to the Corinthians. The first is a meal that follows the pattern of a Jewish fellowship meal with the cup first as an aperitif and the bread second as the food. In 1 Corinthians 10:16-17 Paul writes

10:16 Τὸ ποτήριον τῆς εὐλογίας ὃ εὐλογοῦμεν, οὐχὶ κοινωνία ἐστὶν τοῦ αἵματος τοῦ Χριστοῦ; τὸν ἄρτον ὃν κλῶμεν, οὐχὶ κοινωνία τοῦ σώματος τοῦ Χριστοῦ ἐστιν;
10:17 ὅτι εἷς ἄρτος, ἓν σῶμα οἱ πολλοί ἐσμεν, οἱ γὰρ πάντες ἐκ τοῦ ἑνὸς ἄρτου μετέχομεν.

10:16 The cup of blessing that we bless, is it not a sharing (formation of community) in the blood of Christ? The bread that we break, is it not a sharing (formation of community) in the body of Christ?
10:17 Because there is one bread, we who are many are one body, for we all partake of the one bread.

Sharing in the breaking of bread creates community or fellowship. The cup of wine acts as the liquid appetizer or aperitif that assembles the community before the meal proper.

In 1 Corinthians 11 Paul returns again to the matter of eating together. He speaks critically of a church meal called the Lord's Supper (κυριακὸν δεῖπνον). Because the problems described have to do with equal sharing of food and wine, and because the inequalities reflect potential ruptures in the κοινωνία or fellowship, we can assume the Lord's Supper or agape must be nearly identical with the fellowship meal mentioned in chapter 10.

The agape meal described in 1 Corinthians 11 included, or was followed by, an ἀνάμνησις. Eucharist where the death of Jesus is remembered. The body (bread) is broken first so that the Spirit (the cup) may be released:

> <u>11:23</u> Ἐγὼ γὰρ παρέλαβον ἀπὸ τοῦ κυρίου, ὃ καὶ παρέδωκα ὑμῖν, ὅτι ὁ κύριος Ἰησοῦς ἐν τῇ νυκτὶ ᾗ παρεδίδετο ἔλαβεν ἄρτον
>
> <u>11:24</u> καὶ εὐχαριστήσας ἔκλασεν καὶ εἶπεν· τοῦτό μού ἐστιν τὸ σῶμα τὸ ὑπὲρ ὑμῶν· τοῦτο ποιεῖτε εἰς τὴν ἐμὴν ἀνάμνησιν.
>
> <u>11:25</u> ὡσαύτως καὶ τὸ ποτήριον μετὰ τὸ δειπνῆσαι λέγων· τοῦτο τὸ ποτήριον ἡ καινὴ διαθήκη ἐστὶν ἐν τῷ ἐμῷ αἵματι· τοῦτο ποιεῖτε, ὁσάκις ἐὰν πίνητε, εἰς τὴν ἐμὴν ἀνάμνησιν.

I would translate the passage as follows

> <u>11:23</u> For I received from the Lord what I also handed on to you, that the Lord Jesus on the night when he was betrayed took a loaf of bread,
>
> <u>11:24</u> and when he had given thanks, he broke it and said, "This act of breaking the bread is my body for you. Do this in remembrance of me."
>
> <u>11:25</u> In the same way he took the cup also, after supper, saying, "This act of drinking the cup together is the new covenant in my blood. Do this, as often as you drink it, in remembrance of me."

In both types of Eucharist the emphasis is on action and doing. We have mistakenly supposed the bread was the body of Christ and the wine was the blood of Christ. The translation should read that the breaking of the bread creates the body of Christ and the Spirit of the new covenant is released by the sharing of the cup.[3] Many Christians

[3]Graydon F. Snyder, *First Corinthians: A Faith Community Commentary* (Macon GA: Mercer University Press, 1992) 158.

speak of the *anamnesis* Eucharist as a sacrament. I would rather call it an action symbol.[4] In early Christian art, as we shall see, the bread and the wine are frequent symbols. Even more prevalent is the symbolic breaking of the bread and drinking of the wine. These pictures portray the action that creates the Christian community just as Paul's statements were verbal portrayals.

Lietzmann argues that the fellowship type meal derived from the normal Jewish fellowship meal eaten by Jesus and his disciples, the *chaberah.*[5] The fellowship meal continues in such early Christian literature as the *Didache* but, as we will see, eventually shifts into a meal not only for the living but also for the dead.

The *anamnesis* or remembrance Eucharist, the second tradition to which Paul refers, comes from the Last Supper described in each of the Synoptic Gospels. The Last Supper narrative in the Synoptics purports to be a Passover but, in contrast to the Jewish procedure, ends with a sacrificial cup that promises new life in the coming kingdom.[6] If this does indeed establish the *anamnesis* Eucharist, the bread and cup attached to the Jewish Passover, it must be noted that there are no artistic portrayals of Jesus eating with the disciples until the sixth-century mosaic art of Ravenna (Figure 1). Even then there is no

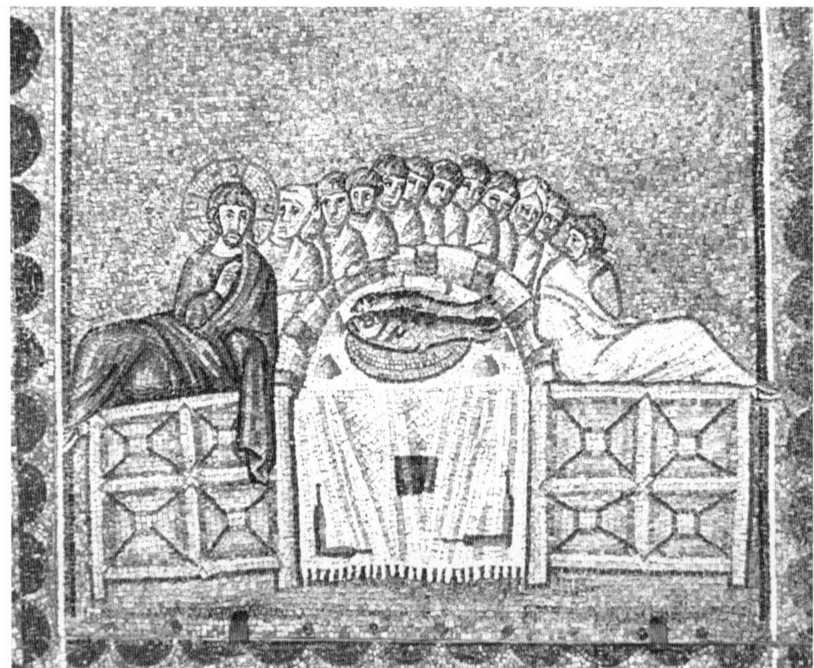

FIG 1.
Last Supper. Sixth century mosaic from S. Apollinare Nuovo, Ravenna.

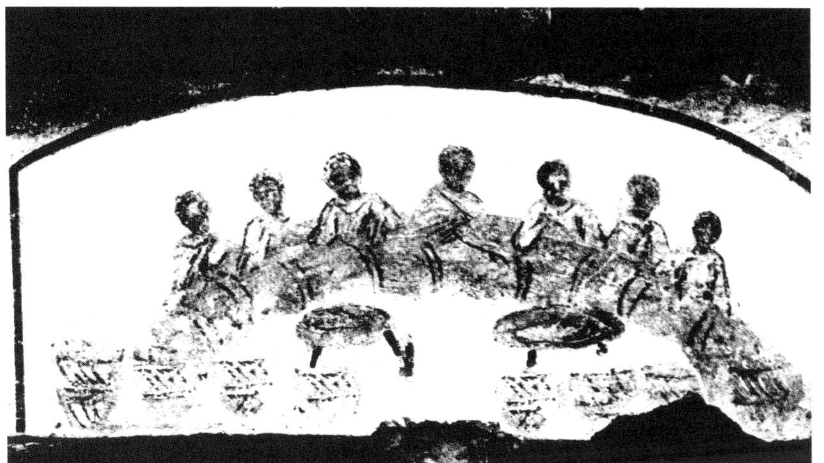

FIG 2.
Early Christian Symbolic Meal. Third century fresco from the Sacrament Chapel A 3, Catacomb of Callixtus, Rome.

Passover menu. The food in Ravenna consists of fish, bread, and wine. Whatever we say about the agape or fellowship meal, the *anamnesis* or remembrance meal (the bread and the cup) does continue throughout Christian history.

In early Christian art we have many representations of Christian meals. The meals normally portray seven people sitting at a lunar table (Figure 2). Their food is bread, fish, and wine mixed with water. There are two fish and a pitcher of wine, while the bread is normally signified by seven baskets or loaves of bread at the table.

The tradition of bread and fish derives from the prominent feeding narrative known as the feeding of the 5,000 or the miracle of the loaves and fishes (Mark 6:35-44; 8:1-10; Matt 14:13-21; 15:32-39; Luke 9:11-17; John 6:5-13):

> <u>Mark 6:35</u> When it grew late, his disciples came to him and said, "This is a deserted place, and the hour is now very late; <u>6:36</u> send them away so that they may go into the surrounding country and villages and buy something for themselves to eat."
> <u>6:37</u> But he answered them, "You give them something to eat." They said to him, "Are we to go and buy two hundred denarii worth of bread, and give it to them to eat?"
> <u>6:38</u> And he said to them, "How many loaves have you? Go and see." When they had found out, they said, "Five, and two fish."

[7]Bo Reicke, *Diakonie, Festfreude, und Zelos* (Uppsala: Lundequistska, 1951) 134.

6:39 Then he ordered them to get all the people to sit down in groups on the green grass.

6:40 So they sat down in groups of hundreds and of fifties.

6:41 Taking the five loaves and the two fish, he looked up to heaven, and blessed and broke the loaves, and gave them to his disciples to set before the people; and he divided the two fish among them all.

6:42 And all ate and were filled;

6:43 and they took up twelve baskets full of broken pieces and of the fish.

6:44 Those who had eaten the loaves numbered five thousand men.

In the Markan account the apostles find the five loaves of bread and two fish (Figure 3). In the Gospel of John it is the boy who presents his resource of five loaves and two fish (John 6:9). These accounts are formal in nature. The multitude sits on the grass in groups of fifties and hundreds. Before the sharing Jesus looks up, blesses the bread, and breaks it. In Matthew's account the breaking of the bread and its distribution by the disciples are more directly attached to the Eucharistic prayer (having given thanks, he broke it and distributed it to the disciples, 15:36). The excess of bread fragments reflects the practice of the early church to share with those in need (he had compassion on the crowd, 15:32).[7]

The multiplication of the loaves itself appears often in early Christian art: Jesus waves a wand over several baskets of loaves (Figure 3). In regard to the meal itself, Passover motifs and the Passover menu are totally missing. We can only assume the Passover played no role in early church worship. In fact, we should assume the Passover as such played no role at all after the Jesus tradition (Synoptic Gospels) had been formed.

On the other hand, the menu and format of the feeding of the 5,000 occur consistently in early representations of the agape/Eucharist. The bread and fish are always present. The cup has been added on a consistent basis. Occasionally the bread and cup are being distributed. The persons who blessed and distributed the bread and

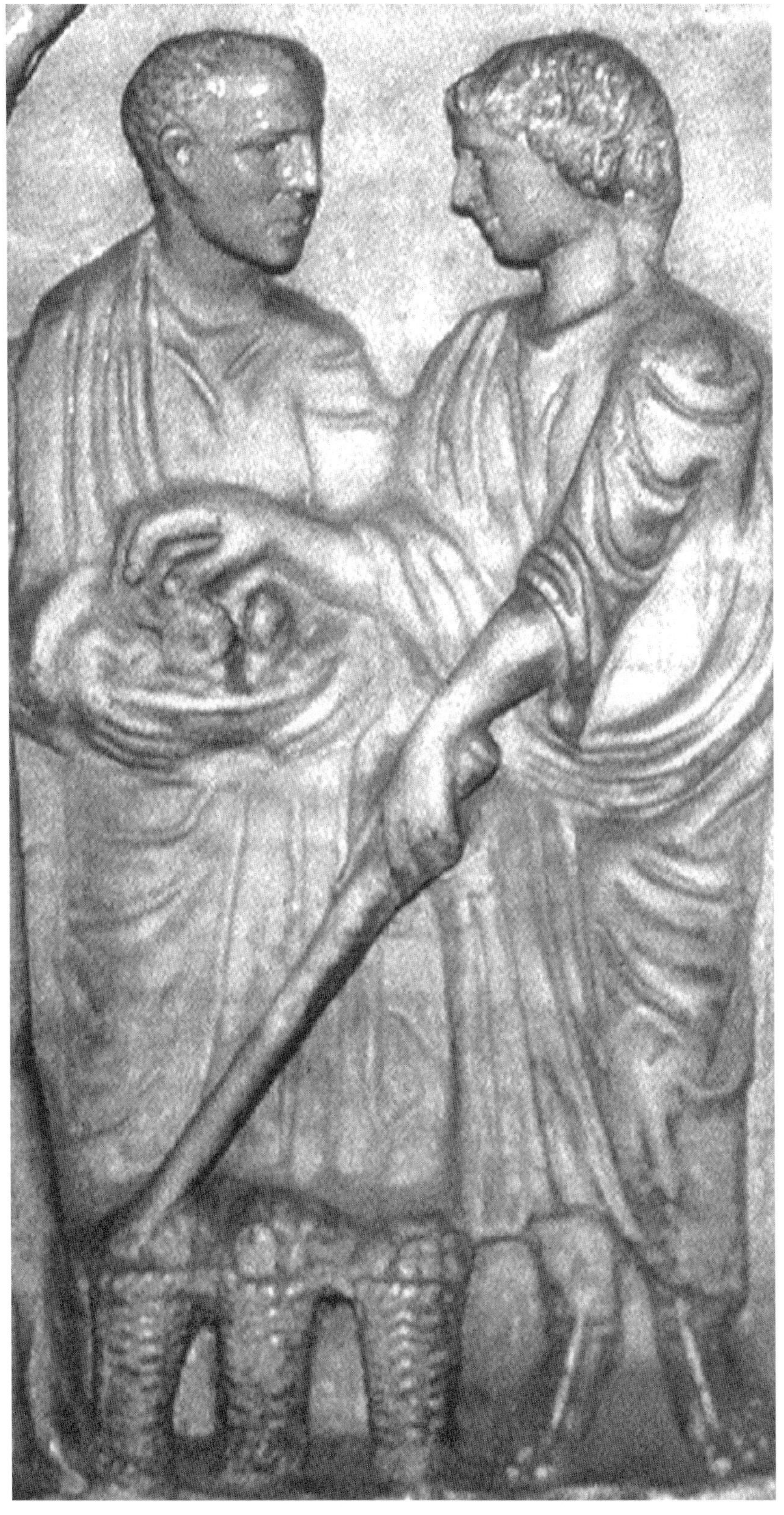

FIG 3.
Multiplication of the Loaves and Fishes. Detail of late fourth century sarcophagus in the Musée de l'Arles Antique, Arles , France.

cup were not necessarily priests, but normally the owner of the house or apartment where the community met. If that owner happened to be a woman, according to artistic representations, she supervised the distribution. There are always five or seven baskets of bread present. Like the fragments in the feeding narrative, the extra baskets of bread will be used to feed the hungry. However, the scenes are clearly symbolic actions. There is no reason to suppose only seven people shared in the Eucharist and that there were always five or seven baskets of bread. Like the text in 1 Corinthians these pictures signify an action symbol that forms the early Christian community.

The cup, bread, and fish found in early Christian art have no apparent connection with the death of Jesus. Actually, the cross is missing from earliest Christian art. The first extant example would be the early fifth-century doors of S. Sabina. Even though Paul's source for the Eucharist connects the bread and cup with the crucifixion, one could more plausibly argue that the use of the bread, cup, and fish simply derives from the menu of common folk in the Mediterranean basin. As such it avoided the problems of table fellowship and kosher food that so separated Jews from Gentiles. At the same time it elevated simple food to a meal that celebrated and created the nascent Christian community.[8]

Instead of the cross, sacrifice in early Christian art may have been portrayed by the sacrifice of Isaac.[9] It has been argued that the sacrifice of Isaac was the prototype for the sacrifice of Jesus. In Romans 8:32 Paul writes about the love of God:

> ὅς γε τοῦ ἰδίου υἱοῦ οὐκ ἐφείσατο ἀλλὰ ὑπὲρ
> ἡμῶν πάντων παρέδωκεν αὐτόν, πῶς οὐχὶ καὶ σὺν
> αὐτῷ τὰ πάντα ἡμῖν χαρίσεται;

> He who did not withhold his own Son, but gave him up for
> all of us, will he not with him also give us everything else?

The phrase "did not withhold your son" is also used of Abraham in relation to Isaac (Gen 22:12).[10] The notion that the Binding of Isaac was a sacrifice (known as the Aqedah) appeared in Judaism about the

[8]Graydon F. Snyder, *Inculturation of the Jesus Tradition: The Impact of Jesus on Jewish and Roman Cultures* (Harrisburg PA: Trinity Press International, 1999) 151–57.

[9]See Robin Jensen, *Understanding Early Christian Art* (London: Routledge, 2000) 143–48.

[10]C. E. B. Cranfield, vol. 1 of *The Epistle to the Romans* (Edinburgh: T. & T. Clark, 1975) 217–18, 436; Luke Timothy Johnson, *Reading Romans: A Literary and Theological Commentary* (New York: Crossroad Publishing, 1997) 134.

time the New Testament was formed. In terms of Jewish art the sacrifice of Isaac appears, for example, to the right of the Torah niche in the third-century BCE synagogue at Dura-Europos.

In the Dura Torah niche Isaac appears as a boy to be sacrificed by his father. The same is true for early Christian portrayals (Figure 4). But deuterocanonical Jewish materials and the Talmud changed the primary emphasis. There, Isaac is described as a grown man. The two so-called young men who accompany Abraham are actually two older, wise advisors. Isaac, as an adult, willingly goes to the altar as a self-sacrifice for the people of God.[11] The popularity of the sacrifice of Isaac in early Christian art likely reflects this later Jewish tradition in which Isaac gives of himself, more than of Abraham who gives up his son.

For their part rabbis saw the Aqedah as a way of countering the sacrifice of Jesus. In terms of early Christian art, however, the sacrifice of Isaac does not always parallel the sacrifice of Jesus. It often stands in the series of deliverance motifs that include Noah in the ark and Daniel in the lions' den.[12] Nevertheless it appears likely that the early Christians, perhaps even as a counter measure, picked up the theme of Isaac as a metaphor for the sacrifice of Jesus on the cross. Even after the cross did appear as a Christian artistic symbol, the sacrifice of Isaac continued to be used.[13] Eventually the sacrifice of Isaac and the Eucharist were combined in the high art of Byzantine Ravenna (Figure 5).[14]

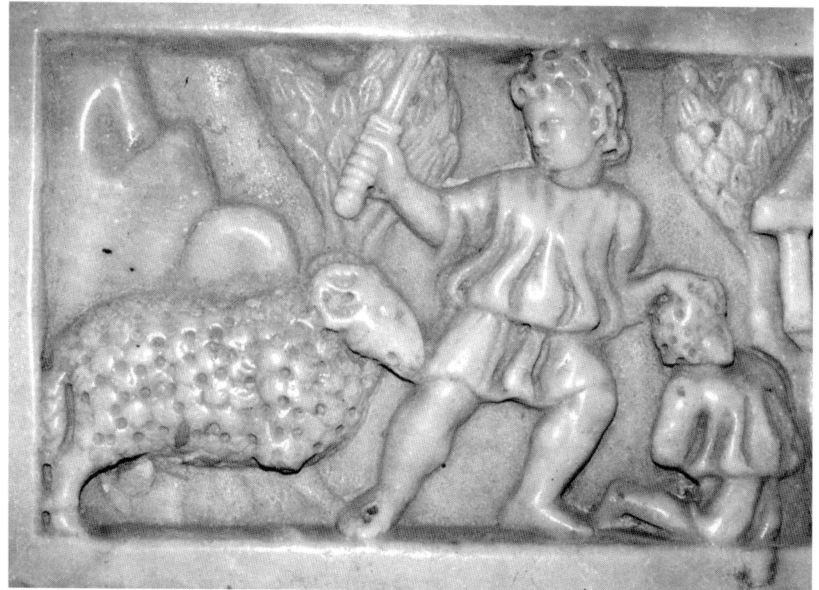

FIG 4.
Sacrifice of Isaac.
Detail of sarcophagus in L'eglise Sainte Quitterie du Mas, Aire-sur-l'Adour, France.

[11]Nils A. Dahl, "The Atonement: Adequate Reward for the Akedah?" *The Crucified Messiah* (Minneapolis: Augsburg, 1974) 146–60. P. R. Davies and B. D. Chilton, "The Aqedah: A Revised Tradition-History," *Catholic Biblical Quarterly* 40 (1978): 514–46.

[12]On the Orante type, see Isabel Speyart van Woerden, "The Iconography of the Sacrifice of Abraham," *Vigiliae Christianae* 15 (1961): 243.

[13]Alison Moore Smith, "The Iconography of the Sacrifice of Isaac in Early Christian Art," *American Journal of Archaeology*, 2/26 (1922): 168.

[14]Giuseppe Bovini, *Ravenna: An Art City* (Ravenna: Edizioni A. Longo, 1967) 40.

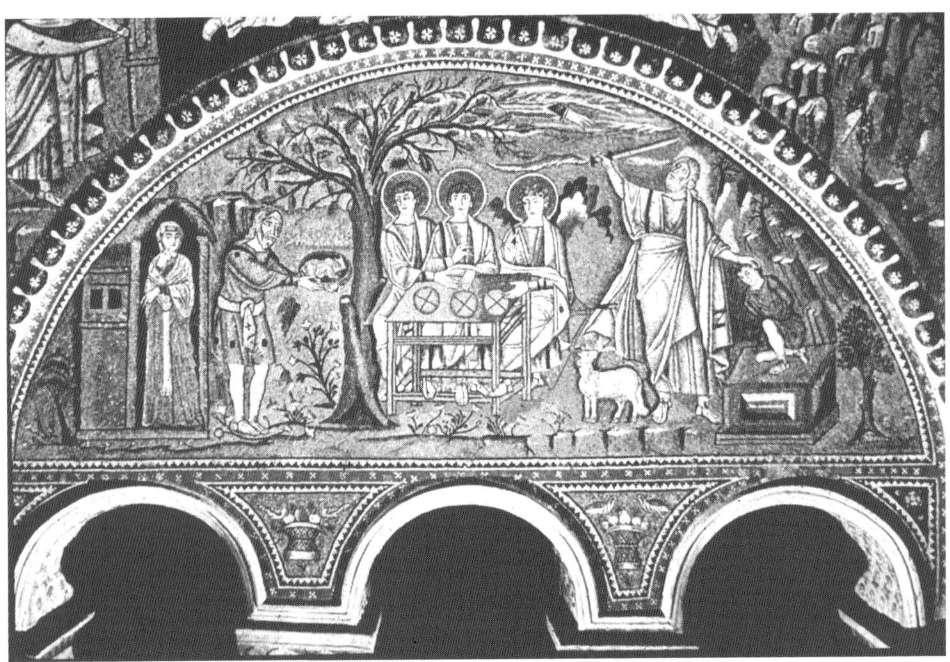

[15]Janos Fedak, *Monumental Tombs of the Hellenistic Age: A Study of Selected Tombs from the Pre-Classical to the Early Imperial Era* (Toronto: University of Toronto Press, 1990); Wolfgang Oberleitner, *Das Heroon von Trysa: Ein lykisches Fürstengrab des 4. Jahrhunderts v. Chr.* (Mainz am Rhein: Verlag Philipp von Zabern, 1994).

[16]Ejnar Dyggve, *Dødekult, Kejserkult og Basilika: Bidrag til Spørgsmålet om den oldkristne kultbygnings Genesis* (København: Branners Forlag, 1943) 13–15.

As for the fellowship meal called the agape, it did not remain simply a fellowship meal, but took over the non-Christian functions of a meal for the dead. In the Greco-Roman world, special dead were buried at a *heroon* and their death dates were celebrated by special meals.[15] A special place was set aside for the meal, close to the tomb, with arrangements for a pleasant meal in honor of the hero. Simpler places for eating with friends and family can be found everywhere in the Greek and Roman world. By the second century, early Christians had adapted the practice of a meal for the dead.[16] The popularity of this meal created special days not only for family dead, but with special Christian dead—specifically the martyrs.

S. Sebastiano is a good example of a building built over a catacomb. In the model (Figure 6) we can see attached places for celebrating the agape, or refrigerium as it was called. Underneath and below ground level, we find a remarkable room built on top of the necropolis and next to the Christian catacomb. In this "meal for the dead" restaurant early Christians met to eat with their special dead as well as Peter and Paul. Fortunately we found on the wall of this bistro over 200 graffiti scratched in by family members as they ate the refrigerium. Many of the graffiti specifically mention Peter and Paul.

Eventually the practice of eating with the dead necessitated the development of special buildings that we call covered cemeteries. At the time of Constantine many such cemetery buildings were built near martyria.[17]

These cemeteries gave rise to the basilica architecture of the early church. San Pietro in Vaticano itself had a cruciform side extension in order to give more access to what was supposed to be the martyrium of St. Peter. By the end of the fourth century, because of severe irregularities, the agape meal for the dead was brought into city churches that had been originally designed for worship rather than meals. A good example of this development would be SS. Giovanni e Paolo in Rome, just a few yards from the Colosseum. Before Christianity there were seven shops along this narrow street (Figure 7). Early Christians found opportunity to meet in one of the shops. About the time of Constantine the hall above the shops was converted into a place of worship. Christians still entered through a narrow shop doorway, but they went to the second floor hall by means of a back staircase. Later, about 410 CE, the relics of John and Paul were placed at the top of the stairs underneath the newly constructed altar. In this manner, the agape—that is, the meal for the dead—combined with the Eucharist to create what we call the Mass.

[17]Theodor Klauser, *Christlicher Märtyrkult, heidnischer Heroenkult und spätjüdische Heiligenverehrung* (Köln und Opladen: Westdeutschenverlag, 1960) 27–38.

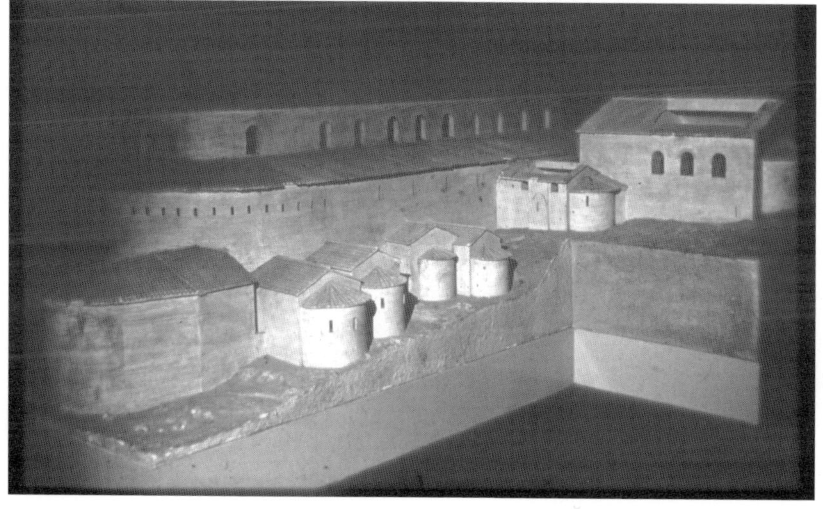

FIG 6.
Model of Covered Cemetery at S. Sebastian, Rome.

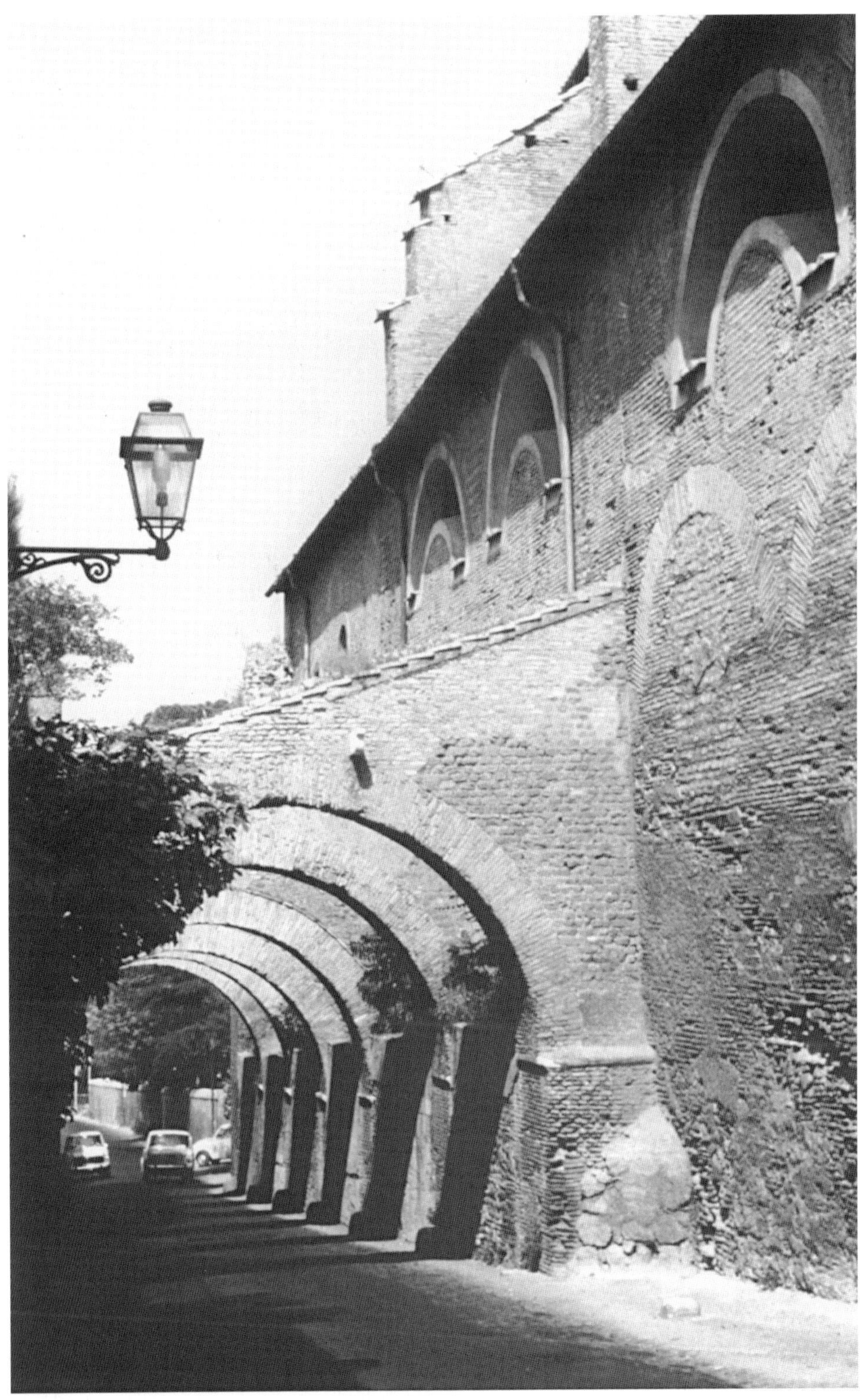

FIG 7. SS. Giovanni e Paolo, Rome, Showing the Shops and the Third Century Christian Hall Above the Shops

4.

A Sufficient Knowledge: Icon and Body in Ninth-Century Byzantium

Charles Barber
University of Notre Dame

The act of interpreting Christian art, as with the interpretation of many other categories of art, has long depended upon a preexisting verbal text to confirm an appropriate reading of the visual evidence. The construction of such contexts provides a rich historical frame that helps to constrain the potential readings of a given work, providing us with the words with which we might make these mute objects speak. Such acts of interpretation, however, imply a hierarchy (one in which the meaning, and perhaps the origin, of a given work of art is determined by the literary texts that have been brought to bear upon that work). In this paper, I will offer an account of ninth-century discussions that make problematic this dependent correlation of prior word and posterior image. As will be seen, the writers introduced in this

[1] Discussions of the use of context in art history are, of course, numerous. Important essays in this regard are: Michael Baxandall, *Patterns of Intention. On the Historical Explanation of Pictures* (New Haven CT: Yale University Press, 1985); Norman Bryson, "Art in Context," *Studies in Historical Change*, ed. Ralph Cohen (Charlottesville: University of Virginia Press, 1992) 18–42; Herbert Kessler, "Medieval Art as Argument," *Iconography at the Crossroads*, ed. Brendan Cassidy (Princeton NJ: Princeton University Press, 1993) 59–70.

[2] Jean Gouillard, "Fragments inédits d'un antirrhétique de Jean le Grammairien," *Revue des etudes byzantines* 24 (1966): 173–74.

[3] This definition of an encomion is drawn from the progymnasmata literature of late antiquity. For a brief introduction, see George Kennedy, *Greek Rhetoric under Christian Emperors* (Princeton NJ: Princeton University Press, 1983) 54–73, esp. 63.

[4] Recent discussions on this topic include Elizabeth C. Evans, *Physiognomics in the Ancient World*, Transactions of the American Philosophical Society 59/5 (Philadelphia: American Philosophical Society, 1969); Gilbert Dagron, "Holy Images and Likeness," *Dumbarton Oaks Papers* 45 (1991): 23–33; Georgia Frank, *The Memory of the Eyes: Pilgrims to Living Saints in Christian Late Antiquity* (Berkeley: University of California Press, 2000) 134–70.

essay were to emphasize a distinction rather than a dependence in the operations of words and images.[1]

My paper will build from one ninth-century text. It is a fragment attributed to the iconoclastic patriarch and leading thinker John the Grammarian. The text can be translated:

> It is impossible for a man to be portrayed by any means, unless one has been led to this by words, through which everyone that exists is definitively captured. As the particularities (τὰ ἰδιάζοντα) of someone have both distinguished him from those of like form (τῶν ὁμοειδῶν) and drawn him near to them in another way, [it follows that] he cannot be grasped in any effective manner by appearance (τῆς ὄφεως). For if the family or the father from which an individual derives are not depicted— bringing forth his deeds and that he is blessed in his companions and the rest of his manners, which are only clearly discernible in the words by means of which one might judge his praiseworthiness or blameworthiness— then the artwork is a waste of time (τὴν ποίαν μετιὼν τέχην διατριβήν). Hence it is impossible truthfully to discern the man by such delineations (εἰκονισμοῖς).[2]

In many ways John is marking a fairly traditional distinction. He argues that words and images differ, and that in the resulting comparison of the two media it can be shown that images are insufficient. This case is built upon one crucial and relatively discrete move. In this passage John makes reference to two rhetorical, that is to say verbal, forms in defining *both* words and images. First, he categorizes verbal representation by invoking the rhetorical power of the *encomion*, which praises its subjects through the presentation of a full account of their background (family, deeds, and so on).[3] In comparison, the work of art is assigned to the category of the *eikonismos*.[4] The latter is a much more restricted form, built primarily upon appearances. The deployment of these two rhetorical analogies proposes a verbal framing for the origins of the work of visual art, in regards to which painting will always be found to be both secondary and deficient.

Now, having categorized words and images in these ways, John is able to define the work of art as a waste of time. It is deemed insufficient because it cannot match the plenitude of a verbal evocation of all that makes a subject worthy of portrayal. He rejects out of hand the value of any interpretation based on morphology. Appearances alone do not tell us enough of their origins and might be confused with those whose appearances are similar. Instead, John argues that words introduce us to a much greater knowledge of a given subject, such that we can understand them more fully. For example, he would consider an icon of Christ to be a mere record of appearance (Figure 1). In the traces marked in the wax of its surface it is unable, by itself, to explain the nature of the incarnation or to invoke Christ's healing powers. As such, John's particular use of the comparison of words and images leads us inexorably to the conclusion that images are in effect useless. One might just as well rid oneself of this unnecessary means of knowing. It adds nothing to that which has already come into existence in words.

Implicit in the Grammarian's challenge is the idea that there is an essential lack in images, one that requires words to interpret the limited vocabulary of visual cues. As formulated by the Grammarian, these words are not understood as a helpful supplement to the images; rather, they render the image, the work of art, redundant.

It is notable how this point is made. John does not evoke a specifically theological argument. His condemnation of images is based upon an evaluation of the relative merits of these media as conveyers of knowledge.[5] It is an iconoclastic challenge that invited iconophiles to demonstrate a value for visual representation, such that its existence was necessary in spite of the possibilities inherent in words. As such they will need to show that an icon is a sufficient medium for the conveyance of Christian knowledge. It is a point that will lead to a more fundamental question, one that asks whether an icon can stand alone as a medium of such knowledge, or whether it requires words to become intelligible.

John the Grammarian's view of art was not an isolated phenomenon but a persistent strand in iconoclastic thought that was built upon an existing spiritual tradition within the Orthodox Church. The

5 The importance of this theme in iconoclasm is explored at length in my forthcoming study *Figure and Likeness: On the Limits of Representation in Byzantine Iconoclasm.*

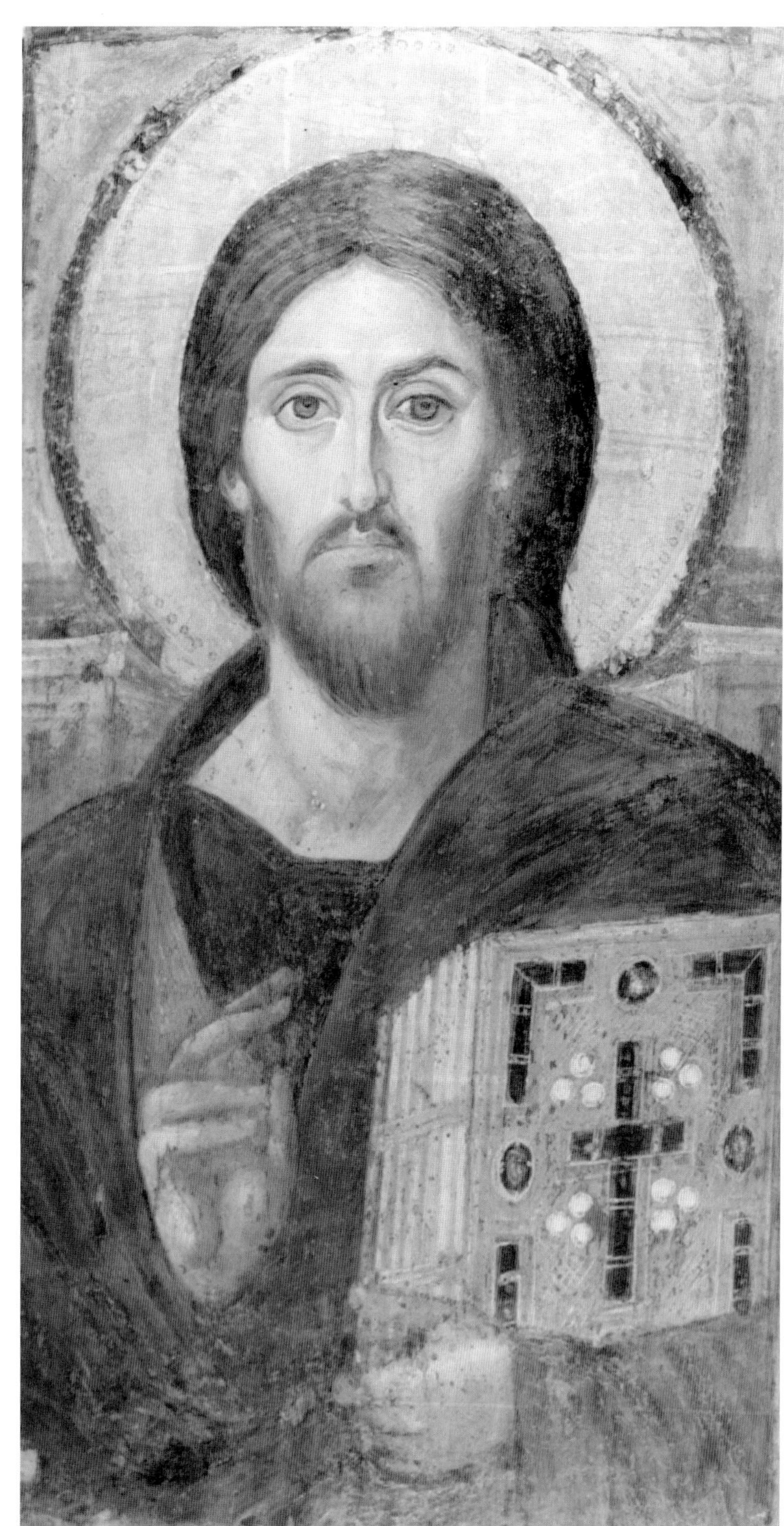

FIG 1.
Christ, Sixth or
Seventh Century, 84
cm x 45.5 cm,
Monastery of St.
Catherine, Mount
Sinai (reproduced
through courtesy of
the Michigan-
Princeton-Alexandria
Expedition to Mount
Sinai).

point of departure for this thinking was an understanding of the location of holiness.[6] Holiness was understood as the gift of participation in the divine. For the iconoclasts, an icon was an inappropriate location for such manifestations of the holy. To them, an icon was simply a material object, whose representation of Christ, for example, was at best partial. An icon might show the outer appearance of Christ or the saints, but it would be impossible for such a base material thing to claim to encompass the holy attributes of these represented bodies. The point is firmly expressed in the *Declaration* pronounced by the iconoclastic council held in 754: "Let, therefore, every mouth that speaks iniquities and blasphemies against our opinion and vote, which have been approved by God, be silent. For the saints who have pleased God and been honoured by him with the dignity of holiness live with him forever, even though they have departed from here. Thus he who thinks to reinstate them on the poles by means of a dead and accursed art which has never been alive but rather has been invented in vanity by the adversary pagans, proves himself blasphemous."[7]

The turning point in this passage is the designation of art as "dead." For the iconoclasts the icon is defined by its dead material nature. This absolutely sets it apart from the ones it seeks to represent. The saints, no longer present on earth, live with God. By definition, this participation in the divine means that they cannot be depicted.[8] The holiness of the saints has therefore taken them beyond the possibility of representation in a medium that is defined as essentially insufficient to convey the entirety of this status. The argument is then taken further in the sixteenth anathema pronounced by the same council: "If anyone ventures to set up profitless figures of all the saints in soul-less, speechless images made of material colours—for this is a vain invention and the discovery of diabolical craft—and does not, on the contrary, reproduce their virtues in himself as actually living icons, with the aid of what has been recorded about them in books, in order to be stimulated to zeal like theirs, as our inspired fathers have said, let him be anathema."[9] Here the same distinction between the dead and the living is drawn. But rather than maintaining an absolute divide that would remove the holy entirely from human experience, the text offers a means of coming close to these saints. It invites the listening

6 The importance of "holiness" in iconoclasm has been stressed by Peter Brown in "A Dark Age Crisis: Aspects of the Iconoclastic Controversy," *English Historical Review* 88 (1973): 1–34.

7 Mansi 13, 276D. This translation is from Daniel J. Sahas, *Icon and Logos: Sources in Eighth-Century Iconoclasm* (Toronto: University of Toronto Press, 1986) 103.

8 Although unrepresentable in images, holiness could, of course, be embodied. Relics memorialized this, even if their holiness was constrained by the iconoclast definition of holiness as a temporary state.

9 Mansi, 13, 345CD. It is based on Theodotos of Ankyra: "We have been taught, not to give shape to the forms of the saints by means of material colours. Rather, with the aid of what has been recorded about them in books, their virtues, which are really living images, so that we may be stimulated in this way to a zeal like theirs" (Mansi 13, 309E-312A).

[10] This so-called "ethical theory of images" has already been well defined by Milton Anastos, "The Ethical Theory of Images Formulated by the Iconoclasts in 754 and 815," *Dumbarton Oaks Papers* 8 (1954): 153–60. For related art-historical discussions, see Henry Maguire, *The Icons of their Bodies: Saints and their Images in Byzantium* (Princeton NJ: Princeton University Press, 1996); Charles Barber, "Writing on the body: memory, desire, and the holy in iconoclasm," *Desire and Denial in Byzantium*, ed. Liz James (Aldershot: Ashgate, 1999) 111–20.

[11] Jeoffrey M. Featherstone, *Nicephori Patriarchae Constantinopolitani Refutatio et Eversio Definitionis Synodalis Anni 815*, Corpus Christianorum, Series Graeca 33 (Turnhout/Louvain: University Press, 1997) 200–201.

believer to become a living icon, stimulated to reproduce the virtues and the zeal of the saints by the things heard in books.[10]

Rather than the image, it is the body of the listening believer that has become the site for imaging holiness. Hence the florilegia attached to the iconoclastic synods of 754 and 815 willingly quote this passage from Amphilochios of Ikonion's fourth-century *Encomion on Basil*:

> The saints are not in need of our written encomia, as they are already inscribed in the book of the living, being the righteous guarded by God. But we desire, through the darkness of writing, to make public that which has been impressed upon our minds in commemoration of them, and to know of them through hearing, so that having been uplifted by this sound we can be transported…. We do not anxiously desire that the flesh of their faces be presented to us by colours on boards, rather to imitate their truth and to repeat their good deeds and to figure the love of God and to be imitators of their good deeds; these post-mortem memories of them are inscribed in those listening so that they might know of their presence in the world.[11]

The iconoclasts therefore propose a model in which the imitation and embodiment of that which is heard is superior to its incarceration in the dead materials of art. The medium for apprehending the holy is understood to be the word alone, whether it is found in books or listened to by an audience.

It is evident, therefore, that John the Grammarian's disdain of the value of visual representation is not an isolated moment in iconoclastic thought. He simply uses a rhetorical framing to redefine the same hierarchical evaluation that is found in these earlier texts. For all of them, the icon is an insufficient medium, unable to compete with the verbal transmission of Christian knowledge.

It should be stressed that the aniconic yet corporeal spirituality explored by these iconoclasts is not an innovation. Indeed, a tradition of imageless prayer had long existed in eastern Christianity. Furthermore, one need only read the ninth-century *Little Catecheses* of Theodore of Stoudios (a leading monastic reformer and iconophile theologian) to understand the importance of this model within the broader patterns of Byzantine spiritual life.[12] The *Little Catecheses* were brief homilies delivered three times a week to the community of the very influential Stoudios monastery.[13] Their wide dissemination attests to their value for a much larger audience. Repeatedly, Theodore invites his audience to listen closely to the saints' narratives that he reads to them. He invites his monks to imitate them, asking them to turn the words heard into virtuous acts to be inscribed and made visible upon their bodies.[14] An image from the ninth-century Khludov Psalter is suggestive in this regard (Figure 2). It shows a monk, identifiable by the megaloschema, which unusually is his only item of dress. For comparison, one can find the dress of a fully clad monk elsewhere in the same manuscript (Figure 3).[15] The state of undress of our first monk calls attention to his body. It is covered in wounds to emphasize

[12] Emmanuel Auvray, *Parva Catechesis* (Paris: apud Victorem Lecoffre, 1891); Theodore Stoudite, *Petites Catéchèses*, trans. Anne-Marie Mohr (Paris: Diffusion Brépols, 1993).

[13] *Patrologiae cursus completus, Series graeca*, ed. J.-P. Migne (Paris: J.-P. Migne, 1857–1866) 99:1712AB.

[14] Auvray, *Parva Catechesis*, 139–42, 278–81; Theodore Stoudite, *Parva Catechesis*, 96–98, 180–81.

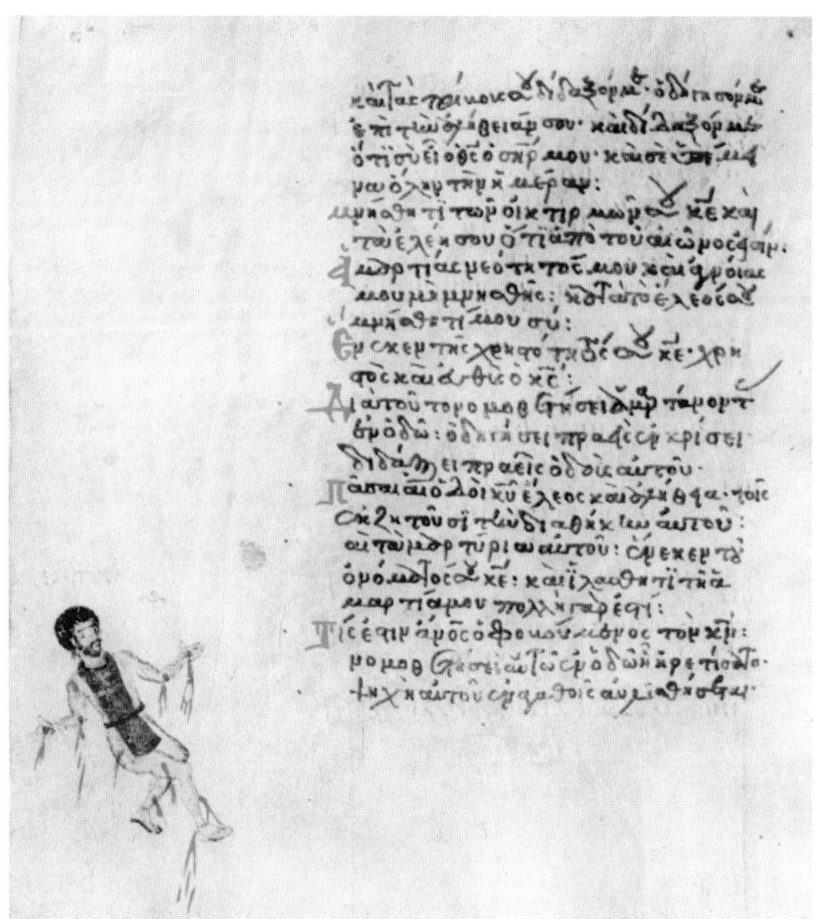

FIG 2.
Monk as Martyr, folio 22v, Khludov Psalter (GIM 86795 or Khlud. 129-d), mid-ninth century, 19.5 cm x 15 cm, State Historical Museum, Moscow (reproduced through courtesy of the State Historical Museum, Moscow).

suffering, and the position of his outstretched arms echoes the appearance of Christ on the cross. He is simply labeled as a witness, a martyr. This echo of the crucified Christ brings us directly to this world of the monastic body that both iconoclasts and iconophiles understood as the site for the inscription of verbal models. Indeed, Theodore compared the monastic life to crucifixion, describing the monks as marked by the cross, their bodies shaped by the painful acquisition of virtue.[16]

Both iconoclasts and iconophiles, therefore, share a sense of the body as a site for the reception and enactment of knowledge. Both strive for a virtuous body and both value verbal sources for this. The primary difference is that the iconoclasts seek to argue that the word alone is appropriate to convey these models, while the iconophiles needed to argue for a positive role for the image itself in this process.

It is to this argument that I will now turn. The difficulties that they and we face in making this iconophile case can be suggested by the following example. In recent writings on Byzantine art, much attention has been focused upon the perception of the image.[17] This

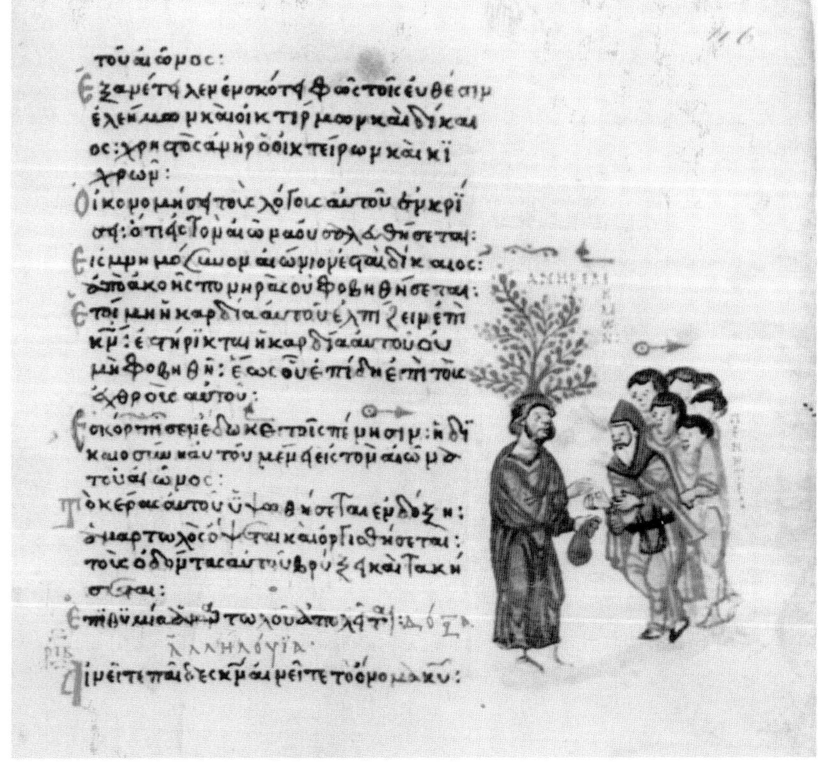

[15] The best introduction to this manuscript is Kathleen Corrigan, *Visual Polemics in the Ninth-Century Byzantine Psalters* (Cambridge: Cambridge University Press, 1992). A partial facsimile of the manuscript is Marfa Scepkina, *Miniatjury Khludovskoi Psaltiri* (Moscow: Iskusstvo, 1977).

[16] Auvray, *Parva Catechesis*, 1–3, 45–49, 242–45; Stoudite, *Parva Catechesis*, 15–16, 41–43, 159–60.

[17] Numerous studies might be cited in this regard. Key works include Henry Maguire, *Art and Eloquence in Byzantium* (Princeton NJ: Princeton University Press, 1981); Leslie Brubaker, "Perception and Conception: Art, Theory and Culture in Ninth-Century Byzantium," *Word & Image* 5 (1989): 19–31; Robert Nelson, "The Discourse of Icons, Then and Now," *Art History* 12 (1989): 144–57; Liz James and Ruth Webb, "To Understand Ultimate Things and Enter Secret Places: Ekphrasis and Art in Byzantium," *Art History* 14 (1991): 1–17; Henry Maguire, *Image and Imagination: The Byzantine Epigram as Evidence for Viewer Response* (Toronto: Canadian Institute of Balkan Studies, 1996).

FIG 3. *Almsgiving*, folio 116r, Khludov Psalter (GIM 86795 or Khlud. 129-d), mid-ninth century, 19.5 cm x 15 cm, State Historical Museum, Moscow (reproduced through courtesy of the State Historical Museum, Moscow).

emphasis has been valuable in helping to train our eyes and minds to reconsider ways of seeing these objects. In this literature, the imaginary Byzantine beholder becomes a factotum for the art historian, situating, embodying, and enacting our omniscient and prescriptive gaze. The danger that lurks in this undoubtedly instructive and important exercise is that we might reiterate the point raised by John the Grammarian. The words we bring to bear will efface the image itself so that, blinded by our own insights and grateful for the presence of preexisting and contextualizing words, we lose sight of one half of the dialogue.

This potential loss can be illuminated when we consider the discussion of a folio from a ninth-century illuminated version of the homilies of Gregory Nazianzos (Figure 4). It is folio 340r of the manuscript and illustrates the martyrdoms of the Maccabees.[18] We see an array of deaths and tortures whose principal actors are portrayed as somewhat phlegmatic figures, who, although being skinned alive or spun on a wheel, crushed, or burned, manage to maintain an impeccable sangfroid, with eyes wide open and mouths firmly shut. We do not see suffering; we see a detached endurance, almost an indifference. Living in an age that expects a more visible display of emotions, we need assistance in learning to look at and comprehend such treatments of this potent and violent subject matter. It has been suggested that this lack would also have been noted by the ninth-century audience, whose culturally conditioned regard of these images, prepared by the verbal narratives already mentioned above, would have supplemented the visual data.

An example cited in regard to this Maccabees folio is worth considering. It is a lengthy and evocative account of scenes of martyrdom found in the ninth-century *Life of Patriarch Tarasios* written by Ignatios the Deacon. I will just quote a portion of this, in order to give you the flavor of this kind of writing:

> Who, beholding a man who has stripped himself to
> face horrible torments and various sorts of tortures
> and is finally beheaded, would not depart smiting his
> breast in contrition of heart?... Who, looking at

18 I am using an example introduced in Brubaker, "Perception and Conception." A full discussion of the folio and the manuscript as a whole can be found in Leslie Brubaker, *Vision and Meaning in Ninth-Century Byzantium: Image as Exegesis in the Homilies of Gregory of Nazianzus* (Cambridge: Cambridge University Press, 1999).

[19] *The Life of the Patriarch Tarasios by Ignatios the Deacon*, introduction, text, translation and commentary by Stephanos Efthymiadis (Aldershot: Ashgate, 1998) 137–38, 195.

another man whose flank and back are being scraped with iron claws because he refused to utter a word unworthy of piety, would not be anointed with the emollient of compassion? Who would not be filled with astonishment and subdued by fear whenever he sees one suffering for the faith measures out each of his limbs as it is cut up and sets aside as a sacrifice and offering to God the parts of the body that are being cruelly divided down to the muscles and thighs and shins and vertebrae and ankles?[19]

The account is not concerned to reiterate the narratives of these martyrdoms. Nor can it be described as an exacting description of a thing seen. Hence, the text should not be thought of as a precise source for an image nor a verbal substitute for it. Rather, the attention of this text is focused upon the effect of these images upon those looking. As such it might be said to forge the link between icon and viewer that would make the beholder an equivalent of the listener. This is an important point of attention, introducing the beholder's share, the beholder's body, into our interpretation of such works. But in this redirection of our attention toward perception and its promise for the interpretative act, one ought to consider the potential of such evocative writings. Notionally, they define a contemporary response to the image, one that we can appropriate and so satisfy our own desires for a contextualized interpretation. Yet, in so doing, we may echo the *ekphrasis's* own combat with the visual and displace the picture itself. Our words, although perhaps provoked by a real depiction, will override this medium, reaching behind it to the things it represents. No longer a tangible screen, the image becomes a window. As such, the words that invoke this transformation do not simply supplement the image; they supplant it.

With this characterization in mind, the iconophiles needed to define how the icon *itself* can provoke these responses and thus mark the necessity of its existence. This entails thinking outside of the model offered by the beholder, returning instead to the conditions of the object itself. One attempt to tackle this issue can be found in the preface to this evocative passage you just read. Here, Ignatios tries to define Tarasios's motivations. He begins by linking the images to their viewing public: "And he did so in order to open a gateway of compunction to the beholders and establish the fighters for the faith, who, by their zeal to imitate them, are eager to take up the same blessed struggle, should circumstances call for it." So far, this implicates the beholder, without offering any qualifications as regards the images themselves. Then the text continues: "For, the eye which

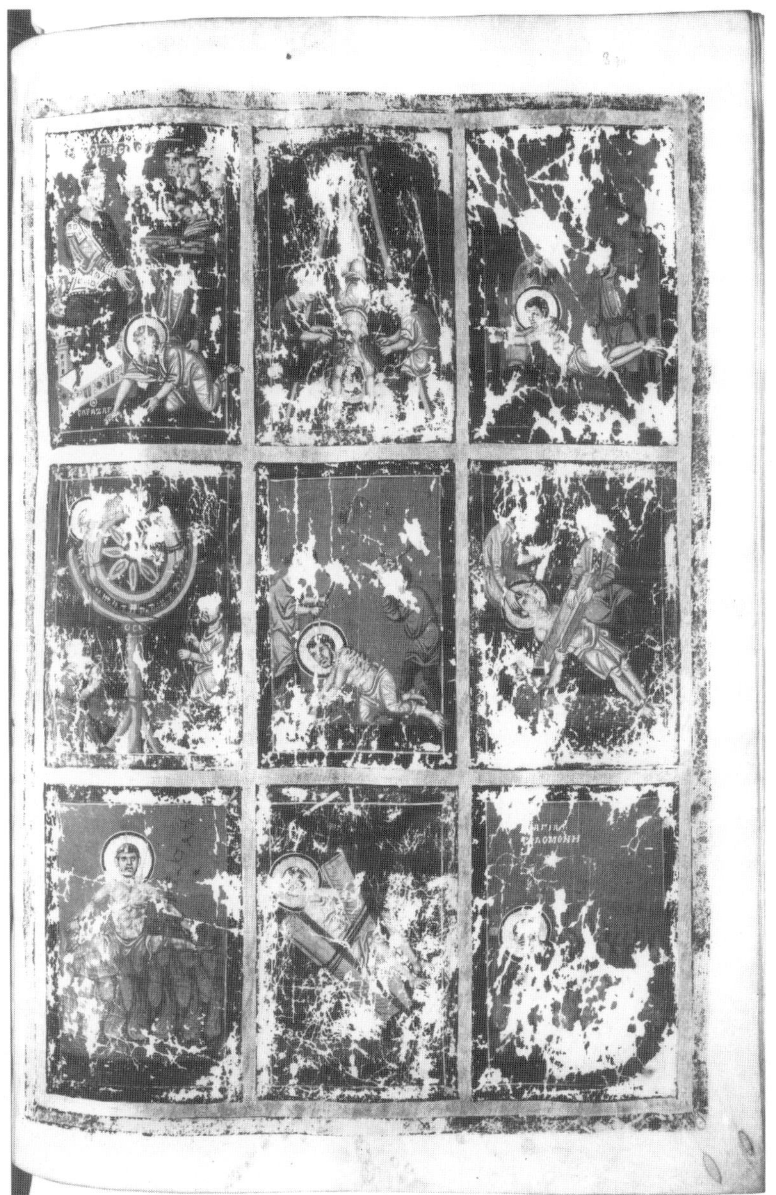

FIG 4.
Martyrdoms of the Maccabees, folio 340r, Homilies of Gregory Nazianzos (Paris, Bibliothèque Nationale, codex graecus 510), ca. 880, 41 cm x 30 cm, Bibliothèque Nationale, Paris (reproduced through courtesy of the Bibliothèque Nationale, Paris).

[20] Ibid., 136, 194.

encounters a good subject is capable of producing such a state of mind, and becomes preferable to hearing, since the latter obtains the second prize after sight and the recipient of teaching is always second to him who receives clear images of realities without any explanation, as a certain wise man said."[20]

Ignatios thus introduces into this account of the beholder's share a distinction between the impact of words and images. This is underlined by his refusal in the following text to name the saints, whose identities would have been written on their images, focusing instead upon the impact of the visual information given within these works. It is here that the defense of art begins, not by excising perceived deficiencies, but by asserting an essential difference between visual and verbal knowing.

By explicitly addressing the word-image comparison that is always present in an *ekphrasis,* Ignatios offers us an inversion of John the Grammarian's critique. He suggests that when one looks at images one has a clear view of "realities without any explanation." Implicit in this phrase is the assumption that an image is sufficient in itself. It has no need of interpretation because its subject matter is indeed recognizable. In so doing, Ignatios leads us to the iconophile response to John the Grammarian's privileging of the visual. Although available in several places, it is perhaps most clearly expressed in these words written by the patriarch Nikephoros. It is a lengthy passage, but it is worth quoting in full:

> But words themselves are the icons of things, and follow on
> from them as from their causes. To begin with they enter
> hearing; for first the sounds of the things spoken encounter
> those listening, then, second, the listener achieves under-
> standing of the given facts through analogy. [Painting]
> directly and immediately leads the minds of the viewers to
> the facts themselves, as if they were present already, and
> from the first sight and encounter a clear and perfect
> knowledge of these is gained. And here I quote the voice of
> a Father, "whatever the word tells of the tale, painting shows
> silently by means of imitation." Just as the deed differs from

the discourse, so too will the imitation and the likeness of the deed differ from the utterance of words when manifesting things. This is why discourses often become more apparent and clearer through such manifestation. For often some difficulties and disputes arise from words, and in all likelihood diverse thoughts are brought forth in souls. Many people produce contradictions and disputes both within themselves and with others, not understanding what is said. But belief is gained from visible things, acquired anywhere free from ambiguity. Up to this point each of them have something in common, so that in one and the same book, as one can see in very ancient documents, inscribed alternately, here the discourse in syllables, there through representation, and they show what is indicated in the writing. Thus the text of the Gospel is itself trustworthy for Christians, not needing another text or another discourse which guarantees it, or which gives witness in its favour as being worthy of veneration or of glory. Similarly, the painting of divine representations, which are of the same things as the Gospel narrative, produces faith by this fact and requires nothing that is extrinsic as proof; painting signifies the facts of the Gospels and requires the same honour.[21]

[21] *Patrologiae*, ed. Migne, 100, 381C-384B. A related discussion of this text can be found in Charles Barber, "The body within the frame: a use of word and image in iconoclasm," *Word & Image* 9 (1993): 140–53.

Nikephoros here presents a different understanding of the icon. He steps outside of verbal models, be they encomiastic, ekphrastic, or that of the *eikonismos*. These rhetorical frameworks are dismissed as potential obfuscations. Instead, he introduces the claim that an image has the greater ability to portray with clarity things that have existed.

Such a position depends upon a strong sense of truthfulness in representation. That is to say that an icon indeed shows in a complete manner the person it purports to represent. This position depends upon the assumption that an icon is able to produce an exact repetition of the thing it purports to show. Returning to patriarch Nikephoros, one can see that this was a primary assumption held by the iconophiles. For example, in his *First Refutation* he defines visual representation in these terms:

[22] *Patrologiae*, ed. Migne, 100, 277A.

[23] The terminology derives from chapter five of Aristotle's *Categories*.

The archetype is an existing origin and paradigm of a form portrayed after it (τοῦ ἀπ᾽ αὐτοῦ χαρακτηριζομένου εἴδους), the cause from which derives the resemblance. Moreover, one may speak of the icon in this definition as of artistic things (τῶν τεχνητῶν τούτων): an icon is a likeness (ὁμοίωμα) of an archetype, having represented in itself by means of likeness the entire form of the one being represented, distinguished only by an essential difference with respect to matter; or an imitation and copy of an archetype, differing in essence and subject (τῇ οὐσίᾳ καὶ τῷ ὑποκειμένῳ διαφέρουσα), or an artifact completely formed in imitation of an archetype, but differing in essence and subject. For if it does not differ in some respect, it is not an icon, nor an object different from the archetype. Thus, an icon is a likeness (ὁμοίωμα) and representation (ἐκτύπωμα) of things being and existing."[22]

This text defines the icon in very precise terms. The fundamental supposition is that an icon differs from the thing it shows both in terms of essence and subject.[23] For example, a painting of Christ will be different from Christ himself, the one being made of wood, wax, and pigments, the other being a divine-human hypostasis. Having drawn this distinction, Nikephoros then insisted that a true icon remains dependent upon the prior existence of the thing shown. This is its formal cause. As such, the true icon cannot show a fictional or imaginary invention. Having established these basic principles of difference and truthfulness, Nikephoros proposed a number of means by which the icon might trace its continuing relation to the archetype. In so doing he has sought to reconcile the claim to an absolute difference with the continuing and linked existence of the two terms, icon and archetype. It is from such an assumption that the iconophiles are able to argue for an immediacy in visual representation that exists without need of interpretation or explanation.

This point is developed further in a letter written by Theodore of Stoudios to a certain Naukratios. In this letter, Theodore seeks to define the truthfulness of visual representation by linking the mimesis (the imitation), which is essential to iconophile notions of representation, to the idea of eyewitness (αὐτοφια).[24] In so doing, he displaces the beholder by the eyewitness of the icon itself. He began by claiming that images were beneficial to those looking at them. In the first place, an icon was an imitation of something and was to be defined in relation to that thing. One consequence of this relationship was that spiritual contemplation addressed to the icon would pass to the archetype represented therein.[25] Similarly, because of this relationship the icon itself was made worthy by that which it represented.[26] A good subject makes for a good image. The immediacy of this relationship is underlined by the definition of the icon as a reflection of actual eyewitness.[27] As such, the icon should be treated as if it were the living eyewitness of the actual events now inscribed upon its surface.[28] He takes this analogy further when he asks, "If such is not possible, then what use is the body of the martyr, which is the imitation of that which is heavenly?"[29] Furthermore an icon could make factual the play of the imaginary, affirming the reality of events that exist only in our minds. First he states that in an icon "imaginary acts are to be seen in their entirety in factual iconic form,"[30] and then he goes on to say that "the imaginary is completed by becoming visible in the enacted form of an icon."[31] The icon is, therefore, an event, a site in which one might find the precise and clear eyewitness of deeds and persons.

John the Grammarian had argued against icons on the grounds that they did less than words. Because of this lack, they were a waste of time and certainly less useful than the traditional verbal site of Christian knowledge. In response the iconophiles argued that icons have to be thought of as existing beyond the domain of words. Visual representation has to be understood as a direct means of communicating the reality of things that have existed. As Christianity is a revealed religion, whose God walked the earth, existing in both space and time, the iconophiles argue that images are the more appropriate account of such a concrete being, opening the way to a visual mimetic economy. The work of art is therefore deemed both sufficient and useful, existing beyond the confusions, doubts, and conflicts inherent in verbal interpretation.

[24] Theodore of Stoudios, *Epistulae*: Georgios Fatouros, *Theodori Studitae Epistulae*, Corpus Fontium Historiae Byzantinae 31/2 (Berlin: Walter de Gruyter, 1992): 515–19.

[25] Fatouros, *Theodori Studitae*, 516 lines 146–51.

[26] Ibid., 516 lines 153–54.

[27] Ibid., 516 lines 157–59.

[28] Ibid., 519 lines 229–31.

[29] Ibid., 516 lines 159–60.

[30] Ibid., 517 lines 179–80.

[31] Ibid., 517 lines 179–80.

5.

The Image of the Word in Byzantium and Islam: An Essay in Art Historical Geodesy

Anthony Cutler

Pennsylvania State University

For the better part of the second half of the twentieth century, one exegetical model largely dictated the ways in which art historians sought to uncover the meanings of images in Western culture. The intellectual basis of iconology, to use the ancient term revived by Erwin Panofsky,[1] its prime practitioner, has been exhaustively analyzed,[2] and subtler methods have been proposed.[3] But Panofsky's method is still used, consciously or otherwise, by the majority of investigators. It has become so pervasive that even those unaware of its roots and method continue to employ them. In order to understand both this endurance and the objectives of the present paper, it is necessary to rehearse (however simplistically) the mechanisms that underlie this interpretative system.

[1] *Studies in Iconography. Humanistic Themes in the Art of the Renaissance* (New York: Oxford University Press, 1939; reprint, New York: Harper & Row, 1962) 3–31.

[2] Michael A. Holly, *Panofsky and the Foundations of Art History* (Ithaca NY: Cornell University Press, 1984); Michael Podro, *The Critical Historians of Art* (New Haven CT: Yale University Press, 1982) 178–208.

[3] Paolo Berdini, *The Religious Art of Jacopo Bassano: Painting as Visual Exegesis* (New York: Cambridge University Press, 1997) 1–35.

Iconology depends upon what can be called "local" positioning—as against the "global" positioning described immediately below. In essence, it consists of a procedure whereby the investigator brings to bear upon an object (of any sort) texts (usually written, but in any case verbal), which, if properly applied, can throw light upon that object's content, nature, and significance. Highly informative as this approach can be, it flirts with the peril of tautology in that repetition ensues when an idea is found to be expressed in another, albeit contemporary, mode, for example, when an image is explicated via sets of words that belong ideally to the time when that image was employed. Various objections have been raised against this method; others are not difficult to discern. Not least among these must be that it tends to ignore the distinction between words and images, that is, signs that operate in different ways and are therefore not entirely interchangeable.[4] Moreover, precisely because they are used systematically rather than as strings of atomic units, one element in a system modifies another: it can clarify or occlude other elements in the same picture or sentence.[5] In geodesy (the science of large-scale land measurement) these occlusions might be the hills and trees that are ignored in plane surveying. Obstacles of this sort, along with disregard for the earth's curvature (in our terms, the often ignored but ineluctable fact that complexity is simplified by its conventional representation on the two-dimensional surface of a page or a canvas), can bedevil attempts to establish the true distance between two points. When these two points are a picture and a text, or an iconography and the words that an investigator attaches to it in the belief that they will elucidate the picture in question,[6] the method can fail precisely because the image and its supposedly explanatory text are too close to each other. Beyond redundancy, then, insufficient distance—historical and/or epistemological—may exist between the commentator and the object of his or her commentary. The result can be a miscalculation, distortion, or, at worst, utter irrelevance.

The science of geodesy has long possessed a tool called triangulation, which minimizes this risk. In this method, the distance of a third point from each of the other two—in the present case, verbal and iconic signs—is used as a control on the supposed relation of one of the first two signs to the other; their relative magnitude is also taken into account, along with the size of the intervening "hills" and "trees." In other words, the stations are globally positioned; or, in terms of our post-Panofskian investigation, the historical and epistemological distance between them allows us to check our initial reading. I intend to look at the problem of discerning intended meaning in Christian imagery with the aid of triangulation. The use of a third set of points—drawn from medieval Islamic art—may allow us to assess both the differences and resemblances between visual expressions of these two cultures (a question which is obvious on its face yet seldom investigated comparatively) and the role played by a text when it is displayed as part, or instead, of an image rather than being taken merely as its generative source.

These two issues are in fact aspects of the same problem. Christianity and Islam, both of which are religions founded upon a "revealed" book, employ inscriptions. The first developed a body of figurative iconography, based upon sacred texts, whereas the second did not. In the Muslim world this placed a heavier burden on the words of the prophet: no body of iconic substitutes replaces these words; as a result, Muslim inscriptions tend to be longer. By contrast, Christian inscriptions that not only reproduce but amplify or comment on a text could generally afford to be pithier. This does not mean that Christian imagery became independent of a verbal source. Indeed, in Byzantine Greek the same term (γραφεῖν) was used to indicate both writing and painting. But the ancillary, rather than central, role of textual allusion in Christian art relieved the word of much of the load that it bears in the Islamic world. Here, we are concerned with the citation of Scripture, not with any or all sets of words that have bearing on an image.

A case in point is the seventh- or eighth-century icon of Christ "made without hands" in the Sancta Sanctorum in Rome under its early thirteenth-century cover as it is encountered by those who gain permission to enter the Pope's private chapel (Figure 1).[7] The doors at the bottom of this cover, which open to allow the annual washing of the image's feet, implicitly allow access to the face of Christ, on the assumption that this is part of the same picture—a degree of entrée

7 Herbert L. Kessler and Johanna Zacharias, *Rome 1300: On the Path of the Pilgrim* (New Haven CT: Yale University Press, 2000) 61–63.

into the holy not even promised to the Muslim pilgrim as he or she approaches the Ka'aba under its cloth at Mecca. But on-site experience suggests a very different state of affairs. Worn as a result of centuries of nocturnal processions and handling during the liturgically prescribed foot washings, the entire upper portion of the icon was recreated at the beginning of the tenth century by order of Pope John X; a new head was painted on a new support. This information is conveyed by an inscription not on but near the image.[8] Does it deter the pilgrim or dismay the faithful?

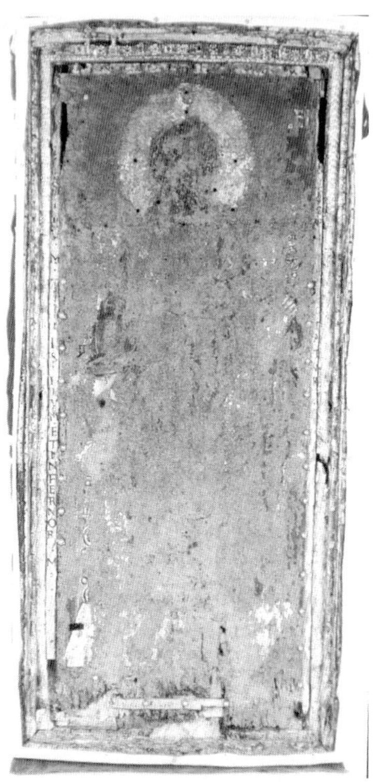

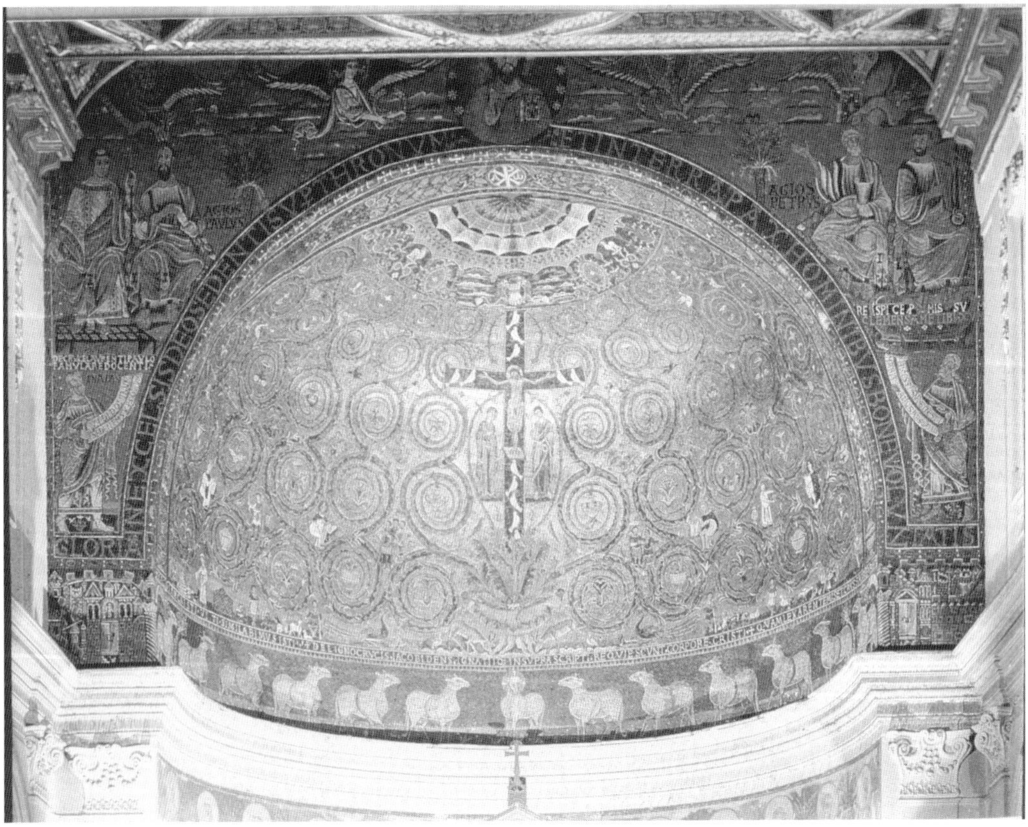

Of course not. Credence is immune to the archaeological datum; the modern word is unavailing in its intent to affect the believer.

But what of ancient words, texts that are materially homogeneous and phenomenologically consistent with Christian images across more than a millennium and a half? Such words do more than identify the subject depicted. In the apse of San Clemente in Rome (Figure 2), for example, they participate in the totality of the work, act as a guarantee of its authority, and certify its authenticity. "I saw the Lord seated on a throne" reads the scroll held by Isaiah on the arch, words that do not literally correspond to the mosaic (unless one reads the cross as a throne), yet which convey not only its letter but its spirit, especially since the scroll points up to the epiphany that is Christ resurrected (in all senses) above the crucifixion. The citation is thus part of the sign as a whole, so that the text of Jeremiah who, to the right, likewise salutes the Lord, offers a surplus of meaning: citing the book of his scribe Baruch (3:35),[9] he declares, "This is our God, there is nothing to compare with him."

Now this is also a thoroughly Muslim sentiment, found in the Koran (*sura* 112) and reproduced as the *shahāda*—"There is no God but God and none is equal to him"—on countless coins and in thousands of mosques from the time of the Dome of the Rock onward.[10] An obvious resemblance links Jeremiah's utterance at San Clemente and the proclamation of God's uniqueness across a myriad of Islamic instances. The *shahāda* and cognate passages are taken directly from the Koran, just as the prophet's declaration in the Roman mosaic derives immediately from the Old Testament. Nonetheless, in quoting the divine word rather than commenting on it, the latter is only one of many kinds of Christian inscription. Put another way, while citation of holy writ characterizes and even identifies the function of inscription in Muslim art and architecture, in Byzantine and Western medieval culture a text serves many purposes and more often than not is the occasion or part of an image but rarely sufficient in itself. This economy of means in the Islamic world is striking. Compared with the almost luxuriant combination of word and image in Christian art, the laconic decision to convey only the essence—thereby, for example, avoiding narrative images—anticipates Voltaire's dictum, "Le secret

[9] Kessler and Zacharias, *Rome 1300*, 87 and fig. 80.

[10] Erica C. Dodd and Shereen Khairallah, *The Image of the Word. A Study of Quranic Verses in Islamic Architecture*, 2 vols. (Beirut: American University of Beirut Press, 1981) 1:24, 27. The parallelism between the title of this book and that of the present study points to the debt owed by the author to Dodd since her initial paper on the topic, "The Image of the Word," *Berytus* (1969): 35–62. Readers of Dodd's book should be aware of the criticisms in the review by Sheila S. Blair in *Arabica* 31 (1984): 337–42.

[11] *Discours en vers sur l'homme*, Bk. VI, lines 174–75.

[12] S. Der Nersessian, *L'Illustration des Psautiers grecs du Moyen Âge: Londres, Add. 19.352* (Paris: Klincksieck, 1970) fig. 255.

[13] For a partial explanation of the genesis of this and similar pictures, see A. Cutler, "Liturgical Strata on the Marginal Psalters," *Dumbarton Oaks Papers* 34–35 (1980–1981): 17–30. The most recent and fullest study is Charles E. Barber, *Theodore Psalter. Electronic Facsimile* (Champaign: University of Illinois Press with the British Library, 2000).

[14] Since pointing—the addition of diacritical signs—is used at least in part to distinguish letters in words with two or even three "teeth" (*hastae*), its presence contributes to the legibility of texts.

[15] The most useful guide to such practices is Sheila S. Blair, *Islamic Inscriptions* (New York: New York University Press, 1998) 76–93.

d'ennuyer est de tout dire."[11] As against this, Christian imagery supplements the content of a biblical passage and instead of functioning simply as its exponent appropriates, absorbs, and amplifies its textual origin. This contrast between the epigrammatic and the synesthetic, which seems at first to be purely formal, in fact affects the ways in which the interior of a mosque and that of a church are experienced; in doing so, the difference meets the congregations' varying expectations of a holy place or object.

In Byzantium examples of the above-mentioned luxuriance are provided by those psalters in the margins of which pictures elaborate the Septuagint text with New Testament imagery. The Theodore Psalter, for example, attaches to Psalm 117:26 ("Blessed is he that cometh in the name of the LORD") a picture of the entry into Jerusalem (Figure 3).[12] Yet the miniature is not just an historical instantiation of the psalm's message but its prime fulfillment and a demonstration of the cognitive stance of the monk who undertook the enormous labor of copying the text only to enfold almost every one of its constituent parts in iconic exegeses.[13] Such books, however, were seen only by a few and thus beg the question of how, on the larger canvas of monumental art, images and the inscriptions that they incorporate would have been perceived by their audience. Any Byzantine who could read would recognize the abbreviated caption as denoting Palm Sunday; and those who could not would be sufficiently alerted by the content—Christ riding side-saddle, the boy laying the cloth in his path, the tree and the city gate—and would thus not miss a verbal definition of the event. The mid-eleventh-century Greek is made legible with accents and breathings. Nearly 300 years earlier, by contrast, at the Dome of the Rock, the Arabic is rarely pointed, and the question remains how many among the literate could decipher the text.[14]

Even after the eighth century, when inscriptions were regularly pointed, they were often complicated by subsidiary decorative elements—knotted, foliated, floriated, interlaced—that made them difficult to read.[15] Fundamentally, however, the issue is one not of literacy or legibility but of social practice. Like Judaism and Christianity, Islam is a "religion of the book," but the Koranic tradition remained essentially one of utterance, a set of declamations intoned aloud, "in mundane circumstances, recited in ritual, and explored in sermon and theological discussion."[16] What is spoken, then, predominates what is read, and one may be permitted to doubt that in ornate architectural settings like the entrance to the *madrasa* of Sultan Hassan in Cairo (Figure 4) the faithful stopped to sound out the calligraphy at the base of the spectacular *muqarnas* ornament. Islamicists are increasingly responsive to the idea that architectural inscriptions func-

[16] Holly Edwards in *The Brocade of the Pen. The Art of Islamic Writing*, exhib. cat., ed. Carol G. Fisher (East Lansing, MI: Kresge Art Museum, 1991) 66.

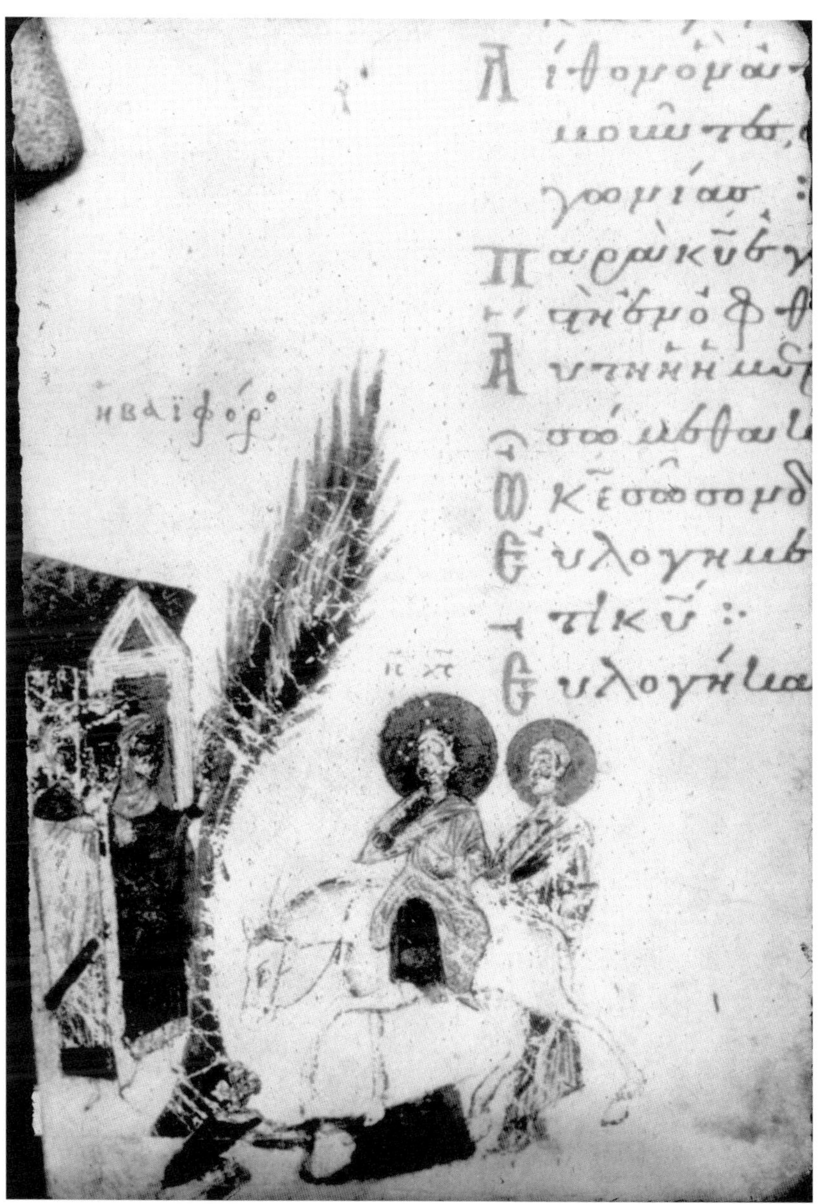

FIG 3.
Entry into Jerusalem,
Theodore Psalter,
1066. London, British
Library, Add. MS
19.352, fol. 157v

17 See, for example, William Diebold, "Verbal, Visual and Cultural Literacy in Medieval Art: Word and Image in the Psalter of Charles the Bald," *Word & Image* 8 (1992): 89–99.

tion as part of a larger visual field rather than as vehicles of theological statement. More than their content, it is the *presence* of these texts that serves to announce and demarcate a sanctified environment.

For medievalists such triangulation on the nature and effect of words in Muslim sacred space raises the question not so much of the relation of art to literacy—a topic that has been widely explored[17]—as of the relation of the inscribed text to the image, a matter less investi-

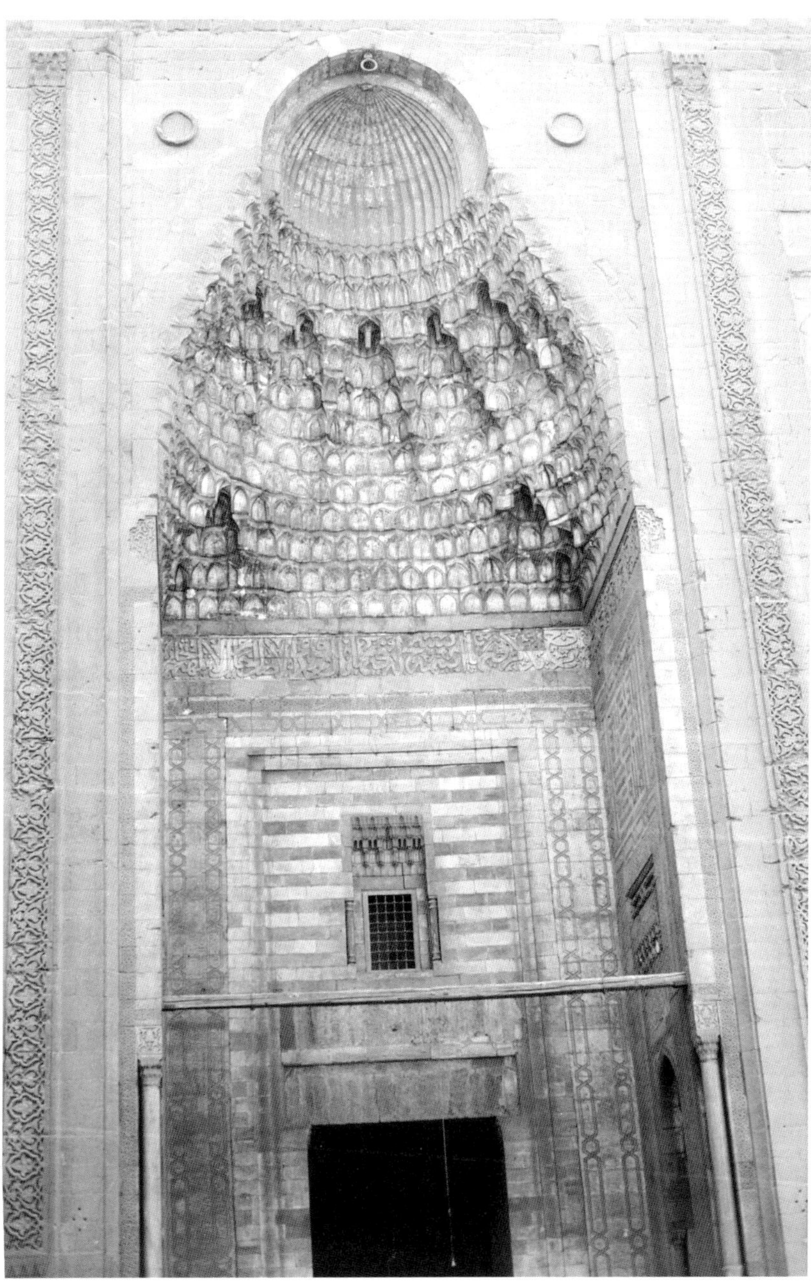

FIG 4.
Madrasa of Sultan Hassan, Cairo, 1362. Entrance

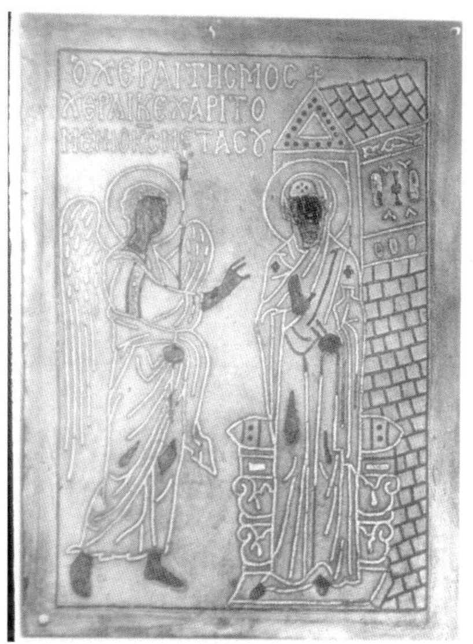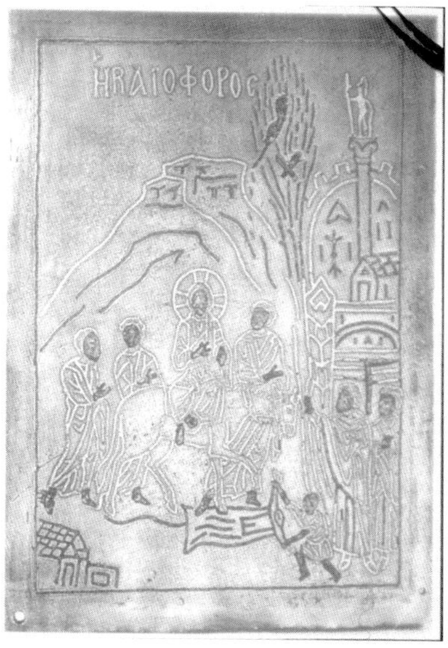

FIG 5.
Annunciation and
Entry into Jerusalem,
1070. Rome, S. Paolo
fuori le mura, door

gated. If, as I have suggested, the words or captions attached to Christian imagery are an intrinsic part of the icon, then why are some pithy in the extreme while others, even on the same monument, are wordy? We can approach this problem via the doors of San Paolo fuori le mura in Rome (Figure 5) made in Constantinople in 1070 at the behest of the abbot Hildebrand, whose epigraphic claim to authorship is set in stone above the details of scenes that he commissioned. Among many economical labels, ʽΗ ΒΑΙΟΦΟΡΟС stands out and not only because, like another miniature of the entry into Jerusalem in the Theodore Psalter[18] painted four years earlier in the Byzantine capital, the city is iconically defined by its statue of Mars. A similarly brief caption, ʽΟ ΧΕΡΕΤΙСΜΟС, denotes the annunciation but in this case the inscription does not end with the identification of the event. Instead, it continues, ΧΑΙ͂ΡΕ, ΚΕΧΑΡΙΤΟΜΕΝΕ, ʽΟ ΚΥΡΙΟС ΜΕΤΑ СΟΥ ("Greetings most favored one, the Lord is with you"). The words of the angel are transcribed and rank in importance with the picture itself first because they constitute a divine message. They are also, of course, a quotation from Scripture, akin in this respect to the passages from the Koran that we have considered.

Inscriptions of this order appear in mosaics and wall paintings, on icons, ivories and many other materials. Precisely because they were so familiar, they were probably left unread. Their function is not to convey the identity of the scene, but to identify as *Orthodox* the images

[18] Der Nersessian, *L'Illustration*, fig. 12.

[19] Blair, *Islamic Inscriptions*, 80. On this entire issue, see Richard Ettinghausen, "Arabic Epigraphy: Communication or Symbolic Affirmation" *Near Eastern Numismatics, Iconography, Epigraphy and History: Studies in Honor of George C. Miles*, ed. D. Kouymjian (Beirut: American University of Beirut, 1974) 297–317.

on which they were written; to do this, they did not have to be read but they had to be *there*. We are not far from the manner in which many Koranic inscriptions operated; increasingly ornate, they were probably recognized visually rather than read literally.[19] But to infer that "symbolic affirmation superseded communication" is to interpret communication in a rather narrow sense. The task, therefore, is to determine not only the ways in which these visual references work but also the role that they were intended to play. Surely, the primary purpose of Christian images and Islamic citations of the Koran was not to send their beholders directly back to holy writ. Compressed allusions to the texts they may be, but the idea that such quotations represent some kind of miniaturized Scripture demands consideration. The Bible or the Koran may be the source, but it is not the end of such performances. Were this the case, we would be faced with a type of mimesis—the depiction of the annunciation, for example, and the words uttered on this occasion, standing in as a sort of surrogate for the text. Yet what would the dutiful reader gain from turning to Luke 1:28 and what follows? He or she would learn nothing that was not already in the image. The picture says it all, and more, for in the succession of scenes on the bronze door the place of the angelic greeting in the overall economy of salvation is demonstrated more clearly than in the discursive narrative of the gospel.

So, too, on Islamic buildings and objects, the context in which Koranic verses are found disqualifies the view that their function was to impel the reader to return to their origin. First, as at the entrance to the *madrasa* of Sultan Hassan (Figure 4) where the famous Light verse and its successor (*sura* 24:36-37) appear, the text refers to "temples God has allowed to be raised up" and is a call to prayer, the injunction to glorify him "in the mornings and the evenings." Secondly, the place where this quotation is set was in many cases occupied not by Koranic verses but by inscriptions commemorating the founder. On mosques, minarets, madrasas, hospitals, and gates, historical information, sayings of the prophet, supplicatory prayers, and the like are carved in the same materials and distributed in the same manner as citations from the Koran. Ignorance of Arabic, Persian, or Turkish is not the only reason why non-Muslims cannot recognize such quotations.

   Interpreting Christian Art

Rather, their position and medium make them visually indistinguishable from texts with other sorts of content.

Certainly the summons to prayer is a call to action, but the nature of the act in question and the notion of mimesis require scrutiny. The worshiper who pauses to contemplate the annunciation on his or her way into San Paolo fuori le mura is not being urged to be unafraid of angels, nor are virgins being driven to conceive. The biographer of the early fourth-century monk Pachomios describes the saint and his brethren as offering "their souls and bodies to God in strict *askesis* and with befitting reverence, not only because they looked day and night to the holy Cross, but also because they saw the martyrs take up their struggles. They saw him and imitated them."[20] Vision, then, can beget imitation. But the very desirability of such behavior means that the viewers of signs and images in a Coptic monastery or the Benedictine one whose doors we are considering were not martyrs but *aspirant*s to such perfection. Because monks, priests, and laypeople sought to imitate Christ, the apostles or angels does not mean that they *become* those heavenly beings. To suppose so would be to confuse the liturgy with the Eucharist and the icons with the elements of that rite. At the Second Council of Nicaea the Orthodox Church declared that the bread and the wine are not images of Jesus but Jesus himself.[21] This was the same council that permitted, indeed required, the pictorial representation of Christ. But this is far from insisting that his likenesses are wee incarnations of him, a position that would justify the charge of idolatry levied by the iconoclasts and Muslims alike. It is true that in later expressions of Orthodoxy there are images that move their beholders to empathize with their content. In his eleventh-century *Protheoria* Nicholas of Andida proclaims a direct relationship between the life of Christ and the events of the Gospels as recounted in the liturgy and depicted in art in their chronological order.[22] But in this doctrine, for all the images that Nicholas had in mind, the relationship is one of analogy, not of ontological identity.

In popular belief, of course, figures on icons could descend from their panels to protect, heal, or otherwise ward off harm. This attitude is neither a Christian invention nor one confined to Christianity. It is expressed early in Philostratos's descriptions of animate sculptures,

[20] Armand Veilleux, *Pachomian Koinonia* (Kalamazoo MI: Cistercian Publications, 1980) 1, 24.

[21] Giovan Domenico Mansi, *Sacrorum conciliorum nova et amplissima collectio*, vol. 13 (Florence 1759; repr. Graz: Akademische Druck, 1960) col. 264.

[22] René Bornert, *Les Commentaires byzantins de la divine liturgie du VIIIe au XVe siècle* (Paris: Institut français d'etudes byzantines, 1966) 202–205. See also the commentary by Hugh Wybrew, *The Orthodox Liturgy. The Development of the Eucharistic Liturgy in the Byzantine Rite* (Crestwood NY: St. Vladimir's Seminary Press, 1990) 139–44.

23 Philostratos, Εἰκόνες = *Imagines*, trans. Arthur Fairbanks (Cambridge MA: Harvard University Press, 1969); *Parastaseis = Constantinople in the Early Eighth Century*, ed. Averil Cameron and Judith Herrin (Leiden: E. J. Brill, 1984).

24 See Blair, *Islamic Inscriptions*, index s.v. *baraka*.

25 *Travels in Hyperreality. Essays* (San Diego: Harcourt Brace Jovanovich, 1986) 19.

still very much alive in the eighth- or ninth-century *Parastaseis syntomoi chronikai*,[23] and continues into the eighteenth century when Mozart's Don Giovanni opens his door to the statue of the Commendatore. But at most such views tell us that an awareness of absence is the functional equivalent of a desire for presence, not that iconic likeness is an adequate substitute for what is lacking. When meditated upon, objects and inscriptions could be instrumental in provoking mental states that allowed them to be seen as transmitting grace or a blessing (in Arabic, *baraka*). But, short of magic, I know of no Christian or Muslim artifact or image that was understood to be the *source* of such a state. Blessings for their usually anonymous owner were a commonplace of legends on metalwork, glass, and ceramics in Islam, and a shroud inscribed with a supplication to God on behalf of the caliph could convey *baraka* to the deceased.[24] So, too, in the Byzantine world grace could pass from a holy object or relic to the place where it was lodged. Thus the church of St. Nicholas at Myra was a destination of pilgrimage long after 1087 when the bones of the (mythical) saint were removed to Bari by Italian sailors. In fact, the basilica was enlarged and redecorated, and the vast majority of Nicholas's icons date from after this event. Yet we are still far from the Californian theology according to which, as Umberto Eco put it in an account of his travels in the Wild West, absolute unreality is offered as real presence. Observing the copies of works by Leonardo and Michelangelo in the so-called Palace of the Living Arts in Buena Vista, Eco remarks that its planners' philosophy was not "we are giving you the reproduction so that you will want to see the original" but "we are giving you the reproduction so that you will no longer feel any need for the original."[25]

In such instances we are dealing with a sort of palimpsest: the original text, without which its surrogate could not exist, is wiped clean and reinscribed with its copy. This perfect replacement not only erases the pristine version but adds values that are missing in the original. Less radical but hardly less transformative were Byzantine responses to some material expressions of Islamic culture. On the one hand, Greeks (or Muslim artisans in their employ) frequently made use of pseudo-Kufic—an ornamental but lexically illegible imitation of an Arabic script—in the decoration of churches and religious objects.[26] On the other, they treated such signs as emblems of the Antichrist, as in the famous story of a cup that found its way up the ladder of gifts into the emperor's presence before its inscription was recognized as Arabic and therefore cast out.[27] Just so, Orthodox holy images were viewed as sacrilegious in Islam either because they were seen to be worshiped and therefore stimuli to idolatry, or because their depictions of the Trinity were read as proofs of polytheism and therefore to be destroyed.

The problem of analyzing reactions of this sort is particularly acute when cultural behaviors overlap without being identical. This is the case with iconoclasm, a practice common at times to both Byzantines and Muslims. Whereas many of the former periodically opposed the representation of sacred figures, the latter objected to the depictions in a sacred context of *any* living form. The distinction is an important one and well brought out by tiles from a frieze decorated with birds that was once in an Iranian mosque and is now in the Hermitage Museum. A detail-photograph (Figure 6) shows that all the heads of the birds perched in the paradisal background to the inscription have been removed. These ceramics date from the late thirteenth

[26] See Anthony Cutler, "A Christian Ewer with Islamic Imagery and the Question of Arab *Gastarbeiter* in Byzantium" *Iconographica. Mélanges Piotr Skubiszewski* (Poitiers: Université de Poitiers, Centre d'etudes supérieures, 1999) 63–69.

[27] George Pachymeres, *Rhomaike historia*, ed. A. Failler, trans. V. Laurent as *Relations historiques*, 2 vols. (Paris: Les Belles Lettres, 1984) 2:572–75. Dread of alien scripts is a seemingly perennial phenomenon among adherents of an established faith. Thus, writing of ill omens, Gregory of Tours (*Historia francorum* 9. 4) records that "many portents appeared at this time [that is, ca. 585] in the homes of a number of people vessels were discovered inscribed with unknown characters which could not be erased or scraped off however hard they tried."

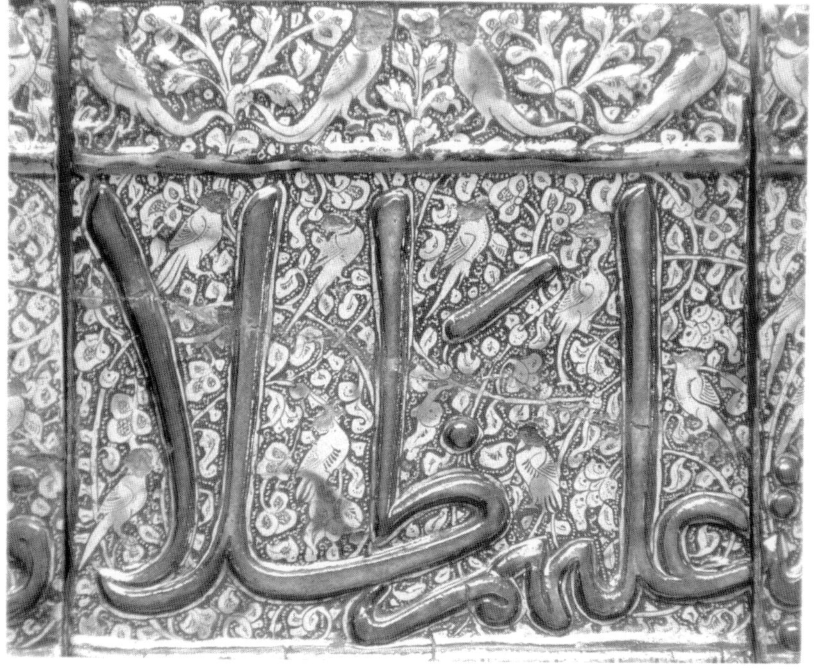

FIG 6.
Inscribed tile from an Iranian frieze, late 13th c. St. Petersburg, State Hermitage Museum

28 That this is an idiosyncratic instance of iconoclasm rather than evidence of a region-wide movement is shown by a similar Iranian tile, dated to March–April 1308, and likewise decorated with birds and bearing an inscription from the Koran, in the Metropolitan Museum of Art (Blair, *Islamic Inscriptions*, fig. 15.88). Here the creatures' heads are left undamaged. Animals were not universally shunned in Muslim religious art. On the façade of the twelfth-century Great Mosque at Diyarbakr (M. van Berchem and A. Strzygowski, *Amida* [Heidelberg: C. Winter, 1910] 61), an image of a lion slaying a bull—an obvious emblem of power—appears below the foundation inscription of the Nisanid vizier al-Hasan. A double-headed eagle and a lion are represented on a lectern in Konya (Blair, *Islamic Inscriptions*, 137–39) on the interior face where the Koran would have been set.

29 Among many discussions of the issue, see Dodd and Khairallah, *The Image of the Word*, 1:15–18.

century; their "purification," therefore, must be even later, which is to say the perception of the danger they posed dates from a time long after the representation of living creatures had been generally eliminated from the holy spaces of Islam.[28]

Such ex post facto cleansing, like the recent destruction of monumental figures of the Buddha by the Islamic Taliban, evokes not the Koran, where only the representation of God is forbidden, but the *hadith*, the sayings of Muhammad, where a general injunction against images is to be found.[29] The quasi-revealed status of this tradition, first written down in the ninth century, is taken as an authoritative prohibition, a text that defines a normative position: how things were should determine how things should be. Those who regard such an attitude as hopelessly archaic (even while it underlies all modern evocations of the US Constitution) might consider the appeal to "ancient" prescription on an item drawn from everyday experience: the array of visual and verbal signs on a Coca-Cola can (Figure 7). Even small things like the hyphen in the brand name—an old-fashioned usage that is fast disappearing from the English language—points to the past. Then, of course, there is the nineteenth-century script used to identify the drink in question. Third, the slightly uneven lettering of the word "always" recalls the misalignment sometimes created by a manual typewriter and stands in clear contrast to the block-letter font used to announce that this is *Classic* Coke. The word "classic" takes us to the heart of the matter. The company is peddling a new form of packaging, but assures us that its content is as good as it ever was. And in case you still miss the point, it is rammed home by the iconography, a picture of the traditional bottle now supplanted by the aluminum can but imprinted on the latter like an unwavering heraldic blazon. The message is conveyed by the synergy of word and image. Despite the changes, this is the good old stuff, "the real thing."

The power of one image to shape another in Byzantium was similarly great, so much so

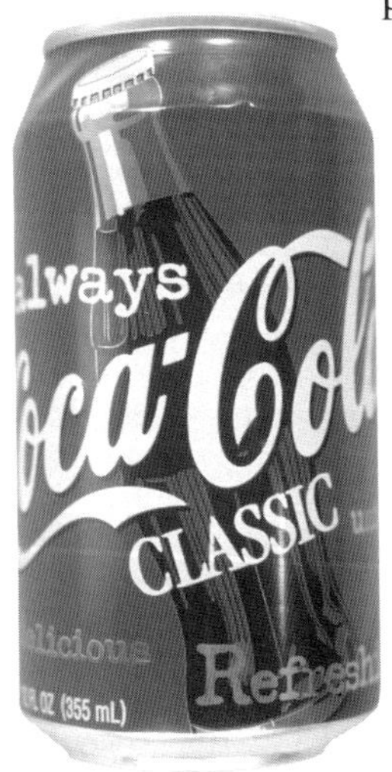

FIG 7. Coca-Cola can, late 20th c.

that scholars have had to come up with a new term—intervisuality—
to account for its aura.[30] What this describes is the absorption of an
earlier motif by a later one and the strength that the second vehicle
acquires by virtue of this incorporation. A good example is the type
usually described as Moses at the burning bush, as it appears on a thirteenth-century icon at Mount Sinai (Figure 8), traditionally, though
not biblically, identified as the site of this event. It shows the prophet
removing his shoes as the Lord instructed him to do according to

[30] Robert S. Nelson, "The
Chora and the Great
Church: Intervisuality in
Fourteenth-Century
Constantinople," *Byzantine
and Modern Greek Studies*
23 (1999): 67–101.

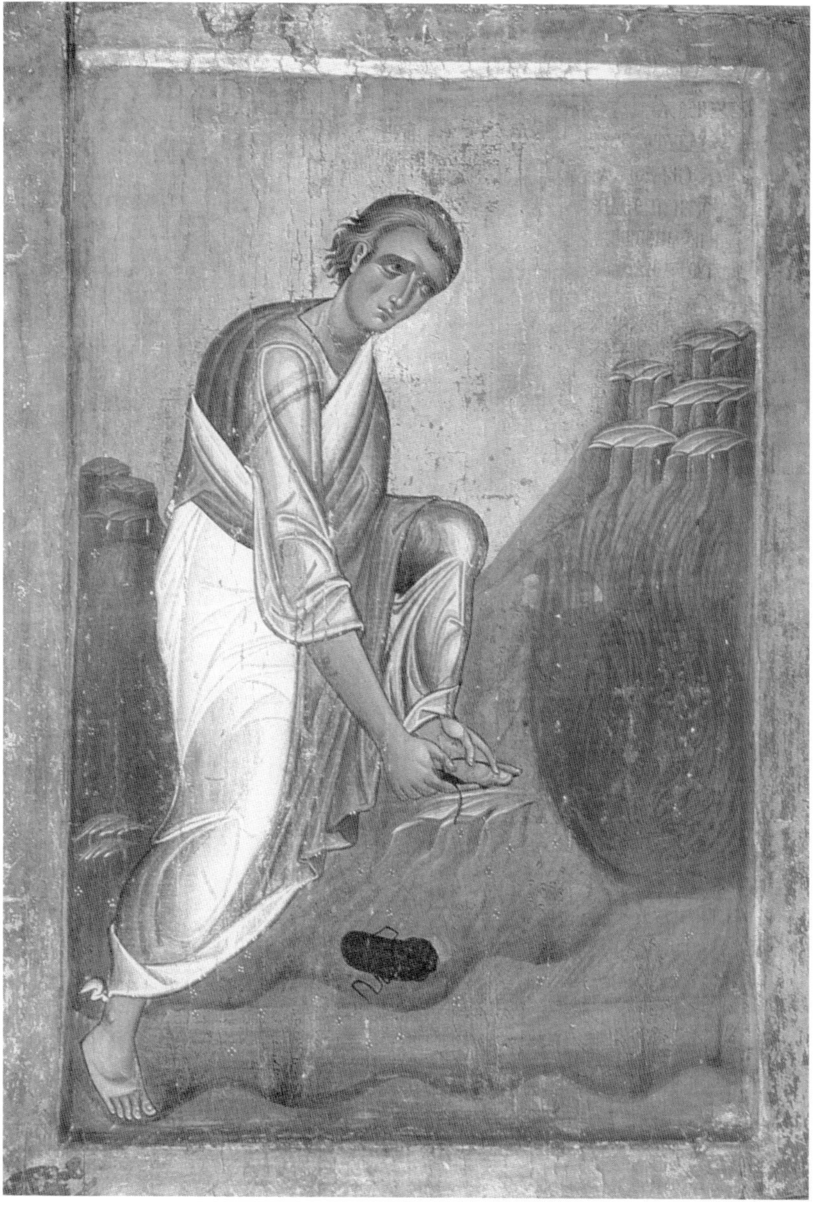

FIG 8.
*Moses at the
Burning Bush,* icon,
late 13th c. Sinai,
monastery of
St. Catherine

Exodus 3:2. What might be called the susceptibility of the motif to further interpretation is apparent in a Russian text called the *Conversation of the Three Hierarchs*[31] where the bush is described as "an image of the pure Virgin" because "as the burning fire by God's will did not burn up the tree, so the Word of God became flesh in the Virgin and did not burn but preserved both." Perhaps contemporaneously, the Logos was given visual form in an early twelfth-century copy of the Homilies of James of Kokkinobaphos where the bush is inhabited by the head of the youthful Christ.[32] And certainly no later than this manuscript, in a roundel on the so-called mantle of St. Kunigunde

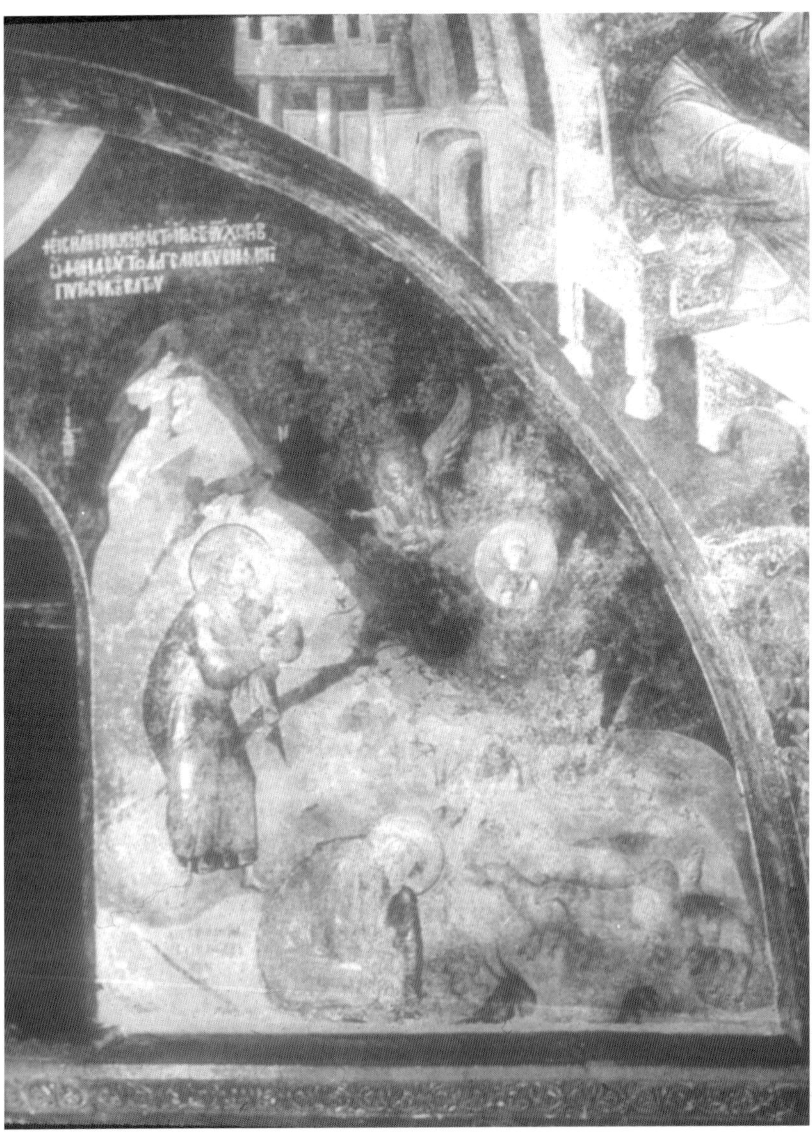

FIG 9.
The Burning Bush,
wall painting, ca.
1320. Istanbul,
Kariye Camii

  Interpreting Christian Art

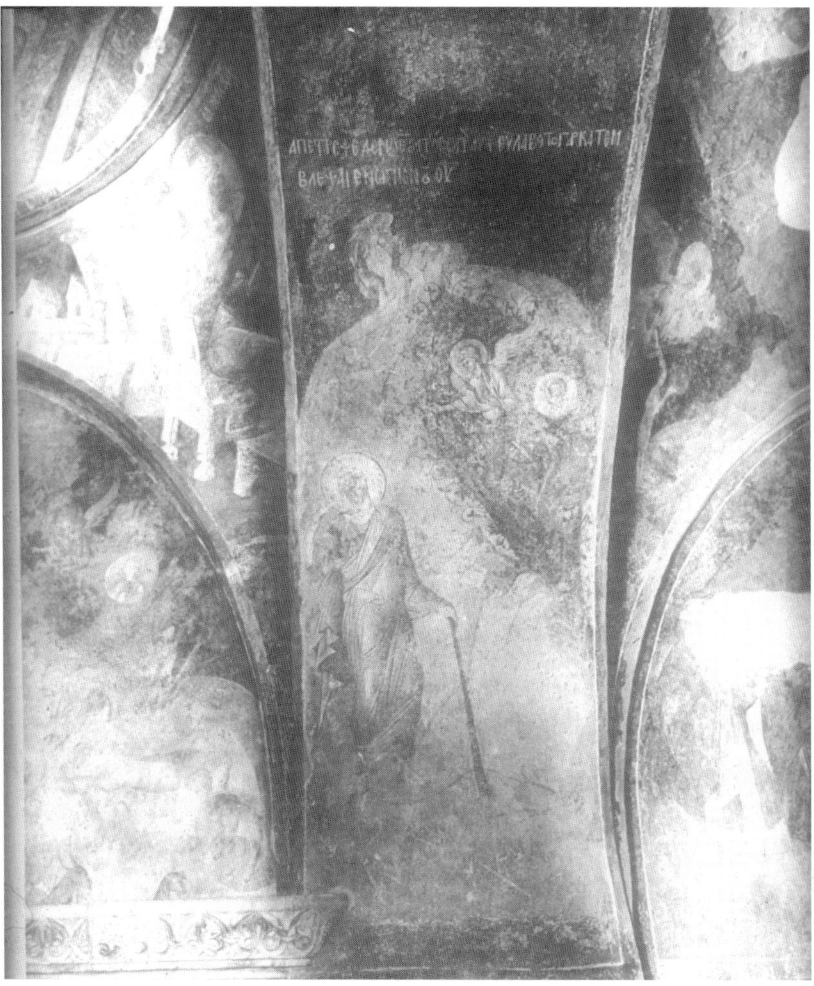

FIG 10.
The Burning Bush,
wall painting, ca.
1320. Istanbul,
Kariye Camii

in Bamberg, Moses encounters an angel in the same setting.[33] Clearly,
we are faced with a situation that in modern linguistic theory is called
catachresis—"the puttings of new senses into old words"[34] and, I
would add, images. Many of these layers of meaning come together in
the compounds that are the two versions of the scene in the early fourteenth-century wall paintings at the Chora in Constantinople.[35] Here
the images are adjacent, and both carry inscriptions based on Exodus
3. In the lunette (Figure 9) Moses gazes at the angel, who looks at him
"out of the midst of the bush" (v. 2)—a situation somewhat hard to
read in the abraded state of the painting—but in the arch (Figure 10)
the prophet averts his head, following the prescription of verse 6. The
visual difference is obvious, but its meaning would be incomprehen-

[33] *Sakrale Gewänder des Mittelalters*, exhib. cat., Bayerisches Nationalmuseum (Munich: Hirmer, 1955) 20, no. 25 and pl. 4.

[34] Max Black, *Models and Metaphors. Studies in Language and Philosophy* (Ithaca NY: Cornell University Press, 1962) 32–33. The meaning attached to the word "catachresis" is itself an example of the process. In the *Oxford English Dictionary* the term is still defined as the "incorrect use of a word or words, as by the misapplication of termi-nology."

[35] Paul A. Underwood, *The Kariye Djami*, 3 (Princeton NJ: Princeton University Press, 1966) 226. See also the commentary by Sirarpie Der Nersessian in *The Kariye Djami*, 336-338 (Princeton NJ: Princeton University Press, 1999)

[36]Both strategies are discussed by Blair, *Islamic Inscriptions*, 216.

[37]Robert Ousterhout, *Master Builders of Byzantium* (Princeton NJ: Princeton University Press, 1999) 24, usefully refers to the rock-cut church of St. Barbara at Göreme, which was of necessity first excavated and its walls painted to look as if made of ashlar.

[38] Crosses: see, e.g., Alexander van Millingen, *Byzantine Constantinople, the Walls of the City and Adjoining Historical Sites* (London:J. Murray, 1889) 98-99, nos. 2, 2b; gates: Ihor Ševčenko, "The Inscription of Justin II's Time on the Mevlihane (Rhegion) Gate at Istanbul," *Zbornik radova Vizantološkog Instituta* 12 (1970): 8 and fig. 1.

[39] Thus the *Ekloga* (*A Manual of Roman Law: The Ekloga*, trans. E. H. Freshfield [Cambridge, Cambridge University Press, 1926] 140), repeating Justinian's *Digest*: "The walls are sanctified, that is to say holy, and it is forbidden for anyone to damage them."

[40] These are identified and amply discussed by Dodd and Khairallah, *The Image of the Word*, 1:30–33.

sible to a beholder who did not read the inscriptions. Typical of the process of catachresis, narrative detail—in this case the removal of the shoes—has vanished from the scene in the arch, and its disappearance shifts attention from a story primarily concerned with Moses to the unconsumed bush presented as a prefiguration of the Virgin. Even so, the prophet still makes an appearance, as he does not in later Russian versions of the subject. There he is often excluded, such icons being customarily identified as "The Virgin of the Burning Bush."

The intellectual stance that lies at the heart of such metamorphoses is the ability and desire to adapt canonical texts and images in the service of an end not envisaged in their pristine application. Their inherent mutability is a necessary condition of these transformations, but no less critical is the mental agility that gives rise to them. We should not expect this of Islam, a religious tradition that made do without images. But cognitive parallels are evident in the dexterous use of different Koranic texts chosen to illustrate the same idea and the corollary process by which the same verse could be applied in different situations.[36] If, as I have suggested, these inscriptions were rarely read, this diversity would no more detract from the sacred character of a mosque than formal or structural variations would deter the faithful worshiping in Orthodox churches. For all their mutability, such buildings had an established and recognizable image, much in the manner of a saint depicted on an icon.[37]

An even more obvious parallel is the treatment of Islamic and Byzantine gates and walls. The former are more often marked with the names of their builders or restorers, but the latter were strengthened with crosses and icons.[38] In any case, these fortifications, indispensable to a city's continued existence as habitation and cultic focus, were regarded as holy, a belief affirmed by inscription and enforced by legislation.[39]

The convergence of secular and sacred ends is a phenomenon common to both Byzantine and Muslim societies and only accelerates after the eighth century. If in the Greek world it is epitomized by the increasingly diverse use of religious iconography on coins, in Islam it can be observed in the Koranic texts introduced by caliphal order into the Nilometer,[40] the great well used to measure the inundation of the river on which all Egypt depended for its food supply. The initial Umayyad inscriptions were pragmatic, concerned only with the height of the water. But 100 years later, in 814, and across the next half-century, a series of monumental inscriptions, citing *suras* that refer to the benefits that derive from the divine gift of water, were carved on the columnar measure at the center of the well and the walls that enclose it (Figure 11). In a sense we have here a foretaste of one of the chief characteristics of Islamic art, a passion for inscriptions that relate, closely or otherwise, to the object that carries them.

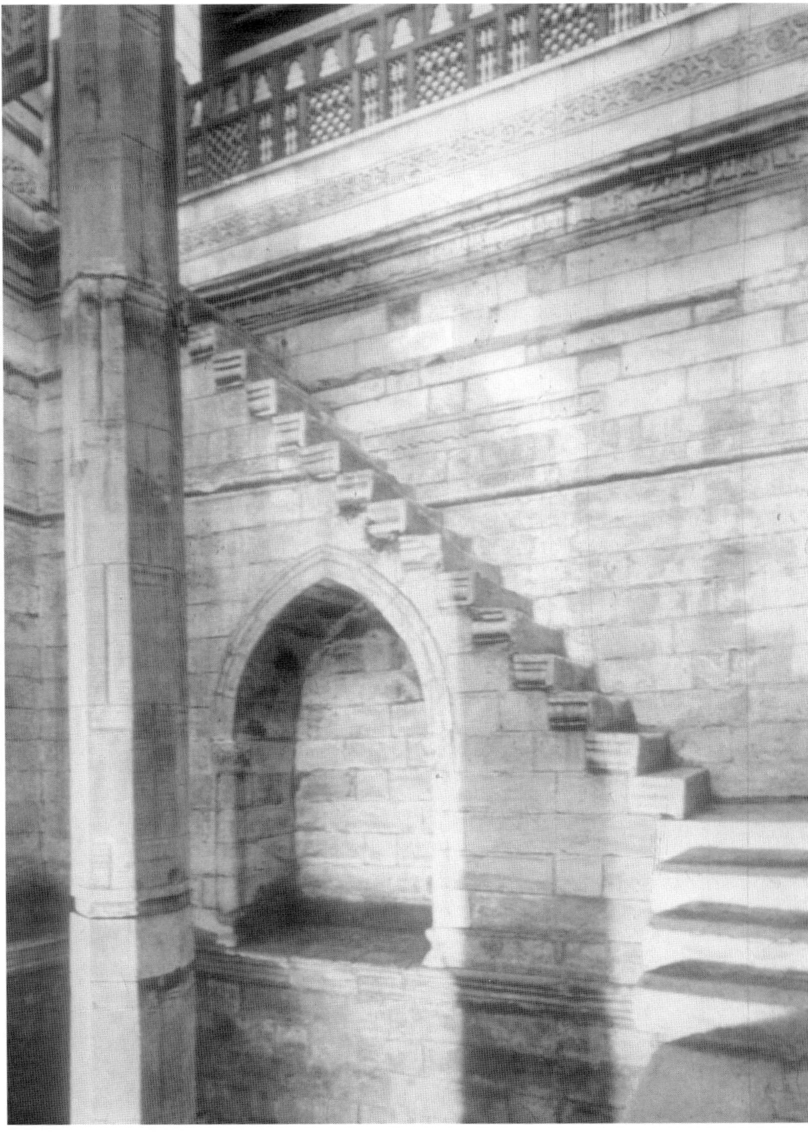

FIG 11.
Nilometer, Cairo, 861, detail

[41] Long associated with the Christian victory at Las Navas de Tolosa (1212), a turning point in the *reconquista*, it is now considered to be a trophy taken in a somewhat later campaign. See Jerrilynn D. Dodds, ed., *Al-Andalus: The Art of Islamic Spain*, exhib. cat. (New York: Metropolitan Museum of Art, 1992), no. 92.

Nonetheless, the Nilometer remains remarkable for the use of religious texts on a structure ostensibly put up for profane purposes.

The sanctification of earthly activity appears perhaps nowhere more clearly than on a banner probably taken from the Almohad sultan, al-Nasir, by Ferdinand III just before the middle of the thirteenth century (Figure 12).[41] As if to comment on the sacred mission of the *jihād*, the bands that surround the field are inscribed with verses from the *sura* (61:10-12) known as the Battle Array, carefully arranged so that some are to be read from the rear. The object, it can be inferred, is a war standard, carried in procession in such a way that it would be legible both to the troops that followed it and the armies they engaged, or else to spectators attendant upon a parade in which it was featured. We have no equivalent artifact from Byzantium, although there survive double-sided icons that may have been carried in a similar fashion.

Foreign traders and envoys to Islamic lands, as well as those who encountered enemy signs on the field of battle, cannot have but picked up some Arabic and, at the very least, would have been familiar with

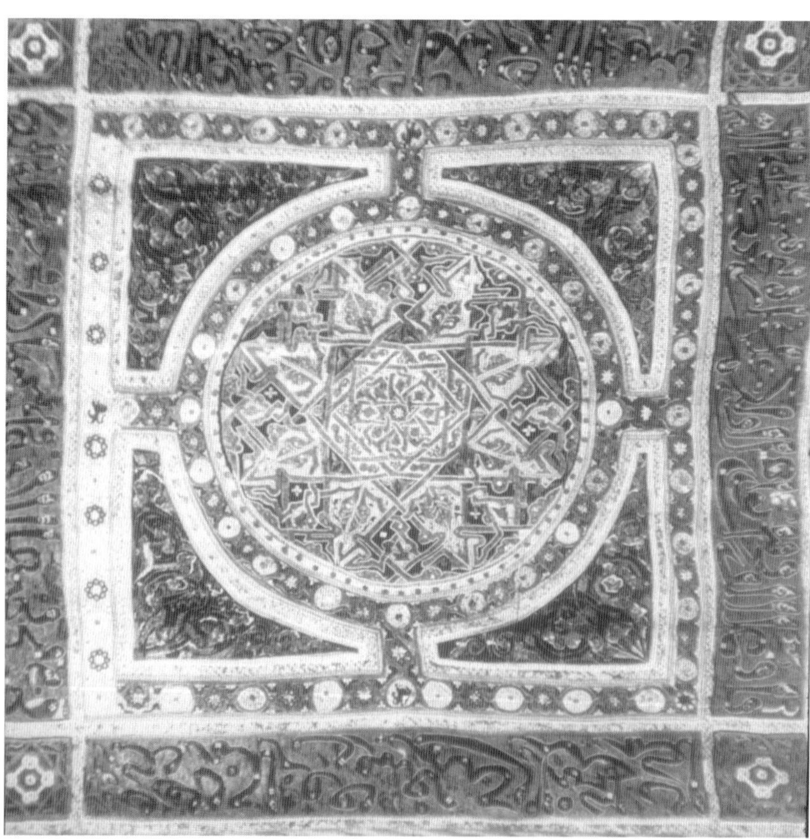

FIG 12. Battle standard, silk and gilt parchment, early 13th c. Burgos, Monastery of Santa Maria la Real de Huelgas

the importance that Muslims attached to inscriptions. The power of words is neatly suggested by a sequence of mosaics in San Marco in Venice that depicts the smuggling of this saint's body out of Alexandria by two Venetian merchants. Alleged to have occurred in 828, the story is reported in a text of no later than the tenth century.[42] Central to the legend is the fact that the Arabs declined to inspect the precious burden because it was concealed beneath a load of salted pork. This stratagem is succinctly conveyed in the mosaics' inscription (Figure 13) by the repetition of the word *kanzir* (pork), a linguistic

[42] Patrick J. Geary, *Furta Sacra. Thefts of Relics in the Central Middle Ages* (Princeton NJ: Princeton University Press, 1990) 93–94 with note 20.

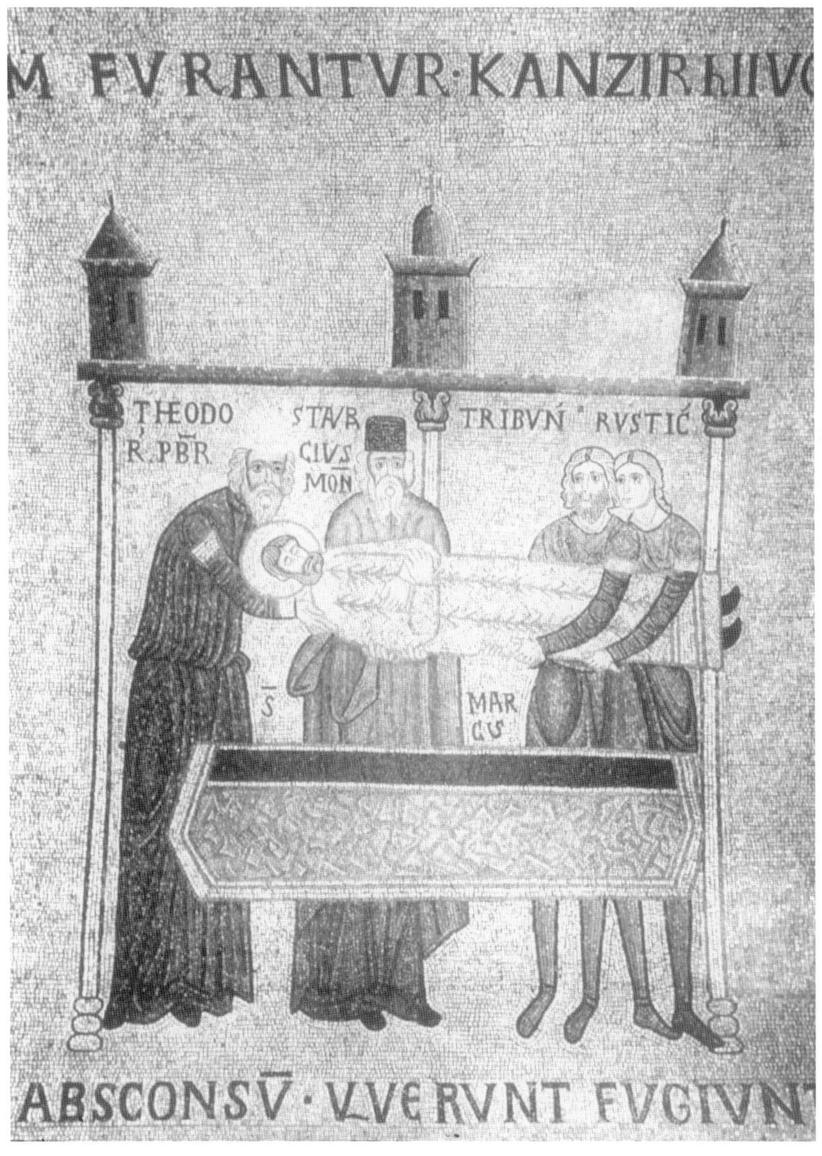

FIG 13.
The body of St. Mark taken from Alexandria, mosaic, 13th c. Venice, San Marco

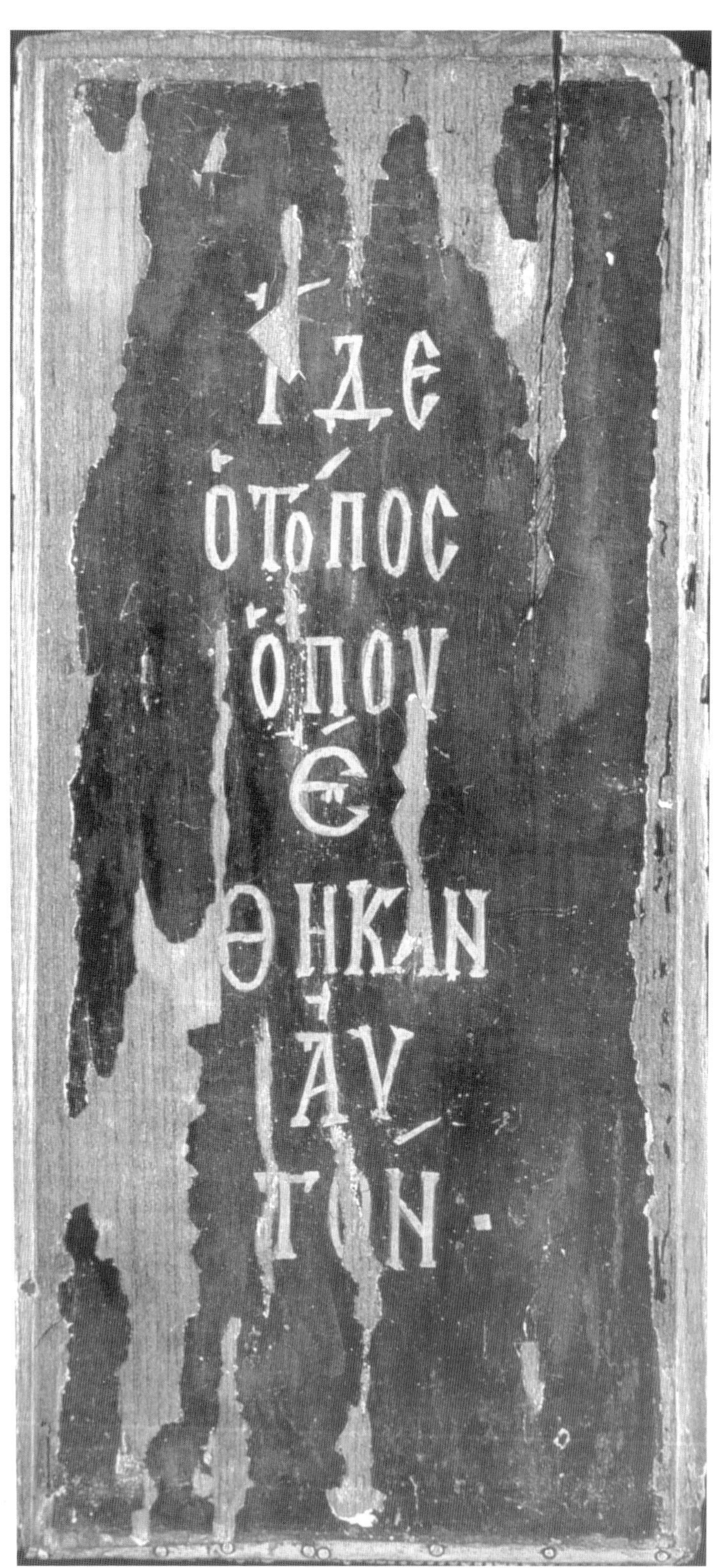

FIG 14.
Reliquary of the
Stone of the
Resurrection, inscrip-
tion on lid, second
half of 12th c. Paris,
Musée du Louvre

borrowing that conveys the ethnicity of the guards no less effectively than the turban sported by one of them in the skiff alongside the Italian merchantman.

It would be wrong, however, to conclude our trigonometric survey of Christian inscriptions with the rather wordy example in San Marco. Even where the designer had available space—obviously the first consideration in determining the amount of text that accompanied an image—the longest and most prominent bodies of words are occasioned not by the impulse to narrative, as in this hagiographical sequence, but, as we saw at the start in San Clemente, by the desire to impress upon the spectator the authority of the image and to achieve this by means of scriptural citation. This is the case with the remains of a reliquary, quite possibly the container of one of the holiest relics of Constantinople brought back from the Byzantine capital by Louis IX in 1241.[43] The two sides of its sliding lid already demonstrate the interplay between word and image with which we have been concerned: on one face, the bejeweled and leaf-flanked cross that was a familiar sign of the resurrection; on the reverse a quotation from Mark (16:6): ἼΔΕ Ὁ ΤΌΠΟC ὍΠΟΥ ἜΘΗΚΑΝ ἈΥΤΌΝ ("Behold the place where they laid him"; Figure 14) These, of course, were the words uttered by the angel to the two Marys when they came to the empty tomb on Easter Sunday morning. It is important to grasp both the dynamics of this shift from symbol to statement and the growing concentration—from general proposition to objectified expression— as the believer proceeds to uncover the successive elements of the box. The cross is a broad allusion to salvation, the inscription an order to look further. Removal of the lid exposes the brilliant luster of the gilded silver plaque that covered the relic itself. This depicts the angel who uttered the command in question and the tremulous women to whom it is addressed (Figure 15).

For all the richness of its imagery, the plaque is quite wordy. Around its perimeter a long stanza taken from the Sunday liturgy remarks on the beauty of the messenger and of his message. Then, above the women there appears a description of their amazement that cites Mark (16:8); in the center, the Matthean version of the inscription on the back of the lid; and, finally, the destination, so to speak: the

43 Jannic Durand, ed., *Byzance. L'art byzantin dans les collections publiques françaises,* exhib. cat. (Paris: Réunion des Musées nationaux, 1992) no. 248.

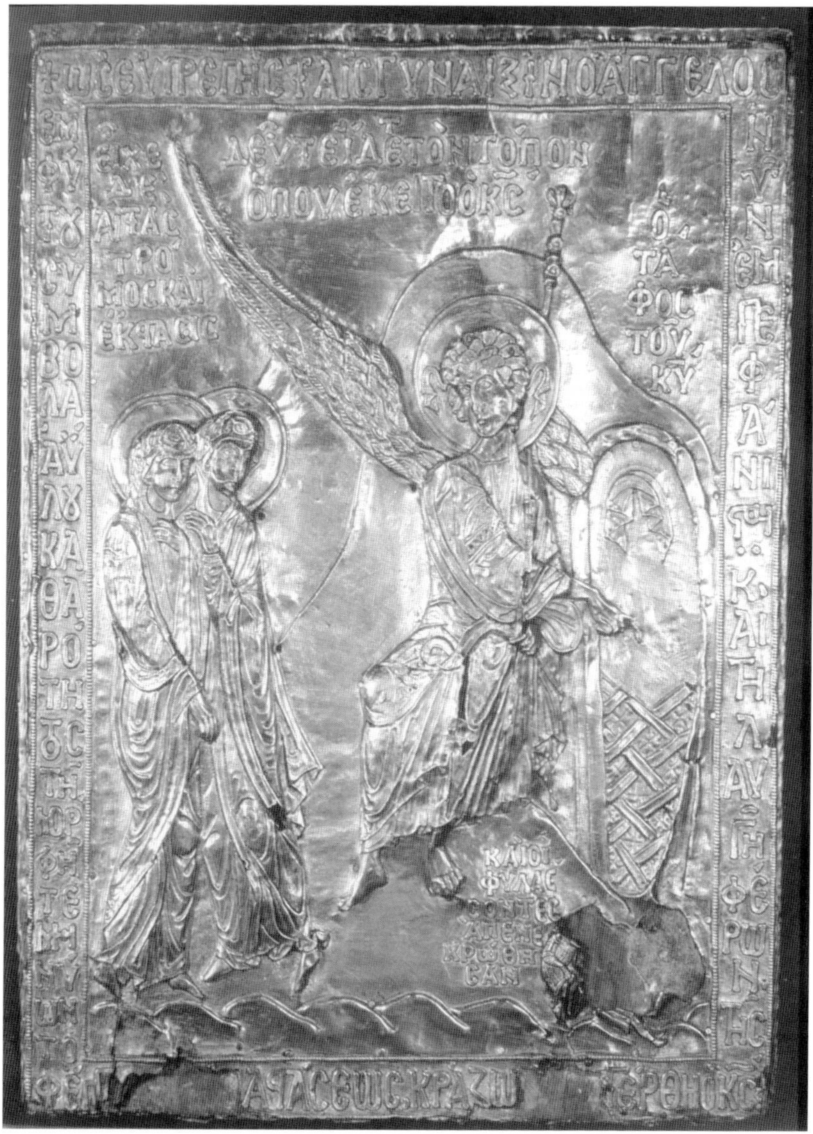

identifying phrase, "the tomb of the Lord," above the shroud and the angel's indexical gesture. His words, like the inscription on the lid, nominally directed to the Marys, are in fact addressed to us, to the beholder who is led from the generalized reference to Christ's apotheosis to the emptiness of the winding sheet and, ultimately, when the box was complete, to the fragment of the stone that closed the tomb, the relic that worked metonymically to concretize the resurrection by substituting this small, hard, material vestige for the extended narrative of the Gospels.

So, too, Koranic texts allude to the object or building on which they are inscribed and thus authenticate it, but they do this without the intervention of pictures, the icons which make present that which has passed. Long ago, Margaret Miles wrote that an "image's universality rests not on its potential for abstraction…but on the capacity of the viewer to grasp in the concrete particularity of the image a universal affectivity."[44] I have suggested that Muslim culture, with its preference for words over images, did not operate in this way. But if by the universal we understand the Christian realm, there is no disputing the observation. The evidence for this consists not of texts brought in from the outside and adduced in order to explicate the meanings of images but the texts themselves that the images bear, inscriptions which, in the Muslim world, were the raison d'être of these fields of display, and, in Christendom, elements no less essential to the objects' apprehension.

[44] *Image as Insight. Visual Understanding in Western Christianity and Secular Culture* (Boston: Beacon Press, 1985) 30.

6.

Who's Missing from Steinberg's "Who's Who in Michelangelo's Creation of Adam"?*

William M. Jensen

Baylor University

(In memory of Margaret and Robert Alexander)

In 1992 Leo Steinberg published a highly original and mostly persuasive interpretation of Michelangelo's *Creation of Adam* in the Sistine Ceiling, a work that was commissioned by Pope Julius II (1503–1513) and executed between 1508 and 1512.[1] Steinberg

* I wish to express my gratitude to my dean, Wallace Daniel, for release time from teaching to conduct research for an early stage of this paper; to my chair, John McClanahan, for his continuous and encouraging support; and to my colleagues, Heidi Hornik and Mikeal Parsons, for their generous invitation to contribute to this volume. The dedication is to the fond memory of two mentors who were instrumental in my decision to pursue a career in art history. An earlier version of this paper was delivered at the Midwest Art History Society meetings in 1995. The present version has been almost completely rewritten and expanded, and it incorporates aspects of another paper given in 1999 to the same society.

---

[1] "Who's Who in Michelangelo's *Creation of Adam*: A Chronology of the Picture's Reluctant Self-Revelation," *Art Bulletin* 74 (1992): 552–66. In a subsequent issue of the same journal (75 [1993]: 340) in a letter to the editor, Marcia Hall criticized Steinberg's Eve identification of the female in God's left arm, proposing instead that she should be identified as the female personification of Wisdom (*Sapientia*) mentioned in Proverbs 8:27. Steinberg (letter to editor in the same volume, 340–44) refuted her argument, persuasively in my view. Hall, however, apparently remains unconvinced since she characterizes Steinberg's Eve identification as "erroneous" in her later *Michelangelo: the Sistine Ceiling Restored* (New York: Rizzoli Art, 1993) 3, n. 11. Since the bibliography on the Sistine Ceiling and Michelangelo is enormous, I have tried to keep my references manageable by selecting the works most relevant to my discussion. The texts of the Bible are from the Douay translation (originally published in 1609–1610), while the Latin is from the Vulgate.

criticized previous interpreters for concentrating almost exclusively on God and Adam, thus ignoring the other figures in the composition, and, more generally, for following an iconographic method that failed to scrutinize the specifics of Michelangelo's imagery. His close reading of most of the other figures in the painting led to the discovery of what he called a "subplot," whose cast of characters included Eve, Christ, the archangel Michael, Lucifer and a companion, and attendant angels. At the end of his article Steinberg threw down the gauntlet, as it were, by noting that a colleague had asked him whether he should "rush into print" before he had identified "the rest of God's entourage in the fresco." Steinberg wryly responded, "Allowing a decent interval to assimilate these late comers should take us past the millennium. And we ought to leave the twenty-first century something to do."² Whether or not we are in the new millennium is debatable. Nonetheless, I feel relatively safe (although somewhat foolhardy) to "rush in where angels fear to tread" with an identification of what might be called the "missing link" in Steinberg's "who's who in Michelangelo's *Creation of Adam*." To see how this link fits (and where it leads) requires first a summary of, then a response to, his remarkable analysis.

Integral to Steinberg's reading of the fresco is the concept of the incarnation (Figure 1). After identifying the pubescent female ensconced in the nook of God's left arm as Eve and her infant companion to our right as Christ, he argues that God's ambidexterity tracks a "continuum," linking the creation of Adam with the creation of Eve and the incarnation of Christ. While Steinberg accounts for the

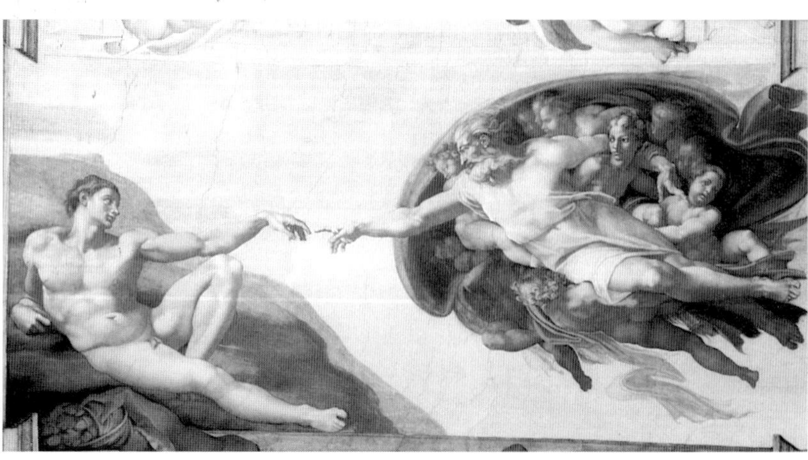

FIG 1. Michelangelo. *Creation of Adam,* 1508-12. Fresco. Ceiling, Sistine Chapel. Vatican, Rome.© Copyright Monumenti Musei e Gallerie Pontifiche.

coeval creation of Adam and Eve by positing Michelangelo's "reconciliation" (in the manner of St. Augustine) of the differing, biblical versions of the first couple's origin—one "simultaneous," the other "sequential" (Gen 1:27 and 2:21-23, respectively),[3] he explains the incarnational reference by means of the perceived "maternal" linkage of Eve and Christ and by a symbolic interpretation of the Lord's left hand, which presses down on Christ: thumb and index finger are "the consecrated two fingers with which alone the celebrant at the Mass touches the *corpus verum*, the Host." Steinberg, therefore, concludes that "the hand conveys more than a message: it not only points to the Incarnation by way of woman; it is the Father's tender of the incarnate Son in sacramental self-sacrifice; see John 3:16. Thus the reserved half of the fresco foreshadows—beyond the creation of Eve and the Son's humanation—the timeless rite of the Eucharist."[4]

The presence of the Redeemer in the fresco, Steinberg logically reflects, entails his need which is found in the two angels significantly placed in the shadows under God's outstretched right arm where they foully abut the derrière of an angel pressed against the upper body of the Creator. One of these degraded angels—little more than a gloomy mask set askew against a knobby shoulder—has his eyes closed; the other—a blond-headed youth likened to the "bright morning star," one meaning of *Lucifer*—defiantly turns his gaze away from Adam, his averting arm echoing his bent leg in ungainly disfigurement. Both of these denizens of the dark are contrasted with the rest of the illuminated angels near God's head who stare in awe at the marvelously formed new man. Given the evidence of the fresco, Steinberg persuasively identifies these umbrageous angels as Lucifer and a follower, relating their existence here to the tradition that ascribed the fall of the angels to Lucifer's envy at the creation of Adam in the image and likeness of God.[5] According to this view, Lucifer, refusing to worship newly created man as commanded by the archangel Michael, led a contingent of his fellow angels in revolt and, after ejection from heaven, revenged his loss of glory by tempting Eve into the first couple's expulsion from paradisiacal bliss. In the fresco the green cloth that curves over Eve's left thigh ("issuing, as it were, from the loins of Eve") and reappears below, crossing the foot of Lucifer in surreptitious

[3]Steinberg, letter to editor, 341. As should be apparent from my interpretation, I think the "reconciliation" of the two accounts of Adam and Eve's creation in Genesis 1 and 2 is due to the need to include Eve as a parallel for the immaculate Mary's role as the co-redeemer in the scheme of salvation. Steinberg's point, however, that the two accounts need to be addressed in any interpretation of Michelangelo's fresco is certainly sound, in my view. While I do not think that Michelangelo followed any specific iconographic tradition in his particular visualization (for nothing close to it exists, to the best of my knowledge), he may have been informed, in a minor way, by representations at the beginning of Italian creation cycles, dating from ca. 700 through the thirteenth century (including the mosaics from the Baptistry at Florence), which have been interpreted as "the Creation of the Souls of Adam and Eve"; Deborah Markow, "The Iconography of the Soul in Medieval Art," (Ph.D. diss., New York University, 1983) 34–42. These odd scenes seem to show a conflation of all the days of creation, a conclusion that Markow assigns to Herbert Kessler (36, n. 10).

[4]Steinberg, "Who's Who," 558.

[5]Steinberg, "Who's Who," 559-64.

[6] Steinberg, "Who's Who," 565.

[7] This may seem like an obvious point, but anyone who reads closely what has been written on the Sistine Ceiling and then looks carefully at what Michelangelo has actually painted will find glaring errors, e.g., that Adam or Eve (or both) grasp or touch the fruit of the Tree of Knowledge in the *Temptation* when they do not, as can be verified by examining the fresco. Hence, the titlement of this painting as the *Fall* is inaccurate. Cf. below n.27 and 30. The central question in interpreting the Sistine Ceiling has been whether or not the Genesis scenes have a christological content. The standard methodology used in the past to address this issue has been "typology," conceived in the sense of Old Testament subjects foreshadowing New Testament ones. In those medieval works, where two subjects from each testament are juxtaposed in the same physical context, this interpretative approach is justified. But the Sistine Ceiling obviously does not follow this artistic practice; instead, it only presents subjects from the Old Testament. Since there are multiple typologies for most of these subjects, it is not surprising that each interpreter has arrived at different conclusions (or has cited several typologies without specifying how such profligacy might relate to what Michelangelo actually painted; this is subject matter to typology in a "bookish" approach that effaces the artist's interpretation). The significance of Steinberg's interpretative method, therefore, which is expanded and contextualized in my analysis, is that a figure of Christ can actually be identified in one of the frescoes. In my view, following Steinberg's approach for the other paintings opens the door to a far more plausible interpretation of the theology of the Ceiling, but this approach requires far more attention to an artist's visualization than what art history is inclined to accept or is prepared to offer. Ettlinger (below n.26, pp. 94–103) analyzed the development of typology and its complexities. Cf. below n.27.

entanglement, Steinberg sees as hinting at the "long train of consequence" of the story which is detailed in the subsequent panels of the ceiling. Finally, Steinberg locates Michael, the only missing character in the "fresco's subplot," in the angel directly beneath God whose "martial posture…defines the figure as the champion of Heaven." As the artist's namesake, he serves not only as an undersigned signature, but as an autobiographical identification with the "defender of Heaven."[6]

Steinberg's approach rests on his insistence that interpretations must agree with the specifics of the image under analysis.[7] On this basis, he criticizes iconography, as sometimes practiced, for being too "bookish," for superimposing texts on images with which they disagree.[8] Put differently, iconography is inclined to attend to the subject matter of a work, not to the specific rendering of the subject as it appears in a particular work. At its extreme, this practice amounts to a type of erasure, analogous to the many anonymous diagrams of the Sistine Ceiling where Michelangelo's actual visualizations of the Genesis scenes running down the spine are replaced by typed titles of their presumed subjects. At issue here is not whether textual material should be used to interpret art (obviously it must if the aim is historical interpretation), but the grounds for its use. As every researcher of Christian art knows, the source material is extensive, varied, conflicting, and even contradictory. How does the interpreter know what, if any, of this information is relevant? Or what prevents the selection of any of this material from being arbitrary? For Steinberg the visual interrogation of the image is what guides and directs the exploration of the textual material and determines its relevance; and I

[8] I have taken the liberty of expanding Steinberg's "bookish" comment (above n.1, 1993, pp. 343–44), which he specifically applied to a particular interpretation by Julian Klaczko, to iconography in general, for that seems to be the sense of his criticism. For a recent collection of essays on iconography from a variety of perspectives, see Brenden Cassidy, ed., *Iconography at the Crossroads* (Princeton NJ: Princeton University Press, 1993). Cassidy's introduction (3–16) is a thoughtful overview. In order to maintain a focus to my discussion I have limited my comments on methodological theory to a minimum. My concern with "contextualization" is an attempt to address the poststructuralist or semiotic criticism of an unqualified empiricist view of perception (the so-called "innocent eye" theory, i.e., that perception in some simple sense gives the viewer "unmediated" or "objective" information of what is seen), which some of my comments at the beginning of my paper might seem to imply. See Mieke Bal and Norman Bryson, "Semiotics and Art History," *Art Bulletin* 73 (1991): 174-208. For an approach from the perspective of reception theory, see John Shearman, *Only Connect…: Art and the Spectator in the Italian Renaissance.* Bollingen Series 35/37: The National Gallery of Art, Washington, DC (Princeton NJ: Princeton University Press, 1992) and Wolfgang Kemp's review in the *Art Bulletin* 76 (1996): 364–67. For an interpretive method more in line with what is argued in my analysis, but framed in a slightly different manner, see Paolo Berdini, *The Religious Art of Jacopo Bassano: Painting as Visual Exegesis* (Cambridge: Cambridge University Press, 1997). Also see Berdini's essay in this volume.

think there is much to commend in this approach, particularly in the case of artists such as Michelangelo, who were regarded during their lifetimes (and subsequently) as being highly "original," that is, unconventional and exploring new territories of artistic expression. At the very least, this approach attempts to make sense of what is seen, rather than interpreting an alleged subject matter which may, in fact, be erroneous precisely because the visual specifics have been ignored or insufficiently examined. A case in point is Steinberg's analysis: if accepted, then Michelangelo's fresco is misnamed, or at least too simply titled. We will return to this issue at the close of our discussion.

For Steinberg, then, specifics matter: gestures, poses, compositional relationships, relative scale, etc. In what follows we will take another look at "St. Michael," the liturgical meaning of God's left hand, "Eve" and "Christ" (with a particular aim of contextualizing their analysis selectively in Michelangelo's art), the imagery of the ceiling, and the art of several Renaissance artists whose work has been widely taken as "sources." This analysis will lead us to the "missing link" and her companions in the back row of the composition (the only figures in God's entourage to escape Steinberg's attention) which, in turn, will raise a broader issue of contextualization: the relationship of the proposed content of the *Creation of Adam* to the dedication, function, and patronage of the Sistine Chapel. A fundamental assumption underlying my methodology is that the meanings we associate with what we see depend on context; if one is interested in a plausible historical interpretation (which I am), then a viable approach is to explore the meaning of Michelangelo's art in terms of what is known about him, his work, and its patronage.[9] Therefore, I will attempt to contextualize Steinberg's assessment of the meaningful ambiguity[10] of Michelangelo's imagery within the Renaissance concept of *ut pictura poesis,* which David Summers has demonstrated is the way his art was viewed and discussed by his contemporaries and the way the artist probably understood it.[11] This artistic concept invites us to understand the unusual, puzzling, and even extravagant features of his art (judged by the artistic norms of the day) as tropes, and especially metaphor.[12] Since many of Michelangelo's visual metaphors are elabo-

[9]What is known about an artist is always an ongoing affair. For a reassessment of biographical information about Michelangelo from the point of view of "self-fashioning," see Paul Barolsky, *Michelangelo's Nose: A Myth and Its Maker* (University Park PA: Pennsylvania State University Press, 1990) and *The Faun in the Garden: Michelangelo and the Poetic Origins of Italian Renaissance Art* (University Park PA: Pennsylvania State University Press, 1994).

[10]Steinberg, letter to editor, 341: "Where Augustine's metaphysics is worded to exclude ambiguity as best he may, Michelangelo's thought orders accurate ambiguities to resist verbal containment."

[11]David Summers, *Michelangelo and the Language of Art* (Princeton NJ: Princeton University Press, 1981).

[12]Bernadine Barnes, "Metaphorical Painting: Michelangelo, Dante, and the *Last Judgment,*" *Art Bulletin* 77 (1995): 65–81; Paul Barolsky, "Metaphorical Meaning in the Sistine Ceiling," *Source* 9 (1990): 19–22; Edgar Wind, "The Ark of Noah: A Study in the Symbolism of Michelangelo," *Measure* 1 (1950): 411–21.

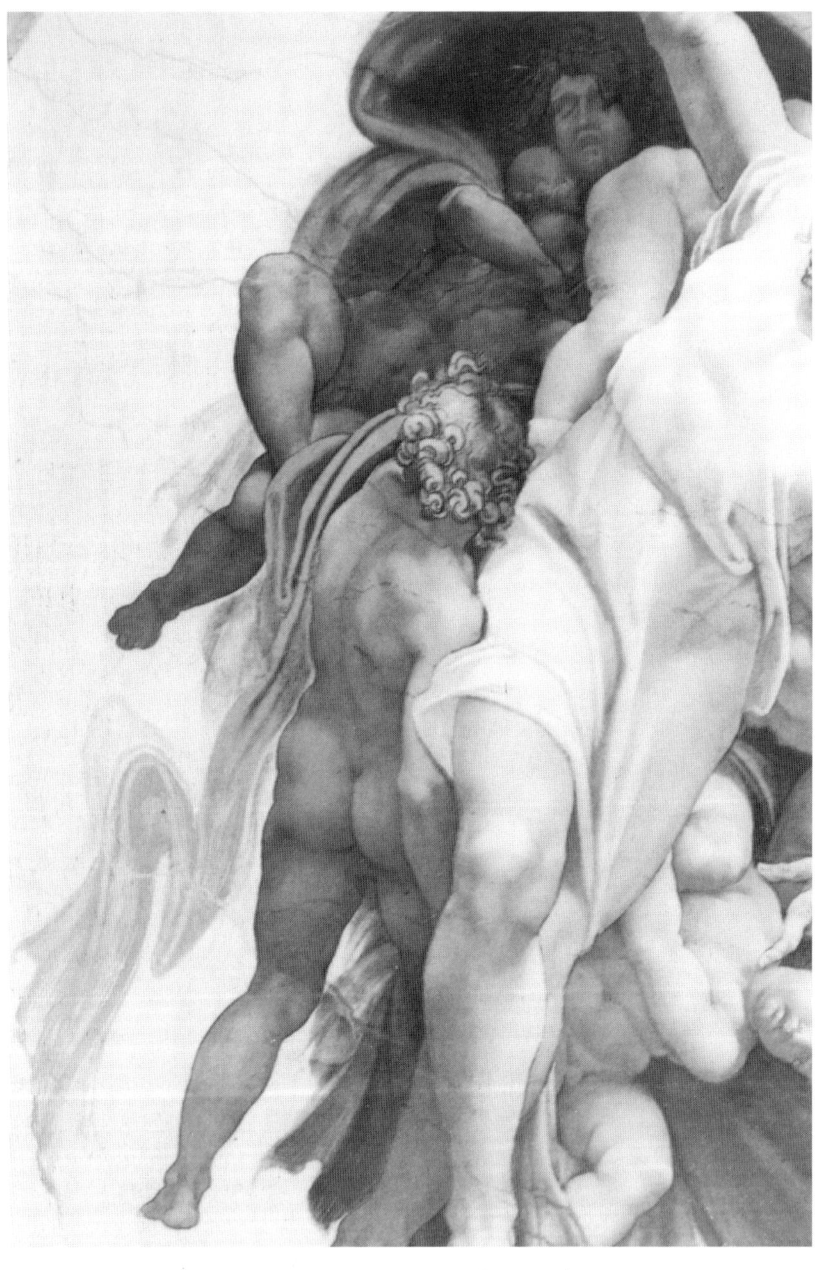

[13]Steinberg, "Who's Who,"
565. A drawing in the
Teylers Museum in Haarlem
(A20v) shows figure studies
of St. Michael, Lucifer, the
angel above him, and the
right knee of Adam. Its
attribution to Michelangelo
is disputed: Frederick Hartt,
Michelangelo's Drawings
(New York: Harry Abrams,
1969) 81, no. 76 and 84,
which has a concordance
with a listing of prior opinions. While accepted by
Hartt, Steinberg, "Who's
Who," 560n.22, rejects it.

rate and esoteric, they can be thought of as analogous to conceits or even metaphysical conceits.

As for the identification of the male nude under God's legs as St. Michael (Figure 2), Steinberg argues that this figure does not literally support the Almighty as commonly thought because the right elbow is "pronated," not "supinated, as it would have to be to produce an upturned palm under a load."[13] Even if one grants this point and concedes that it is fundamental for understanding the meaning of this figure, it still must be said that God's right thigh rests squarely on the biceps, and beneath the deltoid hollow, of this carrier. In short, this figure is ambiguous, performing two functions, one above and one foreword. In its avant-garde role, which is less obvious on immediate inspection and, in effect, future tense, this figure strides to the right with the corresponding arm retracted behind the advanced leg, its hand hidden under God's right calf, while the left arm is bent at an angle in front of the face, its forearm just visible to the right of the figure's head. This left arm ("a gallant arm interposed as though to shield God from Satanic ill-will"[14]) is part of the figure's "martial pose," which, since it faces Lucifer, reveals its identity as St. Michael. Steinberg suggests a comparison with the "Hercules" in Michelangelo's early *Battle Relief* (ca. 1491–1492), that is, the nude youth to the left of center who, seen from the side, raises his left arm in front of his head for protection, while his right, lowered behind him, holds a rock which he is about to hurl.[15]

Although the pose of the "Hercules" is certainly relevant to understanding that of St. Michael in the fresco, a much closer source can be found in a drawing by Michelangelo, which is usually dated ca. 1503–1504 and considered to be an early sketch for the *Battle of Cascina* cartoon[16] (Figure 3; here reversed for comparison). The nude to the left is nearly identical to the St. Michael, except for minor changes. A sword, hanging from an unrepresented belt, identifies the figure as a soldier. In this case, he strides to the left (in our reversal), rather than to the right, and his bent right arm actually does support the leg of the central figure which, as has been recognized, is a free adaptation of the famous *Apollo Belvedere*. This Cascina drawing seems particularly relevant to the *Creation of Adam* in another respect. If it is reversed, as illustrated here, and then rotated ninety degrees to the left, its composition appears as an embryonic version of the nucleus of the fresco, where the supporting warrior is repeated with minor variations and the central figure's biaxial gestures—the extended arm dominant over the trailing one—are transformed into the Creator's ambidexterity. To be sure, the fresco's rendering of God has undergone drastic changes, informed in part by the flying victory

[14]Steinberg, "Who's Who," 565.

[15]Ibid., 565. For the *Battle Relief*, see John Pope-Hennessey, *Italian High Renaissance and Baroque Sculpture* (New York: Vintage Books, 1985) 5, 302, pl. 2; and Giovanni Agosti and Vincenzo Farinella, eds., *Michelangelo e l'arte classica* (exhibition at the Casa Buonarroti, 15 April–15 October 1987), Cantini Edizioni d'Arte (Florence, 1987) 25-27, no. 5.

[16]Johannes Wilde, *Italian Drawings in the Department of Prints and Drawings in the British Museum. Michelangleo and His Studio* (London: British Museum, 1953) 10-14, no. 5, pls. 8 and 11; pl. 9 (the verso, which has a variant of the soldier). Wilde proposed that the soldier is based on the Dioscuri or "Horse-Tamers" on Monte Cavallo in Rome and that a similar figure, except turned in profile to the left, appears in the Cascina cartoon as preserved in the grisaille copy in Holkam Hall. While the Dioscuri compare favorably in several respects with the soldier in the drawing, especially in terms of the classical anatomy of both, their gestures are similar, but not the same; and it is the totality of the pose which demonstrates that Michelangelo's figure is derived fundamentally from the warrior in a defensive posture, however much the specific style may be informed by other works, such as the Dioscuri. Wilde's attempt to understand the actions of the three figures in the drawing in narrative terms, I think, is strained and unconvincing. Also see Hartt, *Michelangelo's Drawings*, 46, no. 27 and 386 (concordance, showing unanimous attribution to Michelangelo). Michael Hirst, *Michelangelo and His Drawings*, New York and New Haven: Yale University Press, 1988, 43, figs. 75-77 observes that the antithetical arrangement of the two supporting figures of Michelangelo's Cascina drawing were inspired by Filippino Lippi's *Crucifixion of St. Peter* in the Brancacci Chapel, S. Maria del Carmine in Florence.

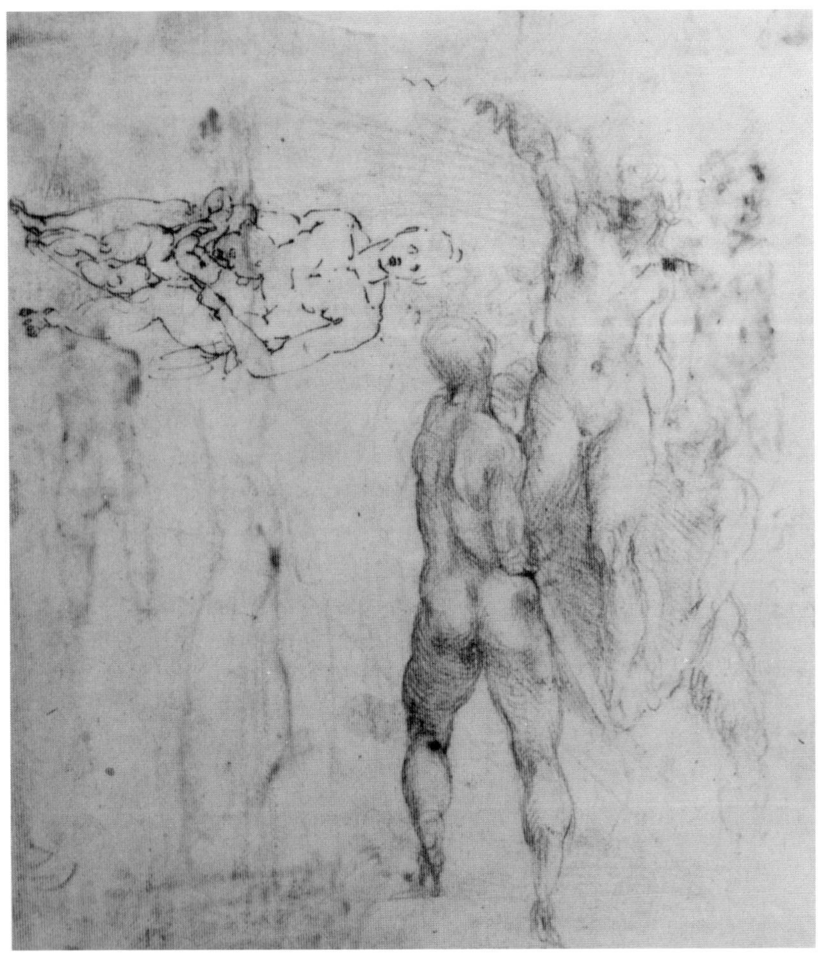

[17]Johannes Wilde, "Eine Studie Michelangelos nach der Antike," *Mitteilungen des kunsthistorischen Institutes in Florence* 4 (1932-34): 63, figs. 20–21.

[18]Oxford, Ashmolean Museum, P. 318 r: Hartt, *Michelangelo's Drawings*, 181, no. 257 and 390 (concordance showing unanimous attribution to Michelangelo).

[19]E.g., see the relief on the Column of Trajan in Ranuccio Bianchi Bandinelli, *Rome: The Centre of Power*, trans. Peter Green (London: Thames and Hudson, 197) fig. 273 (the soldier at the bottom right).

figures found in Roman art.[17] It would seem that this group was to represent a victorious moment of the Cascina battle in Michelangelo's early thoughts for the painting. This trio was apparently a favored motif for the artist since he recycled it in a modified form in a drawing of *The Brazen Serpent* (ca. 1520–1525?),[18] where the central figure is elevated to gaze at the salvific icon, a victorious moment of delivery suggestively analogous to the presence of the Redeemer at the end of God's left hand as he reaches toward Adam.

As the unmistakable classical style of the warrior in both Michelangelo's Cascina drawing and Sistine fresco suggests, its pose is derived from Roman reliefs where, rendered from behind, it is used for a soldier under attack who holds his shield raised protectively in front and his drawn sword in his lowered back hand.[19] A very similar warrior—nude, but with his shield extended out from, rather than across his face—appears in the bronze *Battle Relief* by Michelangelo's teacher, Bertoldo di Giovanni.[20] Since this work is universally acknowledged as a source of inspiration for the pupil's *Battle Relief*, it seems that Michelangelo was first exposed to this warrior motif from Bertoldo; however, after his trip to Rome and his firsthand exposure to more extensive ancient art, he incorporated this experience in his Cascina drawing and the Sistine St. Michael.

As is well known, Michelangelo frequently eschewed attributes (for example, wings for angels and haloes for sacred characters), leaving the figure as formulated to carry whatever meaning it might have within its given context. Deprived of shield, armor, and sword (which is comparable to ellipsis[21]) the Sistine figure is stripped to the bare minimum of the defensive pose of a classical warrior, a suitable embodiment of the "defender of heaven," as Steinberg proposed, but one which taxes the viewer's powers of informed perception, even if it were not further complicated as it is. With his left arm in front of his head and facing Lucifer, who has his right arm across his, St. Michael is, in this respect, a mirror image of his opponent (Figure 2).[22] In regard to Lucifer, Steinberg observed that his pose is "graceless, unbecoming an angel, especially in the bend of the lower limbs which may be mimicking the Almighty's crossed legs, or mocking Adam's—or doing both."[23] Mocking, indeed, for Lucifer, with his left leg extended and his right severely bent, is a very close mirror reversal, at a slightly different angle, of Adam with his right leg extended and his left severely bent (compare Figures 1 and 2). While the foot of the former hangs in front of the extended leg, that of the latter is locked behind it. The altered angle of the two figures ingeniously maintains the look of Lucifer's impending fall, as well as his deformity, in contrast to Adam's earth-created stability and languid grace *ad imaginem Dei*. It seems safe to say that this is a visual parody of a very elevated and learned kind—elevated because of the lofty subject and learned because of its studied expression. Since a mirror image shows both likeness and difference, it is a particularly eloquent means to visualize paradox: angelic agon in the case of Lucifer and Michael, and divergent states of grace for soon-to-fall Lucifer and prelapsarian Adam.

[20]James D. Draper, *Bertoldo di Giovanni, Sculptor of the Medici Household: Critical Reappraisal and Catalogue Raisonne* (Columbia MO: University of Missouri Press, 1992) 133–45, cat. no. 11, illus on p. 138 (detail, showing the warrior), and 40–41 for some of Michelangelo's borrowings in his *Battle Relief* from Bertoldo's. While Bertoldo's relief is a loose imitation of a Roman battle sarcophagus in the Camposanto in Pisa, the warrior in question does not appear in this work.

[21]Cf. Barnes, "Metaphorical Painting," 67.

[22]On the use of mirror reversal in Renaissance art and its connection to the trope of antithesis, see David Summers, "*Figure come Fratelli*: A Transformation of Symmetry in Renaissance Painting," *Art Quarterly* 1 (1977): 59–88.

[23]Steinberg, "Who's Who," 560; the rest of the quotation after the ellipsis is "and yet more, like getting a furtive foot tangled in the green scarf that leaks from above."

[24]Steinberg, "Who's Who," 557–58, cites an unpublished undergraduate paper by Michael Stolbach to support his interpretation. The evidence can be found in Joseph A. Jungmann, *The Mass of the Roman Rite: Its Origin and Development*, trans. Rev. Francis A. Brunner (Westminster MA: Christian Classics, Inc., 1986) 2/205ff. For the twelfth–thirteenth century controversy on transubstantiation, see V. L. Kennedy, "The Moment of Consecration and the Elevation of the Host," *Mediaeval Studies* 6 (1944): 121–50.

[25]Representations of the Elevation of the Host: *The Mass of S. Giles* by the Master of S. Giles (London, National Gallery), ca. 1500, clearly illustrated in color in Martin Kemp, ed., *The Oxford History of Western Art* (Oxford: Oxford University Press, 2000) 69, fig. 86; John Pope-Hennessy, *Italian Gothic Sculpture* (New York: Vintage Books, 1985) pl. 58 (the *Eucharist* on the Campanile, Florence); Roger S. Wieck, *Painted Prayers: The Book of Hours in Medieval and Renaissance Art* (New York: George Braziller, 1998) 122–23n.96; Jonathan J. G. Alexander, ed., *The Painted Page: Italian Renaissance Book Illumination 1450–1500* (London/Munich: Royal Academy of Arts and Prestel-Verlag, 1994) 239n.128, (illus. on p. 241).

[26]Cf. Steinberg, "Who's Who," 558: "Stolbach perceived this godly gesture not as overemphatic, forced, cramped, heavy-handed, or proto-mannerist, but as Christian." The two readings, however, are not mutually exclusive.

The evidence to support Steinberg's liturgical interpretation of God's left hand in the *Creation of Adam* can be traced back to the eleventh century, where reference is made to the celebrant holding the consecrated host between the forefinger and thumb.[24] This specific feature is also visible in late medieval and Renaissance representations of the "Elevation of the Host," the display of the consecrated *corpus Christi* to the congregation for adoration.[25] That Michelangelo's gesture should be seen as alluding to the very moment of transubstantiation, or rather its equivalence in the context of the *Creation of Adam*, is indicated by one aspect of the fresco to be addressed now and others to be discussed later. The rendering of the Lord's left hand is extraordinarily artificial in that both its wrist and elongated index finger are exceptionally double-jointed (Figure 4). Since this distortion is strikingly at odds with the natural flexion and proportions of the rest of God's body, it calls attention to itself; and it is quite inexplicable why it seems hardly to have been commented on before.[26] But that is not quite accurate. Michelangelo has supplied an internal witness in the cherub directly behind the Almighty's hand, who stares at it in amazement (Figure 4), a transient acknowledgement of the mystical moment of transmutation as it applies to the incarnation (see below). Since Michelangelo was schooled by Poliziano, who was an admirer of Alberti, it seems credible that the visual function of this figure is derived from Alberti's recommendation that painters of *historia* (the category to which *the Creation of Adam* belongs) should include in the composition an interlocutor who by expression or gesture "tells the spectator what is going on."[27]

Steinberg's interpretation of the Lord's left hand captures its basic meanings: it has a soteriological sense in regard to the subject portrayed in the painting and prefigures "the timeless rite of the Eucharist." However, since this sacramental gesture appears in the papal chapel, it surely must be seen as also having an ecclesiological import. It would seem to foretell the divine institution of the church,

[27]Leon Battista Alberti, *On Painting and On Sculpture: The Latin Texts of De Pictura and De Statua*, trans. Cecil Grayson (London: Phaidon Press, 1972) 83 (*De Pictura*, 42: *Tum placet in historia adesse quempiam qui earum quae gerantur rerum spectatores admoneat*) and 143 on Poliziano and Alberti. The irony of Michelangelo's cherub is that his expression is not clearly visible from the floor of the chapel. It was, however, clearly visible to those on the scaffolding: the artist, his assistants, Julius II, and Alfonso d'Este (and possibly others). William E. Wallace, "Michelangelo's Assistants in the Sistine Chapel," *Gazette des Beaux-Arts*, 6/110 (1987): 203–16.

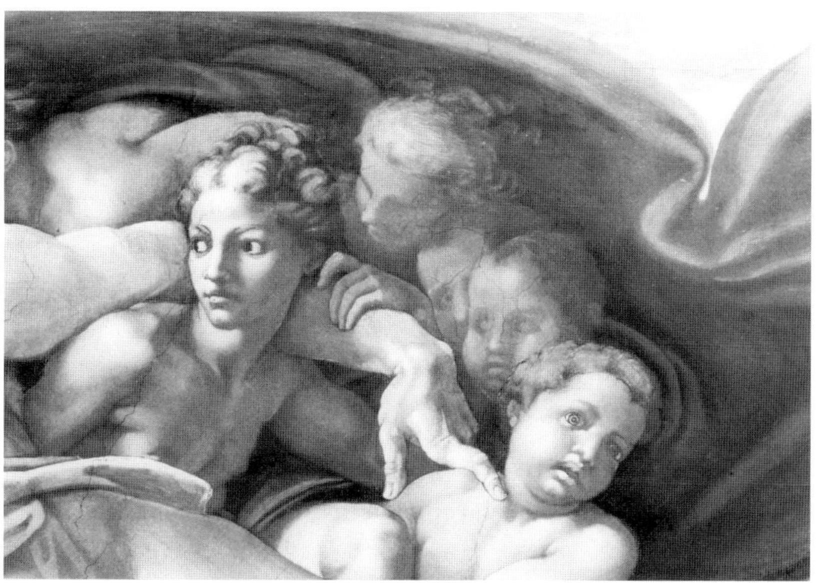

FIG 4.
Michelangelo.
Detail. *Creation of Adam.* 1508-12.
Fresco. Ceiling,
Sistine Chapel.
Vatican, Rome. ©
Copyright
Monumenti Musei e
Gallerie Pontifiche.

headed by the vicar of Christ, in which case it would complement the theme of the frescoes on the lower walls of the Sistine Chapel, executed under Sixtus IV (1471–1484) between 1481 and 1483, by projecting their assertion of papal primacy[28] back to the incarnation and God's providential plan. This intimation, suggested by the chapel's function, returns us to Michelangelo's imagery.

In the fresco, directly beneath Adam's thigh, a hand of the *ignudo*, the male nude, above the Persian Sibyl and the end of an acorn swag overlap the frame and intrude into the field[29] (Figure 1). The right hand of the *ignudo* virtually duplicates the shape of the left hand of God, even including the disjointed wrist (Figure 4). Here, then, the sacramental gesture is married to the emblem of the *Della Rovere* (*rovere* means "oak") family, which included Pope Sixtus IV, the founder of the Sistine Chapel, and his nephew Pope Julius II, Michelangelo's patron. Acorns, garlands of oaks, and the papal coat-of-arms with the *Della Rovere* oak tree are prominently exhibited in the dynastic decoration of the chapel. Partridge and Starn have concluded that in the Sistine Ceiling the "garlands of oak and acorns were entertwined in a message of salvation and redemption through the Church Universal," based on their study of Julian iconography where the acorn was associated with the golden age and the oak tree

[28]L. D. Ettlinger, *The Sistine Chapel before Michelangelo: Religious Imagery and Papal Primacy* (Oxford: Oxford University Press, 1965) 104–19. John Shearman, "The Chapel of Sixtus IV," *The Sistine Chapel: The Art, the History, and the Restoration*, ed. Massimo Giacometti (New York: Harmony Books, 1986).

[29]Cf. Frederick Hartt, "*Lignum vitae in medio paradisi*: the Stanza d'Eliodoro and the Sistine Ceiling," *Art Bulletin* 32 (1950): 191: "And to remind us that the body of Christ is the fruit of the Tree of Life, Michelangelo has introduced a mass of *rovere* leaves and acorns below Adam, almost touching his body." Hartt's interpretation of the Sistine Ceiling and his methodology were castigated by Edgar Wind, "Typology in the Sistine Ceiling: A Critical Statement," *Art Bulletin* 33 (1951): 41–47, to which Hartt responded (262–73), "Pagnini, Vigerio, and the Sistine Ceiling: A Reply." In my opinion, both sides in this debate made valid criticisms of the other's work, but I would criticize both of their methodologies for being primarily "too bookish" in Steinberg's sense (for an exception see Wind, "The Ark of Noah," above n. 12). Nonetheless, I think there are aspects of their research and analysis that are relevant for a historical interpretation of some of Michelangelo's imagery in the *Creation of Adam,* and thus I will cite from their work selectively.

[30]Loren Partridge and Randolf Starn, *A Renaissance Likeness: Art and Culture in Raphael's Julius II* (Berkeley: University of California Press, 1980) 56–57, 142–43 (for golden age); and Hartt, "*Lignum vitae*," 133; cf. Wind, "The Ark of Noah," 43.

[31]For Julius and the golden age, see John O'Malley, "Fulfillment of the Christian Golden Age Under Pope Julius II: Text of a Discourse of Giles of Viterbo, 1507," *Traditio* 25 (1969): 265–338 (an expanded version of a sermon delivered in the presence of Julius II in St. Peter's on 21 December 1507); and Elisabeth Schröter, "Der Vatikan als Hügel Apollons und des Musen. Kunst und Panegyrik von Nikolaus V. bis Julius II," *Römische Quartalschrift für christliche Altertumskunde und Kirchengeschichte* 75 (1980): 208–40; and her "Raffaels Parnass: Ein ikonographische Untersuchung," vol. 3 of *Actas del XXIII Congresso Internacional de Historia del arte. Espana entre el Mediterraneo y el Atlantico, Granada, 1973* (Granada: University of Granada, Department of the History of Art, 1978) 593–605.

[32]Partridge and Starn, *A Renaissance Likeness*, 32.

[33]Ettlinger, *The Sistine Chapel*, 77–88. Ettlinger does not mention the octagonal shape (actually half of an octagon) of the room of Rossellini's *Institution of the Eucharist*, but it should be related to the octagonal church that appears at the center of *The Delivery of the Keys to St. Peter* in Perugino's fresco, which Ettlinger recognized (p. 91) as a symbol of the universal church. Thus, the divine justification of petrine succession with Peter as the first *Vicarius Christi* of the universal church is joined with the Eucharist (Christ's sacrifice as establishing the New Covenant, superceding the blood sacrifices of the Old, or Christianity replacing Judaism).

with the Tree of Life and the crucifixion, a symbol of universal renewal.[30]

If mirror reversal is a signifying device in Michelangelo's painting, as argued above, then the right hand of the *ignudo* is the paradoxical counterpart of God's transmutative left hand; joined to the *Della Rovere* oak with its multiple symbolisms it must refer to the earthly transubstantiating hand of Julius II, vicar of the church in its golden age.[31] This conclusion agrees with Partridge and Starn's assessment of Julius's concept of his pontificate: "Julius contemplated and adored the host. He witnessed and confirmed the miracle of Transubstantiation which sanctioned in turn his spiritual power and his office as Christ's vicar."[32] The content of Michelangelo's fresco again correlates with the frescoes on the lower walls where the theme of the Eucharist, combined with the centralized plan, symbol of the universal church, underpins the sacred authority of the vicar of Christ.[33]

The *ignudo*-oak image can be thought of as a visual metaphor that collapses its eucharistic, ecclesiological, and papal meanings into a single sign that can carry the burden of polyvalence in its context because of its potent ambiguity. Since this image is next to Adam, is there more to its polysemy? Frederick Hartt observed that the acorns of the swags arguably could be seen as visually punning on the genitals of the *ignudi* and that the same pun exists in the Latin *glans*.[34] His observation has died on the exegetical vine of the ceiling, perhaps because it seemed too outrageous to count as serious subject matter. However, if this visual punning is transferred to Adam, it makes sense, and the composition juxtaposes the two, inviting such a comparison (Figure 1). Since Steinberg's publication of the *The Sexuality of Christ*,[35] which documents the incarnational theology behind the *ostentatio genitalium* of Christ in Renaissance art, Hartt's observation as applied to the first Adam finds an explanatory historical context.

[34]Hartt, "*Lignum vitae*," 218; cf. Frederick Hartt, *History of Italian Renaissance Art*, 4th ed., rev. David G. Wilkins (New York: Harry Abrams, 1994) 500. In regard to Hartt's claim, it should be noted that only eight of the twenty *ignudi* have exposed genitals (and one of them only barely so). I cite this fact not to quibble, but as a reminder of the value of Steinberg's insistence that interpretations agree with what Michelangelo actually painted. Overgeneralizations are fairly common in interpretations of the ceiling and probably no place more than in regard to the *ignudi*. Having tried to follow Steinberg's lead over the last decade in my examination of the ceiling, I greatly sympathize with past interpreters and their inclination to oversimplify.

[35]Leo Steinberg, *The Sexuality of Christ in Renaissance Art and in Modern Oblivion*, 2nd ed. (Chicago: University of Chicago Press, 1996).

Since it is combined with the transubstantiating hand of Julius II, the visual analogy would certainly seem to forecast the *corpus mysticum*, the mystical body of Christ (the "New Adam") both in the sense of the church and the consecrated host, the sanctifying power of Julius's pontificate.[36]

What we are seeing in Michelangelo's seemingly innocuous detail tucked in the corner of the *Creation of Adam*, so I would propose, is more than a visual metaphor. It is the visual analogue of something more akin to a compound metaphysical conceit[37] that attempts to communicate perceived Christian universals in a highly ingenious set of analogies. In contrast to the sequential nature of language, art can collapse these analogies into a condensed sign that defies easy perception and verbal explanation; and in contrast to the syntax of language, the demonstrative nature of art must show the extended analogies by visual devices: juxtaposition, punning, reversal, pairing, alignment, etc. It is no wonder that Michelangelo's art was praised by some for being Dantesque and criticized by others for containing "profoundly allegorical meanings understood by a few" in the manner of "those great philosophers, who hid the greatest mysteries of human and divine philosophy under the veil of poetry, so that they would not be understood by the common people."[38]

The absence of Mary from the cast of characters in the *Creation of Adam* has troubled art historians in the past. Aware of this point, Steinberg observed that the tendency in recent scholarship has been to accept the identification of the child at the end of God's left hand as Christ, but to reject the identification of the female embraced in his left arm as Eve.[39] Given what was perceived as the fresco's maternal joining of a female with an infant Christ, the mother of God seemed

[36]Sebastian Tromp, *The Body of Christ, Which Is the Church*, 2nd ed., trans. Ann Condit (New York: Vantage Press, 1960; orig. published as *Corpus Christi Quod Est Ecclesia*, 2nd ed., 1946). While the medieval expression *corpus mysticum* seems to have lost its meaning as the consecrated host in the latter Middle Ages when it was used as a metaphor for the church, I think the evidence of Michelangelo's fresco warrants seeing both meanings as being present. As indicated in my text, this union already seems clearly present in the frescoes of Sixtus IV. For the later medieval development of *corpus mysticum* as an expression of the church see Ernst H. Kantorowicz, *The King's Two Bodies: A Study in Medieval Political Theology* (Princeton NJ: Princeton University Press, 1957) 193–206 and Brian Tierney, *Foundations of the Conciliar Theory: The Contribution of the Medieval Canonists from Gratian to the Great Schism*, enlarged new ed., Studies in the History of Christian Thought 81 (Leiden/New York/Köln: Koninklijke Brill, 1998): 121–40.

[37]S.v. "conceit" in *The New Princeton Encyclopedia of Poetry and Poetics*, ed. Alex Preminger and T. V. F. Brogan (Princeton NJ: Princeton University Press, 1993) where a distinction is made between two main types of conceit, Petrarchan and metaphysical. Although Michelangelo's poetry is well known for its tropic borrowings from Petrarch, I think the image in the fresco possesses features more characteristic of the intellectual nature of a metaphysical conceit, which is closely related to allegory. The other major source for his poetry, Dante, is relevant in this regard.

[38]Barnes, "Metaphorical Painting," 66; her translation of Lodovico Dolce's comment made in 1556 on Michelangelo's *Last Judgment*. For the Italian, see Mark W. Roskill's *Dolce's "Aretino" and Venetian Art Theory of the Cinquecento* (New York: New York University Press, 1968) 164.

[39]Steinberg, "Who's Who," 558–59 (with bibliography).

[40]Steinberg, "Who's Who," 554. To support his argument he illustrates the *Crouching Venus* in the *Museo Nazionale delle Terme*, which, however, was not known in the Renaissance. It was excavated at Hadrian's Villa, Tivoli in 1914: see Orietta Vasori, "Statua di Afrodite accovacciata (inv. n.108597)," in *Museo Nazionale Romano*, Rome, vol. 1, pt. 1 (*Le Sculture*, Antonio Giuliano, ed.), Rome, 1979, 141-44n.100; and Reinhard Lullies, *Die Kauernde Aphrodite* (Munich, 1954) 12n.6. However, this fact does not negate Steinberg's observation since other examples of the "Doidalsas" type were known to the Renaissance (see our fig. 5 and the following footnote).

the most logical choice. But Steinberg countered that the specifics of the fresco simply will not support this identification. In addition to her nudity, "no female crouched like an Aphrodite and fascinated by Adam may be the Blessed Virgin."[40]

Included in this argument is Steinberg's convincing observation that the basic pose of the female in the fresco, but not her gestures, is based on the antique statue of the *Crouching Venus*, as seen from a somewhat more frontal (and hence more erotic) view, which is not illustrated here. This antique, however, seems clearly to have been used by Michelangelo both for Eve as well as Mary in two works that predate the *Creation of Adam.* In the so-called "Doidalsas" version of this ancient statue (Figure 5) the head is turned sharply to the viewer's left in opposition to the right arm, which crosses over the chest in a V pattern with the hand near the far shoulder.[41] This contrapposto motif of head and arm, as seen from a more frontal view, appears in the figure of Eve in the *Expulsion* (Figure 6) from the Sistine Ceiling, which was painted before the *Creation of Adam.* Eve's left arm, devi-

[41]For my discussion I have selected the *Crouching Venus* in the British Museum (the so-called "Lely Venus" since it once belonged to the painter Peter Lely) because it is the best preserved of the examples known to the Renaissance: Phyllis Pray Bober and Ruth Rubenstein, *Renaissance Artists and Antique Sculpture* (New York: Harvey Miller, 1987) 18–19; and Selma Holo, "A Note on the Afterlife of the Crouching Aphrodite in the Renaissance," *The J. Paul Getty Museum Journal* 6–7 (1978–1979): 23–36. For its Renaissance history, see Holo, 24-25 and fig. 4, a print by Marcantonio Raimondi, dating 1509, which is based on the "Lely Venus." While Michelangelo is not likely to have seen this antique firsthand, he probably was aware of Raimondi's print. He surely must have known of one of the *Crouching Venus* variants that was adapted by Pietro di Puccio for both Adam and Eve in the Camposanto, Pisa and by Ghirlandaio for the maidservant at the center of the *Birth of the Virgin* in Sta. Maria Novella in Florence (Holo, pp. 28-29, figs. 9-10). Given the latter, it is very likely that Michelangelo was first exposed to the *Crouching Venus* when he was an apprentice in Ghirlandaio's workshop. Michelangelo also must have known the "Doidalsas" example, today in the Naples museum, which was in the Loggia of the Palazzo Madama-Medici, Rome probably at the beginning of the Cinquecento. The Medici purchased this palace in 1505. The early sixteenth-century appearance of the Naples Venus is extremely well preserved in three drawings, showing the statue from five different vantage points, by Marten van Heemskerck, made when he was in Rome (1532-1535): Holo, 23-24, figs. 2a-c. Holo's article excludes Michelangelo's art, except for a brief comment in n.23. Karl Kilinski II, "Thoughts on the Crouching Aphrodite," *Source* 12 (1992): 1–6, argues the interesting thesis that the *Crouching Venus* was developed in antiquity from the Capitoline Venus type by, in effect, collapsing the latter.

[42]Erwin Panofsky, *Renaissance and Renascences in Western Art* (New York: Harper & Row, 1969) 167n.2, expressed the opinion that Masaccio's Eve in the *Expulsion* in the Carmine Chapel is not based directly on an antique *Venus pudica*, but on "such derivations of the latter as Giovanni Pisano's *Prudence*" in his pulpit in the Duomo at Pisa; cf. John Pope-Hennessey, *Italian Gothic Sculpture*, 179 (this figure "depends from a classical Venus Pudica") and pl. 21. Even if one accepts Panofsky's (and apparently Pope-Hennessey's) assessment, it seems certain that Michelangelo would have recognized the *Venus pudica* as a model for Masaccio's and Jacopo della Quercia's Eves since he must have known the antique example in the Medici collection, which Botticelli used in his *Birth of Venus*; cf. James Beck, *Jacopo della Quercia* (New York: Columbia University Press, 1991) 1/129 and 2/fig. 102 (*Expulsion* from the main portal of San Petronio, Bologna). Beck does not mention the *Venus pudica* as a model for Jacopo's Eve; cf. his brief discussion of the antique sources (pp. 48–49). Jacopo's Eve may also be based more on Pisano's *Prudence* than on an actual antique example, but for my purposes it is Michelangelo's perspective that is important (see n.38 above). It should be noted that in Jacopo's adaptation Eve's right hand does not cover her breasts, but is placed up to the base of her neck with her head modestly lowered and tilted to our left. Her left hand, however, is squarely over her genitals, and her right leg is also forward for further coverage. As in the case of Masaccio's *Expulsion*, Adam's genitals are exposed.

ating from the position in the *Crouching Venus*, angles under her right, to form crossed arms—a potent gesture in Renaissance art. In using an antique Venus as a partial model for Eve in the *Expulsion*, Michelangelo clearly seems to be following the precedent set by both Masaccio and Jacopo della Quercia, who, directly or indirectly, based their expelled Eves on another antique, the *Venus pudica*, in which the arms and hands cover the figure's breasts and genitals.[42] Both of these artists are frequently cited as major iconographic and stylistic sources for some of the Genesis scenes of the Sistine Ceiling, while Masaccio's

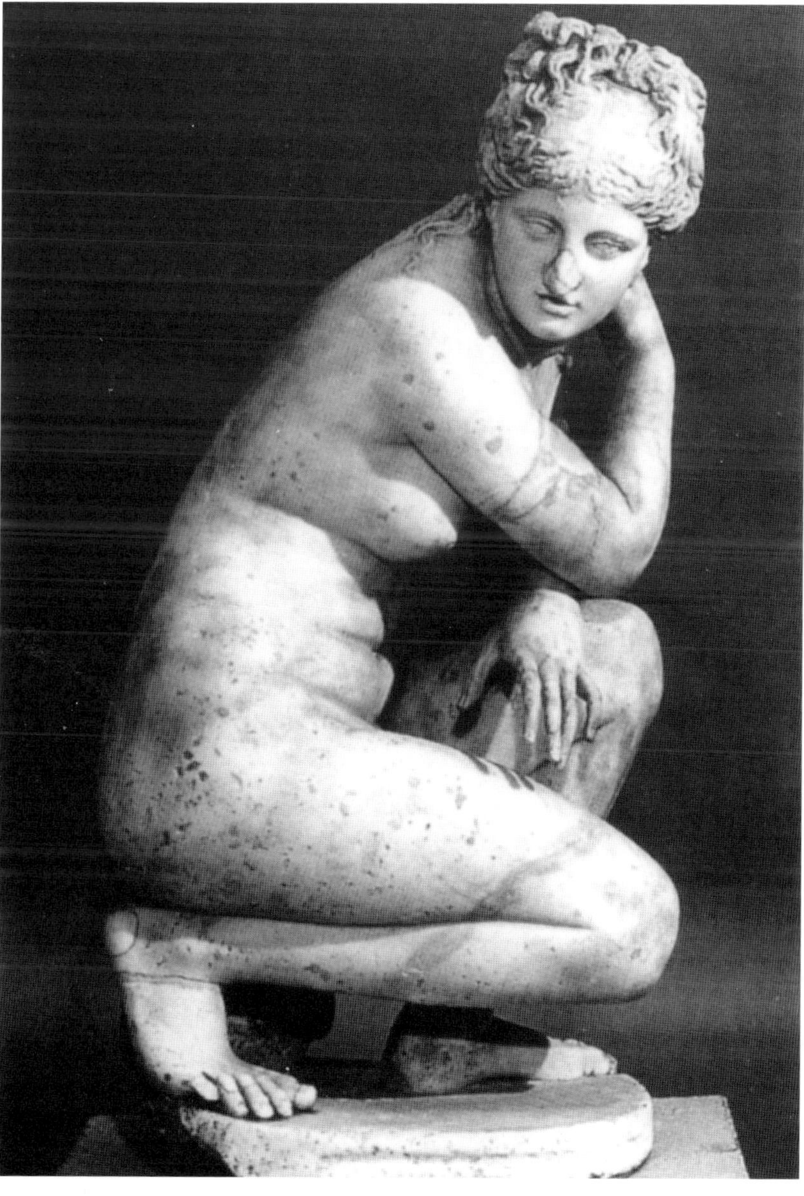

FIG 5.
Crouching Venus.
Greek, Hellenistic.
Marble. British
Museum, London.
© Copyright The
British Museum.

[43]Charles de Tolnay, *The Sistine Ceiling* (Princeton NJ: Princeton University Press, 1969) s.v. "Masaccio" and "Quercia" in index (numerous references).

[44]Leo Steinberg, "Eve's Idle Hand," *Art Journal* 35 (1975/1976): 135 persuasively, in my view, sees proleptic aspects in Eve's representation in the *Temptation*. More could be added to his analysis, and I plan to return to this fresco in a future discussion that contextualizes Michelangelo's imagery in the theology of the papal court and in Julian iconography.

Expulsion in particular has been justly considered a proximate model for aspects of Michelangelo's rendition of the same subject.[43]

The adaptation of the *Venus pudica* for expelled Eve appears to be a rather obvious Renaissance modernization *alla antica* of the fig leaf, animal skin, or clothed coverage standard, if not universal, in medieval iconography of the expulsion. The same cannot be said for Michelangelo's partial adaptation, which unconventionally leaves the genitals of Eve exposed (Figure 6). While her hunched posture and arms covering the breasts can be understood in terms of the traditional theme of bodily shame (but see below), her genital display and mature female hips and pelvis can be credibly related to the narrative theme of God's curse of painful childbearing and sexual attraction to her husband (Gen 3:16) toward whom she turns. This point seems graphically driven home by the emphatically male hips (androgynously combined with female breasts) and genital concealment of prelapsarian Eve (Figure 6) on the other side of this antithetically composed fresco ("before" and "after," if you will).[44] In the *Expulsion* Adam and Eve are shown as a couple, walking side by side in unison, left foot in advance of the right, shoulder to shoulder and foot to foot. Their mutual genital exposure, therefore, can be reasonably understood to foreshadow their parentage of the human race (Genesis 4:1ff.) and along with their aged faces, creased with wrinkles, to convey the concupiscence and mortality resulting from original sin.

Although it has mostly passed unnoticed, the pose of the Virgin in a drawing of the *Madonna and Child with St. Anne* (ca. 1500–1505, or possibly earlier) by Michelangelo (Figure 7) is an exceptionally close adaptation of the *Crouching Venus*.[45] The angle of the right leg has

[45]Paris, Louvre, 685 r: Charles de Tolnay, *The Youth of Michelangelo*, 2nd rev. ed. (Princeton NJ: Princeton University Press, 1969) 189–90, no. 33, dates this drawing 1505–1506 on the basis of style and cites opinions for both an earlier and later dating. Hartt, *Michelangelo's Drawings*, 65–66, no. 57 dates "probably 1505"; and 392 (concordance showing unanimous attribution to Michelangelo). Alexander Perrig, *Michelangelo's Drawings: the Science of Attribution*, trans. Michael Joyce (New Haven CT: Yale University Press, 1991) 38, 41n.49, and 111–14, fig. 4: he offers a *terminus ante quem* of July or August of 1497 for the St. Anne group because it seems to have been on the page before the sketch of the nude male below, which Perrig argues shows Michelangelo's lost Hercules statue, which, he thinks, can be most plausibly assigned to this date, and not earlier as commonly believed. He also supplies evidence, visual and documentary, that the hatching was added by Antonio Mini, Michelangelo's pupil. He sees the relationship between St. Anne and the Virgin as "a mute dialogue referring to the fate of the child" with the Virgin turning in alarmed response to her mother's foreboding gaze on Christ. Anton Hekler, "Michelangelo und die Antike," *Wiener Jahrbuch für Kunstgeschichte* 7 (1930): 219, fig. V, 4b-c, suggested that the virgin in the drawing was based on the *Crouching Venus*. Unfortunately, his comparison was marred by an inadvertent reversal of the photograph of the drawing and by his use of a *Crouching Venus* in the Louvre, which is missing its head and arms. Wilde, *Italian Drawings*, 61, figs. 18-19, rejected Hekler's proposal and suggested instead that the pose of the Virgin was inspired by a sibyl in Giovanni Pisano's Pistoia pulpit. For whatever reason, Wilde's conclusion has been followed by subsequent researchers, wrongly, as I try to show in my text.

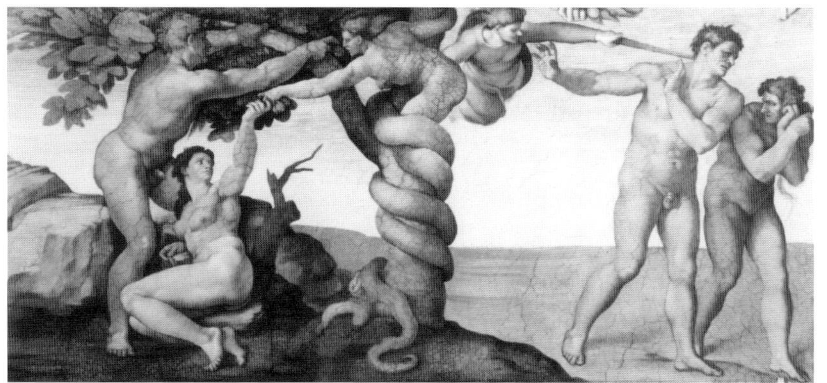

been slightly expanded to accommodate Mary to the lap of her mother, who sits on the ground, while the right arm has been lowered so that its hand presses on the Virgin's left breast as she nurses the foreshortened Christ child (whose angled position substitutes for the left arm of the *Crouching Venus*) reclining in the hollow of her legs. While the unusual composition of piling one figure upon another is thought to be Michelangelo's response to a lost cartoon by Leonardo da Vinci, it seems to have been overlooked that the content of Michelangelo's drawing almost certainly entails the concept of the Immaculate Conception, that is, the belief that Mary was free of original sin because she was predestined from the beginning of time to be the unstained vessel of the incarnation and was conceived in historical time by her mother, St. Anne, without sexual intercourse.[46] The adaptation of the Madonna of Humility[47] for St. Anne is telling, for this iconography normally stresses the incarnation by placing Mary on the ground (earth) and in the natural act of nursing. Transferring the former aspect to St. Anne implicates her in a fundamental way in Christ's incarnation. So, too, does her downward-cast gaze, which in images of the Madonna and Child is a means of presaging the passion of Christ and his mother's future sorrow. Visually, the composition of the drawing stresses the matrilineal generation of the incarnated

[46]For the thorny question of the lost cartoon, see Martin Kemp, *Leonardo da Vinci: The Marvelous Works of Nature and Man* (Cambridge MA: Harvard University Press, 1981) 215–27. Another drawing by Michelangelo is also thought to be a response to Leonardo's cartoon; see Jack Wasserman, "Michelangelo's Virgin and Child with St. Anne at Oxford," *Burlington Magazine* 111 (1969): 122–31. For the interpretation of the image of St. Anne, the adult Mary, and infant Christ as an Immaculate Conception theme, see Mirella Levi d'Ancona, *The Iconography of the Immaculate Conception in the Middle Ages and Early Renaissance*, Monographs on Archaeology and Fine Arts 7 (New York: College Art Association of America, 1957): 18, 39.

[47]Millard Meiss, *Painting in Florence and Siena After the Black Death* (New York: Harper Torchbooks, 1964) 134–56, esp. 145ff for "the meaning of the image." While many of the trecento examples of this iconography also show Mary with the symbols of the Apocalyptic Woman (sun, moon, stars), Meiss does not think there is any reference to the Immaculate Conception. For a broader cultural interpretation of this iconography with a focus on "messages received rather than messages given," see Margaret R. Miles, "The Virgin's One Bare Breast," *The Expanding Discourse: Feminism and Art History*, ed. Norma Broude and Mary D. Garrard (New York: HarperCollins, 1992) 27–37. Also see her contribution to this volume.

FIG 7.
Michelangelo.
Drawing of Madonna and Child with St. Anne. c. 1500-05. Pen, ink, and black chalk. 32.5 x 26.1 cm. Paris, Louvre. © Copyright Réunion des Musées Nationaux/Art Resource, NY.

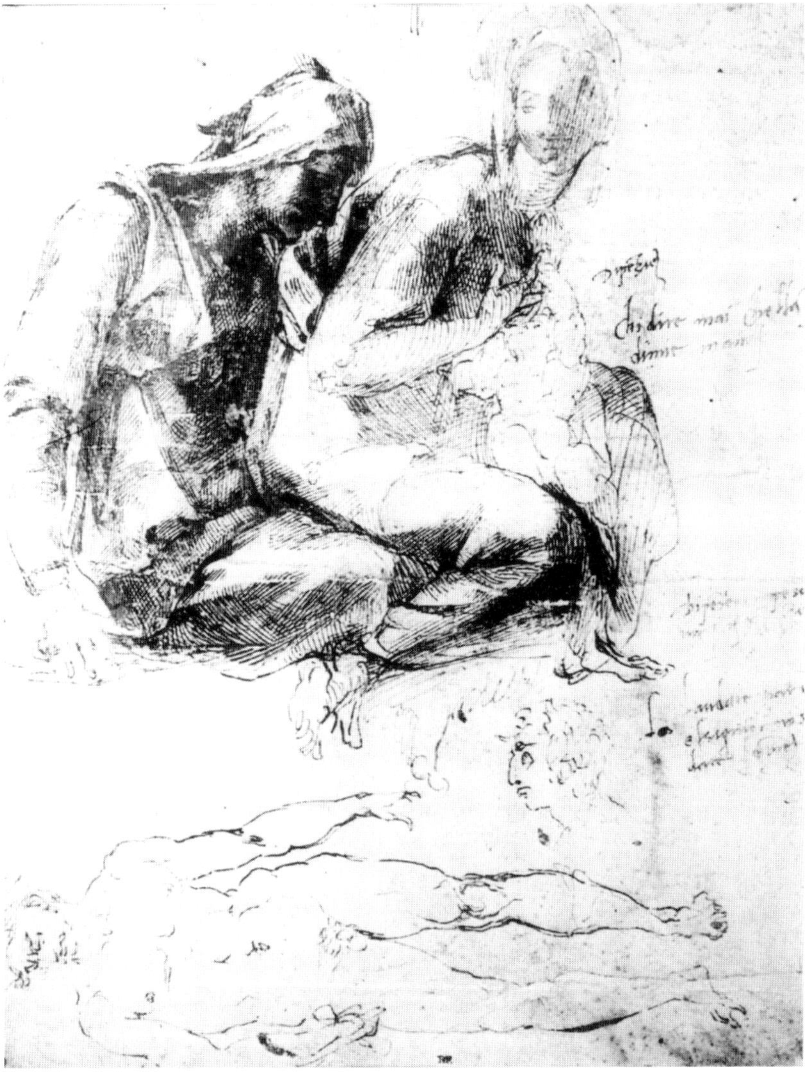

Christ; as he is nurtured from the body of the Blessed Virgin from which he has issued, so she rests (or arises?) directly on (or from) the lap of her mother from which she has been born *sans père.*

In this context it is relevant to note that Michelangelo again employed the *Crouching Venus* for the Virgin Mary (Figure 9) in his much later *Last Judgment* (ca. 1536–1541) on the altar wall of the Sistine Chapel.[48] In this adaptation the pose has been considerably attenuated, the upper and lower halves of her body twisted more against each other and the back leg lowered and crossed in front of the angled right leg. The representation of her head and right arm, taken from the *Crouching Venus,* is combined with her left arm angled

[48]Charles de Tolnay, *Michelangelo, the Final Period* (Princeton NJ: Princeton University Press, 1960) 113, figs. 283–84, crediting the observation to Dr. Gertrude Coor.

underneath to form a crossed motif—the whole image is remarkably similar to the expelled Eve in the ceiling (Figure 6). As Bernadine Barnes has keenly observed, in one of Michelangelo's early sketches for the *Last Judgment* a crescent moon appears at the foot of the Virgin, but in the finished painting this detail has been omitted in favor of placing her in the golden aureole surrounding Christ, thus identifying her as the Apocalyptic Woman "robed with the sun" (Rev 12:1, *mulier amicta sole et luna sub pedibus eius*).[49] This text was widely cited in support of the Immaculate Conception.[50] Thus, the two cases examined, in which Michelangelo based the image of the Virgin on the *Crouching Venus*, can be plausibly taken to refer to her immaculacy—a connection which certainly seems to have been inspired by the act of bathing or cleansing represented in the classical model.

Michelangelo's art shows that the *Crouching Venus* could be used for either Eve or Mary. On the one hand, this usage is not surprising since in Christian thought the two are related as antithetical mothers, the first and second Eve, the one having introduced death, reproductive suffering, and concupiscence into the world, the immaculate other having given virginal birth to the Savior.[51] On the other hand, it is rather remarkable that the same antique source (adapted in each recension) was employed for such diametrically opposed identities.[52] This practice relates to the use of mirror images and compound invention (discussed above) as evidence of the paradoxical nature of some of Michelangelo's Christian imagery. Of course, the central tenets of Christianity are thoroughly paradoxical: Christ is both human and divine, his birth is virginal, he must die to achieve salvation, etc. The paradoxical dimension of Michelangelo's art equally testifies to one of its metaphorical tendencies, that is, the merging of compared entities, even contrary ones (such as male and female as in the case of Eve in the *Temptation*, which was discussed above).[53] The latter, given their contrived nature and contrariety, could be justifiably called paradox-

[49]Bernadine Barnes, *Michelangelo's Last Judgment: The Renaissance Response* (Berkeley: University of California Press, 1998) 65–69. While Barnes acknowledges that Revelation 12:1 is most often associated with the Immaculate Conception, she argues instead for a connection with Mary's assumption because of the dedication of the chapel to *Maria Assunta*. However, as pointed out in our text, it is probably better to see these concepts as closely intertwined in the Sistine Chapel. Barnes (69) also observes the similarity between the head and arm gestures of Mary in the *Last Judgment* and Eve in the *Expulsion*, but considers it "purely visual."

[50]D'Anconna, *Iconography of Immaculate Conception*, 17, 24–28, and 56; and Ernst Guldan, *Eva und Maria: Eine Antithese als Bildmotiv* (Graz-Koln: Hermann Bohlaus Nachf., 1966) 102–105.

[51]Guldan, *Eva und Maria*, 117ff.

[52]Relevant for this issue is the allegorical tendency of the Renaissance to understand classical subjects in Christian terms and the Neoplatonic view of the two Venuses, for which see Marsilio Ficino, *Commentary on Plato's Symposium on Love*, trans. Sears Jayne, 2nd rev. ed. (Dallas: Spring Publications, 1985) 2/7/53-54 and 6/7/115-18.

[53]Summers, *Michelangelo*, 267–68: a contextual analysis of Michelangelo's *Bacchus*, which quotes Vasari: "It is known that he wished to achieve a certain marvelous mixture of members, and particularly to have given it the smoothness of a male youth and the fleshiness and roundness of a woman." For a recent analysis of Michelangelo's "cross-gender images" from primarily a feminist perspective, but with brief references to iconographic and psychoanalytic views (with relevant bibliography) see Yael Even, "The Heroine as Hero in Michelangelo's Art," *Woman's Art Journal* 11 (1990) 29–33.

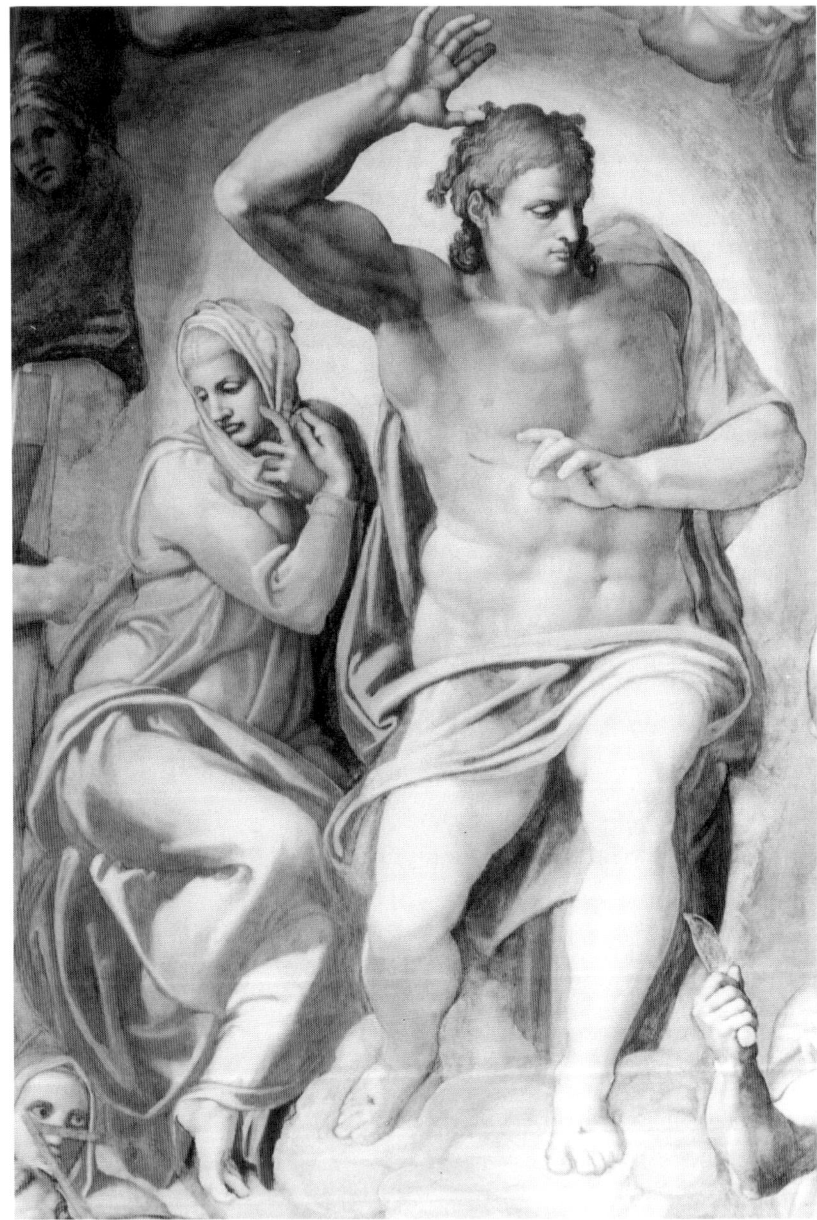

[54]James Saslow, *The Poetry
of Michelangelo: An
Annotated Translation* (New
Haven CT: Yale University
Press, 1991) 41–44; cf.
Summers, *Michelangelo*, 10:
"Paradox and the dialectical
intricacies of paradox were
the favored terrain over
which the deeply Christian
mind of Michelangelo
moved. In his mind every-
thing generated its
opposite, and it is this deep
sense of contrariety that
underlies his irony."

[55]Summers, *Michelangelo*,
33–282. Also see Paul
Joannides's comments on
the "combinatory image" in
Michelangelo's *Crucifixion
of Haman* and *Brazen
Serpent* in *Michelangelo and
His Influence: Drawings
from Windsor Castle*
(Washington, DC/London:
National Gallery of Art and
Lund Humphries
Publishers, 1996) 132n.40.
For "combinatory fantasy"
see Summers, *Michelangelo*,
109ff. For Leonardo and
fantasia see Kemp, 152–202.

ical conceits, and, unsurprisingly, the same or similar tropes (for
example, antithesis, paradox, and oxymoron) frequent Michelangelo's
rime.[54] In Renaissance art theory, compound invention belongs to the
sophistic tradition of poetic license and testifies to the creative powers
of the artist's *fantasia*.[55]

The evidence just cited might seem to undercut Steinberg's identification of the female in the *Creation of Adam* as Eve. However, the
other reasons he cited (the figure's nudity and attentive focus on

Adam) seem more than sufficient to exclude seeing her as the Virgin Mary. In the above cases where Michelangelo used the *Crouching Venus* for Mary, she is clothed. But since they seem to refer to her immaculacy and given Michelangelo's penchant for metaphor, one might wonder about the meaning of Eve's nudity. In terms of her presence at the creation of Adam it can be understood to indicate her prelapsarian state, which is identical to Mary's immaculacy (namely, her freedom from original sin). As for her age, she has "the shy mimillae of a pubescent girl."[56] Her budding womanhood is potently ambiguous, evoking gynecological innocence on the one hand, but also presaging the fall and God's curse on the other. In this regard her left-hand grasp—the same *sinister* which Eve extends in the Sistine *Temptation* (Figure 6) to receive the forbidden fruit—of God's incarnating arm certainly would seem to prefigure the fall, Eve's instrumental role in original sin, and the need for the Redeemer. Cause and effect, as it were, are metaphorically joined in somatic signing. What, then, are we to make of the suggestive placement of the infant Christ next to Eve's raised left leg? Is this also an intimation of God's future imprecation (and Mary's instrumental role in its negation—see below), or is there a better reading of it?

Since Steinberg agrees with others that this juxtapositioning suggests a maternal union, it leaves him in the rather awkward situation of explaining how Eve can be considered the "mother" of Christ. His solution follows:

> Michelangelo's coupling of Eve and Christ is no scandal at all. For the Trinity's Second Person bears the epithet "Son of Man" because, born of woman, he is son of Eve. And since "Son of Eve" is a trope, a metaphor to denote ultimate derivation, Michelangelo makes the metaphoricity of the trope all-apparent, almost palpable. The boy's sonship is presented as *sic et non*, so and not so. While his clinging reach links him to the Eve figure as to a mother, his inordinate size in relation to hers denies direct filiation. So that, respecting the visual data, we understand him to be her son, yes, but not in the literal sense.[57]

56Steinberg, "Who's Who," 554.

57Ibid., 559.

Following Steinberg's lead in "respecting the visual data," one might be inclined to respond likewise with the words of Peter Abelard: *sic et non*. On the one hand, Christ's "reach" ("clinging" seems inexact) can be seen as connecting him with the image of Eve (or with that of God—more on this below); but on the other, the rest of Christ's contrapposto pose, if anything, gives the impression of pulling away or separating from these figures (Figure 1). Less than a third of his body falls under the touch of God and less yet is in contact with Eve. By virtue of this detachment the head of Christ is far more intimately united in the composition with those of three others in the back row of God's celestial mantle.

All four of the heads in this back row are set on a diagonal directly behind the left forearm and hand of God (Figure 4). Christ's head is the fourth and terminal one in the group, which is seen as descending because *inter alia* it follows the downward pointing of God's gesture. At the top of the diagonal is the head and part of the shoulders of a female. Subsequent to the publication of his article, Steinberg reported that he received an unsigned letter in which it was proposed that this figure is the Virgin Mary.[58] In support of this identification, it was observed that this female, while more mature than Eve, is linked to her by her downward gaze, juxtaposed placement, and similar blond hairstyle. In contrast to Eve's nudity, however, she is dressed in a modest, roundneck garment (barely visible in most photographs) whose color matches that of God's heavenly cloak. I think there is further and more compelling evidence to support the identification of this female as the Virgin Mary.

With her head cocked left and declining, this female looks down at Eve (Figure 4). The two intervening heads are of putti or cherubs; the topmost—pupils and head rotated right— apprehensively stares at his companion who, head now rotated left and pupils painted bottom left, gazes in amazement at God's miraculous, incarnating left hand, as noted earlier. Completing the series, Christ's head rotates and inclines to the right, while he stares out at the viewer as a premonition of what his incarnation will mean.[59] This back row is twice implicated in the incarnation, once by the expression of the foremost cherub and once by the presence of the Son of God. Thus, the enclosure of these rearguard protomes in the descending, internal fold of God's heavenly veil indicates that it, too, is incarnational in meaning.

Rolling over the back of the angel above Eve's head, this internal fold disappears behind the mature female, bumps up ever so slightly atop the crown of the first putto, disappears again, and then emerges triumphantly in two prominent circular swirls that enframe the head of Christ. This "double halo" surely confirms the identity of this figure as the Second Person of the Trinity (the Logos), as does the way in which the outer contour of God's mantle (Figure 1) subdivides directly above him with its suggestive momentary flutter to form a smaller but comparable heavenly veil for the Son of God.[60] Even its trailing end, behind Christ's knee, nearly duplicates its counterpart in God's royal tunic as it streams behind God's right foot where it elides the juncture of Christ's left foot with that of the Lord's right. Thus, this juncture shows a seamless fusion—the consubstantiality—of Father and Son, while the pulling away or separation from God of the upper part of Christ suggests the development of a separate "person."[61]

In Michelangelo's theologically informed representation, the visual analogies between God, Christ, and Adam—the protagonists who, as Steinberg perceived, are all in the same scale to convey the shared dimension of their ontology[62]—are accompanied by disanalogies to show their distinct natures (Figure 1). As God the Son (Logos) both unites with and separates from God the Father, so his reclining pose (including *ostentatio genitalium* which conveys his full humanation) echoes, but does not duplicate that of Adam to show that he is the Second Adam.[63] Human and divine in one Christ is the hypostatic union of orthodox christological doctrine.[64] But if we accept the presence of both God the Father and his Son in the fresco, as Steinberg and others have, then are we to imagine that Michelangelo gives us a heretical twofold Godhead? Is it not evident that the Holy Spirit (*spiritus* means "breath" or "wind") is visualized in the aerodynamic Creator enclosed in a pneumatic mantle, which swirls around him and the Logos?[65]

In expression of the paradoxical "image and likeness" of Scripture (Gen 1:26), God and Adam are likened in size and scale, virile physiques, and the "graceful" curvature of their extended bodies, but

[60]Cf. Steinberg, "Who's Who," 566 observed that God's outer mantle "is twice disturbed: by a nick, bottom left, where the Devil makes his grab for a portion of it; and at the upper right where it gathers in a *nota bene* pointed to the Redeemer."

[61]Henry Denzinger, *Sources of Catholic Dogma*, trans. Roy Deferrari, 13th ed. (St. Louis: B. Herder Book Co., 1957) 225-28 (from the Bull "Cantata Domino," 4 February 1442).

[62]Steinberg, "Who's Who," 559.

[63]Leo Steinberg, "The Line of Fate in Michelangelo's Paintings," *Critical Inquiry* 6 (1980): 438: Christ rests "in Adamic pose…to represent the Second Adam."

[64]Above n.54; also O'Malley (below n.78), 138.

[65]The windswept mantle has been often enough associated with the Holy Spirit, but without relating it to a trinitarian interpretation of the fresco: e.g., Esther Gordan Dotson, "An Augustinian Interpretation of Michelangelo's Sistine Ceiling," *Art Bulletin* 61 (1979): 243; Paul Barolsky, "Michelangelo and the Spirit of God," *Source* 17 (1998): 15; and Partridge, *Michelangelo*, 48. Staale Sinding-Larsen, "A Re-reading of the Sistine Ceiling," *Acta ad Archaeologiam et Artium Historiam Pertinentia* 4 (1969): 143–57 advanced a trinitarian reading of the early Genesis frescoes. I think his interpretation fails to take into account Michelangelo's specific imagery and thus goes awry; I plan to return to this topic in the near future. Also see Adelheid Heimann, "Trinitas Creator Mundi," *Journal of the Warburg and Courtauld Institutes* 2 (1938–1939): 42–52. For related issues in early Christian art see Robin M. Jensen, "The Economy of the Trinity at the Creation of Adam and Eve," *Journal of Early Christian Studies* 7 (1999): 527–46; and her contribution to this volume.

[66]Cf. Loren Partridge, *Michelangelo: The Sistine Chapel Ceiling, Rome* (New York: George Braziller, 1996) 48. Steinberg, letter to editor, 341–42 questions Adam's ontological status since the fresco is devoid of plants, which is at odds with Genesis 2:8 (and 2:15). As always, his ever thoughtful probing raises an important question, which I plan to address in a subsequent study since space does not allow a response here.

[67]On the androgyny of God see Barnes, "Metaphorical Painting," 76 (comparing God the Father in the ceiling, particularly in the *Separation of Light and Dark*, to Minos in the *Last Judgment*), and Partridge, *Michelangelo*, 42 (also the *Separation* fresco). Neither of these authors draws any theological conclusions from their observations.

[68]Patricia Emison, "Michelangelo's Adam, Before and After Creation," *Gazette des Beaux-Arts* 112 (1988): 115–18 conveniently summarizes the opinions of six specialists on Michelangelo (Esther Dotson, Frederick Hartt, Herbert von Einem, Rudolf Kuhn, Sidney Freedberg, and Charles de Tolnay) before she offers her view based on Marsilio Ficino and a sonnet by Michelangelo, which Saslow (*Poetry of Michelangelo*, 236) dates ca. 1535–1541. Emison's analysis is potentially relevant for understanding a personal, artistic dimension to Michelangelo's fresco, which I have mostly ignored here.

are contrasted in age, energy, and gravitation—in sum, matter versus spirit.[66] Since Genesis 1:27 states that both male and female were created *ad imaginem Dei*, a theologically inclined viewer might ponder if Michelangelo's Eve is congruent with Scripture. Her rightward tilt and placement behind the Lord's side not only metaphorically suggest her later creation from godlike Adam's side, but can be seen as visually echoing the angle of Eve's body in the adjoining fresco in the ceiling (Figure 9), where her husband's curved outline and his extended legs mime, respectively, the sweep of Adam's reclining body and the legs of the Lord in the *Creation of Adam*. And the same theologically inclined viewer might wonder if Michelangelo's God is congruent with the same passage. Are God's mimillae less "shy" than pubescent Eve's?[67]

The separation of God and Adam's hands has been often and variously commented on, but never (to the best of my knowledge) with an eye on both the painting and the biblical text.[68] Michelangelo's visualization shows that Adam possesses a body and is sentient but notably lethargic. In mood he appears expectant, longingly looking toward his Creator and extending a heavy listless arm, which requires the support of his bent leg, which, in turn, is anchored like a mortise and tenon joint by the insertion of its foot under his right lower thigh. Genesis 2:7 stipulates three acts or stages in Adam's creation: formation, enlivenment, and animation (*formavit igitur Dominus Deus hominem de limo terrae et inspiravit in faciem eius spiraculum vitae et factus est homo in animam viventem*). Michelangelo's Adam shows the first two of these stages, but in contrast to Christ he has not yet been divinely touched. Adam's somnolent flesh, in poignant counterpoint to its heroic potential (and God's pneumatic majesty), awaits the spiritual animation of the Creator's outstretched finger so that he will become "a living soul." The oxymoronic punning of Adam and his Maker's hands is bred in their very bones by the near mirror reversal of one with the other and their inverted extrusion into enervation versus animation[69] (Figure 1). God's binary gesturing, therefore, antithetically pairs two acts of unequal incarnational signing: "the Word made

[69]Tolnay, *The Sistine Chapel*, 36, thought that Adam and God are mirror reversals, "broadly speaking." Dotson's ("An Augustinian Interpretation," 234) comment that Adam was the "mirror" of God was criticized as being theologically flawed, since it implied identity, by Thomas Martone, letter to the editor, *Art Bulletin* 64 (1982): 484–85; cf. Dotson's response, letter to the editor, *Art Bulletin* 64 (1982): 655–57.

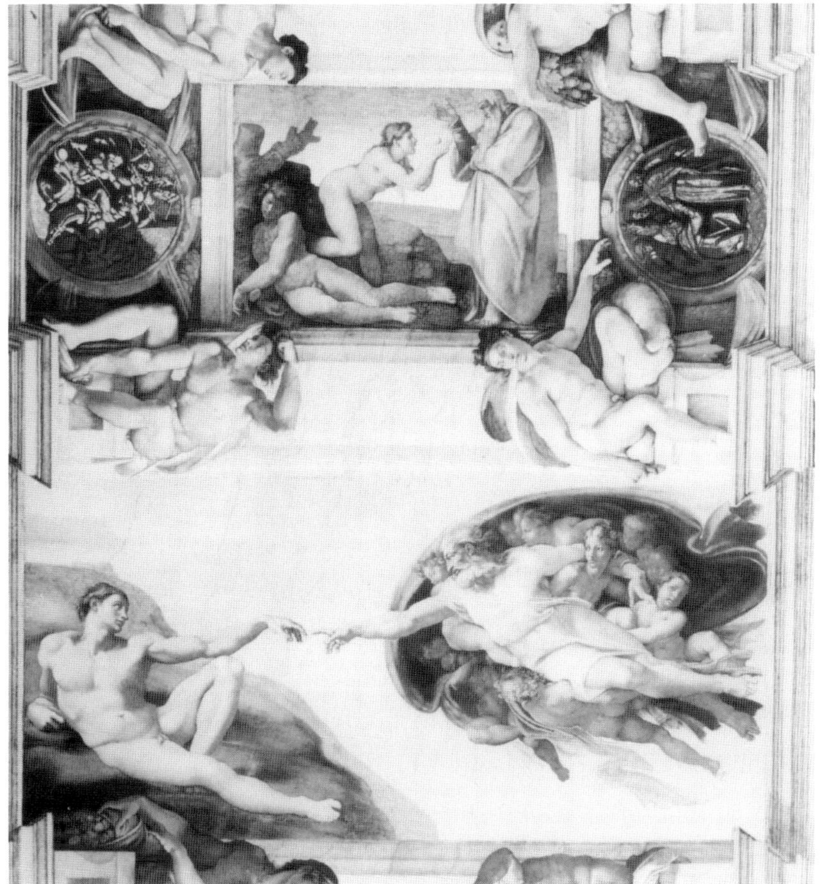

FIG 9. Michelangelo. Creation of Eve (top) and Creation of Adam (bottom). 1508-12. Fresco. Ceiling, Sistine Chapel. Vatican, Rome.© Copyright Monumenti Musei e Gallerie Pontifiche.

flesh" (John 1:14) and flesh not yet inspirited (compare 1 Cor 15:45: *Factus est primus Adam in animam viventem, novissimus Adam in spiritum vivificantem*). The temporal distinction between the two demonstrates that the incarnation of the Word, by anteceding the animation of the first man, was part of the divine plan.[70] By extension, the subplot enclosed in the Lord's heavenly mantle is also providential and an epiphany—artistically a literal showing—of God's saving grace.

The only missing figure from this incarnational drama is the Virgin Mary. On the basis of the evidence of the fresco, she can be identified as the more mature female in the back row. By her gaze and placement she is linked to Eve as the "Second Eve"; and by her enclosure in the incarnating veil, placement at the head of a descending diagonal composed of the parturient effect of the background to foreground overlapping of heads, and the quickened rhythm of the tonal

[70]Cf. Steinberg, "Who's Who," 555, where Alfred Higgins is quoted: "Thus are finely indicated at the very moment of Adam's creation the further and final purposes of God in the creation of the Mother of Mankind, and in the incarnation of the Son of God."

[71]More could be added to support this interpretation. I plan to return to it in a future publication. Erick Wilberding, "Embracing the Cross: A Liturgical Gesture," *Source* 8 (1989): 1–5.

progression from the dusky first cherub, to the warm embers of the second, and finally out to the climatic radiance of the *lux mundi*—she is shown to be the mother of God. (In John 1:4-5 and 3:19-21, the Logos is identified with light.)

The existence of the Virgin Mary in the back row supplies the "missing link" in the fresco's subplot. How, then, does her presence fit with the interpretation of the rest of the fresco? Does she belong with the creation of Adam and Eve and the impending battle between Michael and Lucifer? Indeed she does, but obviously in a theological sense since she appears in a creation scene long before her historical debut as recorded in the Gospels. Only one concept fits with Mary's portrayal as the mother of Christ, the "Second Eve," and in some sense extant from creation: the Immaculate Conception. This concept harmonizes with proposals made above. The prelapsarian significance of Eve's nudity (derived along with her pose from the *Crouching Venus*) parallels Mary's original grace. The placement of the infant Christ at the juncture of the background diagonal and Eve's raised leg visually links the Blessed Virgin with the prefiguration of God's curse and indicates the instrumental role of the former's virginal womb in the negation of the latter's corrupted one. And the striking similarity between the apocalyptic Mary in the *Last Judgment* and the expelled Eve in the ceiling—both based on the *Crouching Venus* and both with arms crossed on the chest, a *gratia plena* gesture common for Mary in scenes of the annunciation which in some Renaissance paintings is typologically linked with representations of the expulsion in the back-ground— would seem to convey the same message, making of the latter a paradoxical metaphysical conceit (original sin redeemed by the immaculate Mary's plenitude of grace at the incarnation—all collapsed into a single dense sign[71]) and demonstrating, as we should expect, that Michelangelo's Sistine frescoes as a whole are theologically coherent.

What, then, is to be made of the green drape that prominently streams through the composition (Figure 1)? Is it to be seen as a purely ornamental flourish, or can it plausibly carry the weight of a signifier in what has been proposed so far without contradicting the visual evidence? The color green, of course, can signify various things in art, but in the story of creation it is associated with earthly vegetation and, most particularly, with the garden of Eden and the fecundity of its two trees, the Tree of Knowledge and the Tree of Life. In Michelangelo's fresco the drape curves over Eve's thigh and up under her bicep, disappearing at this point, which indicates an origin behind her in the back row (Figure 5). Its foreword path is as Steinberg observed it: It descends through Eve's loins, then separates St. Michael from Lucifer below. Earthly in color and fertile in symbolism, it can be reasonably taken to foretell the birth of the Redeemer from the immaculate Mary and their triumphant defeat of original sin and Satan—a standard theme in the iconography of the Immaculate Conception.

Two texts were commonly cited in support of this idea, one of which was Genesis 3:15, the second verse of God's imprecation of the serpent.[72] Since the maculists, as the advocates of the doctrine were called, identified "the woman" as Mary in her predestined role as the unstained vessel of the incarnation, the passage was understood to forecast the ultimate triumph of her and "her seed" over Satan. It reads, "I will put enmities between thee and the woman, and thy seed and her seed: she shall crush thy head, and thou shalt lie in wait for her heel."

The second text, and by far the most popular, was the well-known twelfth chapter of the book of Revelation where the account of the apocalyptic woman is interwoven with St. Michael's war with Satan, his expulsion from heaven accompanied by the proclamation of the salvation of God and Christ, and the subsequent conflict between Satan and the woman. For the maculists the celestial vision of the pregnant apocalyptic woman, identified as the Blessed Mary, was understood to show her predestined role from creation to be mother of the Redeemer; and the conflict between Mary and Satan was seen as alluding to her and Christ's ultimate victory.[73] A third text, less commonly cited than the previous two, was also taken to associate the immaculate Mary with Lucifer: *Ex utero ante Luciferum genui te*, "I generated you from my womb and before Lucifer" (Psalm 109:3—Vulgate).[74] This passage seems particularly relevant to understanding the incarnational fold in God's mantle (argued above on the basis of independent evidence) as a uterine symbol that encloses the immaculate Mary and her redemptive progeny, the Logos.

[72] D'Anconna, *Iconography of Immaculate Conception*, 17, 22–23; and Guldan, *Eva und Maria*, 90–102. Genesis 3:14-15: et ait Dominus Deus ad sepentem quia fecisti hoc maledictus es inter omnia animantia et bestias terrae super pectus tuum gradieris et terram comedes cunctis diebus vitae tuae [15] inimicitias ponam inter te et mulierem et semen tuum et semen illius ipsa conteret caput tuum et tu insidiaberis calcaneo eius.

[73] See above n.46.

[74] D'Anconna, *Iconography of Immaculate Conception*, 28–29, 51–52 (this psalm was incorporated into the feast of the Immaculate Conception). *Lucifernum*, of course, could be translated as "morning star," which is what is found in most English Bibles.

[75]Rona Goffen, "Friar Sixtus IV and the Sistine Chapel," *Renaissance Quarterly* 39 (1986): 229–30; Ludwig Pastor, vol. 5 of *The History of the Popes*, 5th ed. (London: Routledge and Kegan Paul, 1949) 394–95; and Denzinger, *Catholic Dogma*, 236–37 (*Grave Nimis*). On the probability of Sixtus granting indulgences for praying in front of an image of the immaculate Mary see S. Ringbom, "*Maria in Sole* and the Virgin of the Rosary," *Journal of the Warburg and Courtauld Institutes* 25 (1962): 326–30.

[76]As quoted by Partridge and Starn, *A Renaissance Likeness*, 51.

[77]Edgar Wind, "Sante Pagini and Michelangelo: A Study in the Succession of Savonarola," *Gazette des Beaux-Arts* 6/26 (1944): 22n.31.

[78]Rona Goffen, *Piety and Patronage in Renaissance Venice: Bellini, Titian, and the Franciscans* (New Haven CT: Yale University Press, 1986) 91–94.

[79]Goffen, "Friar Sixtus IV," 230.

[80]John O'Malley, *Praise and Blame in Renaissance Rome: Rhetoric, Doctrine and Reform in the Sacred Orators of the Papal Court*, Duke Monographs in Medieval and Renaissance Studies 3 (Durham NC: Duke University Press, 1979); the information in the two paragraphs of my text is primarily a summary of pp. 36–76. O'Malley notes (52) that further work needs to be done on the tropes and diction used in the sermons.

It was standard practice during the Renaissance for artists to adapt their commissioned works to the dedication of the religious buildings in which they appeared and to the interests of their patrons. From the aspects of the Sistine Ceiling examined here, it seems clear that Michelangelo followed this principle of decorum. The Franciscans were the major proponents of the Immaculate Conception and both Sixtus IV and his nephew Julius II belonged to this order. Extremely well documented is Sixtus's perpetuation of the Immaculate Conception. Among other things, he commissioned two new offices to commemorate it, one from Leonardo Nogarolo when he was the head of the Franciscan Order, another from Bernadino de Busti after he became Pope; his private funerary chapel in the choir of St. Peter's was dedicated to the *Immaculata*, and he himself celebrated the office there in 1481. He also issued the bull *Grave Nimis* on 4 September 1483, asserting that it was heresy and a mortal sin to preach or write against the belief.[75] As for Julius II, his papal master of ceremony, Paris de Grassis, wrote that he aimed "in many, almost all things, to imitate his uncle Sixtus."[76] The Sistine Chapel is dedicated to *Maria Assunta*, and this cult was closely allied with the Immaculate Conception, even being combined in some chapels.[77] Franciscan theologians understood Mary's assumption to be evidence of her freedom from original sin.[78] Since the Immaculate Conception was controversial at the time, especially with the Dominicans who rejected it, it seems that the dedication of the Sistine Chapel to *Maria Assunta* was a way of worshiping the immaculate Mary without provoking dissension.[79]

At this point in our analysis, it can be proposed that the titlement of Michelangelo's fresco the *Creation of Adam* is, at best, a synecdoche, for its actual subject certainly seems to be the *Creation and Redemption of Humankind*. Its celebratory message is remarkably consonant with the "incarnational theology" of the sermons delivered at the papal court between 1450 and 1521, as studied and named by John O'Malley.[80] Since the truths of Christianity were considered decided, the task of the preacher was not to dispute in the manner of scholastic sermons, but to praise God's works and deeds in order to arouse the audience to the appreciation, wonder, and contemplation of divine mystery. To achieve this end epideictic rhetoric was employed, the art of formal praise for a select audience, such as existed at the papal court and in the Sistine Chapel, one of the locations for these sermons.

The two great deeds that were celebrated in this sacred oratory were the creation and incarnation. The view of the latter was soteriological, so that the incarnation and redemption were closely allied with each other. Thus, the sermons placed less emphasis on the passion of Christ than on the redemptive moment of his incarnation in the Virgin's womb. John 1:14 ("the word became flesh and dwelt among us"), the moment of hypostatic union, was frequently cited by the preachers, and this incarnational moment—conceived soteriologically, associated with the Virgin Mary, and signaled by the Lord's transmutative gesture which foreshadows the transubstantiation of the earthly rite of the Eucharist—is at the heart of Michelangelo's visual exegesis of the biblical story.

As for the mystery of creation, the papal orators associated it with the Trinity and the making of man in terms of the "image and likeness" theme: the beauty and harmony of the Triune God were visible in all of reality, and most especially in the excellence and dignity of man, a popular subject of the sermons. Casting an eye on Michelangelo's fresco, O'Malley notes that the glorious portrayal of Adam as a reflection of the divine harmonizes with the theology of the court sermons.[81] The identification of the Trinity, proposed above, is also in agreement, as is also the acorn-penis pun. Explicit and even erotic references to Christ's genitals or the relic of his foreskin in St. John in the Lateran occur in two of the sermons, dating 1484 and 1495, on the circumcision (1 January) in the context of "the wonderful paradox of true-god-true-man" theme of the incarnation.[82] Delivered before an educated audience, the sermons were subtly erudite on the Ciceronian model, blending without emphasis quotations, paraphrases, and allusions from both Christian and classical sources, which implied the universality of the church. In the *ut pictura poesis* tradition, the preachers used verbs of vision (for example, *intueri, videre, aspicere*) to paint in the manner of *ekphrasis* "word pictures" to encourage the audience to visualize the wonders of God's creation.

While many corollaries exist between the "incarnational theology" of the sermons of the papal court and the interpretation of

[81]John O'Malley, "The Theology behind Michelangelo's Ceiling," *The Sistine Chapel: The Art, the History, and the Restoration*, ed. Massimo Giacometti (New York: Harmony Books, 1986) 124; he associates a sonnet by Michelangelo with the "image and likeness" theme of Adam, which Saslow (*Poetry of Michelangelo*, 238, #106) dates ca. 1536–1546: "né Dio sua grazia mi si mostra altrove/ più che'n alcun leggiadro e mortal velo;/ e quel sol amo perch'in lui si specchia."

[82]John O'Malley, "Postscript," in Steinberg (above n.35), 215.

[83]O'Malley, *Praise and Blame*, 61–62.

[84]First advanced by Julian Klaczko, *Rome and the Renaissance: The Pontificate of Julius II*, trans. John Dennie (New York: G. P. Putnam and Sons, 1903) 294; but expanded and systematically developed by Charles Seymour Jr., ed., *Michelangelo: The Sistine Chapel Ceiling*, Norton Critical Studies in Art History (New York: W. W. Norton and Co., 1972) 93–94.

[85]Seymour, *Michelangelo*, 93–94.

Michelangelo's fresco presented in this paper, there are also differences, the most notable being the presence of the immaculate Mary. The sacred orators avoided disputed subjects and only one sermon on the Immaculate Conception is recorded. As to be expected, it was delivered before Sixtus IV on 8 December 1472 in S. Maria del Popolo in Rome.[83] It has been argued that the presence of the immaculate Mary in the fresco accords with the specific Franciscan theology of Sixtus IV and Julius II; her placement in the very background of the composition, where she is almost hidden, agrees with the controversial nature of the doctrine. Another aspect of the painting that relates to Michelangelo's patron is its ecclesiological and papal import.

Using the visual evidence in conjunction with the biblical account, the separation of the hands of God and Adam was interpreted earlier as conveying the idea of soul infusion. Employing an iconographic method, others have come to the same conclusion, associating God's extended forefinger of his right hand with the metaphor of the finger spirit, *digitus paternae dexterae*, found in the medieval hymn *Veni Creator Spiritus* ("Come, Holy Spirit").[84] In the Roman rite this hymn was sung at vespers of Whitsunday (Pentecost, the birth of the church); it was also sung before each afternoon vote when the Sistine Chapel was used for the conclave to elect a new pope, the morning vote having been preceded by the singing of the Mass of the Holy Spirit.[85] This contextual information demonstrates that the Lord's right finger was associated with the selection of the head of the church as well as its very foundation by means of the sanctifying grace of the Holy Spirit.

This information leads us back to Michelangelo's painting and to a detail that has been overlooked in previous analyses. Directly over Adam's head (Figure 1) is a two-tiered rock arising on the distant horizon above the wavy blue strip that borders the green earth. Surely this detail, which has nothing to do with the biblical story of Adam's creation, must be a reference in the papal chapel to Matthew 16:18-19 ("And I say to you that you are Peter and upon this rock I will build my church"), which is the scriptural justification for papal authority. As such, it appeared in Perugino's *The Delivery of the Keys to St. Peter* as part of the frescoes executed under Sixtus IV on the lower walls of the chapel. Relevant to understanding the placement of this rock is the common metaphor for the church: Christ is the head (supreme authority) of his mystical body, the church.[86] In the bull *Consueverunt Romani Pontifices*, 1 March 1511, Julius II stated that Christ and his vicar form a single head of this body.[87] In Michelangelo's visualization the providential foundation of the church headed by Peter and his successors is foreshadowed by the sanctifying grace of God's finger spirit at the moment of the creation of godlike Adam, who prefigures the *corpus mysticum* of the Second Adam.

Throughout this paper I have argued that Michelangelo's art conceals the divine mysteries of creation under "the veil of poetry" so as not to profane their sublime message. Although lofty styles in general were expected of court panegyrists and artists in keeping with the period's notion of decorum, the style of Michelangelo's Sistine Ceiling acquired the elevated appellation of *terribilità*, "the terrible style," which was considered appropriate for Olympian subjects entailing the supreme mastery of challenging difficulties.[88] The term was also applied to the character of individuals who achieved such imperial goals and displayed such godlike fearsomeness. Both Michelangelo and Julius II, the militant and messianic pope, were considered "terrible."[89] There is something fitting, therefore, to Steinberg's suggestion that St. Michael in the fresco is both a signature and a self-identification. It would be a suitable conceit for his perceived role as the militant archangel and divine messenger of Pope Julius, head of the universal church in its golden age. Apparently, something along these lines was actually in circulation at Rome already in 1510, for Francesco Albertini in his guidebook to Rome, dedicated to Julius II, recorded that in the Sistine Chapel "*superiorem partem testudineam pulcherrimis picturis & auro exornavit* [sc. Julius] *opus praeclarum Michael. Archangeli floren.*"[90] Albertini's perfect tense for the unfinished Sistine Ceiling in 1510 is perhaps the perfect way to finish my incomplete study, for "we ought to leave the twenty-first century something to do."

---

[90]Francesco Albertini, *Opusculum de mirabilis novae & verteris Vrbis Romae*, as quoted in John Shearman, "The Vatican Stanze: Functions and Decoration," *Proceedings of the British Academy* 57 (1973): n.91; and n.5. Sherman dates Albertini's book to 3 June 1509, but Creighton Gilbert observes that the colophon, indicating the end of the printing, is 4 February 1510 (*Michelangelo, On and Off the Sistine Ceiling* [New York: George Braziller, 1994] 165n.48 [the full Latin text] and n.49.). He translates the complete quotation: "Your holiness provided [the chapel] with iron chains, and adorned the upper ceiling part with very beautiful paintings and gold, the admirable work of Michel Archangel the Florentine, extremely admirable in the art of painting and sculpture."

[86]Tromp, *The Body of Christ*. The metaphor "mystical body of Christ" for the church figures prominently in the writings of Giles of Viterbo, an intimate of Julius II, in connection with his eschatological thinking about church reform. He believed that the authority and sacramental power of the church was derived from the animating grace of Christ and that the supreme means of sanctification was the Eucharist: John O'Malley, *Giles of Viterbo on Church and Reform* (Leiden: E. J. Brill, 1968) 97–99, 110, 118–19, 189.

[87]Tromp, *The Body of Christ*, 201. Cf. Hartt, "Lignum vitae," 128n.97 (cf. 134), quoting from Bernardo Zane's oration, referring to Julius II who was present, which opened the first session of the Lateran Council on 10 May 1512:

sicut enim humanum corpus ex capite multusque membris conficitur as diversa naturae munera ubeunda, ita & ecclesia militaris ex te sanctissimo pontifice tamquam capite, caeterisque christicolis tamquam membris integratur, testante apostolo; 'Sicut in uno corpore multa membra habemus, omnia autem membra non eundem actum habent; ita multi unum corpus sumus in Christo'. (Rom 12:4-5)

[88]Summers, *Michelangelo*, 234–41.

[89]Partridge and Starn, *A Renaissance Likeness*, 5; Hartt ("*Lignum vitae*," 215–16) argued that the figure of God in the ceiling should be understood as referring to Julius II.

7.

Luke and Pontormo: The Visitation in the Third Gospel and at SS. Annunziata

Heidi J. Hornik

Mikeal C. Parsons

Baylor University

This essay is based on research conducted for a monograph, *The Lukan Infancy Narrative in Italian Renaissance Painting*, itself part of a projected three-volume study, *Illuminating Luke*, in which we examine scenes unique to the Gospel of Luke that were popular subjects in Italian Renaissance and Baroque art, especially with an eye toward their theological meaning then and now.[1] We begin with a brief word about method. This essay is not primarily an application of a theoretical model; thus, methodological considerations, while certainly present, run beneath the text like an underground stream rather than appearing constantly on or near the surface. Nonetheless, our methodology is generally indebted to the vocabulary of German

[1]The first volume is scheduled for publication in 2003 by Trinity Press International under the title *Illuminating Luke: The Infancy Narrative in Italian Renaissance Painting.*

[2]See Wolfgang Iser, *The Act of Reading: A Theory of Aesthetic Response* (Baltimore: The Johns Hopkins University Press, 1978) esp. 85. On the history of reception theory and especially on the contributions of Robert Jaus and Wolfgang Iser to its theoretical foundations, see Robert C. Holub, *Reception Theory: A critical introduction* (London: Metheun, 1984). Among art historians influenced by reception theory, we have found the work of John Shearman particularly helpful; cf. John Shearman, *Only Connect…Art and the Spectator in the Italian Renaissance* (Princeton NJ: Princeton University Press, 1992).

[3]See Jaraslov Pelikan, *Jesus through the Centuries* (New Haven CT: Yale University Press, 1985); and Margaret R. Miles, *Image as Insight. Visual Understanding in Western Christianity and Secular Culture* (Boston: Beacon Press, 1985).

[4]John Drury, *Painting the Word: Christian Pictures and Their Meaning* (New Haven CT: Yale University Press, 1999).

[5]In the brief history of interpretation of the text, we are following the lead, for example, of commentators like François Bovon (*Das Evangelium Nach Lukas. 2. Teilband Lk 9:51-14.35*, EKKNT [Zürich: Benziger Verlag, 1996]) and Ulrich Luz, (*Matthew: A Commentary*, trans. Wilhelm Linss [Minneapolis: Augsburg, 1989]), both of whom write of the "Wirkungsgeschichte" of the text, which may be roughly translated as the "history of influence."

Rezeptionsgeschichte, or reception theory, especially as articulated in Wolfgang Iser's notion of the reader actualizing a text.[2]

We are interested in the reception of the biblical text in two moves. First and foremost, we attend to the way in which the artist himself has actualized the text in the production of a visual image. This part of the exercise requires that we examine the work of art in stylistic, historical, and iconographical terms. While most of our efforts are spent on this first aspect of reception history, our methodology is also explicitly hermeneutical, and herein lies our second move of reception history. We are interested in how this "visual exegesis" might enrich our understanding of Luke's Gospel and at the same time inform the contemporary faith community's interpretation of Scripture.

We propose to include examples of visual interpretations as part of the *Nachleben,* the "afterlife," of these stories as they are reconfigured for a different time and place. Of course, we are not the first to examine visual depictions of religious art for its theological content. The efforts of Jaraslov Pelikan and Margaret Miles, for example, to track the development of the Christian tradition through analysis of both verbal *and* visual texts have been rightly lauded, but unfortunately seldom followed.[3] One exception is the recent work of John Drury, who examines the religious meaning of various works of art from the National Gallery, London.[4] Our project, while deeply indebted to the approach of Pelikan and Miles, differs from theirs and Drury's in scope and emphasis. We attempt to trace portrayals of individual artists of specific scenes unique to Luke's infancy narrative. This limited scope has enabled us to examine our topic in much more detail, and hopefully has prevented us from making some of the overgeneralizations often associated with such interdisciplinary studies.

Though we allow each text and its visual depiction to determine the particular issues to be pursued, in the book from which this essay is drawn we follow a common strategy for each painting. Each of those chapters begins with an overview of the biblical passage and its subsequent interpretation, noting significant rhetorical features and the overarching theological argument of the text, as well as outlining a brief summary of its subsequent interpretation in the ecclesiastical literature.[5] Next, we contextualize the selected work of art by giving a brief biography of the artist, placing the work within the artist's own *oeuvre*, discussing what is known of the patronage of the specific image, and exploring important social, political, and religious factors that may facilitate our understanding of the painting. A stylistic and iconographic analysis is followed by brief hermeneutical reflections about how this visual interpretation might inform the church's reading of Scripture. We follow this pattern in this essay as well.

OVERVIEW OF THE BIBLICAL TEXT
AND ITS SUBSEQUENT INTERPRETATION

[39]In those days Mary set out and went with haste to a Judean town in the hill country, [40]where she entered the house of Zechariah and greeted Elizabeth. [41]When Elizabeth heard Mary's greeting, the child leaped in her womb. And Elizabeth was filled with the Holy Spirit [42]and exclaimed with a loud cry, "Blessed are you among women, and blessed is the fruit of your womb. [43]And why has this happened to me, that the mother of my Lord comes to me? [44]For as soon as I heard the sound of your greeting, the child in my womb leaped for joy. [45]And blessed is she who believed that there would be a fulfillment of what was spoken to her by the Lord."

In visual depictions, Luke 1:39-45 is a discrete scene, "The Visitation," distinguishable from Luke 1:46-56, which is often depicted and titled in visual renderings, "The Madonna of the Magnificat."[6] In the rhetorical flow of the Third Gospel, Luke 1:39-45 is part of a larger unit, 1:39-56, which itself functions as a kind of bridge between the annunciations of John and Jesus (1:5-38) and the births and early lives of John and Jesus (1:57–2:52).[7] Luke 1:39-56 is comprised of a narrative introduction (39–41), two hymns (42–45; 46–55), and a narrative conclusion (56).[8] Just as Mary is the object of attention in 1:26-38, so also she is the focus of this passage.[9] The unit begins and ends by narrating Mary's arrival in and departure from the hill country (cf. 1:39, 56). Mary serves as the subject of all the verbs in verses 39-40— Mary "arose"; "went with haste"; "entered the house of Zechariah"; and

[6](1444/5–1510), *Madonna of the Magnificat*, 1482, tempera on panel, Uffizi, Florence, as illustrated in, "*Aureola super auream*: crowns and related symbols of special distinction for saints in late Gothic and Renaissance iconography," *Art Bulletin* 67 (1985): 567–603.

[7] Charles H. Talbert, *Reading Luke: A Literary and Theological Commentary on the Third Gospel* (New York: Crossroad, 1982) 22.

[8] Ibid.

[9] On this emphasis on Mary, see Mark Coleridge, *The Birth of the Lukan Narrative: Narrative as Christology in Luke 1–2*, JSNTSS 88 (Sheffield: Sheffield Academic Press, 1993) 76.

[10] See below, however, on the manuscripts that replace Mary with Elizabeth as the speaker in Luke 1:46.

[11] See Coleridge, *Birth of the Lukan Narrative*, 79–80.

[12] R. Alan Culpepper, "Luke," vol. 9 of *The New Interpreter's Bible* (Nashville: Abingdon, 1995) 54.

[13] Talbert, *Reading Luke*, 22.

[14] Coleridge, *Birth of the Lukan Narrative*, 85.

[15] Culpepper, "Luke," 54–55.

[16] Robert C. Tannehill, *Luke* (Nashville: Abingdon, 1996) 53. Mary's speech also echoes many of the themes found in Hannah's song recorded in 1 Sam 2:1-10.

[17] Talbert, *Reading Luke*, 22.

"greeted Elizabeth." Even when the subject changes to Elizabeth in verse 41, Mary remains the focal point. The sound of Mary's greeting causes the babe in Elizabeth's womb to "leap," and Elizabeth is filled with the Holy Spirit. Mary is the subject of Elizabeth's speech (vv. 42-45), and then Mary is the speaker of the hymn in 1:46-55.[10] Visual depictions notwithstanding, in 1:41 the scene moves into "aural mode," and there is no mention in the text of any physical contact between the two women, nor is any mention made of Zechariah (both important iconographical details in Pontormo's painting). It is Mary's greeting that triggers the subsequent action of the narrative.[11] The importance of this greeting is seen in the detail of the leaping babe in verse 41. Elizabeth's quickening recalls other examples of "prenatal signs" in the Jewish Scriptures—Jacob and Esau's embryonic struggle causes Rebekah to lament, "If it is to be this way, why do I live?" (Gen 25:22; cf. Gen 38:27-30).[12] The importance of Mary's greeting is seen also in the mention again of the greeting in Elizabeth's speech (v. 44). Still, the narrator says nothing about its content.

The first hymn by Elizabeth celebrates Mary as the "ideal believer."[13] The absence of Mary's name from the canticle suggests that Coleridge is correct in arguing that it is "not Mary in her own right who appears in the speech, but Mary in relation to God's plan."[14] Elizabeth's speech contains four oracles.[15] The first declares that both Mary and her unborn child are "blessed" (1:42; cf. 11:27). The second oracle is in the form of a question ("Why?") but contains in it a reference to the "mother of my Lord," a thoroughly Christian confession (1:43). The third oracle gives Elizabeth's interpretation for why her babe moved in the womb: "The baby in my womb leaped for joy" (1:44—"joy" is an important motif in the Lukan infancy narrative, cf. 1:14; 2:10). The last oracle is a beatitude on Mary and her faith and underscores her depiction as the ideal disciple.

If Elizabeth praises Mary in the first speech, Mary praises God in the second.[16] This second hymn, the Magnificat, "clarifies the links between what God has done for one individual and what he will do for the structures of society at large."[17] In this light, the canticle divides into two strophes: The first is Mary's declaration of what God has done for her (1:47-50); the second is concerned with God's activity in the larger society (1:51-55).[18] As such, the Magnificat is not a direct response to Elizabeth's hymn of praise, but rather a theological reflection of the work of God throughout the Lukan infancy narrative to this point.[19] There are important links between the two parts: Mary speaks of her own "lowliness" (v. 48) and later talks of what God has done for the "lowly" in general (v. 52). In the first strophe, God is the "Mighty One"; in the second, God brings down the "mighty" (v. 52). In both parts, God shows both his strength (vv. 49, 51) and his mercy (vv. 50, 54). The most powerful language about the social reversal that God effects is found in a chiastic pattern in vv. 52-53:

> A God brought down the *powerful*;
>
> B God lifted up the *lowly*;
>
> B¹ God filled the *hungry*;
>
> A¹ God sent the *rich* away empty.

These themes are repeated in Jesus' "messianic woes" recorded in Luke 6:20-26. Mary's speech ends with reference to the "remembrance of his mercy" in relationship to "Abraham and his descendants" (1:55).[20] The Abrahamic covenant is mentioned also in Zechariah's prophecy (1:73-75) and in Peter's temple sermon in Acts 3:25 (cf. also 3:8; 7:2-17; 19:9).[21] The end of Mary's speech is rarely given much consideration in the biblical commentaries, but in light of the prominence Pontormo gives to the connection between Abraham and the unborn Christ, we shall return to this theme in the discussion of the iconography of the *Visitation*. The scene concludes, as we noted, with Mary returning to her home.

In terms of the reception history of the story, the Visitation scene was popular in the visual arts, depicted as part of a Nativity cycle as early as the sixth century and finally claiming an independent position in pictorial history in the late Middle Ages.[22] In subsequent Christian literature and liturgy, however, the Visitation and its characters did not

[18]Tannehill, *Luke*, 54.

[19]Although some Latin manuscripts attribute this speech also to Elizabeth, it is generally agreed that the original text of Luke read Mary (or perhaps had no named subject). On the textual problem, see Bruce M. Metzger, *A Textual Commentary on the Greek New Testament*, 2nd ed. (New York: United Bible Societies, 1994) 109, and on the history of interpretation regarding the identity of the speaker of the Magnificat, see especially Stephen Benko, "The Magnificat: A History of the Controversy," *Journal of Biblical Literature* 86 (1967): 263–75. What concerns us is whether or not the Latin text naming Elizabeth as the speaker might have influenced Pontormo or his patrons. Since Pontormo's *Visitation* seems to depict the introductory part of the episode with Elizabeth's lips parted as if in speech, the extent of Elizabeth's speech (e.g., whether it ends in v. 45 or 55) would affect in part the iconographic interpretation. Since the Vulgate includes the name of Mary, we shall limit the focus of our attention to 39-45, though we shall still pay some attention to the mention of Abraham and his descendants in v. 55.

[20]The Greek at this point is difficult and there is some question about its translation. Some take Abraham in apposition to the fathers: "He remembered mercy, even as he spoke to our fathers, that is, to Abraham and to his seed forever." Others view 1:55a as parenthetical, rendering the following translation, "Because he remembered mercy for Abraham and his seed forever, even as he spoke to our fathers." On the history of the translation difficulties, see Darrel L. Bock, *Luke 1:1–9:50* (Grand Rapids: Baker, 1994) 159–60. In either case, Mary chooses to end her speech with a reference to the Abrahamic covenant.

[21]Abraham is mentioned a total of twenty-two times in Luke and Acts. See Nihls A. Dahl, "The Story of Abraham in Luke–Acts," *Studies in Luke–Acts: Essays Presented in Honor of Paul Schubert*, ed. Leander E. Keck and J. Louis Martyn (Philadelphia: Fortress, 1966) 139–58; Robert L. Brawley, "For Blessing of All Families of the Earth: Covenant Traditions in Luke–Acts," *Currents in Theology and Missions* 22 (1995): 18–26.

[22]See Gertrud Schiller, vol. 1 of *Iconography of Christian Art*, trans. Janet Seligman (Greenwich CT: New York Graphic Society, 1971) 55.

[23]In the *Protevangelium of James* (12.1-2), we are told that Elizabeth (like Mary) was spinning thread for the temple veil when Mary arrived at her home.

[24]Cited by Mary Lee Wile, "Elizabeth," *Daughters of Sarah* 22 (1996): 45–59.

[25]See the *Life of John according to Serapion*, cited in vol. 1 of *New Testament Apocrypha*, ed. Wilhelm Schneemelcher, trans. R. McL. Wilson (Louisville KY: Westminster/John Knox, 1991) 467–68.

[26]Schiller, *Iconography*, 55.

[27]Feminist studies and/or studies that focus on the female characters include Jean-Pierre Ruiz, "Luke 1:39-56: Mary's Visit to Elizabeth as a Biblical Instance of Mentoring," *Apuntes* 17 (1997): 103–105; Loretta Dornisch, "A Woman Reads the Gospel of Luke: Introduction and Luke 1: The Infancy Narratives," *Biblical Research* 42 (1997): 7–22; Turid Karlsen Seim, "Searching for the Silver Coin: A Response to Loretta Dornisch and Barbara Reid," *Biblical Research* 42 (1997): 32–41; Arie Troost, "Elisabeth and Mary—Naomi and Ruth: Gender-Response Criticism in Luke 1–2," *A Feminist Companion to the Hebrew Bible in the New Testament*, ed. Athalya Brenner (Sheffield: Sheffield Academic Press, 1996) 159–96; Krister Stendahl, "And Why Is This Granted to Me?" *Harvard Divinity Bulletin* 24/2 (1995): 23–24; Ben Witherington III, *Women in the Earliest Churches* (Cambridge: Cambridge University Press, 1994); Tina Pippin, "The Politics of Meeting: Women and Power in the New Testament," *That They Might Live: Power, Empowerment, and Leadership in the Church*, ed. Michael Downey (New York: Crossroad, 1991) 13–24; Janice Capel Anderson, "Mary's Difference: Gender and Patriarchy in the Birth Narratives," *Journal of Religion* 67 (1987): 183–202.

fare quite so well. Apart from Mary, whose popularity continued to increase with the development of the cult of the Virgin, neither the scene itself nor Elizabeth, the other major character, received much attention among the ecclesiastical commentators. The *Golden Legend* and Pseudo-Bonaventure's *Meditations on the Life of Christ*, both well known for their embellishments of the biblical narrative, add little to the Visitation scene or to the development of the character of Elizabeth.[23] Augustine's reference to Elizabeth's role as primarily that of the mother of John the Baptist was fairly typical of the church fathers.[24] That is not to say that Elizabeth was neglected altogether. We are told the name of Elizabeth's mother (Hismeria according to the *Golden Legend*; Sobe according to St. Hippolytus) and that she— Elizabeth's mother—was the sister of Anna, Mary's mother (thus explaining the blood relationship mentioned briefly in Luke). And according to the *Protevangelium of James* (22.3), Elizabeth protected John from the slaughter of the innocents by fleeing to the desert, where a rock opened up to conceal them until danger had passed. In another medieval document, we are told that when John the Baptist was seven-and-a-half years old, Elizabeth died on the same day as did her nemesis Herod, and Mary and Jesus came to comfort John the Baptist and assist in Elizabeth's burial.[25]

Likewise the Visitation scene itself has not been totally neglected. In 1263, Bonaventure introduced the feast of the Visitation into the Franciscan calendar, and from 1389 it was celebrated as one of the Marian feasts in the entire Roman Catholic Church.[26] Analyses of the Visitation, however, have mushroomed in the latter half of the twentieth century as feminist scholars have noted the importance of the scene of two women, meeting in a private home but discussing matters profoundly public, political, and theological.[27] Likewise, advocates of liberation theology have noted the profound political and social implications of Mary's Magnificat.[28] Any hermeneutical reflection on this

[28]From the perspective of liberation theology, see Ernesto Cardenal, *The Gospel in Solentiname*, trans. Donald D. Walsh, 4 vols. (Maryknoll NY: Orbis, 1982) and the accompanying *The Gospel in Art by the Peasants of Solentiname*, ed. Philip and Sally Scharper (Maryknoll NY: Orbis, 1984) esp. 8–9 where the Visitation is discussed and depicted; Gustavo Gutiérrez, *A Theology of Liberation: History, Politics and Salvation* (Maryknoll NY: Orbis, 1973); Gail R. O'Day, "Singing Woman's Song: a Hermeneutic of Liberation [Ex 15:21; 1 Sam 2:1-10; Lk 1:46-55]," *Currents in Theology and Mission* 12 (1985): 203–10; D. Sölle, "Meditation über Lukas 1," *Die Revolutionäre Geduld* (Berlin: Gedichte, 1974) 26.; also the brief treatment of recent interpretations of the Magnificat in François Bovon, *L'Évangile Selon Saint Luc (1,1–9,50)* (Geneva: Labor et Fides, 1991) 94–95.

text (or its visual depictions) would need to take into account our contemporary context of interpretation.

THE ARTIST AND THE PAINTING

Jacopo Pontormo

Jacopo da Carucci was born on 26 May 1494 in Pontormo and died in Florence on 31 December 1556 at the age of sixty-two.[29] Pontormo, as he was known to his contemporaries, was a skilled painter and draughtsman and the leading artist in mid-sixteenth-century Florentine Mannerism. According to Giorgio Vasari, Pontormo (1494–1556) probably received his first artistic training with Leonardo in 1508[30] and would have been very familiar with his master's *Annunciation*.[31] Pontormo's *Visitation*, 1514–1516 (Figure 1), is located *in situ* at the Chiostrino dei Voti or atrium of SS. Annunziata, Florence.[32] Pontormo's training probably continued in the workshop of Mariotto Albertinelli (1474–1515)[33] and finally was completed with Piero di Cosimo.[34] Pontormo became the assistant to Andrea del Sarto around 1512.[35] His earliest surviving work, a collaborative effort with Andrea, is the *St. Catherine of Alexandria*, 1512, today in the Uffizi, Florence.

The first independent works are a group of frescoes reflective of the high Renaissance classicism of Andrea and Fra Bartolommeo.[36] Pontormo's collaboration with the Medici begins in 1515 with Pope Leo X's visit to Florence.[37] He is commissioned to paint a lunette fresco of St. Veronica and the vault frescoes of God the Father and Putti with the Arms of Leo X in Santa Maria Novella.[38] The dramatic

[29]Major monographs and exhibition catalogs on the artist and his paintings include Fritz Goldschmidt, *Pontormo, Rosso und Bronzino. Ein Versuch zur Geschichte der Raumdarstellung* (Lipzig: Klinkhardt and Biermann, 1911); Frederick Mortimore Clapp, *Jacopo Carucci da Pontormo: His Life and Work* (New Haven CT: Yale University Press, 1916); Luciano Berti, *Pontormo e del manierismo fiorentino*, exh. cat. (Florence: Tipografia guintina, 1956); Luciano Berti, *Pontormo* (Florence: Edizione d'Arte il Fiorino, 1966); Kurt W. Forster, *Pontormo: Monographie mit kritischem Katalog* (Munich: Bruckman, 1966); Luciano Berti, *L'opera completa del Pontormo* (Milan: Rizzoli, 1973); Luciano Berti, *Pontormo e il suo tempo* (Florence: Banca Toscana, 1993) 190; Philippe Costamagna, *Pontormo* (Milan: Electa, 1994); Carlo Falciano, *Il Pontormo e il Rosso. Guida alle opere* (Florence: Giunta regionale toscana, 1994); Anna Forlani Tempesti and Alessandra Giovannetti, *Pontormo* (Florence: Octavo, 1994); Roberto Ciardi and Antonio Natali, *Pontormo e Rosso: atti del covegno di Empoli e Volterra progetto Appiani di Piombino* (Florence: Giunta regionale toscana, 1996).

[30]Giorgio Vasari, *Le Opere di Giorgio Vasari: Le Vite de'più eccellenti pittori, scultori ed architettori scritte da Giorgio Vasari pittore Aretino, (1568)*, ed. Gaetano Milanesi, 9 vols. (Florence: Sansoni, 1885) 6:246.

[31]Janet Cox-Rearick, *Dictionary of Art*, ed. Jane Turner, 34 vols. (New York: Grove's Dictionaries, 1996) 25:221–24. See also, S. J. Freedberg, *Painting in Italy, 1500–1600* (Harmondsorth: Pelikan History of Art, 1971, rev. 1983) 102–104, for a detailed synopsis of the artist's life and works.

[32]The fresco painting is 13' x 11'2".

[33]Freedberg (*Painting in Italy*, 102) states that Pontormo served as an apprentice to Albertinelli ca. 1508–1510 and then continued with Piero di Cosimo.

[34]Giorgio Vasari, Le Opere di Giorgio Vasari, VI:246.

[35]Scholars agree that Pontormo was about eighteen when he began his association with Andrea.

[36]These include a *Faith and Charity*, 1513–1514 (Florence, Gallerie), originally surrounding the arms of Pope Leo X over the portico of SS. Annunziata, Florence; *The Hospital of St. Matteo*, ca. 1514 (Florence, Accademia); and the *Virgin and Child with Saints*, ca. 1514 (Florence, SS. Annunziata) for S. Ruffillo. For a summary of Pontormo's work in Florence, see Eva Darragon, "Pontormo à Florence," *Revue de l'Art* 51 (1981): 51–60.

[37]For the relationship between Pontormo and the Medici, see Janet Cox-Rearick, *Dynasty and Destiny in Medici Art: Pontormo, Leo X and the Two Cosimos* (Princeton NJ: Princeton University Press, 1984). For the cultural and historical settings in contemporary Florence and its influence on Pontormo, see Paolo Simoncelli, "Pontormo el la cultura fiorentina," *Archivio storico italiano* 153 (1995): 488–527, and J. N. Stephans, *The Fall of the Florentine Republic 1512–1530* (New York: Oxford University Press, 1983) respectively.

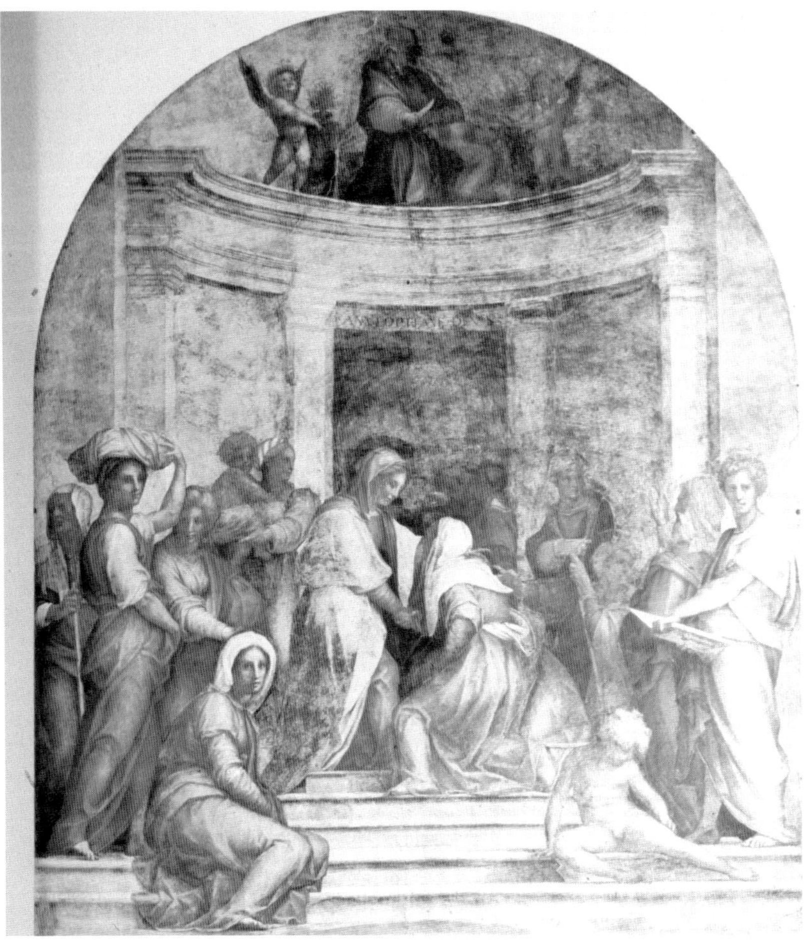

[38]Cox-Rearick, *Dictionary*, 222. This commission will be discussed below as part of the preparation for the visit of Leo X on 15 November 1515.

[39]Panel paintings executed immediately following the Florence *Visitation* include three scenes from the Story of Joseph painted for the bridal chamber of Pier Francesco Borgherini, 1515–1517 (London, National Gallery), a *Portrait of a Jeweller*, ca.1518 (Paris, Louvre), a *Portrait of a Musician*, ca. 1515–1516 (Florence, Uffizi) and a *Portrait of Cosimo de' Medici il Vecchio*, 1519 (Florence, Uffizi).

[40]For San Michele Visdomini, see David Franklin, "A Document for Pontormo's Michele Visdomini Altarpiece," *Burlington Magazine* 132 (1990): 487–89.

rhetoric and classical amplitude of form of the High Renaissance is also found in the *Visitation*, 1514–1515, a part of the cycle of the Life of the Virgin in SS. Annunziata, Florence.[39]

The *Visitation*, therefore, is an early work but its importance in Pontormo's *oeuvre* is best understood by discussing not only what he did before it but also what came after it. Around 1517, Pontormo experimented with spatial relationships, increased the visible signs of emotion in the figures, and destabilized the compositional forms. His incorporation of these aspects of the new style of the day, Mannerism, into his paintings is first apparent in the *Virgin and Child with Saints*, 1518, in San Michele Visdomini, Florence, and the *Joseph in Egypt*, 1518 commissioned for the Borgherini family and today located in the National Gallery, London.[40]

The mature works are usually dated 1520–1530 and include his masterpieces of *Vertumnus and Pomona*, painted in the Gran Salone of the Medici villa at Poggio a Caiano (1520–1521), the fresco series of the Passion at the Certosa del Galluzzo (1523–1526), and the *Lamentation* altarpanel and fresco decoration for the Capponi Chapel in S. Felicita, Florence (1525–1528).[41] The artificial elegance and emotionality of the figures, the spatial uncertainty, and the vibrant color palette used in the *Lamentation* define a Mannerist composition. Also painted during this period of Mannerism is the *Visitation* from S. Michele in Carmignano, dated to the late 1520s.[42] Pontormo also devised a typical Florentine Mannerist portrait type that is pursued and then abandoned by other Mannerists, such as his pupil in the 1520s, Agnolo Bronzino (1503–1572), Francesco Salviati (1510–1563), and Giorgio Vasari.[43] The late works, 1530–1556, are heavily influenced by Michelangelo. He painted frescoes in two Medici villas at Careggi (1535–1536) and Castello (1537–1543) and in the choir of S. Lorenzo, Florence.[44]

Pontormo was an advocate of the concept of Florentine *disegno* and participated in the *paragone* (debate) on the primacy of painting or sculpture in 1546.[45] Much is known about the eccentric and often depressed character of Pontormo through his own diary.[46]

[41]For Poggio a Caiano, see J. Kliemann, "Vertumnus und Pomona: Zum Program von Pontormos Fresko in Poggio a Caiano," *Mitteilungen Kunsthistorisches Institut, Florenz* 16 (1972): 293–328 and M. Winner, "Pontormo's Fresko in Poggio a Caiano," *Zeitschrift für Kunstgeschichte* 35 (1972): 153–97. More recently see, Litta Mari Medri, *Pontormo a Poggio a Caiano* (Florence: Octavo, 1995). For the Certosa del Galluzzo, see Elizabeth Pilliod, "Pontormo and Bronzino at the Certosa," *Getty Museum Journal* 20 (1992): 77–88. For the Capponi Chapel, see John Shearman, *Pontormo's Altarpiece in S. Felicita: The 51st Charlton Lecture, University Newcastle-upon-Tyne* (Westerham: University of Newcastle-upon-Tyne, 1968); Leo Steinberg, "Pontormo's Capponi Chapel," *Art Bulletin* 56 (1974): 385–99.

[42]Comparison and further examination of the two *Visitation* paintings will be the subject of a future study. For recent scholarship on the *Visitation* in Carmignano, see Mariano Apa, *Pontormo. La Visitazione a Carmignano* (Carmignano-Florence: Arti Grafiche Albano, 1994); Rosanna Caterini Proto Pisani, Maria Grazia Trenti Antonelli, and Litta Medri, *Il Pontormo: le opere di Empoli, Carmignano e Poggio a Caiano* (Venice: Marsilio Editori, 1994) 31–50; *Pontormo e Rosso. La 'maniera moderna' in Toscana: Empoli and Volterra*, 1994 (Florence: Giunta regionale toscana, 1996); Christoph Bertsch, *Jacopo Pontormo Le Quattro Donne di Carmignano* (Florence: Edizioni Medicea, 1998).

[43]See the exhibition catalogs on paintings, *Mostra del Pontormo e del primo manierismo fiorentino*, ed. U. Baldini, Luciano Berti and Luisa Marcucci (Florence: Palazzo Strozzi, 1956) and on drawings, *Mostra di disegni dei primi manieristi italiani*, ed. U. Baldini, Luciano Berti and Luisa Marcucci (Florence: Uffizi, 1954) for a discussion of the first Mannerists. For Bronzino, see Robert B. Simon, "Bronzino's Portraits of Cosimo I de'Medici" (Ph.D. diss., Columbia University, 1985).

[44]For the frescoes at San Lorenzo, see Charles de Tolnay, "Les Fresques de Pontormo dans le choeur de San Lorenzo à Florence," *Crit A.* 33 (1950): 38–52; Janet Cox-Rearick, "Pontormo, Bronzino, Allori and the lost Deluge at S. Lorenzo," *Burlington Magazine* 134 (1992): 239–48.

[45]Pontormo's written letters to Benedetto Varchi requesting that he be permitted to participate in the debate are published by Varchi in *Due lezioni di M. Benedetto Varchi* (Florence, 1549) 132–35.

[46]See Jacopo Carucci Pontormo, *Diario: Codice Magliabechiano VIII 1490 della Biblioteca nazionale centrale di Firenze* (Rome: Salerno, 1996) or *Pontormo's Diary*, ed. Rosemary Mayer (New York: London Press, 1979).

Luke and Pontormo   **147**

[47]John Shearman, "Rosso, Pontormo, Bandinelli and Others at SS. Annunziata," *Burlington Magazine* 102 (1960): 152–56. For the life of Andrea di Cosimo Feltrini, see Vasari, 5:204–10.

[48]Ibid., 154. A payment of 3 lire, 15 soldi, dated 31 January 1513, to "*porto Jacopo di bartolomeo dipintore.*"

[49]Clapp, *Pontormo*, 9.

[50]Vasari, VI:248.

[51]Shearman, "Rosso, Pontormo, Bandinelli and Others at SS. Annunziata," 154.

[52]Ibid.

[53]Vasari, VI:248. Shearman, "Rosso, Pontormo, Bandinelli and Others at SS. Annunziata," 154, focusing on archival documentation, calls this story "legendary embroidery," which does not concern his study. For additional commentary on the probability and/or possibility of Vasari's story see Clapp, *Pontormo*, 9 n.15.

[54]Clapp, *Pontormo*, 10.

[55]Shearman, "Rosso, Pontormo, Bandinelli and Others at SS. Annunziata," 154, clarifies the previous scholarship regarding the documents related to Pontormo's payments for this work.

[56]Vasari, 6:250.

[57]Clapp, *Pontormo*, 10, cites the following sources as contemporary evidence of the popularity of the putti: Vasari, VI:248; Francesco Bocchi, *Le bellezze della città di Firenze*, 1581, ed. M. Giovanni Cinelli (Florence: Gugliantini, 1677) 415; Giuseppe Richa, *Notizie istoriche delle chiese fiorentine divise ne'suoi Quartieri* (Florence: P. G. Viviani, 1754–1762) 5:52.

The Commission and the Servites

The Servites, or the Ordine dei Servi di Maria, were founded in 1234 by seven Florentines. The church of SS. Annunziata was built in 1250 and reconstructed by Michelozzo between 1444 and 1481. Andrea di Cosimo Feltrini, an artist held in high esteem for his own limited field of pure decoration (much of which might be considered menial tasks, such as painting candles), occupied a position of general factorum at the Servi even before the election of the Medici pope.[47] Shearman cites documentation that Pontormo, most likely hired by Feltrini, received payment on 31 January 1513 for painting candles.[48]

The decoration of several areas, including the façade and the Chiostrino dei Voti, began in celebration of the election of Cardinal Giovanni de'Medici to the papacy (Leo X) on 11 March 1513. In the summer following that election, Andrea del Sarto, Franciabigio (1482/3–1525), and Rosso Fiorentino were all working in the Chiostrino dei Voti.[49]

Vasari tells a story about Pontormo's selection to work in the Annunziata.[50] Feltrini had been assigned to paint a new stone coat of arms for the Pope to be placed over the principal arch of the façade that required gilding, grotesques, and the figures of *Faith* and *Charity*.[51] Feeling inadequate for the allegorical figures, he called on Pontormo.[52] According to Vasari, after hiding himself in Sant'Agostino alla Porta a Faenza and producing a series of drawings for the stem, Pontormo showed them to a "stupefied" master, Andrea del Sarto. From that point forward, Pontormo was no longer allowed to attend the master's *bottega*.[53] Although this may be one of Vasari's famous tales, it does indicate the solitary and whimsical character of Pontormo.[54] Pontormo finished the stem, received payment, and then almost immediately destroyed it.[55] He replaced it with a now nearly destroyed *Faith and Charity*, which contains two putti. Vasari thoroughly enjoyed this fresco (he discusses it for two pages),[56] especially the putti, which became famous throughout the sixteenth century.[57]

The frescoes in the Chiostrino dei Voti—six dedicated to scenes from the life of the Virgin and six to the life of St. Filippo Benizzi— were not completed by the time of Pope Leo X's arrival on 15

November 1515.[58] The entrance to the atrium is in the center of the structure. The door to the nave is opposite it. The frescoes from the life of the Virgin, beginning from the right side of the atrium door in a counter-clockwise direction and continuing to the church entrance, are *Assumption, Visitation, Marriage, Birth of the Virgin, Adoration of the Magi*. The *Nativity of Christ* is located on the other side of the nave entrance and had been painted earlier, 1460–1462, by Alesso Baldovinetti. Fra Mariano dal Canto alle Macine[59] commissioned Franciabigio to execute the *Marriage of the Virgin*, which was completed by September 1513,[60] and Andrea del Sarto to paint the *Birth of the Virgin* from 1513-1514.[61] According to Forlani Tempesti and Giovannetti, Fra Jacopo de'Rossi preferred the talents of the younger artists, Rosso Fiorentino and Pontormo.[62] Rosso Fiorentino began to paint the *Assumption of the Virgin* toward the end of 1513.[63] Pontormo was paid by the Servites from December 1514 to June 1516 to conclude the cycle.[64] It has been suggested that instead of for the Pope's arrival, the painting was completed by 17 January 1516 for the new consecration of SS. Annunziata.[65]

STYLISTIC AND ICONOGRAPHIC ANALYSIS OF THE PAINTING

Artistic Sources and Composition

The stylistic sources are clearly his masters, Andrea del Sarto and Mariotto Albertinelli. Albertinelli's *Visitation* (Figure 2) of 1503 indicates a loving rapport between the two women that Pontormo maintains in his composition of the same subject over ten years later. Pontormo's training with Albertinelli, sometime around 1506 at the age of twelve, would have been in the classical Renaissance style.[66] Andrea's *Birth of the Virgin* (Figure 3), painted in the same cloister between 1513 and 1514, is a compositional source.[67] Pontormo's varia-

[58]Clapp, *Pontormo*, 12, states that Pontormo also worked with Ridolfo del Ghirlandaio in the Papal Chapel of S. Maria Novella during the summer of 1515. Pontormo painted a *St. Veronica Holding the Sudario* in fresco in a lunette above the door. In the center of the ceiling, he painted a tondo of God the Father descending. He also painted the four medallions (each with a putto) and squares (the arms of Leo supported by putti) on the ceiling. These are completely repainted.

[59]Forlani Tempesti and Giovannetti, *Pontormo*, 110–11.

[60]Sherman, "Rosso, Pontormo, Bandinelli and Others at SS. Annunziata," 154–55.

[61]The date on the fireplace: A. D. M. D. X. IIII.

[62]Forlani Tempesti and Giovannetti, *Pontormo*, 111.

[63]Elisabetta Marchetti Letta, *Pontormo. Rosso Fiorentino* (Florence: Scala, 1994) 9.

[64]Shearman, "Rosso, Pontormo, Bandinelli and Others at SS. Annunziata," 154, reviewed and updated the accuracy of the documentation: "Here again Milanesi (Vasari, VI:258 n.1) had spotted some of the payments, but simply stated that between April 1515 and June 1516, Pontormo received on various occasions 73 lire. Clapp, *Pontormo*, 275–76, again published in full a series of payments from December 1514 to June 1516, missing only one." Shearman published the final document to be discovered. Clapp (Ibid.) also states that Fra Mariano dal Canto alle Macine commissioned Andrea del Sarto and Franciabigio. Five of the six scenes from the life of San Filippo Benizzi (the *Calling and Ordination* was painted by Cosimo Roselli ca. 1476) were commissioned solely to Andrea del Sarto.

[65]Berti, *Pontormo e il Suo Tempo*, 190. For more on why the particular scene of the Visitation was chosen for this cycle, see Jack Wasserman, "Jacopo Pontormo's Florentine *Visitation*," *Artibus Et Historiae* 32 (1995): 39–53.

[66]James Beck, "The Young Pontormo and Albertinelli," *Burlington Magazine* 122 (1980): 623–24, argued that Clapp misread the documents that enabled him to claim Pontormo entered into Albertinelli's bottega at the age of nine in 1503. Given this evidence, an entrance of the young boy into his first workshop probably occurred between twelve and fourteen years of age.

[67]Vasari, 5:67.

[68]Clapp, *Pontormo*, 18, discussed several sketches by Pontormo drawn between 1513 and 1518 that have their source in the Michelangelo. Luisa Marcucci, *Quaderni Pontormeschi: Vol. 3. La "Maniera" del Pontormo* (Florence: Tipografia Giuntina, 1956) 9, also finds the Battle of Cascina to be a source for the Pontormo *Visitation*.

[69]Letta, *Pontormo. Rosso Fiorentino*, 13.

[70]Salvatore S. Nigro, *Pontormo. Paintings and Frescoes* (New York: Harry N. Abrams, 1994) 2:2. See also Irving L. Zupnick, "Pontormo's Early Style," *Art Bulletin* 47 (1965): 345–53, esp. 347, 349, and 352, for a discussion of the stylistic influences on the *Visitation*.

[71]See Heinrich Wölfflin, *Classic Art: An Introduction to the Italian Renaissance*, trans. Peter and Linda Murray (New York: Phaidon Publishers; distributed by Oxford University Press, 1961) 153–54.

[72]Ibid. On the possible iconographic significance of this architectural space, see Wasserman, "Jacopo Pontormo's Florentine *Visitation*," 45, 48–50.

[73]See Frederick A. Cooper, "Jacopo Pontormo and Influences from the Renaissance Theater," *Art Bulletin* 55 (1973): 380–92, for a discussion of Pontormo's part in various Florentine *feste* and theatrical decorations.

tion in gesture and the female facial types is similar to Andrea's painting. Andrea's monumental figures are fewer and positioned well within the frescoes' space while Pontormo's figures seem crowded and their positioning recalls another master of the classical high Renaissance, Fra Bartolomeo. The *Mystical Marriage of St. Catherine*, 1512, today located in the Galleria Accademia of Florence, represents a stepped composition with a cylindrical niche placed behind the central scene. The static quality of the Fra Bartolomeo figures is not copied by Pontormo, but instead the younger artist turns to Michelangelo's cartoon of the *Battle of Cascina*.[68] It should also be noted that Raphael's frescoes in the first two of the Vatican Stanze are nearly contemporary and may justify the hypothesis of a first journey to Rome in 1515.[69] The influence of Raphael can be found in the soft colors, natural movements, and certainly with the placement of the figures in front of an illusionistic architectural setting open to the front and made of marble.[70]

Heinrich Wölfflin was among the first to write about the classicism of this work.[71] He notes the triangular area of the central figures and the semi-cylindrical architectonic frame behind them, the verticals of the side figures, and then the circular movement back to the center of the composition.[72] Mary and Elizabeth are centered and "staged" in this event.[73] Mary's gown is pinkish-orange, and she wears a pale blue mantle, worn almost as a long coat over the right side of her body, and then gently draped over her left arm as it extends to the kneeling figure of Elizabeth. Elizabeth is aged and grasps Mary's right hand with hers. Elizabeth's left hand falls to her lap to assist her balance as she falls to her knees after the realization that Mary is carrying the Lord Jesus. Elizabeth's head is covered, as is Mary's, and both Elizabeth's gown and Mary's head covering consist of a radiant yellowish-orange colored drapery, which moves the spectator through the painting. This color, brightest in the picture, appears in the gown of the male figure holding the book on the right side of the composition, the upper half of the gown of the seated female figure on the steps, and finally in the gown of the female figure directly behind this seated woman.

There is a strong diagonal that also brings the audience from Mary to Elizabeth and continues to the seated boy on the steps.[74] The foot of the boy, who seems to be focused on a brown indeterminate object, is placed directly below the male figure holding the book whose drapery catches the eye and moves the viewer back into the center. Once at the top of the Virgin's head, which is covered in the same colored drapery,

74Janet Cox-Rearick, "The Drawings of Pontormo: Addenda," *Master Drawings* 8 (1970): 363–78, discusses a preparatory drawing of the boy on the steps identified by I. Fenyo, "Sur Quelques Dessins italiens du XVIe siècle," *Bulletin di Musée National Hongrois des Beaux-Arts* 19 (1961): 59–60, fig. 45. See Cox-Rearick, "Drawings of Pontormo," cat.11-13a, for additional drawings related to the *Visitation*. Drawings are not the focus of our study, but we find it necessary to mention the specific drawings related to the fresco in discussion. Some have identified the figure of Diogenes in Raphael's *School of Athens* as a possible compositional source.

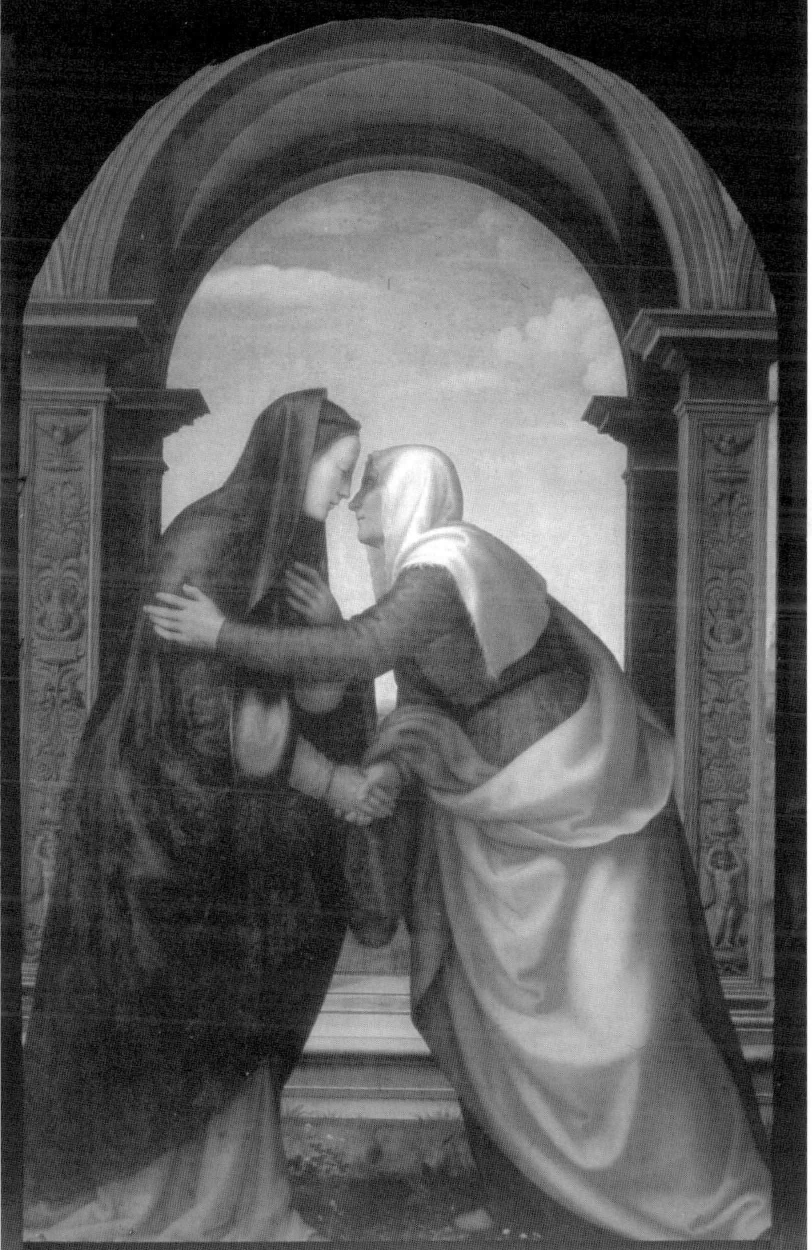

FIG 2.
Visitation. Mariotto Albertinelli. 1503. Panel. Uffizi, Florence. Photo. With permission from the Ministero dei Beni e le Attività Culturali.

the viewer may follow the curve of her back around to the standing woman holding a child whose left arm has just a sleeve visible of this orange drapery, to the standing figure of the woman with the orange gown and rose mantle, and finally down to the seated woman on the left side of the steps whose legs guide the spectator back into the center.

Iconography

The sacrifice of Isaac depicted above the architecture suggests a parallel between the faith of Abraham and that of the Virgin Mary, united by the common sacrifice of their sons. The first public recognition of the moment of incarnation occurs when Elizabeth identifies Mary as the mother of her Lord. We will begin our study of the

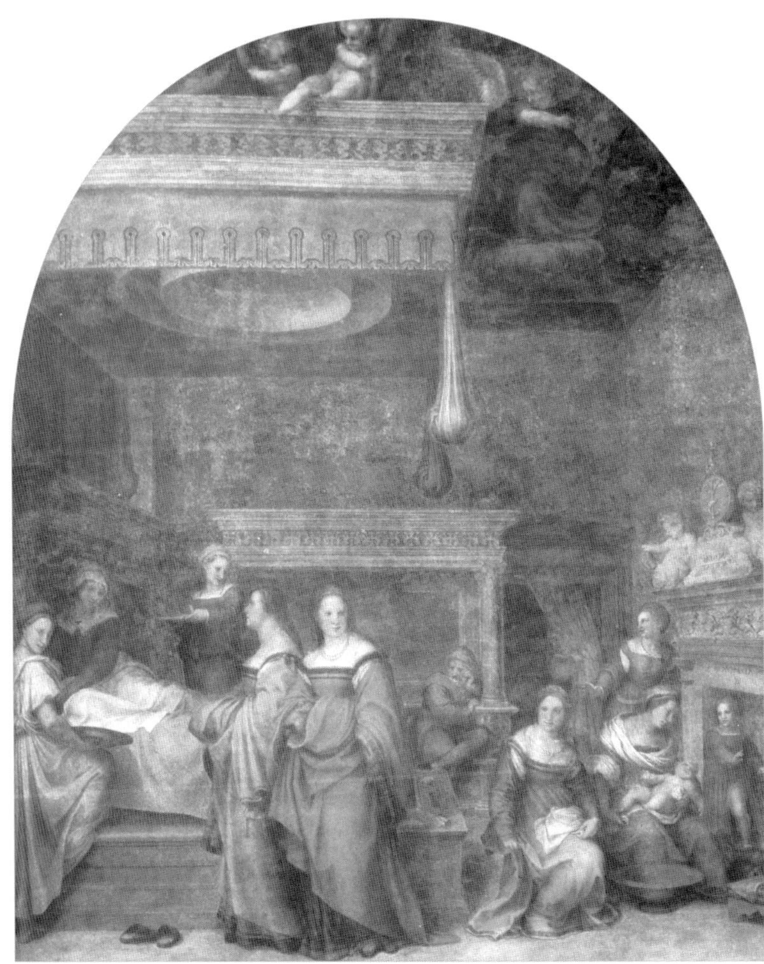

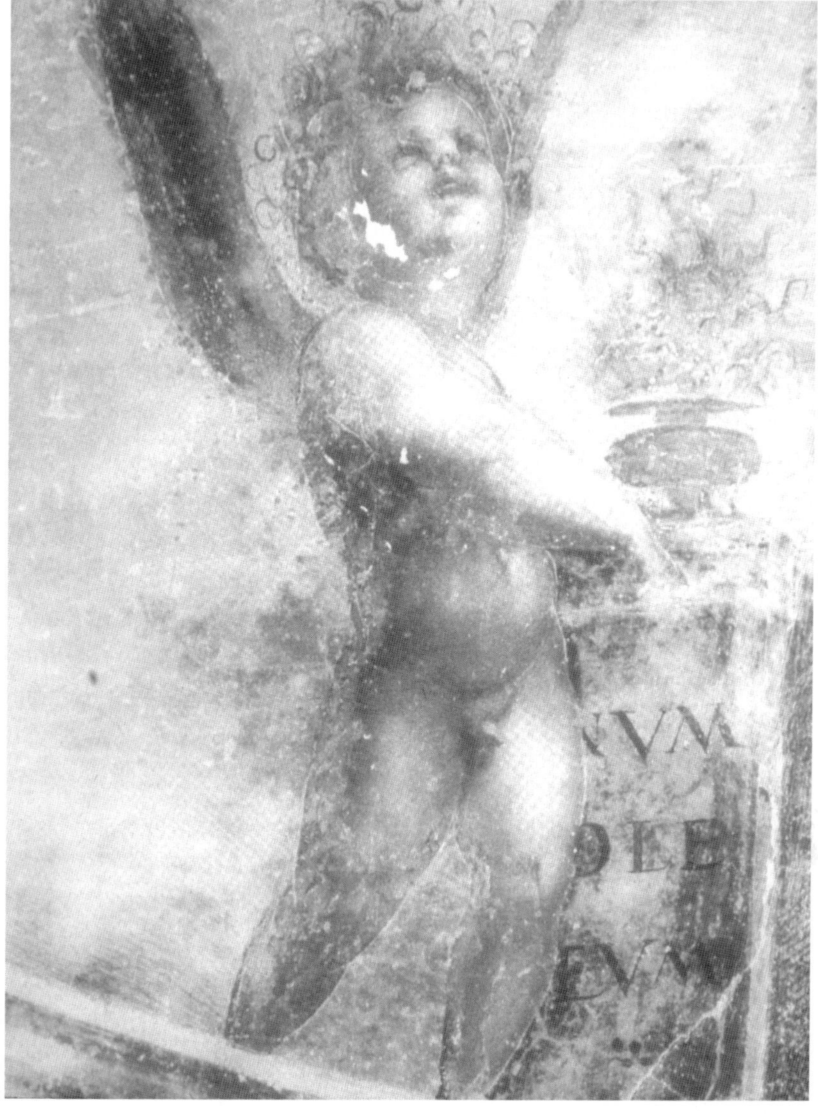

FIG 4.
Visitation.
Pontormo. Detail of inscription on the left. Before restoration. Gabinetto Fotografico, Florence. Photo. With permission from the Ministero dei Beni e le Attività Culturali.

iconography of this painting by returning for a moment to the figures on the left of Mary, whose compositional function we have just described. In fact, when these figures are treated at all, it is almost always in terms of their composition and style.

Inattentive Figures. A recent study by Robert Gaston suggests that these "minor" figures may play a more important role in the meaning of the painting than is generally acknowledged.[75] Drawing on the work of Vasari and other Renaissance observers of art, Gaston concludes, "In most narrative pictures a high degree of inattentiveness to the principal personages was regarded as appropriate."[76] Gaston explores the

[75]Robert W. Gaston, "Attention and Inattention in Religious Painting of the Renaissance: Some Preliminary Observations," *Renaissance Studies in Honor of Craig Hugh Smyth* (Florence: Giunti Barbera, 1985) 253–68. Gaston does refer to Pontormo's work, though his attention is directed toward Pontormo's "other" *Visitation* at Carmignano. The study of figures in religious painting seen in contemplation was the subject of an informative article by Giancarlo Fiorenza on "Dosso Dossi, Garolfalo, and the *Costabili Polyptych*: Imaging Spiritual Authority," *Art Bulletin* 82 (2000): 252–57.

[76]Ibid., 264.

various functions of these figures in visual art who are seemingly inattentive to the main action of the protagonists.[77]

Some figures, whose gaze takes them to another minor character or some unfocused spot in the narrative "have more to do with the artist's ability to create such an impression of naturalness in his groups, and in their interaction that the beholder is, in a sense, induced to 'forget about' the inattentive figures."[78] Nonetheless, these figures contribute to the "very naturalness of his [the artist's] depiction. The courtiers' behaviour seems inappropriate only to someone who does not share the painter's knowledge that courtiers were permitted to chat among themselves while their lords executed the affairs of state. Their inattentive behaviour is decorous within special limits."[79] This is an apt description of the four female figures (and child) who stand to Mary's left; they contribute to the "naturalness of the depiction," yet are ignored in most iconographic analyses.

Second, Gaston observes that some figures "look out at the viewer and 'invite his attention.'"[80] The result is that "the beholder is flooded with attention, which induces unease if his expectation is to be merely the observer of interaction by others."[81] Both the woman seated on the steps and the prophet holding the open book look out to the audience and invite their participation in this scene.

Finally, Gaston notes that many figures neither gaze at another "minor" character on the canvas nor stare out at the viewer, but rather "remain deeply absorbed." He adds, "One might conclude that they are thus highly attentive to the *means* by which the heavenly vision can be attained by the beholder of the painting. Such a picture requires the beholder to divide his attention between the saints who show the way of attentive prayer and contemplation, and the Madonna and Child [and here with Pontormo, Elizabeth and John] who represent the object of that process."[82] The curious nude figure on the right, as we have observed, is shown here deeply absorbed by something other than the action taking place behind him. We will explore his possible identity later, but here we point out that the child seems to function as one of these inattentive figures who models the means—contemplation—by which one can attain the vision offered here, namely a fuller understanding of the sacrificial dimensions of the Visitation scene.[83]

[77]Ibid.

[78]Ibid.

[79]Ibid., 263.

[80]Ibid.

[81]Ibid., 265.

[82]Ibid., 263.

[83]Gaston also discusses the "chorus effect," which we will take up below under the discussion of the figures of Joseph and Zechariah.

Flanking Inscriptions. Three inscriptions offer potential assistance in the interpretation of this moment of recognition, though interpreters have often despaired in deciphering their meaning.[84] Jack Wasserman has recently explored the iconography of this painting, paying close attention to these inscriptions.[85] The Latin of all three inscriptions "is of Renaissance origin, vaguely imitating classical Latin but intended to 'explain the composite image.'"[86] The flanking inscriptions most probably contain phrases that refer to the sacrifice of Isaac, which is depicted between the two putti.

The putto on the left holds a tablet with an inscription. The first problem is to decipher what the letters are. Working from a photograph of the fresco taken on 9 September 1958, before the painting was removed and restored (Figure 4), and also drawing on Frederick Mortimore Clapp's reconstruction of the inscription, Wasserman has reconstructed those letters NUM/ DEE/ EVM.[87] Based on a fifteenth-century inscription from a monument in the church at Domjulien, France, that reads VNVM CREDE DEVM NE IVRAS VAN,[88] Wasserman suggests that the left inscription can be amended to read [V]NVM [CRE]DE [D]EVM, which he translates, "Believe in one God." Wasserman further comments, "In this case, we must assume…that the final 'E' in DEE must have been a 'D' originally which is to say, the first letter of the succeeding word DEVM. This assumption is easily made, because incomplete words, and letters of words distributed on separate lines, occur frequently in Renaissance inscriptions."[89]

This reconstruction is certainly plausible and made all the more attractive by the existence of a chronologically close (though geographically distant) antecedent. We wish, however, to offer an alternative interpretation for this inscription. Following a lead by Timothy Verdon, we suggest that the original inscription read NUM/DEB/EUM and should be reconstructed as NUM[INI] DEB[ET] EVM: "He [Abraham] owes him [Isaac] to God." That is, Abraham, who owes his son to God, the son originally given to him in fulfillment of the ancestral promise, is now giving him back (cf. Gen 12). This reconstruction does not require amending the inscription to place the beginning of the third word at the end of the second line. Though undoubtedly this

[84]Forster, *Pontormo* 129, for example, considered the flanking inscriptions indecipherable.

[85]See Wasserman, "Jacopo Pontormo's Florentine *Visitation*," 59.

[86]Quoted by permission from private correspondence with Monsignor Timothy Verdon, Canon of the Florence Cathedral, dated 17 October 1999. Mnsgr. Verdon is also cited (with no details) for his interpretation of these inscriptions by Tempesti and Giovannetti, *Pontormo*, 111. We are most grateful for Mnsgr. Verdon's assistance with these inscriptions.

[87]Wasserman, "Jacopo Pontormo's Florentine *Visitation*," 42.

[88]The inscription was published by William Forsyth, *The Entombment of Christ* (Cambridge: Cambridge University Press, 1970).

[89]Wasserman, "Jacopo Pontormo's Florentine *Visitation*," 42. Wasserman goes on to cite "from among innumerable examples" Cosimo Tura's *Enthroned Madonna*. See Frederick Hartt, *History of Italian Renaissance Art*, 4th ed., rev. David G. Wilkins (New York: Harry N. Abrams, 1994) 450, cp 81.

occurs in other Renaissance inscriptions, it does not occur with any of the other five words in *this* one. This reconstruction also makes more sense in the immediate context. [90]

Inscription	Wasserman	Hornik & Parsons
NVM	[V]NVM	NVM[INI]
DEE or DED or DEB	[CRE]DE[D]	DEB[IT]
EVM	EVM	EVM
	"Believe in One God"	"S/He owes him to God"

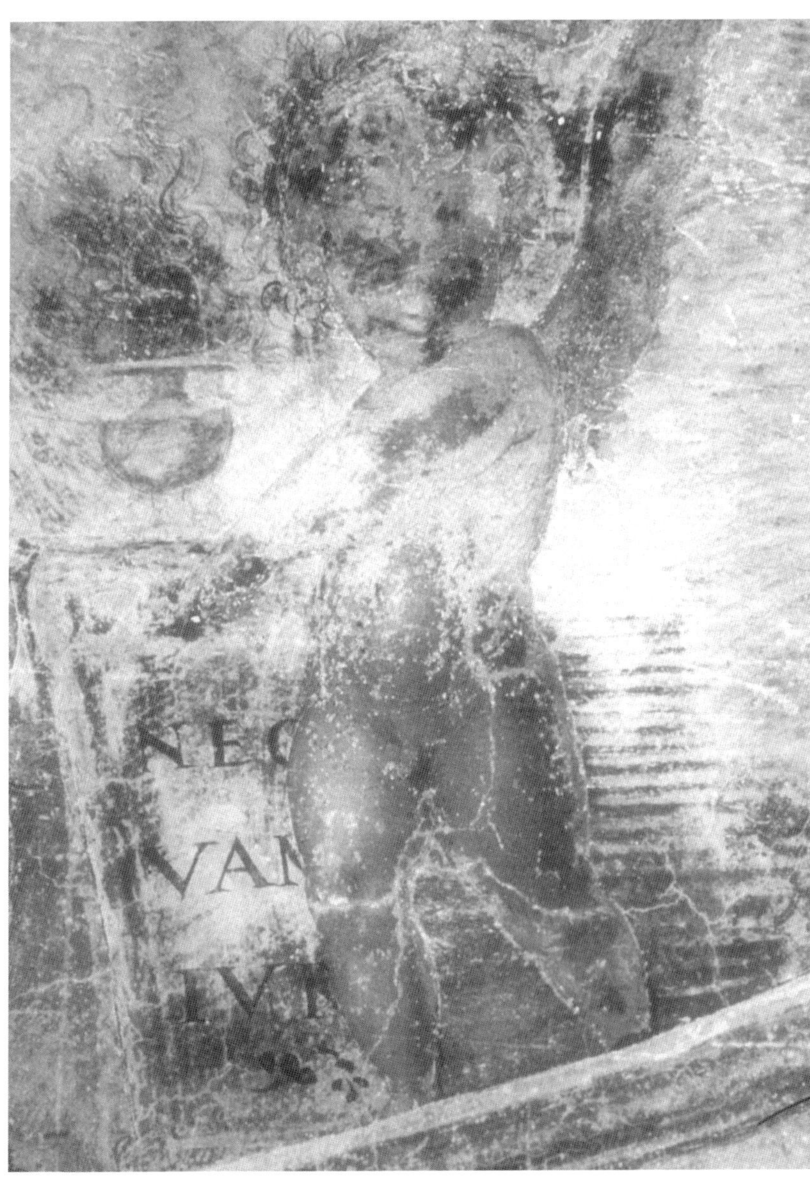

FIG 5. *Visitation.* Pontormo. Detail of inscription on the right. Before restoration. Gabinetto Fotografico, Florence. Photo. With permission from the Ministero dei Beni e le Attività Culturali.

156   *Interpreting Christian Art*

NEC/VAN/IVR is inscribed on the putto's tablet on the right (Figure 5). Here we are in agreement with Wasserman who reconstructs NEC/VAN/IVR as NEC VAN[E] IUR[AT]: "Nor does he swear (or promise) in vain."[91] This inscription has two possible meanings. The sense could be that Abraham does not swear in vain to obey God, or God did not promise in vain to grant Abraham a glorious legacy.[92] Both meanings should probably be kept in mind. In fact, Genesis 12–25 is moved along by a series of threats to God's promise to make of Abraham a mighty nation, and no threat was more severe than the near death of Isaac at the hands of Abraham himself.[93] The inscription echoes the Vulgate translation of the words spoken by Zechariah at John the Baptist's birth: *salutem ex inimicis nostris et de manu omnium qui oderunt nos ad faciendam misericordiam cum patribus nostris et memorari testamenti sui sancti iusiurandum quod iuravit ad Abraham patrem nostrum* (Luke 1:72-73, authors' emphasis).[94] Here in Pontormo's interpretation, then, God's promise to Abraham (to give him offspring through which the nations would be blessed) on the one hand is preserved when God's angel stays Abraham's hand from sacrificing Isaac. On the other hand, the promise is brought to full fruition in the birth of Christ himself, anticipated in the main scene of the Visitation. Thus, "he [God] did not swear in vain [to bless Abraham with offspring,] and—behold—Christ now enters the scene."[95]

Isaac and Christ. Reflection on the relevant New Testament passages makes the connection between Isaac and Christ even clearer. Isaac is mentioned explicitly by name forty-one times in the New Testament, though references to Abraham's seed, covenant, promise— references in which Isaac is embedded—would dramatically increase allusions to him and the ancestral promise he represented to the Jews, including Christian Jews. For example, in Romans 8:32, Paul alludes to the Genesis 22 scene when he claims, "He [God] who has not spared his own Son but has given him for us all, how should he not also give us every other gift." The function of the occurrences vary from giving a place to Isaac in Jesus' genealogy (Matt 1:2; Luke 3:34; cf. Acts 7:8), listing in reports by Paul of Isaac as the fulfillment of the ancestral promise made to Abraham (Rom 9:7, 10; Gal 4:28), as evidence of Abraham's righteous work (Jas 2:22), and as the middle term of the

[91]Wasserman, "Jacopo Pontormo's Florentine *Visitation*," 42. Interestingly, at this point, Wasserman (in our opinion, rightly) abandons the Domjulien inscription (which read "NE IVRAS VAN" and is rendered as a second-person imperative, "nor swear in vain"). The second half of the Domjulien inscription not only reads NE instead of NEC, but it reverses the order of the last two words. Verdon (private correspondence) offers the slightly different reconstruction "NEC VANE IURAVIT" ("Nor *did* he swear in vain").

[92]See Wasserman, "Jacopo Pontormo's Florentine *Visitation*," 42. Verdon (Ibid.).

[93]On the development of this theme of the threats to and fulfillment of the ancestral promise, see Walter Brueggemann, *Genesis* (Atlanta: John Knox Press, 1982).

[94]Translation: "that we should be saved from our enemies and from the hand of all who hate us in order to perform the mercy with our fathers and to remember the holy covenant which he promised to Abraham our father."

[95]Verdon, private correspondence.

[96]On this point, see now Robin Jensen, *Understanding Early Christian Art* (London: Routledge, 1999).

[97]Ambrose, *De Cain et Abel,* i.8. Latin: "Isaac ergo Christi passuri est typus."

[98]See Irenaeus, *Adversus Haereses,* iv.5; Origen, *In Genesim,* ix; Tertullian, *Liber adv. Judaeos,* x; Melito, *Frag.* ix, x, xi, xv; Augustine, *De Civitate Dei,* xvi, 32. Other references may be found in volume 209 of Migne's *Patrologia Latina* in the Index of Old Testament figures, col. 245. On the history of the christological interpretation of the sacrifice of Isaac, see especially David Lerch, *Isaaks Opferung Christlich Gedeutet: Eine auslegungsgeschichtliche Untersuchung* (Tübingen: J. C. B. Mohr, 1950).

[99]Alison Moore Smith, "The Iconography of the Sacrifice of Isaac in Early Christian Art," *American Journal of Archaeology* 26 (1922): 160.

[100]Ibid., 168–69.

formula characterizing God as the "God of Abraham, Isaac, and Jacob" (Matt 22:32//Mark 12:26//Luke 20:37; Acts 3:13; 7:32; cf. Matt 8:11//Luke 20:37 where the triad also occurs). Abraham's sacrifice was not employed typologically by any New Testament writer, though the writer of Hebrews comes the closest: "By faith Abraham, when put to the test, offered up Isaac. He who had received the promises was ready to offer up his only son, of whom he had been told, 'It is through Isaac that descendants shall be named for you'" (Heb 11:17-18). The use of the term "only son" (μονογενής) is a favorite expression, especially in the Gospel of John, to describe the relationship of God to Jesus. Jesus is God's "only" (μονογενής) son (cf. John 1:18; 3:16, 18; 1 John 4:9). Possibly some christological echoes may have been heard in the use of the term to describe Isaac's relationship to Abraham here in Hebrews as well.

From the patristic period on, however, Christian theologians did see Isaac's experience as a foreshadowing prefigurement of Christ's cruxifixion.[96] Ambrose wrote, "Isaac is therefore a type of the suffering of Christ."[97] Irenaeus, Origen, Tertullian, Melito, Augustine, and many others also saw in the Isaac story the foreshadowing of various details from Christ's passion.[98] Each was a "beloved son" offered as the consummate sacrifice by his father. Both sacrifices took place upon a hill. The thorns of the bush that trapped the ram were the thorns of Christ's crown. The ram in the bush was Christ on the cross; Isaac was Christ in the Eucharist.

The linkage between the sacrifice of Isaac and the crucifixion was found in early Christian art as well. As Alison Moore Smith has noted, "A story regarded as of such importance by the Church had frequent representation in Early Christian art. It is depicted on Early Christian monuments of all classes; frescoes, sarcophagi, mosaics, glasses, gems, and lamps."[99] Smith isolated five different "types" of representation through about the sixth century. From the sixth to the eleventh century, "the sacrifice was seldom reproduced in art," a point Smith explains by noting that "the Crucifixion, which it [the sacrifice of Isaac] had symbolized, began to appear upon monuments at this time."[100] She goes on to note that "during the four centuries [twelfth–sixteenth] following that period it had renewed and widespread popularity in representation, owing no doubt to a revival of interest in its symbolic connotations."[101]

Pontormo's depiction fits what Smith has called the "Hellenistic Type": "Usually he [Abraham] is bearded. Holding the knife in his right hand, with his left he often grasps the head of Isaac who kneels on the ground or stands beside the lighted box-shaped altar with hands shackled as Christ's were in the apocryphal version of the Crucifixion."[102] So even taken on by itself, the sacrifice of Isaac depiction could contain visual elements that echo the crucifixion and, in Pontormo, did so.

Often, these links were much more explicit. In chapter twenty-five of the medieval, illustrated manuscript, the *Biblia Pauperum*, the sacrifice of Isaac was the subject of a visual illustration to the left of the central subject, Christ on the cross.[103] This sacrifice of Isaac was titled "the father sacrifices his son, who typifies Christ" and was accompanied by a quote from and interpretation of Genesis 22:10: "We read in Gen. xxii, that when Abraham had stretched forth his hand to slay his son, the angel of the Lord from heaven prevented him, saying, 'Stretch not forth thine hand against the child.' Abraham signifies the heavenly Father, who sacrificed His Son, to wit, Christ, for us all, on the Cross, that thus He might show us a sign of His fatherly love."[104]

At some early point, the typological interpretation of Isaac's sacrifice made its way into the liturgy of the Mass, prefiguring the sacrifice of Christ in the Eucharist. As the priest extended his hand over the host, he would pray: "Supra quae propitio ac sereno vultu respicere digneris et accepta habere, sicuti accepta habere dignatus es munera pueri justi Abel et *sacrificium Patriarchae nostri Abrahae*."[105] Rosemary Woolf has further observed that a number of illuminated medieval sacramentaries have as their second most frequently illustrated subject (next to the crucifixion) the sacrifice of Isaac.[106] In fact, the sacrifice of Isaac was frequently found as an illumination tucked into the rounded, Carolingian T of the first words of the canon of the Mass, *Te igitur,* visually uniting the Tau cross (symbolizing the crucifixion of Christ) with the sacrifice of Isaac in the Mass.[107]

The linkage of the sacrifice of Isaac to the Eucharist prepares the way for connecting the sacrifice of Isaac not just to the sacrifice of

[101]Ibid., 169.

[102]Ibid., 162. Interestingly, Smith (169) claims that "a cursory examination of western monuments down to the fifteenth century seems to show an almost universal adoption of the Asiatic-Hellenistic Isaac on the altar [*the* invariable element] in representations of the scene." While this may be true of monumental art, it does not seem true of Pontormo's fresco.

[103]For a facsimile, see *Biblia Pauperum, Faksimileausgabe des vierzigblättrigen Armenbibel-Blockbuches in der Bibliothek der Erzdiözesee Estrergom* (Hanau/Main: Werner Dausien, 1967).

[104]Translation from A. N. Didron, vol. 2 of *Christian Iconography* (London: Henry G. Bohn, 1891) Appendix III. The Latin text of the quotation reads: Legitur in Genesi xxii capitulo, cum Abraham gladium extendisset ut filium immolaret angelus domini ipsum de delo prohibuit, dicens ne extendas manum tuam super puerum. Abraham patrem celestem significat qui filium suum scilicet Cristum pro nobis omnibus in cruce immolavit ut per hoc innueret signum amoris paterni. On the right side of the central subject are the Brazen Serpent and a quotation from Numbers 21:9. In keeping with the pattern of the *Biblia Pauperum*, quotations from the Old Testament prophets were found in the upper left and right, in this case from Psalm 22:16 ("They pierced My hands and My feet") and Job 41:1 ("Canst thou draw out Leviathan with a hook?").

[105]J. Wickham Legge, ed. *The Sarum Missal* (Oxford: Clarendon Press, 1916) 223. Authors' ours.

[106]Rosemary Woolf, "The Effect of Typology on the English Mediaeval Plays of Abraham and Isaac," *Speculum* 32 (1957): 806–807.

[107]Ibid.

[108]See Leah Sinanoglou, "The Christ Child as Sacrifice: A Medieval and the Corpus Christi Plays," *Speculum* 48 (1973): 491–509.

[109]See Woolf and Sinanoglou. While both Woolf and Sinanoglou focus on the English medieval plays, their ideas can be extended also to those plays whose origins are Italian; see Luigi Grotto, *Lo Isach* and *La rappresantaxione d'Abraam e d'Isaac suo figliuolo*; see A. D'Ancona, *Origini del teatro italiano* (Turin: E. Loescher, 1891).

[110]Sinanoglou, "The Christ Child as Sacrifice," 502; Woolf, "The Effect of Typology," 813. Petrus Comestor (b. 1100–1110) defends the view that Isaac was a man of twenty-five or thirty years in *Historia Scholastica* and appeals to Josephus as his authority on this point. The minority view among the commentators (that Isaac was a child) is defended by Nicholas of Lyra in *Additio*, ii, and *Replica* for Genesis, xxii, by arguing that had Isaac been an adult his consent would have been required for the sacrifice; cited by Woolf, "The Effect of Typology," 814n.44a. Woolf comments, "It is interesting to notice how, although in exegesis the idea of Isaac as a child was associated with a non-allegorical interpretation of the text, in art and literature it particularly served the purposes of typology."

[111]Shearman, "Rosso, Pontormo, Bandinelli and Others at SS. Annunziata," 154.

[112]A. D'Ancona, *Sacre Rappresentazioni dei secoli XIV, XV, XVI* (Florence: Successori Le Monnier, 1872) 1:43f.

[113]On this point, see also Cooper, "Jacopo Pontormo and Influences from the Renaissance Theater," 381.

Christ on Calvary but to his re-sacrifice in the Mass. As Leah Sinanoglou has demonstrated, the sacrifice in the Mass is that of the Christ child in the elements of the Eucharist.[108] The link between Isaac and the infant Christ was one especially exploited in the medieval Corpus Christi plays.[109] This connection may explain in part why Isaac is almost always depicted in these plays as a child even though medieval commentators were generally uniform in placing Isaac's age at the time at twenty-five or thirty.[110]

Abraham and Isaac plays were also connected to performances of the *Rappresentazioine dell'annunziazione*, and this point brings us closer to Pontormo's depiction. As we noted earlier, John Shearman established that in 1513 Pontormo was working under Andrea di Cosimo Feltrini, refurbishing SS. Annunziata for the forthcoming presentation of the *Rappresentazioine dell'annunziazione*.[111] Of special interest is the fact that D'Ancona has documented that other *sacre rappresentazioni* were featured as interludes within the *Rappresentazione dell'annunziazione*.[112] Among those often featured was *Abraam e Isaac*.[113] Through his participation in the preparation for this observance of the festival at SS. Annunziata (which as we have already observed coincided also with the arrival of Leo X in Florence), Pontormo may have had first-hand exposure not only to a performance of *Abraam e Isaac* and its christological overtones, but would have viewed it within the context of the marvelous spectacle of the *Rappresentazione dell'annunziazione*, where the annunciation was dramatically performed. And just as importantly, Pontormo's audience would have had the same opportunity of viewing Abraham and Isaac within a larger framework of the infancy narrative.

Linking the Sacrifice of Isaac with the Visitation. Already a witness to the connection between the sacrifice of Isaac and the annunciation to Mary, Pontormo (most likely upon the advice of his patrons, the Servites) relocates the link between Isaac and Christ backward from the crucifixion (as in the *Biblia Pauperum*) and forward from the annunciation to the scene of Mary's visitation. Such a connection appears to be unprecedented in the history of art,[114] and Pontormo secures the linkage through several different strategies.

First, the central inscription, ANVE OPTIME DEUS, links the two scenes together. As Wasserman has noted, "Previous attempts to deal with the inscription have been unsatisfactory."[115] Especially problematic is Kurt Forster's conjecture (widely followed) that the ANVE be read as A[N]VE, echoing the angel's greeting to Mary at the annunciation (and part of the liturgical Ave Maria), and rendered "Hail, Best God."[116] As Wasserman observes, "Making a letter irrelevant is not an option when dealing with Medieval and Renaissance inscriptions."[117]

Wasserman suggests, in light of the fact that words are often abbreviated in Greek and Latin inscriptions, that ANVE is actually missing a letter and should be reconstructed as ADNVE ("look favorably").[118] This word is the second-person imperative of *adnuere*. Wasserman bolsters his argument by noting that an 1834 engraved copy of the fresco has an abbreviation sign above it (Figure 6).[119] We

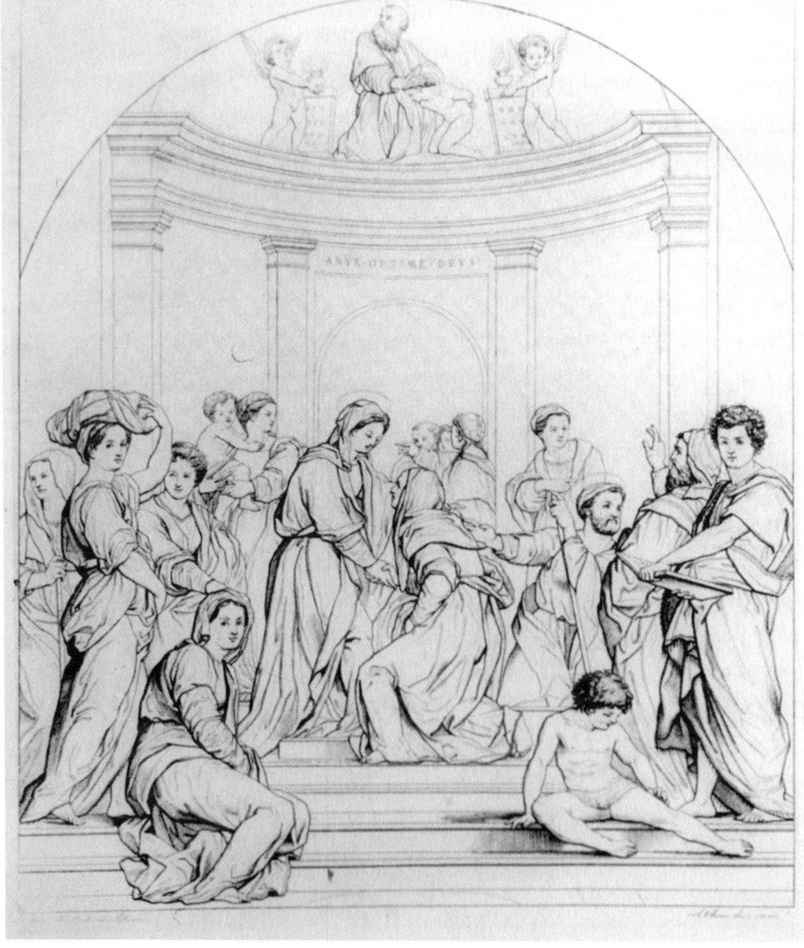

FIG 6.
1834 Copy of Pontormo's *Visitation*. From *Pittura a fresco di Andrea del Sarto e d'altre celebri autori disegnate e incise a contorni da Alessandro Chiari con illustrazion del Professore Melchior Missirini*, Florence, unpaginated.

114Forster, *Pontormo* 129, for example, suggests, "Die Parallele von Isaaks Opferung (Bild im Bilde) mit der Heimsuchung ist ikonographisch merkwürdig."

115Wasserman, "Jacopo Pontormo's Florentine *Visitation*," 43. We wish to express our thanks to Professor Jeff Fish, classics department, Baylor University, who along with Fr. Timothy Verdon, provided invaluable assistance in working on this inscription.

116Forster, *Pontormo*, 129, argues further that the greeting AVE "gibt in ihrer vokativen Form Elisabeths Anrede wieder, während sich die bis zur Unentzifferbarkeit abgekürzten Inschriften in der Kalotte der Deutung enziehen."

117Wasserman, "Jacopo Pontormo's Florentine *Visitation*," 44.

118Ibid., 45.

119Ibid.

accept Wasserman's reconstruction with one slight emendation. In our opinion, the abbreviated word should probably be rendered ANNVE, the favored term for "look favorably" in ecclesiastical Latin.[120] Further, close examination of the engraved copy reveals that the abbreviation siglum is placed above and between the letter N and V, suggesting that it is the second "N" that has been omitted. One might wonder why the artist would omit a letter in this inscription. The best answer may be simply one of symmetry. By reducing the word ANNVE to ANVE, Pontormo is able to balance ANVE on one side with DEVS on the other. This symmetry matches the symmetry of the two flanking inscriptions, each with three rows of three letters each.

We would also slightly modify Wasserman's translation ("Look favorably [upon us], O Best Lord, [for we are of faith]")[121] to something like, "Look favorably, most excellent God," since the vocative, *optime*, is used three times in the Vulgate translation of Luke and Acts to render the honorific Greek term, *kravtiste* ("most excellent Theophilus," Luke 1:3; "most excellent Felix," Acts 24:3; "most excellent Festus," Acts 26:25) and is best rendered this way here as well.[122] The inscription's intention seems to be to invoke divine favor upon both Abraham's and Mary's faithfulness.[123]

Inscription	Forster	Wasserman	Hornik & Parsons
ANVE	A[N]VE OPTIME	ADNVE OPTIME	ANNVE OPTIME
OPTIME	DEVS	DEVS	DEVS
DEVS			
	"Hail, Best God!"	"Look favorably [upon us], O Best Lord, [for we are of faith]"	"Look favorably, most excellent God"

[120]Our examination of the Latin Vulgate, for example, showed no occurrences of *adnuere*, while various forms of *annuere* occurred a number of times. In most instances, the word connoted "motion" (waving of the hand, Luke 5:7; Acts 12:17; 21:40; 24:10; winking the eye, Proverbs 6:13; 10:10), but at least twice the term was used to connote "approval," as in 2 Maccabees 11:15a: "annuit autem Macchabeus precibus Lysiae in omnibus utilitati consulens" (cf. 2 Macc 14:20). This same word is, of course, found on the reverse of a dollar bill, ANNUIT COEPTIS ("he looked favorably on our beginnings").

[121]Wasserman, "Jacopo Pontormo's Florentine *Visitation*," 45.

[122]We should note also that the use of the nominative DEVS with the vocative OPTIME avoids the rather awkward construction DEE. This case is similar to the use in Greek of the nominative "θεо" where a vocative "θεε" is expected.

[123]Our interpretation of the inscription in light of the fresco does not agree in detail with that of Wasserman, who spends more time on the role of John the Baptist in the iconography. Still, there are some interesting connections to John the Baptist. Not only has the "most Excellent God" provided a sacrificial lamb to take Isaac's place, at the Visitation, Christ in the womb is himself acknowledged as "the most excellent God" by John the Baptist (1:44), the first time in Scripture in which Jesus' divinity is explicitly recognized. And this recognition is by John the Baptist, who is the future prophet of his Passion ("Behold the Lamb of God who takes away the sins of the world," John 1:29). The Lamb of God's provision, often a detail in visual depictions of the sacrifice of Isaac, is not missing from this scene as some suggest; rather the ultimate provision is to be found in the Lamb of God. Thus, the sacrifice of a father and of the Father are brought into relationship with Christ's forthcoming passion.

Second, the two scenes are united by the cluster of complex gestures of the figures to the right of Mary and Elizabeth. The figure kneeling to the right of Elizabeth is presumably Joseph, who turns to the standing figure of Zechariah. With his right hand, he points to the scene of Elizabeth and Mary and with his left hand points upward toward the sacrifice of Isaac.[124] Likewise, Zechariah points to the Old Testament scene overhead,[125] and a third female figure behind Joseph directs the viewer's attention toward Zechariah as well. That the viewer is to interpret these scenes in light of each other is made unmistakably clear by these characters in the lower part of the fresco.

Finally, and more tentatively, one may wonder about the identity of the nude child seated on the steps in this light.[126] The figure, when mentioned, is usually treated as a compositional figure and as an example of Pontormo's indebtedness to classicism.[127] There is a remarkable similarity in features between this figure and that of Isaac above. Not only are both nude, but both are also ruddy-complexioned and red-headed. If this figure is meant to represent Isaac, then he, seen in tandem with the prophet holding an open book,[128] standing to the right of the nude, may be taken as a visual reminder that the ancestral promise that God made to Abraham first realized in Isaac's birth has now reached its complete fulfillment in the arrival of the Christ child, a truth to which Mary bears witness.

Role of Mary. Mary also plays an important role in Pontormo's *Visitation.* In addition to standing at the center of the scene and receiving the adoration of Elizabeth, there is a sense in which the inscriptions described above also portray Mary's actions as well. *Numini debet eum* ("He owes him to God") refers to Mary as well: she owes him (Christ) to God. As Timothy Verdon has observed, "With a faith equal to Abraham's—she [Mary] acknowledges her debt to God, offering her son (i.e., emotionally accepting the necessity of his self-oblation, attuning her heart to his own willingness to accept the cross)."[129]

Likewise the second flanking inscription applies to Mary as well: NEC IVRAT VANE, "She does not promise in vain." Earlier in Luke's story, Mary had promised to accept what Gabriel proclaimed God had planned for her: "Behold, I am the handmaid of the Lord; let it be to

[124]We are following here the work of Lorenzo Gnocchi, *Il Pontormo e il Rosso* (Marsilio: Comune di Empoli, 1994) 26, who identifies the kneeling figure as Joseph and notes the significance of the gestures. See also Wasserman, "Jacopo Pontormo's Florentine *Visitation*," 39.

[125]Such gestures are, of course, especially appropriate for Zechariah since he was earlier struck mute because of his disbelief over the oracle of Elizabeth's pregnancy (Luke 1:20). That curse is not removed until John's birth (see Luke 1:67).

[126]For an alternative interpretation, see Wasserman, "Jacopo Pontormo's Florentine *Visitation*," 45.

[127]See Wölfflin, *Classic Art.*

[128]Wasserman, "Jacopo Pontormo's Florentine *Visitation*," 41, makes the tentative suggestion that the figure may represent St. Luke, since, though lacking the stock iconographical symbols, "he alone among the Evangelists describes the Visitation."

[129]Verdon, private correspondence.

me according to your word" (Luke 1:38). Furthermore, Forster also notes certain verbal links between the Latin text of Genesis 22:17 and the earlier annunciation to Mary: *"benedicam tibi et multiplicabo semen tuum"* ("I will bless you and multiply your seed," Gen 22:17); "Ave, gratia plena, Dominus tecum, *benedicta tu in mulieribus*" ("Hail, [you who are] full of grace, the Lord is with you, you are blessed among women," Luke 1:28).[130]

Finally, the plea "ANNVE OPTIME DEUS" ("Most excellent God, look favorably") applies also to Mary. Mary's faithfulness in recognizing her debt to God and in promising to be obedient to God is no less deserving of the same divine approval that falls upon Abraham's faithfulness. This emphasis on Mary (a point made also in Luke) is important because it was precisely Pontormo's patrons, the Servites of SS. Annunziata, who in the early sixteenth century developed to a maximum the theology of Mary as "Mother of Sorrows."[131]

Hermeneutical Reflections

More and more Christian theologians are turning to the rich resources of patristic and medieval interpretation in order to address the vexing questions of modernity and postmodernity.[132] In this light, Jacopo Pontormo's *Visitation* is an unusually rich visual and theological fare. We may reflect briefly on the hermeneutical significance of our painting, especially for heirs of the free church tradition, who face serious challenges from the cultural right and from the cultural left. The intent here is to give a specific, though hopefully not provincial, example of the incorporation of Christian art into the life of contemporary faith communities. Over the past several summers the major denominational expression of Baptist thought in America, the Southern Baptist Convention, has modified its confession of faith in terms of the role of women in marriage and ministry. Women are to be "graciously submissive" to their husbands, and "the office of pastor is limited to men as qualified by Scripture."[133] For those who wish to resist such interpretations on biblical and historical grounds, the visual aspects of the Christian tradition provides relatively unexplored resources. Of course, any hermeneutic dealing with ancient visual texts must reckon with the facts that (1) most of these depictions of women are commissioned,

[130]Forster, *Pontormo*, 129.

[131]See William M. McLoughlin, "Our Lady of Sorrows—a Devotion within a Tradition," *Mary and the Churches* (Dublin: Columbia Press, 1987) 114–21.

[132]See, e.g., David Burrell, *Knowing the Unknowable God: Ibn-Sina, Maimonides, Aquinas* (South Bend IN: University of Notre Dame Press, 1986); Ellen T. Charry, *By the Renewing of Your Minds: The Pastoral Function of Christian Doctrine* (New York: Oxford University Press, 1997); Bruce D. Marshall, *Trinity and Truth* (Cambridge: Cambridge University Press, 2000); John Milbank, *The Word Made Strange: Theology, Language, Culture* (Oxford: Blackwell, 1997); Rowan Williams, *Christian Spirituality: A Theological History from the New Testament to Luther and St. John of the Cross* (Atlanta: John Knox, 1980).

[133]Relevant news articles, opinion editorials, and various responses to the SBC votes may be found in the archives of the Associated Baptist Press. Their web site is http://www.abpnews.com/abpnews/.

executed, approved, and paid for by men and that (2) *our* interests and concerns were not necessarily those of the original audience.[134]

For Pontormo the message *given* is determined to a large degree by the guidance provided by the three inscriptions. Those inscriptions make clear that in this scene, Mary is not defined only or perhaps even primarily by her role as mother. Rather, she, like her ancestor Abraham, is admired for her confession of faith. Like Abraham, Mary too owes her child to God, and the recognition that this child belongs to God, indeed *is* God, is the Epiphany in which both Luke and Pontormo invite their respective audiences to participate. The centrality of Mary is underscored also by the fact that the two male figures, Joseph and Zechariah, are reduced to roles of silent gesturing, roles, ironically, often associated in the biblical tradition with female characters.

But the message *given* is not always exactly the same as the message *received*.[135] Although the inscriptions limit the possible meanings of the *Visitation*, and even if we have deciphered their cryptic messages accurately, there remains a delightful ambiguity. Given the Servites' interest in Mary, the historical meaning given probably does have to do, as we have argued, with the parallels between Abraham and Mary, Isaac and Christ. But, for example, the meaning received by Renaissance women, no doubt a significant part of the worshiping community at the Annunziata, need not have been limited to those parallels. And, of course, the third-person singular verbs allow for either a male or a female subject. Thus, we imagine that some beholders of the Visitation might have applied the inscriptions also to Elizabeth.[136] In this case, Elizabeth, too, owes her unborn child to God, and God has not promised a child to her and Zechariah in vain. Nor is her two-fold confession that Mary is blessed because of her faith (1:45) and that the pre-natal Jesus is "her Lord" (1:43) made in vain. And finally Elizabeth, too, is one upon whom God can look favorably. The appeal of Elizabeth to Renaissance women may be in her relatively ordinary existence.[137]

Mary, from the beginning to the end of her life, was different from other women. She was from a wealthy family, immaculately conceived, had herself a virginal conception, painless birth, perpetual virginity,

[134]Miles, *Image as Insight*, 83.

[135]The language of "message given" and "message received" is that of Miles, *Image as Insight*, 30–35, passim.

[136]We need not conclude that these female viewers were necessarily literate, since over time, the inscriptions could and most likely were interpreted for those illiterate (both male and female) either formally by priests and other ecclesiastical officials or informally by literate friends and companions.

[137]Of course, Elizabeth is not totally obscure, since she is the mother of John the Baptist, patron saint of Florence. Hartt (*History of Italian Renaissance Art*, 556) suggests that the central scene may also be read allegorically. She pays homage to Mary, who in Hartt's reading, represents Rome. Such a reading is, of course, possible, especially given the political and ecclesiastical struggles between Fra. Girolamo Savonarola of Florence and Pope Alexander VI that culminated in Savonarola's martyrdom on 28 May 1498, just a few years before Pontormo's work for the papal visit of 1516. On this conflict, see Donald Weinstein, *Savonarola and Florence: Prophecy and Patriotism in the Renaissance* (Princeton NJ: Princeton University Press, 1970). Savonarola's influence on the art of his day has often been overblown; we have not found any direct connection between Pontormo's *Visitation* and Savonarola's sermons or theology. For a judicious reading of the relationship between Savonarola's preaching and Florentine art, see Ronald M. Steinberg, *Fra Girolamo Savonarola, Florentine Art, and Renaissance Historiography* (Athens: Ohio University Press, 1977).

and at the end of her life was assumed into heaven. Remember that the story of Elizabeth, on the other hand, was little embellished in the literary sources. Nothing much about her own birth or parentage survives, save the name of her mother (which was confused in the tradition). Granted that her advanced age made the conception of John the Baptist an impressive miracle, nonetheless that conception took place in the "old-fashioned" way (even if the emphasis here was on "old"!). And despite the fact that in one late medieval work the angels Michael and Gabriel dig Elizabeth's grave while the souls of Zacharias and Simeon sing, Elizabeth dies as she lived, in an ordinary manner.[138] Evidently her frequent appearance in visual depictions is dependent almost entirely on someone else—John the Baptist, Zechariah, or in this case, Mary—and the importance of this scene, here placed as it is in a sequence of the Virgin's life, is for Mary's, not Elizabeth's, life. Nonetheless, Elizabeth is the first human character in Luke to recognize the true identity of Jesus, calling him "her Lord," and that before he was even born. She functions as a prophet even though she is not explicitly called one. The point here is that in Elizabeth, the early sixteenth-century community of women had a resource for evoking an emotionally satisfying, spiritually edifying, and politically powerful interpretation that if God could look favorably on the rather ordinary saint Elizabeth because of her faith, God could look favorably also on the now anonymous but faithful lives of women who first experienced this painting. Thus, the *Visitation* is also a potential resource for those interested in drawing on ancient sources to address contemporary issues, in this case, the role of women in the faith and practice of contemporary Christian communities.

On the other hand, Pontormo's *Visitation* provides a resource for addressing the interpretations of the cultural left. In her recent book *Abraham on Trial: The Social Legacy of Biblical Myth*, Carol Delaney has argued that the Abraham story is the foundational myth that lies at the root of much if not all child abuse and violence against women and children in the West.[139] Part of the problem with Delaney's work is that she does not take into account sufficiently the history of biblical interpretation that has struggled with precisely the same issues she has raised about this and other texts. Luke Timothy Johnson has observed,

[138]Cf. *The Life of John according to Serapion.*

[139]Carol Delaney, *Abraham on Trial: The Social Legacy of Biblical Myth* (Princeton NJ: Princeton University Press, 1998). Delaney's conclusion is opposite that of Jon Levenson (*Death and Resurrection of the Beloved Son* [New Haven CT: Yale University Press, 1993], who argues that the Abraham story works against a pattern of child sacrifice that was sporadically practiced in the ancient Near East, even among some Israelites.

"The function of such interpretation within both Judaism and Christianity has not been to reinforce the violent tendencies of the stories, but to mitigate and transmute them. Midrash and allegory represent strategies of reading within religious traditions that seek to combine loyalty with criticism, that try to save those aspects of the text that give life while also challenging those elements that are morally questionable."[140] Pontormo's *Visitation* represents one allegorical reading that emphasizes the life-giving aspect of the Abraham story, and as such functions as a kind of Christian midrash on Genesis 22—a midrash that could still well serve contemporary communities of faith in their theological reflection and liturgical appropriation of these sacred texts.

CONCLUSION

Drawing on liturgical, visual, and exegetical sources, Jacopo Pontormo stands in a long tradition of interpreters who have connected the suffering of Christ with the sacrifice of Isaac. What is new in Ponormo's work is the parallel between Abraham and Mary. The Renaissance worshiping community, prompted to contemplate the Epiphany by the minor figures in the scene, may have thus first experienced Pontormo's and his patrons' visualization of the Visitation text. So also may the modern worshiper add his or her voice to the petition ascribed to Abraham, Mary, and yes, even Elizabeth: "Most Excellent God, look favorably" upon us as well, in the confidence that God "does not promise in vain"!

[140]Luke Timothy Johnson, "How Not to Read the Bible," *Commonweal* 126 (July 1999): 24.

8.

Jacopo Bassano: A Case for Painting as Visual Exegesis

Paolo Berdini
Stanford University

When presented with the task of visualizing a text, the painter is engaged firstly, and quite naturally, as a reader. We know that reading, rather than being subject to patterns of universal validity, registers at any moment the prerogatives—of gender, class, or belief among others—that the reader brings to the text. These prerogatives are historical and phenomenological and in that capacity affect the reader's reading of the text. Conversely, reading is conditioned by the circumstances under which a text reaches its reader. If it is a book, for example, its production is such that the text itself requires an apparatus of rituals and codes that makes it readable while conditioning its reading. The ways in which a preface, an introduction, or a footnote (not to mention the format, possible illustrations, production, and even the price) can condition the reading of a book are easy to recognize.[1] These procedures constitute the intermediary zone, which

[1] See G. Genette, *Introduction à l'architext* (Paris: Seuil, 1979), and particularly idem, *Seuils* (Paris: Editions du Seuil, 1987) 7: "Mais ce texte se présente rarement à l'état nu, sans le renfort et l'accompagnement d'un certain nombre de productions, elles-mêmes verbales ou non, comme un nom d'auteur, un titre, une préface, des illustrations, dont on ne sait pas toujours si l'on doit ou non considérer qu'elles lui appartiennent, mais qui en tout cas l'entourent et le prolongent, précisément pour le *présenter*, au sens habituel de ce verbe, mais aussi en son sens le plus fort: pour le *rendre présent*, pour assurer sa présence au monde, sa 'réception' et sa consommation, sous le forme, aujourd'hui du moins, d'un livre."

activates reading by mediating access to the text from the outside and by conditioning movements within it.[2] They are relevant to the experience of any reader, and there is no reason to believe that the painter is an exception. If I insist on the importance of the circumstances of reading and the prerogatives of the reader at the risk of restating the obvious, namely that a text cannot exist outside its reader, it is because I believe—and this is my thesis—that fundamentally painting visualizes a reading and not a text. Translated into simpler and linear terms, what I am referring to is a process that goes something like this: the painter reads a text and translates his reading into a problem in representation, to which he offers a solution—the image. In that image, the beholder encounters not the text in the abstract, but the painter's reading of the text, so that the effect the image has on the beholder is a function of what the painter wants the beholder to experience in the text. This process could be called the trajectory of visualization.

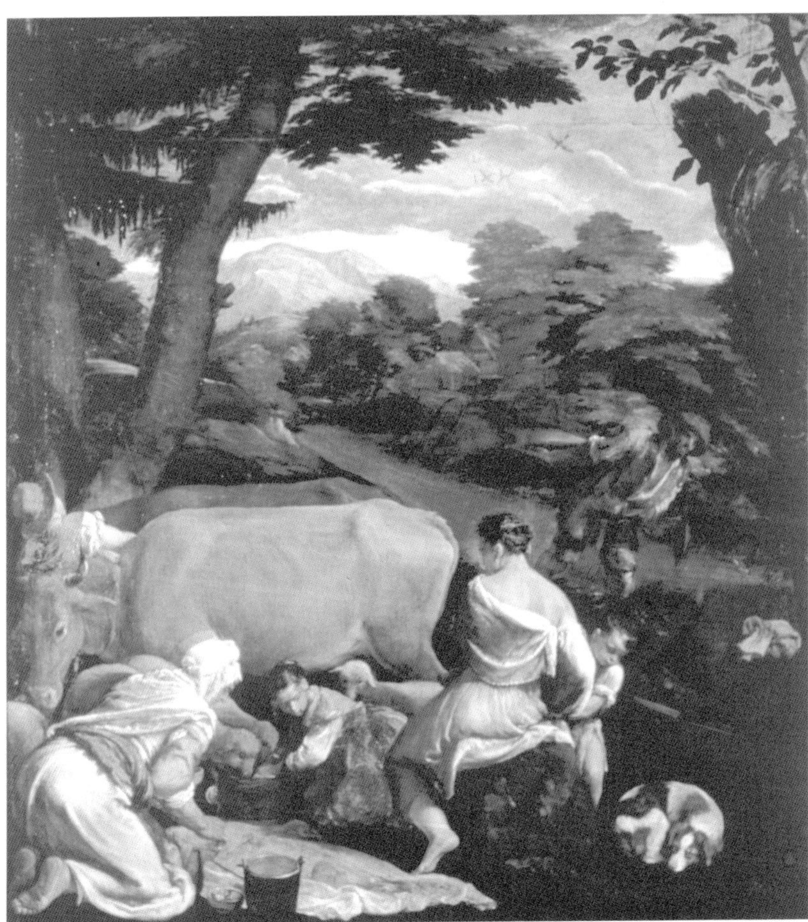

FIG 1.
Jacopo Bassano,
The Parable of the Sower, c. 1561.
Madrid, *Thyssen-Bornemizsa Collection.*

Before presenting my case, which will consist of a discussion of two paintings by Jacopo Bassano which, for different though related reasons, bear a problematic relation to the text they visualize, *The Parable of the Sower* of circa 1562 in the Thyssen Collection now in Madrid (Figure 1),[3] and *The Baptism of Christ* of 1592, in a private collection in New York (Figure 2),[4] I need to be a little more specific about reading: reading of Scripture in general, and reading of Scripture in the second half of the sixteenth century in the Veneto in particular.

Beginning with the first generation of Christians, scriptural reading has been described as a mode of comprehension that is hierarchical and highly formalized, that is, as a gradual engagement with the text intended to guide the reader from an advocacy of the text's meaning to an assertion of its existential significance.[5] What is important to observe is that in order to achieve its goal, this form of reading, Christian exegesis, is constructed in such a way as to be able to monitor the effect of the text on its reader. It does so by addressing several dimensions of the text, of which the narratival is just the initial one. It is followed by others—allegory, tropology, and anagogy—that gradually depragmatize, so to speak, the reader's response and eventually spiritualize it. Ideally, scriptural reading should resolve into sacramental desire, so that in the end the text or, more precisely, the reading of the text will have taken the reader quite far from the mere apprehension of what it tells as a story. It follows that what a painting visualizes is not necessarily limited to the narrative component of the text. My point is that painting does not aim at simply substituting the narrative of the text, at showing what the text tells as a story, but rather at presenting the beholder with an experience that, like reading for the reader, exceeds the narratival aspect of the text and proposes itself as a form of exegesis, a visual exegesis. If the narrative of the text is the same for any period, society, or painter, not so its exegesis, which is subject to discursive strategies of various kinds. In the Veneto in the second half of the sixteenth century, the project that historians have

3 See Alessandro Ballarin, cat. no. 189, in *Le siècle de Titien*, exh. cat., ed. Michel Laclotte (Paris: Réunion des Musées nationaux, 1993) 741–42, with bibliography; cf. D. Ekserdjian, *Old Master Paintings from the Thyssen-Bornemizsa Collection*, exh. cat. (London-Milan-Lugano, 1983) 28–29.

4 The picture may be identical with the one described by G. Verci, *Notizie intorno alla vita e alle opere de' Pittori, Scultori e Architti della citta' di Bassano* (Venice: Apresso Giovanni Gatte, 1775) 92, at no. 64: "Il battesimo di N. S. da S. Gio. Battista, cioe' una Tavola d'altare sbozzata," in the inventory dated April 27, 1592, drawn up in Jacopo's house, and/or with the one with the same title mentioned by C. Ridolfi, *Le maraviglie dell'arte* (Venice: Presso Gia, Battista Sgaua, 1648) 389: "una pala del Battesimo di Christo, che fu una delle ultime opere sue non finita." It should be noted that neither Ridolfi nor Verci, surprisingly enough, describes the picture as a nocturne. The canvas was first published by L. Frohlich-Bume, "Unbekannte Gemälde des Jacopo Bassano," *Belvedere* 10 (1931): 121–25, and later by W. R. Rearick, "Jacopo Bassano's Last Painting, the 'Baptism of Christ,'" *Arte Veneta* 21 (1967): 102–107, who claimed that the New York *Baptism* "is the only extant treatment of this theme to be painted by any member of the dal Ponte family with the single exception of Leandro's later signed altar at the Catecumini in Venice...." Another version does, however, exist and is presently in the Museo di Castelvecchio in Verona (Inv. 828). This second version, which seems "sbozzata" as well—particularly in areas which are dark in the New York version—is, however, not a nocturne. Recently, Rearick, in "Life and Work of J. B.," 170, has acknowledged the presence of the Verona version, and attributed it to Gerolamo Dal Ponte.

5 On the theory and history of Christian exegesis, see the fundamental study by H. De Lubac, *Exégèse médiévale*, 2 vols. (Paris: Aubier, 1959); see also B. Smalley, *The Study of the Bible in the Middle Ages* (Oxford: Clarendon Press, 1941); G. R. Evans, *The Language and Logic of the Bible* (Cambridge: Cambridge University Press, 1984) esp. 72–124; H. Caplan, "The Four Senses of Scriptural Interpretation and Medieval Theory of Preaching," *Speculum* 4 (1929): 282–90; and W. Dilthey, "Die Enstehung der Hermeneutik," in *Schriften* (Leipzig, 1924) 5: 7–23.

called the Christianization of the countryside advocated specific forms of exegesis that served to actualize the scriptural text for the rural populations.[6] What is historical about the paintings that I am going to discuss is above all the specific quality of attention to the text that motivates their visualization.

I have suggested that both *The Parable of the Sower* and *The Baptism of Christ* bear problematic relationships to the scriptural text. I should specify that they are problematic from the standpoint of standard art historical notions of text. In the case of *The Parable of the Sower* the relation of the image to scriptural text has previously been denied altogether, and the image is not even considered religious;[7] as for *The Baptism of Christ* its main visual characteristic, that of being a nocturne, is dismissed as an extra-textual stylistic license.[8] What is at stake, however, is not merely the restitution of these images to proper textual status, but, and more importantly, the form of beholding that they advocate, and what it tells us about the dynamic of beholding in general. The literature is unanimous in labelling *The Parable of the Sower* simply a pastoral.[9] The reasons for doing so are easy to under-

[6]The notion of Christianization (*Christianisierung* in German historiography and *Cristianizzazione* in Italian) has been the focus of debate among historians of early modern Europe since the 1970s. Independent research on "social discipline" and "ecclesiastical discipline" has revealed the presence of similar attitudes and patterns in religious and secular contexts so as to justify the belief that a common form of discipline (*Disziplinierung* in the original German formulation) underlies both. The term Christianization (less felicitous in English than in German) is intended to convey the sense of discipline, both social and institutional, grounded on religious discourse. *Konfessionalisierung* is also a related term, indicating the form of social control exerted by confession and similar forms of discipline of the conscience. The literature on the theory and applicability of notions is predominantly German. Italian studies have focused particularly on Lombardy and the Veneto in years before and after the Council of Trent (The Istituto storico italo-germanico di Trento and its publications have played a leading role in Italian scholarship). For the theory and historiography, see W. Reinhard, "Gegenreformation als Modernisierung? Prolegomena zu einer Theorie des konfessionellen Zeitalters," *Archiv für Reformationsgeschichte* 68 (1977): 226–51; idem, "Konfession und Konfessionalisierung in Europa," in *Bekenntnis und Geschichte. Die Confessio Augustana im historischen Zusammenhang*, ed. W. Reinhard (Munich: Vögel, 1981) 165–89; J. C. Spalding, "Discipline as a Mark of the True Church in its Sixteenth Century Context," in *Piety, Politics and Ethics. Reformation Studies in Honor of G. W. Forell*, ed. C. Lindberg (Kirksville, MO: Sixteenth Century Journal Publishers, Northeast Missouri State University, 1984) 119–38; W. Schulze, "Gerhard Oestreichs Begriff 'Sozialdisziplinierung' in der frühen Neuzeit," *Zeitschrift für Historische Forschung* 14 (1987): 265–302; P. Blickle, ed. *Kommunalisierung und Christianisierung. Voraussetzungen und Folgen der Reformation 1400–1600*, Zeitschrift für Historische Forschung Beiheft 9 (Berlin: Duncker & Humblot, 1989); W. Reinhard, "Disciplinamento sociale, confesionalizzazione, modernizzazione. Un discorso storiografico,"in *Disciplina dell'anima, disciplina del corpo e disciplina della società moderna*, ed. P. Prodi, Annali dell'Istituto storico italo-germanico di

Trento. Quaderno 40 (Bologna: Società editrice il Mulino, 1994) 101–23; H. Schilling, "Chiese confessionali e disciplinamento sociale. Un bilancio provvisorio della ricerca storica," ibid., 125–60. The attempt to frame artistic patronage within these notions has produced remarkable materials in terms of documentary findings, though the persistence of outdated conceptualizations (the notion of Mannerism as the style of the Counter Reformation, for example) has inhibited new critical acquisitions. Cfr. the art historical contribution to important symposia such as P. Prodi, ed. *Bernardo Clesio e il suo tempo*, 2 vols. (Rome: Bulzoni, 1988) and L. Dal Prà, ed. *I Mandruzzo e l'Europa. I principi-vescovi di Trento tra Papato e Impero 1539–1658* (Trent: Castello del Buonconsiglio, 1993).

[7]The most recent attempt to de-Christianize Bassano's image has been made by R. W. Rearick, "From Arcady to the Barnyard," in *The Pastoral Landscape*, ed. J. Dixon Hunt (Washington: National Gallery of Art, 1992) 137–59: "Jacopo might well have painted the biblical parable of the sower, as has generally been thought since the Jacopo Bassano exhibition in Venice in 1957. However, an attentive reading of Virgil's passage in the *Georgics* that treats the plowing techniques necessary to prepare soil for the field crops, the best procedures for sowing various types of seed, and the dangers to these seeds for voracious birds shows that much more of Jacopo's picture can be accounted for in that text than in the Bible." There are no signs in Bassano's picture of such pedagogic intentions and, moreover, it is hard to take Virgil's *Georgics* for the sort of agricultural manual implied by Rearick. As Pliny explains in his *Historia naturalis*, liber XVIII, Virgil is not concerned in the *Georgics* with the practice of agriculture—for which purpose he recommends the reading of Varro's *Re Rustica*—but with its virtues. Moreover, the notion of *labor* in Virgil seems to require some further observations. Virgil's language of *labor* is analogous to the language of *bellum*, that is, of war, and in fact, the work of the farmer in the *Georgics* evokes images of constant struggle against asperities. The work of the sower, in particular, is often described in military terms, such as *semen iacere*, an evocation of the belligerant *tellum iacere*. The notion that "the Georgic farmer is a destroyer, like a soldier in war" (A. Betensky, "The Farmer's Battle," in *Virgil Aschrean Song. Ramus' Essays on the Georgics*, ed. A. Boyle [Victoria: Berwick, 1979] 108–19) is what gives agriculture the "Roman" virtue, perfected in the battlefield, of overcoming hostile forces. This notion of struggle against nature is what appealed to Christian exegetes of Virgil, as it corresponded to the concept of labor as a form of redemption advocated in Scripture. On Virgil's notion of *labor* as unrelated to agricultural competence and dependence on human struggle for survival, see particularly W. Richter's commentary in *Georgica* (Munich: M. Hueber, 1957) 134–41; L. Habermann, "Varro and two Military Similes in Virgil's Georgics," *Classical Bulletin* 53 (1977): 54–56; M. Carilli, "Aspetti lessicali dell'umanizzazione di elementi naturali nelle Georgiche: la terminologia del 'labor' e del 'bellum,'" *Civiltà classica e cristiana* 7 (1986): 171–79. Rearick had previously referred to the picture as a biblical pastoral, and his hermeneutic backpedaling is somewhat surprising; see W. R. Rearick, "Jacopo Bassano's Later Genre Paintings," *Burlington Magazine* 110 (1968): 241–49; idem, "Tiziano e Bassano," in *Tiziano e Venezia. Atti del Convegno Internazionale di Studi, Venezia 1976* (Vicenza: N. Pozza, 1980) 371–374; and idem, "Life and Works of Jacopo dal Ponte," 110: "*The Parable of the Sower* in which the biblical text…is freshly illustrated with the device that would become a Dal Ponte trademark."

[8]E. Panofsky, *Problems in Titian. Mostly Iconographic* (New York: New York University Press, 1969) 53, offered a definition of the nocturne as "a picture in which the illumination is exclusively provided by artificial sources of light and/or the moon." Though restricted to conditions of illuminations, the definition was open to accepting the symbolism and iconography of light.

[9]See D. Rosand, "Giorgione, Venice, and the Pastoral Vision," in *Places of Delight: The Pastoral Landscape*, ed. R. C. Cafritz et al. (Washington: Phillips Collection in association with the National Gallery of Art, 1988) 20–81, who observed that "Titian, whose inclination was to energize the landscape, took a leading and influential role in transposing pastoral into georgic, particularly in

stand once one accepts what Ernst Gombrich has called "the primacy of genre," an attitude according to which recognition of the genre of an image is the primary and conditioning act in the experience of beholding it. Given the absence of any religious motif, labelling this image a *pastoral* may seem initially justified.[10] What I would like to argue is that the visualization of a parable contains a critique of that attitude; and ultimately the opposite is true: it is the beholding of an image that determines its genre.

The parable is a literary form in which language and images derived from ordinary life become the metaphorizing agents of religious discourse.[11] But if the ordinary aspect of the parable, its narrative form, contains no religious signs, how does it manage to *refer to* something outside what it actually states as narrative? In other

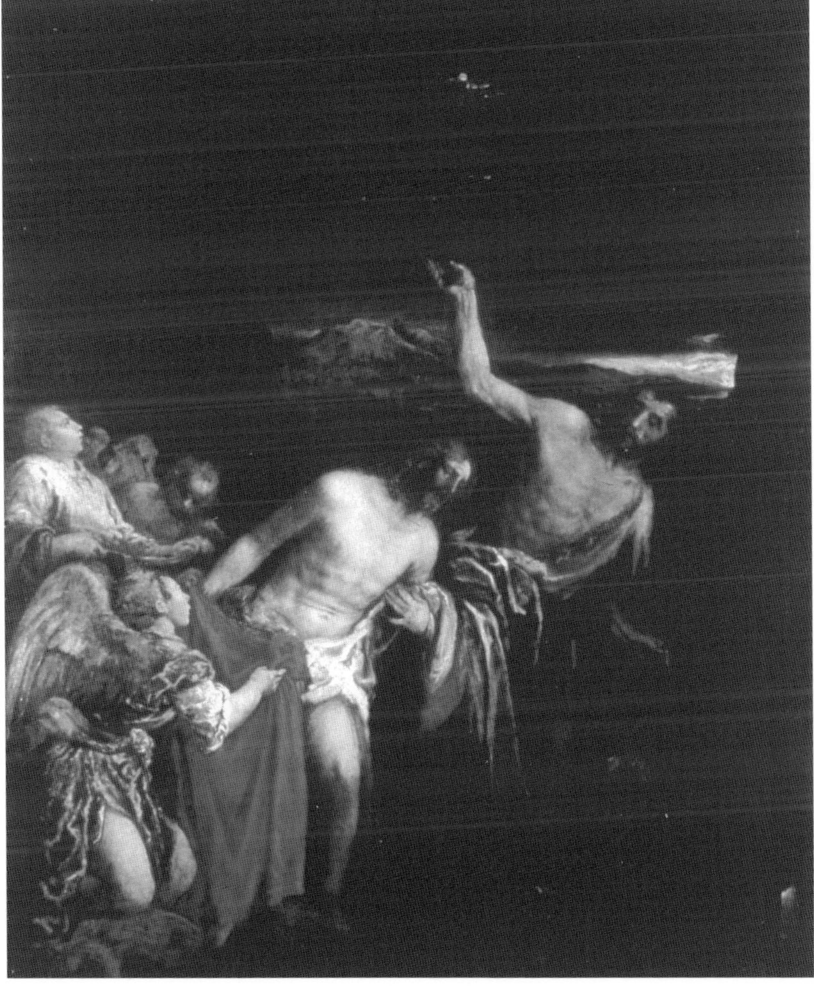

FIG 2.
Jacopo Bassano,
*The Baptism
of Christ*. 1592.
New York,
Private Collection.

his woodcut design of *Landscape with a Milkmaid*. . . . The basic structure of this landscape, with its distance between foreground figures and the fortified town on the horizon, may evoke certain pastoral values, but the figures themselves hardly have any time to enjoy any escape from the cares of life: no idyllic nostalgia here, no music, no love. This couple—rather, family—must tend the flocks and cattle, feed the goats and milk the cows. Whatever escape from urban care may continue to inform the georgic landscape, it assumes the form of a practical alternative: labor in the country. Jacopo Bassano (1510–1592) and his studio made a specialty of catering to the growing urban taste for such imagery (*The Parable of the Sower*). When such labor is freely chosen, however, that freedom assigns work a very positive value indeed" (67–69). Thematically the parable is closer to the *Georgics* than to the *Eclogues*, yet in the parable labor has no value, since it is just a metaphor for religious discourse. The problem with a search for correspondence with classical (Virgilian) sources is that it overlooks the parable as a literary genre.

[10]E. H. Gombrich, "Introduction: Aims and Limits of Iconology," in *Symbolic Images: Studies in the Art of the Renaissance II* (London: Phaidon, 1972) 5.

[11]According to C. H. Dodd, *The Parables of the Kingdom* (New York: Scribner, 1936) 16: "At its simplest the parable is a metaphor or simile drawn from nature or common life, arresting the hearer by its vividness or strangeness, and leaving the mind in sufficient doubt about its precise application to tease it into active thought."

words, how does a reader become aware that the text reveals something else besides its evident narrative content?

The parable is contained within another narrative, that of the Gospels, and may thus be understood as a component, a unit that needs only to be properly situated within that larger whole to acquire sense and order. But it could also be argued that, as a literary form, the parable activates a metaphorical process that makes the reader gradually aware of the religious import of the text.[12]

As a problem in visualization, this alternative presents itself to the painter in analogous ways. He can remit to the larger narrative the task of disclosing the religious *referent* to the viewer by representing Jesus as speaker, for example, in the very act of preaching, and thus rendering the nature—and message—of the image unequivocal. In Erhard Schön's print of the *Parable of the Sower*, the presence of Christ and Martin Luther, not to mention the inscription above the image, militate against any possible misreading of the scene (Figure 3).[13]

The painter may also take a different approach, by giving an image of ordinary life—an image, again, that is not *explicitly* religious—metaphorizing traits that activate a process of what could be called referential response, thereby allowing the viewer to complement the narrative with what he or she comes to experience as the religious content of the image. In such cases, the question confronting the

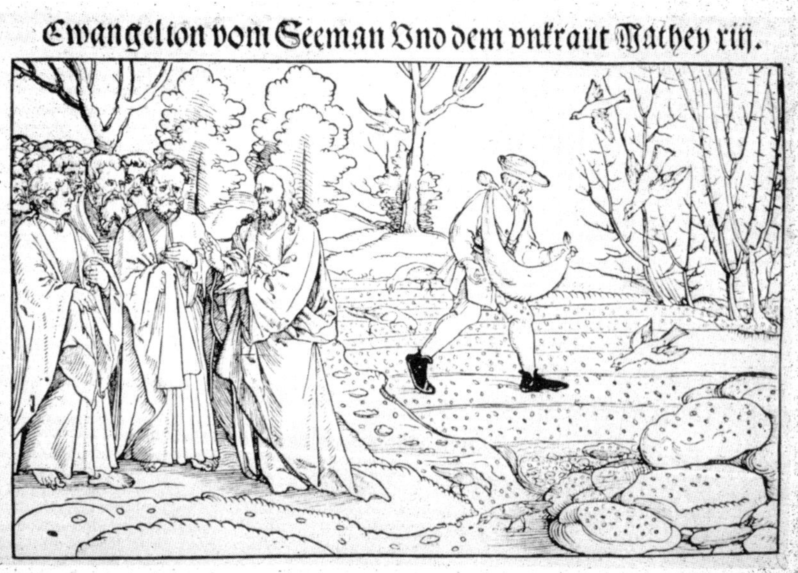

FIG 3. Erhard Schön, *The Parable of the Sower*, c. 1525. Woodcut.

174   *Interpreting Christian Art*

beholder becomes analogous to the question addressed to the reader: how to recognize an image of ordinary life as a religious image? Essentially, the painter has to put in motion a set of responses that eventually lead the viewer to reconsider what he or she sees in light of what he or she knows or suspects. This involves the ability to activate the metaphor, and thereby rescue religious discourse from literal obliviousness.

Bassano's *Parable of the Sower* represents a scene of country life with women and men engaged in outdoor activities. The ordinary nature of such activities is affirmed by the quasi-random placement of the figures within the landscape. At first sight, no organizing narrative or hierarchy of performance seems detectable aside from the figures' plausible, if not entirely self-evident, actions. The gazes of the three women in the foreground converge towards the loaf of bread, placed quite emphatically on the white cloth on the ground. Behind them, a man sows seed and a young boy attends to the oxen drawing the plough; together they present the instrument and the labor necessary for sowing the soil. The sack containing seeds on the ground to the right completes the display of equipment required for such agricultural activities. The landscape is also attuned to this construction. The brown color of the trees, the crisp air, the cloudy sky, and the cold light falling on the figures signal the season, even the month, and time of the day customarily chosen for sowing. Whereas in the middle ground the full range of tools, expertise, and labor required by this practice— which is traditionally left to men to enact and coordinate—is presented with a kind of meticulousness, in the foreground the activities of the women are not displayed with the same coherent didacticism germane to a single operation like sowing. Their actions are logically unrelated and only spatially coordinated; and what actually unites them is the sudden interruption of their actions motivated, without apparent cause, by the presence of the loaf of bread on the cloth.

Since the activities of the women are not overtly productive, they have been considered an appendix of the sowing project, such that the subject of the painting has been reduced to a farmer at work with his family standing by. As sowing and harvest, seed and bread, are

[14] The parable's employment of so-called "shock tactics" has been discussed by J. J. Vincent, "The Parables of Jesus as Self-Revelation," *Studia Evangelica* 18 (1959): 84–109; J. Jeremias, *The Parables of Jesus* (New York: Scribner, 1963) 29–34; A. N. Wilder, *The Language of the Gospel* (New York: Harper & Row, 1964) 85; and R. Funk, *Language, Hermeneutics, and the Word of God* (Philadelphia: Fortress, 1964) 160.

[15] P. Ricoeur, "Biblical Hermeneutics," 30: "The parable, it seems to me, is the conjunction of a *narrative form* and a *metaphorical process*".

[16] Funk, *Language, Hermeneutics, and the Word of God*, 158–59: "Metaphorical language, it was suggested, does not look *at* the phenomenon, but *through* it. Metaphor seeks to rupture the grip of tradition on man's apprehension of the world in order to permit a glimpse of another world, which is not really different but a strangely familiar world. Metaphor, moreover, remains temporally open-ended, thus permitting the hermeneutical potential of the vision conjured up to make its own claim upon the future. It is in these senses that parabolic imagery is genuinely metaphorical."

certainly consequential acts and their relation unquestionably one of cause and effect, they have been taken to present the requisite components of a statement about the essential dynamics of agrarian existential determinism: work and reward.

There are incongruities in Bassano's picture that resist surrender to literal description. First, the image actually says little about sowing, and what it does show is incongruous from the standpoint of agrarian practice. The farmer is sowing with peculiar randomness, and seeds are cast onto portions of the ground that are ill-disposed to fertilization. Some fall victim to voracious birds ready to snatch them up; some are thrown absent-mindedly on a path; others fall on rocks and among thorns. The sower's incompetence is suspicious, and makes it apparent that the image neither illustrates nor provides instruction in the practice of sowing. Supplementing this observation with attention to the dramatic—and ostentatious—presentation of the harvest in the foreground, the viewer begins to suspect that the image may not be about the practice of sowing but rather about its outcome and, more specifically, about the receptivity of the soil. The relationship between inadequacy of performance and abundance of results signals that the logic and discursive position of the ordinary and the out-of-the-ordinary have been deliberately reversed: the unusual behavior of the sower is taken as ordinary, while the good harvest, an expected consequence of any rational sowing, is valued as out-of-the-ordinary.[14] What this situation activates in the beholder is a gradual awareness of being in the presence of a peculiar representation of ordinary life, in which internal incongruities may be the vehicle of a critique of literal manifestations. The presence of parabolic discourse becomes evident as soon as the figures in the image are seen to contradict rather than fulfill the roles that realism assigns to them. That is, what ultimately makes the parable in Bassano's picture recognizable is the tension between the representation of the ordinary *vis-à-vis* an insufficient compliance with those modalities of customary behavior that would make that reality characterizable as ordinary.[15] And if the parable fulfills its *mimetic* requirements, it is only as a function of a *metaphorical* reality, so that ultimately the beholder can only make sense of the image by engaging a metaphorical register.[16]

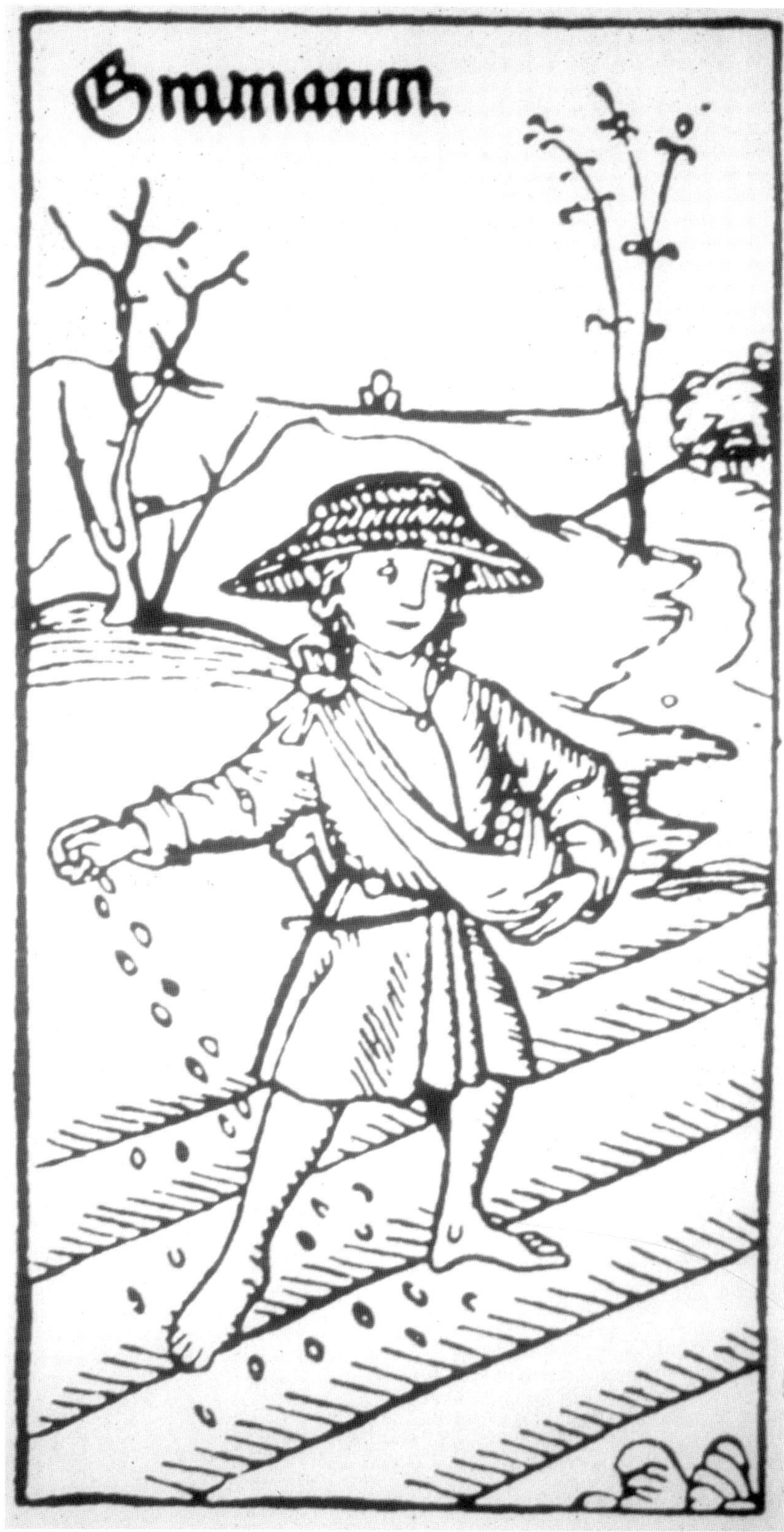

FIG 4.
Anonymous,
Grammatica.
fifteenth-century
woodcut.

Disclosure of the metaphor comes from a closer look at the convergence of the three women's gazes on the loaf of bread. The women's simultaneous and sudden torsion indicates an unexpected response to sound, not to vision. That is, the women's gaze is stimulated by a call, and what it in fact discloses is the parabolic equivalence of seed and word. The three female figures witness the emergence of the fructified word; they are the good soil on which the seed falls. What Bassano visualizes is their hearing the word. That the equivalence seed=word possesses a visual tradition of its own is attested by this fifteenth-century woodcut of the sower as *Grammatica* (Figure 4).

The complex visual status of the woman in *contrapposto* at the center of Bassano's picture plays a key role in the metaphorizing process. She is the agent of metaphor, participating with her gaze in the shock of recognition of the fructifying effect of the heard word and enacting, at the same time, a logical and visual link between the seed and the word. She is strategically located between sowing and harvest, between emission and reception; and the diagonal that her averted gaze establishes between the farmer and the bread on the white cloth makes her the agent of the parabolic beholding of the picture. Her *contrapposto* is what prevents a literal view of the image from prevailing and forces its replacement by a metaphorical one grounded on the equivalence of seed and word.

Seen from the rear, the figure draws the beholder's attention from right to left and, in so doing, gives cohesion to the whole image by twice subverting the prerogative of narratival representation. First, she inverts the viewer's sense of direction, at least that which is posited by apologists of left to right reading of pictures. Secondly, contrary to the Albertian notion of the figure who addresses the beholder from within the narrative, the figure seen from behind blocks the beholder's view, impelling a crisis of intelligibility in and of the narrative. The figure breaks the pictorial continuity that typifies humanist representations of dramatic narrative and demands from the beholder a different mode of unification of what is present in the visual field. The figure that stages a *crisis* of the narrative, she is also the figure of *dénouement,* for she resolves the crisis of the literal intelligibility of the picture by encouraging the beholder to adopt a metaphoric register in order to make sense of it.

The presence of the three women is not mentioned in the biblical text of the parable. Their inclusion is due to Bassano, though there is nothing arbitrary about it, quite the contrary. The parable is in fact an open form that leaves to the reader the task of complementing its narrative in light of its metaphor. The question at this point is: Why are women chosen to disclose the metaphor? Before the word was understood and processed through *intelligentia scripturarum*, it had to be heard, received, accepted, and passed along. Traditionally, woman is not the agent of speech—she does not preach, and thus has no place in either the elaboration or the delivery of the word. She is the agent of hearing, of the initial process of activating the word without which all the rest would not be possible; there would be no Scriptures had not the woman *heard* the word. Hers is the power—and agency—of reception and transformation, as she is in fact the good soil in which the seed is fructified. The agrarian metaphor is justified by the notion that she possesses the yeast necessary for the transformation of the seed into bread, a train of argument that inevitably leads to the mariological notion of *Virgo fermentata*, where the word becomes flesh.

To test the notion of painting as visual exegesis one must ask then whether it also holds true for images that visualize unproblematic texts, by which I mean texts that pose no apparent challenge either in finding them or in interpreting them.

When we consider an image like Bassano's *Baptism of Christ* and proceed in the iconographic practice of checking the image against the text, to use Panofsky's expression, that is against the narrative of the synoptics, we are presented not with textual riddles but only with the relative problem of having to account for an unexpected discrepancy. In Bassano's picture the event of Christ's baptism is represented as nocturnal, even though it is not so recorded in the text. I spare you the rationale that students of the Venetian Renaissance have offered as explanation: short-sightedness of the elderly painter, congenital darkening of a painter's late style, Counter-Reformatory gloom and the like. The alternative posed by the image to the beholder seems to be quite radical: should the primary visual interest of Bassano's *Baptism*

[17] L. B. Alberti, *La Pittura* (Venice, 1547) 19.

of Christ—its being a nocturne—be considered just another form of illumination, such that everything represented would remain the same no matter how it is illuminated, and light, therefore, be understood as having no effect on beholding? Or should the nocturnal illumination be taken as an indication that the image visualizes dimensions of the text that exceed its narrative and may, therefore, pertain to the painter's specific reading of it? Ultimately, to ask why the representation of the event is nocturnal even though the event does not take place at night is to ask whether light plays an exegetical role in the painter's visualization of the text and, conversely, in the beholder's experience of the image.

In the case of Bassano's *Baptism of Christ* the initial act of beholding may consist of an acknowledgment of the ways in which the image invites [asks] the beholder to reconcile his/her response to the dark with the knowledge that the event represented is not recorded in the Gospels as having taken place at night. The nocturne engineers a contrast between response and narrative—a contrast that may find the beholder initially unprepared—and rather than dismiss that which disagrees with the narrative of the text as artistic license, the beholder might work out his/her modified expectations, following the instructions given by the image as indicative of the specific encounter with the text that the painter proposes. Initially, and as a hypothesis, we may ask to what extent the nocturne is a narratival strategy, and look for explanation in Renaissance theories of narrative painting, from Alberti to Armenini. But we won't find any. Such theories propose that the function of illumination is simply to adhere to the mutual interplay of textuality and vision implicit in the primacy of the *historia*. From these texts we learn that light is not an agent *per se,* but a component of the picture that is entirely subject to the controlling agency of *disegno* and the ethical and aesthetical agenda of *historia.* As Alberti explained, the "use of white and black without much discretion" is to be avoided because it is capable of diverting the narratival drive.[17]

To answer our pending question—of why the baptism of Christ is represented as nocturnal—we may turn to the picture, investigating first the phenomenology of its beholding.

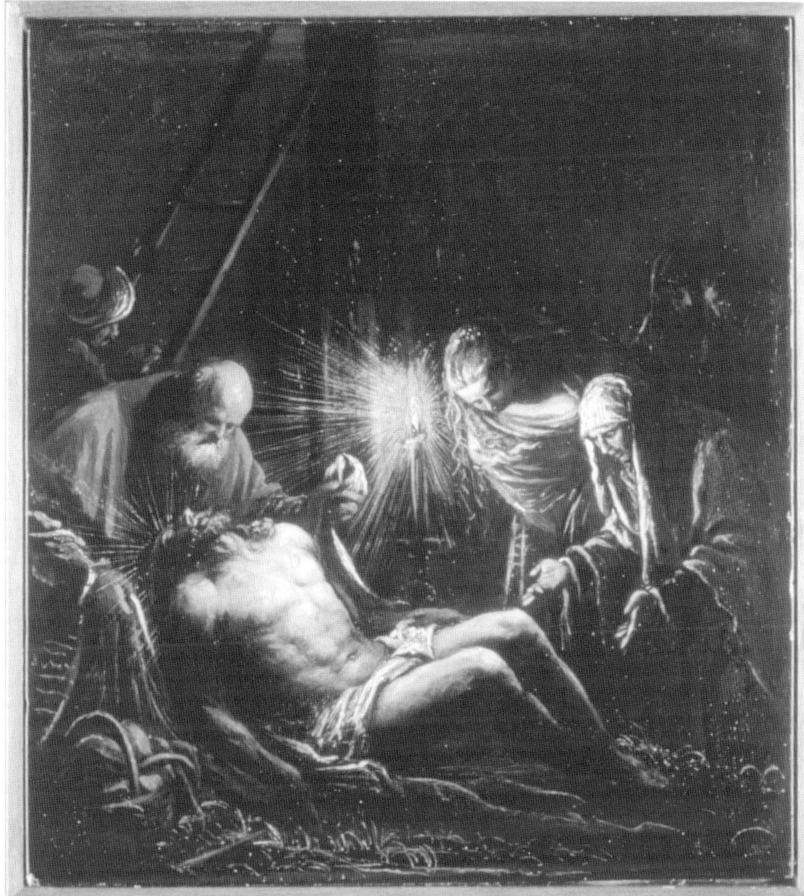

FIG 5.
Lamentation,
c. 1585. London,
Trafalgar Gallery.

As we do so, we come to realize that, first of all, the nocturne is not a picture like any other, differentiated only by lesser illumination. No supplementary lighting could reveal that which appears to be undisclosed in the nocturne. The nocturnes that Bassano's biographers describe as such were actually painted on black stone, a ground that starts dark. Surviving examples include the *Lamentation* (Figure 5).[18] It should be clear from this example that the dark of the nocturne does not obscure something that, better lit, might become visible. That is, the nocturne does not hide things; it conditions viewing, and this is so because the nocturne enables the painter to direct and sustain the beholder's attention towards and in those areas of the pictures that are selectively illuminated. This condition, moreover, valorized Jacopo's celebrated *tocco,* his rapid and localized brushstroke. When we compare Jacopo's painting with his son Gerolamo's diurnal version of *Baptism of Christ* (Figure 6) we note that the originally darker areas of

[18]The *Lamentation* was on view at the Trafalgar Gallery in London in 1998. I thank the gallery personnel for inviting me to see it and for granting me permission to reproduce it.

the picture become amorphous and nearly incomprehensible as a result of Gerolamo's effort to discern what was *not* hidden in the dark in his father's picture.[19]

Thus the nocturne emerges as an aesthetic object that requires from a beholder not a supplement of illumination, but one of imagination: beholding is a critical operation, not an optical one. Once the nocturne is recognized as a problem in aesthetics, light, its agent, can be addressed in terms that are neither astronomical nor symbolic but rather exegetical.

In Bassano's *Baptism of Christ*, the night obscures those elements—the trees, the water of the Jordan River, and the river bank—that traditionally provide the beholder with the identifying circumstances of the event. The truncated tree at the right edge of the

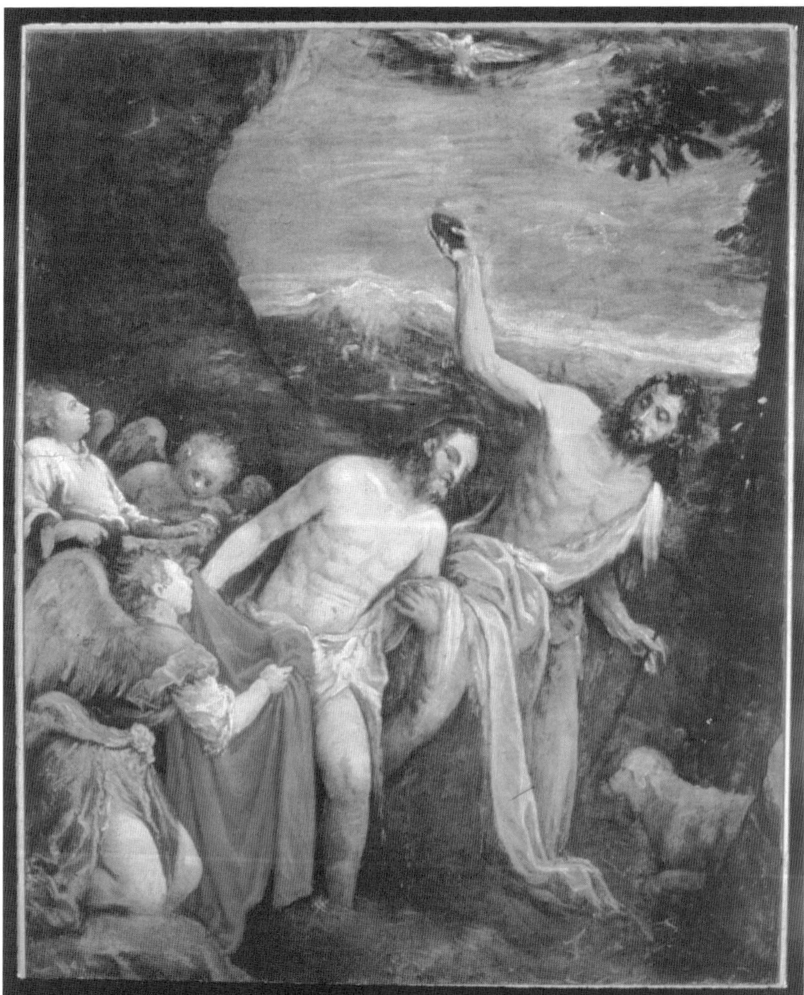

FIG 6. Jacopo Bassano, *The Baptism of Christ, 1592*. New York, Private Collection.

canvas for example, an iconographic attribute of the Baptist, is rendered barely visible by a dash of white paint signalling its profile against the dark background. By undermining the elements on which an iconographic reconstruction of the narrative depends, the darkness detours the beholder's response towards the illuminated bodies of the figures. Specifically, the nocturnal illumination emphasizes the perception that the body of Christ is a suffering body. In Bassano's image Christ carries his body with difficulty: he is pale, unsteady on his legs, out of breath, and dark in the face. His inclining posture represents quite literally the theological notion of submission to God's design that Émile Mâle has characterized as "the voluntary submission of Christ" ["l'abaissement volontaire du Christ"].[20]

Whereas throughout the Renaissance the figure of Christ at his baptism had been consistently represented as hieratic, frontal, and vertical as in Piero's famous picture, in Bassano's painting the figure of Christ has undergone a rotation resulting in a posture that is now semi-frontal and inclined. If we observe carefully and deconstruct, so to speak, the new stance, we will discern a dual force at play: a movement downwards in response to the pressure of light, which irradiates from the dove above, and a lateral thrust initiated by John the Baptist. The bowl *per infusionem* that the Baptist holds between the head of Christ and the radiant dove establishes the vertical axis of descent to which the lateral thrust of ascent operates as a counterpoint. The two forces that determine the instability of the new posture are indicative of Christ's dual attitude: the vertical of humility in accepting baptism, the lateral of submission to God the Father's design. The lateral thrust also emphasizes the Baptist's role in *leading* Christ into the wilderness, and represents the fulfillment of his role as the last prophet of the Old Testament, which Christ's baptism brings to an end. Entrance into the wilderness effectively introduces the story of Christ as a story of his passion. The lateral thrust indicates that Christ has begun his Passion; figuratively he is about to assume the profile of the carrier of the cross. In Bassano's picture it is darkness itself, which the reader of the Gospel knows to be conclusive, that confirms the allusions to the Passion, and acts as the *sign* of the incumbent tragedy of the cross. In summary: both Christ's suffering body and the darkness of the image conspire to

[20]E. Mâle, *L'art réligieux de la fin du Xve siècle, du XVIIe siècle et du XVIIIe siècle* (Paris,1950) 260: "Le Baptême etait donc pour le moyen age un *mystère de grandeur*; le XVIIe siècle en fit un *mystère d'humilité*. Mystiques et theologiens s'accordent sur ce point; ce qu'ils admirent tous, c'est l'abaissement volontaire du Christ...." Citing Marie-Madaleine de' Pazzi, Mâle interprets the kneeling posture of Christ in some seventeenth-century Baptisms of Christ as an indication of his humility towards John the Baptist. It seems proper to say, however, that John the Baptist is the instrument (as a priest) of that humility rather than its recipient.

[21]Cornelio Musso, *Prediche sopra Il Simbolo degli apostoli, Le Due dilettationi di Dio e del Prossimo, Il Sacro Decalogo, & La Pasione di nostro Signor Giesu' Christo, descritta da S. Giovanni Evangelista* (Venice, 1590) 171: "Non sapete che nella primitiva Chiesa, se a San Paolo crediamo, era tanto il desiderio di giovare ai morti, che insino alcuni, quando si battezzavano, si battezzavano prima per se', e poi per l'anime de' loro defunti, (nel modo pero' che San Paolo intende del battesimo in quell luogo) pensando che il battesimo giovasse non solo ai vivi, ma a' morti ancora?" See in particular W. E. Wilson, "The Development of Paul's Doctrine of Dying and Rising again with Christ," *Expository Times* 42 (1930–31): 562–65; J. W. Bally, "Gospel for Mankind: The Death of Christ in the Thinking of Paul," *Interpretation* 7 (1953): 163–74; P. Roulin and G. Carton, "Le Le Bapteme du Christ," *Bible et vie chretienne* 25 (1959): 39–48; R. Schnackenburg, *Baptism in the Thought of St. Paul* (Oxford: Basil Blackwell, 1964) 139–69; R. Tannehill, *Dying and Rising with Christ* (Berlin: Töpelman, 1967); E. Schweizer, "Dying and Rising with Christ," *New Testament Studies* 14 (1967): 1–14; E. Dinkler, "Romer 6, 1–14 und das Verhaltis von Taufe und Rechtfertigung bei Paulus," in *Battesimo e giusizia in Rom. 6 e 8,* ed. L De Lorenzi (Rome: Abbazia S. Paolo fuori le mura, 1974) 83–103; F. Morgan, "Romans 6,5a: United to Death like Christ's," *Ephemerides Theologiae Lovaniensis* 59 (1983): 267–302, offers a survey of major previous interpretations. The possible dependence of Paul's exegesis on the Gospel of Mark is explored by R. Scroggs and K. Groff in "Baptism in Mark: Dying and Rising with Christ," *Journal of Biblical Literature* 92 (1973): 531–48.

[22]In *Lib. Jesu Nave Homelia IV* (GCS Origenes VII, 309), Origene states: "Si enim omnes, qui baptizantur, in morte ipsius baptizantur, mors autem Jesu in crucis exaltione completur, merito unicuique fidelium tunc primum Jesus exaltatur, cum ad mysterium baptismi pervenitur, quia sic et scriptum est quod exultavit illum Deus, et donavit ei nomen, quod est super omne nomen, ut in nomine Jesu genu flectatur coelestium et terrestrium et infernorum."

alert the beholder that certain dimensions of the Baptism, extra-narrative and metaphorical, are present and in need of explanation.

That the regeneration alluded to by baptism was the result of Christ's sacrifice on the cross, and that immersion in baptismal water was a sign of participation (or co-action) in Christ's death was stated by Paul in one of the most controversial lines of the entire New Testament: "Do you know that all of us who have been baptized into Christ were baptized into his death?" (Rom 6:3).[21] This was further clarified by Origen, who considered baptism a sacramental gift that should be conceived of, and accepted, as an anticipatory participation in the sacrifice of the cross.[22] In discussing the Baptism of Christ in the Jordan River, Ambrose notes that after his death on the cross, Christ had descended into Hades. His consequent ascent, the resurrection, was made equivalent to the regeneration that baptism gives the catechumen. Ambrose speaks of baptism as an act of "imitation" of Christ's death, and of the catechumen as being "co-crucified," and in full accordance with Paul, conceives of baptism as the sacrament of the cross.[23]

Returning to Bassano's painting we begin to perceive why darkness, as the *signifier* of the Passion of Christ, is brought into representation: it constitutes the essential circumstance for visualizing Paul's metaphor of baptism as a "likeness of Christ's death." The nocturne operates as an exegetical tool: as the agent of the metaphor, it emancipates the text from its narratival constrictions, it liberates its potentials, it expands, and quite dramatically, its narrative in the direction of the reader. In short, the nocturne offers the text to the reader for appropriation. But what are the circumstances of such existential appropriation of the text? How can the trajectory from event to sacrament, implicit though still locked in the Pauline metaphor, be represented? The observations made with regard to *The Parable of the Sower* apply to *The Baptism of Christ* as well. The painter cannot

[23]"Mortis et sepulturae similitudinem" (*De sacramentic, PL* 2, 23). According to W. Ledwich, "Baptism, Sacrament of the Cross: Looking Behind St. Ambrose," in *The Sacrifice of Praise. Studies on the Themes of Thanksgiving and Redemption in the Central Prayers of the Eucharistic and Baptismal Liturgies in Honour of Arthur Hubert Couratin,* ed. B. D. Spinks (Rome: C.L.C., 1981) 199–211, "We have then two images of baptism: the one in the east sees the pattern of baptism to be the Lord's baptism in the Jordan, and it is celebrated primarily at the Epiphany. The other, the western pattern, sets baptism in the context of Easter celebration. What is striking about the comparison is not, however, the contrast in pattern and images, but the similarity in theological theme. For the cross is at the center of both. Both see baptism as the sacrament whereby men may be delivered from the tyranny of death and this world, and share in Christ's resurrection. St. Ambrose, with his enormously comprehensive mind, superbly intergrates eastern and western liturgical traditions, and shows their theological unity" (210).

visualize a metaphor; he can only make the beholder recognize one. As he aims at making the event in the text the event of the reader, it is liturgy that presents the faithful with the modalities of the exegetical transformation of textual event into sacramental experience. And I should say a few things about liturgy, for it is essential in understanding how the Pauline metaphor running through Bassano's painting can be recognized and experienced by the beholder.

Liturgy provides the reader with a temporal frame. By relativizing and existentializing the text for the reader, it appropriates the temporal condition of the faithful, dictating the forms of that appropriation. Not only does the text acknowledge the time of the reader, it synchronizes his/her daily life with the events and circumstances of the text. Liturgical reading aims at making the text significant for the reader, and for that purpose it relocates, so to speak, the event for the reader. A nocturne, then, is an image whose circumstances are nocturnal either because the event it visualizes occurred at night, or because its celebration is nocturnal. Night may pertain thus both to the event and to its celebration, which explains why an image like Bassano's *Baptism of Christ* is nocturnal even though the event it visualizes is not.

In the sixteenth century it was customary to baptize at night, on Easter Vigil night, that is, between the Death and the Resurrection of Christ.[24] The choice of that particular night underlined the transitional quality of the sacrament as the end of the old life and the beginning of the new one bestowed on the celebrant by Christ's sacrifice.[25] The Pauline metaphor of baptism as "a likeness of Christ's death" offered the rationale for the nocturnal celebration of baptism, for its liturgical representation as a nocturnal event, which is what Bassano's painting visualizes: the particular reading of a text which, though not nocturnal, is represented as such in liturgy in order to make it significant for the reader.

A beholder familiar with the liturgical practice of baptizing at night—a practice that was discontinued in the 1660s—would experience in Bassano's nocturnal image the vividness and significance of the Pauline metaphor. Bassano's painting reminds the beholder that the analogy between the Baptism of Christ and that of the ordinary

[24]According to E. C. Ratcliff, "The old Syrian Baptismal Tradition and its Resettlement under the Influence of Jerusalem in the Fourth Century," in *Liturgical Studies*, ed. A. C. Couratin and D. H. Trapp (London: S.P.C.K.: 1976) 135–54: St. Cyril of Jerusalem's *Mystological Lectures* mark a reversal to Paul's theology, in which not Jordan but Golgotha was the archetype of baptism. Consequently baptism was not to be considered (or approached as) a "rebirth and womb" (evoking Jordan) but a "burial and tomb" (evoking Golgotha). "What has been done physically in the redemptive events of Christ's passion, death, and burial on the first Easter Eve was done symbolically in the baptismal liturgy on the anniversary of events, and on the very site which had witnessed their occurrence. Sixteen centuries after Cyril delivered his exposition, it is still possible to sense the powerful appeal which the rite, the night, and the site combined to exercise upon imagination of the persons being baptized" (144). The practice of baptizing at Easter Vigil night is recorded in Rahmani, *Testamentum*, PL 17, 141: "Ab initio vesperis baptizandi baptizantur post unam lectionem," St. John Chrisostom, *Homili. In resurrectione Domini*, PL 49, 439b: "Qui heri vesperi baptismate digni habiti sunt," and by St. Cyril, *Mystag. I*, PG 33, 1069: "Opertionem cognoscatis quae in vobis illa baptismatis vespera effecta est."

[25]Lactantius, *De divinarum institutionum*, PL 6, 797–98: "Haec est nox, quae a nobis propter adventum regis ac Dei nostri pervigilio celebratur: cujus noctis duplex est ratio, quod in ea et vitamtum recepit, cum passus est, et postea regnum orbis terrae recepturus est." Onuphrij Panvinij Veronen, *De baptismate paschali et origine ac ritu consecrandi Agnos liber* (Rome, 1656) 19: "Tempus autem Baptizandi erat Pascha potisimum, & Pentecoste cum sex diebus sequentibus" and "Oratio Sabbati Sancti Deus cuius antiqua mirabilia etaim nostris saeculis coruscare sentimus, dum quo uni populo, & a persequatione Aegyptiaca liberando, dexterae tuaepotentia contulisti, id in salutem gentium, per aquam regenerationis operaris" (28). On the use of lamps in the baptismal liturgy, see D. R. Dendy, *The Use of Lights in Christian Worship* (London: S.P.C.K., 1959) 120–27; E. C. Whitaker, *Documents of the Baptismal Liturgy* (London: 1960); idem, *The Baptismal Liturgy* (London: Faith Press, 1965) 52–59.

[26]Agostino Valier, like St. Charles Borromeo, belonged to that generation of prelates that brought to the Council of Trent ideas first elaborated in a spirit of reconciliation by Gasparo Contarini and Reginald Pole. His doctrinal and political stance lacked their vision, as it lacked Borromeo's militant zeal, though it possessed a pointed pedagogic clarity. On Valier see B. Navagerio, *Augustini Valerii patrici veneti S. R. E. Cardinalis, Episcopi Veronensis…vita* (Padua, 1719); A. Ventura, "Vita Augustini Valerii," in vol. 25 of *Raccolta di opuscoli scientifici e filologici*, ed. A. Calogerà (Venice, 1741) 49–115; L. Valpolicelli, *Il pensiero pedagogico della Controriforma* (Florence, 1960); G. Mantese, "Il card. Agostino Valier e l'origine delle Compagnie della Carità," *Archivo Veneto* 101 (1970): 5–26; G. Santinello, *Politica e filosofia alla Scuola di Rialto: Agostino Valier* (Venice: Centro Tedesco di Studi Veneziani, 1983); F. Segala, "Introduzione," in A. Valier, *Vita di Carlo Borromeo card. di S. Prassede arcivescovo di Milano* (1586) (Verona, 1988) 13–33; A. L. Puliafito, "Filosofia aristotelica e modi dell'apprendimento. Un intervento di Agostino Valier su 'Qua ratione versandum sit in Aristotele,'" *Rinascimento* 30 (1990): 153–72; A. Niero, *Valier*, in vol. 16 of *Dictonnaire de Spiriualité*, (Paris: G. Beauchesne, 1992) 183–90. Valier's political views, his admiration of Paruta, and the very special relationship he entertained with the Venetian Signoria emerge from his *Lettere ai dogi di Venezia*, published in Verona in 1862, and in. *Relazioni dei Rettori veneti in Terraferma. IX: Podesteria e Capitaniato di Verona*, ed. A. Tagliaferri (Milan, 1977). Bishop of Verona, Valier had visited extensively the dioceses of the Veneto, and his manual was in fact designed to Christianize the population of the Terraferma. On Valier's visitation of the dioceses of Vicenza, see C. Fanton, *La riforma tridentina a Vicenza nella seconda metà del sec. XVI* (Vicenza, 1941); G. Mantese, *Memorie storiche della Chiesa vicentina*, vol. 3 (Vicenza: Scuola tip. Istituto S. Gaetano, 1958) 319–54; idem, "Nota d'archivo sull'attuazione dei decreti tridentini a Vicenza," *Rivista di storia della Chiesa in Italia* 13 (1959): 102–106; and for the other dioceses, F. Masotto, *Agostino Valier vescovo di Verona e la sua attuazione dei decreti del Concilio di Trento* (Milan: Tesi di Laurea, Università Cattolica, 1936–1937); M. M. Tacchella, *Il cardinale Agostino Valier e la riforma tridentina nella diocesi di Trieste* (Udine: Arti grafiche friulane, 1974); G. Castioni, *La situazione religiosa a Chioggia nella visita apostolica del Valier del 1580 e la construzione spirituale* (Rome, 1972).

celebrant lies not merely in the ritual but in the metaphorical co-experience of Christ's passion, a "likeness of his death."

I have claimed that what is historical about painting as visual exegesis is the specific quality of attention to the text that motivates its visualization. My argument would not be complete, then, without reference, however sketchy, to the historical circumstances of Jacopo Bassano's readings. *The Parable of the Sower* and *The Baptism of Christ* visualize scriptural readings promoted in the course of what historians have called the Christianization of the Venetan countryside. Bassano's images were in fact specific instruments of that project whose executor was Agostino Valier,[26] disciple and biographer of Carlo Borromeo, bishop of Verona, visitor to the Venetan dioceses, and secretary at the Council of Trent.[27] In a methodological volume, *Rhetorica Ecclesiastica*, published in 1570, Valier summarized the precepts of that campaign.[28] In Chapter XLV, *Quo modo impellendi sint ruri habitantes* [On how to address the rural populations], Valier specifically advocated the use of parables as the ideal form of instruction for rural populations on the ground of the efficacy of agrarian metaphors. As for the massive campaign of baptizing in the Veneto, his instructions informed the clergy and the laity that administration of baptism on Easter Vigil night was to be considered the culmination not only of the holy week but of the entire liturgical year.

[27]On Christian rhetoric after the Council of Trent, see F. Zanotto, *Storia della sacra eloquenza* (Modena: Tip. Pontifica ed Arcivescovile, 1899); E. Santini, *L'elonquenza italiana dal concilio tridentino ai nostri giorni. I. Gli oratori sacri* (Milan: R. Sandron, 1923); E. Ortiguez, "Écritures et traditiones apostoliques ou Concile de Trente," *Recherches de science religieuse* 37 (1949): 271–99; R. Rusconi, *Predicazione e vita religiosa nella società italiana, da Carlomagno alla Controriforma* (Turin: Loescher, 1981); idem, *Predicatori e predicazione (secoli IX-XVIII)* in *Storia d'Italia Einaudi. Annali 4, Intellettuali e potere* (Turin: Giulio Einaudi, 1981) 951–1035.

[28]A. Valier, *Rhetorica ecclesiastica* (Verona: Apud Sebastianum & Ioannem à Donis, 1570). Valier's ideas reflected the experience of reform of the Veronese dioceses conceived and conducted by G. M. Ghiberti within the context of what later came to be called Catholic Reform. On Giberti's program of reform of the dioceses of Verona, see the studies by A. Prosperi, "Note in margine ad un opuscolo di Gian Matteo Giberti," *Critica storica* 4 (1965): 367–402; idem, "Di alcuni testi per il clero nell'Italia del primo Cinquecento," *Critica storica* 7 (1968): 137–68; idem, *Tra evangelismo e controriforma. G. M. Giberti (1495–1543)* (Rome: Edizioni di storia letteratura, 1969); idem, "La figura del vescovo tra Quattrocento e Cinquecento," in *Storica d'Italia-Annali 9* (Turin: Giulio Einaudi, 1986) 216–62; idem, "Le visite pastorali del Giberti," in *Riforma pretridentina della diocesi di Verona. Le visite pastorali di Gian Matteo Giberti*, ed. A. Fasani (Verona: Instituto per le ricerche di storia sociale e di storia religiosa, 1989); and O. Viviani, "Note su G. M. Giberti e i primi capitoli della 'Societa Caritatis,'" *Atti e Memorie dell'Accademia de Agricoltura, Scienze e Lettere de Verona* 127 (1950–1951): 133–66; H. Jedin, *Il tipo ideale de vescovo secondo la riforma cattolica* (Brescia: Morcelliana, 1950); A. Grazioli, *Gian Matteo Giberti, vescovo di Verona, precursore della riforma del Concilio di Trento* (Verona: Stamperia Valdonega, 1955); P. C. Brownell, "La figura di committente del vescovo Gianmatteo Giberti," in *Veronese e Verona*, ed. S. Marinelli (Verona: Il museo; Distribuzione, Valdonega, 1988) 53–83; Bibliotexa Capitalare di Verona, *Gian Matteo Giberti* (Verona: Stamperia Valdonega, 1989).

9.

What Is Christian about Christian Art?

John W. Cook

President Emeritus, The Henry Luce Foundation, Inc.

INTRODUCTION

Having taught the history of the visual arts in the Christian tradition for twenty-five years, there is at least one approach to the question, "What is Christian about Christian art" that deserves to be answered. It seems timely, at the beginning of the twenty-first century to pose this question for at least two reasons. First, the subject matter that is the evidence at hand needs to be looked at seriously as religious information by the historians of Christianity and by the historians of art. Second, the Christian religious climate, in the United States at least, tends to need certainty and security. In the face of an increasing pluralism of religions in this country and a pervasive globalization for culture generally, dominant Christian forces in this society have drifted toward fundamentalism and a kind of religious protectionism. This essay addresses its topic in order to show that the Christian tradition has taken many forms through the centuries, and each has produced art forms of great strength, integrity, and insight.

Over the years, Christianity has produced a material culture that, while being largely ignored today, is full of encouraging surprises that call for our devoted attention.

The origins of Christian art can be traced to a slow process and a set of carefully selected dominant images. The process of an emerging Christian art lies somewhere between a natural human activity know as art making and the convictions of the earliest Christian communities investing their beliefs in material cultural forms. Those early years indicate a certain reluctance to trust the forms of material culture to carry the weight or impact of Christian beliefs and practices, and they indicate a tendency to rely on symbols to carry exclusive messages between members of the early Christian communities. There is at the same time a trial and error period as a vocabulary of forms emerges and tentatively establishes a secure set of references. Those early symbols, figures, and narrative scenes give exciting evidences of a sect seeking adequate visual forms to meet its own needs. The early Christian sects borrowed images from their cultural context, and that early trial and error period reaches from the awkward beginnings of Christian imagery throughout the so-called "pre-Constantinian" period of art in the West.

The evidence from the pre-Constantinian period shows both the hesitancy and aggressiveness of Christianity to give form to its scriptures, practices and beliefs. Our first answer to the question "What is Christian about Christian Art?" must take into account that period of early struggle to find and adopt the cultural forms that were adapted to the needs of the early believers. Consider, for instance, a sarcophagus fragment from Rome dating from the third century.

THE SARCOPHAGUS

Rather than a clear narrative scene made up of figures relating a story with stable sculptural maturity, it records a collection of individual scenes that appear to tell different stories, but they, nevertheless relate specifically to Christian beliefs and practices. The compositions naturally take on the art forms of the period while they simultaneously maintain a sense of selectivity that reflects a thoughtful community embodying its priorities in figural compositions for specific purposes.

The point is illustrated in a series of scenes that are presented in low-relief carvings across the front of a sarcophagus. The sarcophagus (Figure 1), dated to be about A.D. 270, is identified as being from the church of Santa Maria Antiqua at Rome. The scenes across the front are identified, left to right, as Jonah reclining under the arbor, a female figure standing in the orans position, hands raised in a posture of prayer, a seated male figure reading from a scroll, a good shepherd figure with a horned goat on his shoulders, and a baptism scene in which an older bearded male figure baptizes a child-like figure as a dove, representing the spirit, descends.

This accumulation of figures and scenes does not convey a continuous story. Rather, they symbolize resurrection, prayer, study, benevolence, and baptism. While each of these types of figures can be found in earlier, non-Christian compositions, they appear here together as Christian imagery in funerary art that relates the believer(s) who was buried in this sarcophagus with the biblical witness, especially the life of Jesus: his baptism, ministry, and resurrection. Following the Roman cultural practice of decorating sarcophagi with images of the character and values of the ones to be buried, this piece characterizes the dead as being at one with the risen Lord, Jesus.

It may be that, for this sarcophagus specifically, a man and wife were buried together. Note the blank faces of the female and male figures at the center of the composition. They may have originally

FIG 1.
Roman Sarcophagus,
C. 270 C.E. Marble,
low relief carving
Santa Maria Antiqua,
Rome, Italy

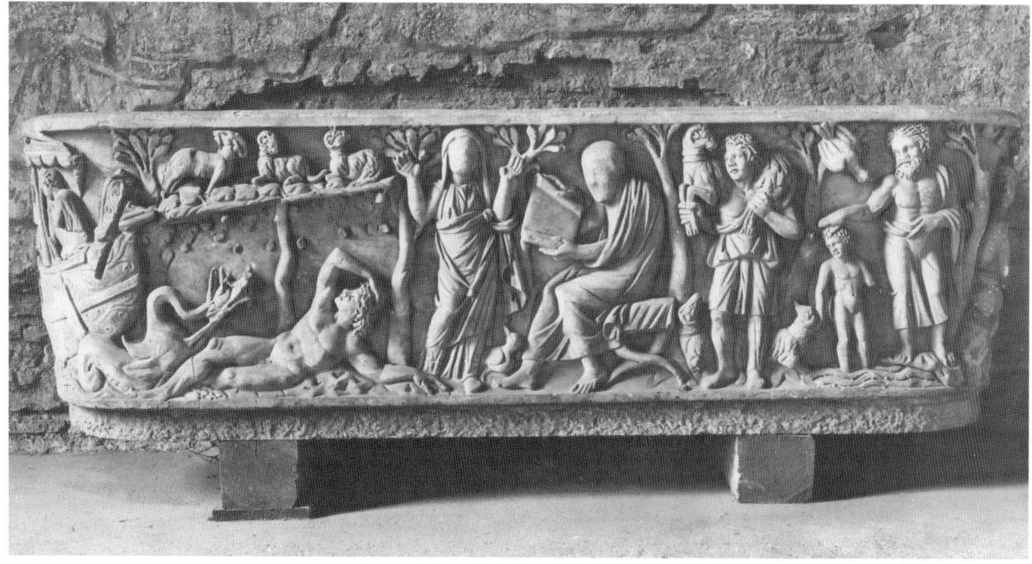

been filled in with wax to create a portrait-likeness. If so, those details have been lost over time. Or it may be that this sarcophagus was never finished, therefore the faces were left blank. In any case, the Christian nature of the piece is preserved.

Having identified the way the figures on the sarcophagus seem to have worked for the early Christian community that created them, it is important to note that, for the last century at least, art historians have traditionally treated this material as unimportant, ugly, and immature. The concentration by art historians, when it does appear, has been primarily on style, thereby missing the functional significance of this work and works similar to it.

It is also the case that historians of the Christian tradition have ignored the evidence provided in the material culture of the early Church. For the most part the art of the early Church is ignored by church historians even though, when examined carefully, it (the art) can be seen as an essential part of the Church's religious vocabulary. It seems that today the academic study of the arts and religion, in this case the Christian religion, ignores the traditional and transitional vocabularies of artistic forms that belong to religious inquiry.

What is Christian about the work of art, the low relief sculpture above, is precisely the identification in funerary art of the believer seen following in the example of the liberator or redeemer who set the norms of behavior. To put it another way, buried in the sarcophagus, were early Church members whose iconography shows that they, in their religious practice, were to be identified with Christianity's leader. This artistic example makes another point. The example emphasizes the identification of the individuals as those who have followed the examples of the leader and are to be identified with him.

Such an emphasis on personal identity was slowly changed as the tradition turned its corporate attention to establishing itself according to a consolidated scripture, an organized leadership, and growing uniformity of practice.

After the "pre-Constatinian" phase of development occurred in the arts, the so-called "Early Christian Art" as defined by art historians evolved into a highly sophisticated language of power over political deities and rulers. Whereas the earliest forms present an art of believers who followed the examples and teachings of their divine leader, it is at the turn of the fourth through the fifth and sixth centuries that a political dimension shows up in the material culture of Christianity. The leader who was at one with the follower in the earlier period becomes one above all, a divine, heavenly ruler who stands at the pinnacle of a hierarchy that includes priests, princes, kings, rulers, and emperors. In the iconography of the later years of the so-called "Early Christian Art" period, Jesus Christ as miracle worker, dispenser of justice, ruler of all, above emperors, and a hierarchy of angels, resides equal to God and is equated with God.

It seems obvious from an early twenty-first century perspective that the art of the early Church should find it necessary to compete with earthly powers and place its leader above all leaders as reigning eternally over all that is and ever shall be.

THE APSE OF SAN VITALE AT RAVENNA, ITALY

Look for instance at the manner in which such a complex ideology was presented in the mosaic art of San Vitale at Ravenna, Italy (Figure 2) in the middle of the sixth century. A political theology, a liturgical theology, and a metaphysical theology are all expressed in the complicated program of that mosaic decoration. The compositions envelop the Eucharistic space, that is, the stage for the ongoing enactment of the liturgical action that pulled the entire decorative program into the act of worship. The liturgical action gave the iconography of the mosaic composition its meaning.

The focal point is the reigning, young-beardless, Adonis-type Jesus who sits above the heavens, enthroned on the universe as it was conceived in the sixth century. All the players, and their actions are acted out at his feet, down to the floor of the apse where clergy sat and out to the imagery beyond. Emperor and Empress, court, church officials, the military, believers, and servers are under the command and rule of the one above all others, Jesus the Reigning Lord. The scene in which the figure of Jesus is enthroned on the globe of the universe, includes two angels to his right and left who present St. Vitalis on the left, receiving a crown of victory, and the Bishop Ecclesius on the right, presenting a model of the church building in which the composition appears. This example of sixth century iconography suggests that the subjugation of all earthly powers are under one rule, one ruler, therefore one God who reigns eternally above all. The rectangular panes below the Christ figure and to the left and right of the three central windows present the Emperor Justinian on the left as a presenter in the liturgy, and the Empress Theodora on the right entering the church with ladies of the court. The entire chamber that provides the place for the altar is covered with a total iconographic program that houses the liturgical action. This discussion has selected out of that, the program,

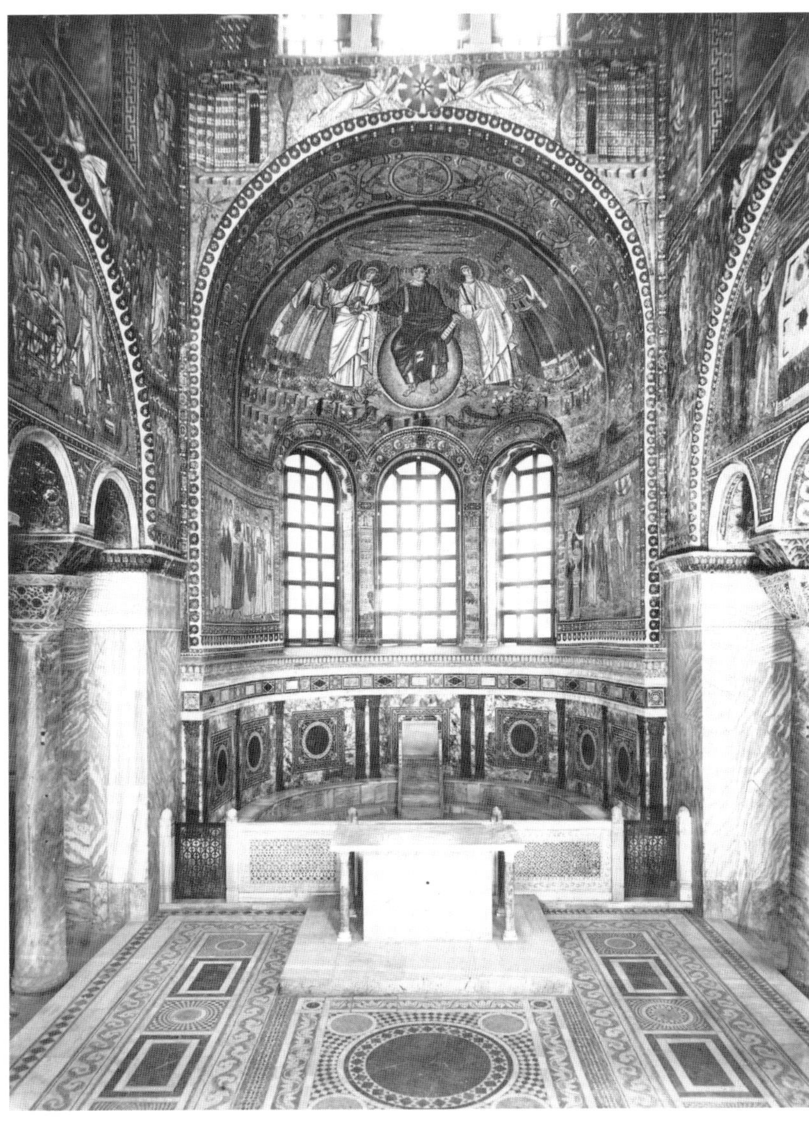

FIG 2.
Mosaic décor of the Sanctuary of The Church of San Vitale at Ravenna, Italy, C. 560 C.E.

the apse, and area for clergy in order to emphasize the importance of the hierarchy over which is the central figure of Jesus.

What is Christian about Christian Art in this example is the Christology that is implied in the composition. It served a distinctly different purpose than that served by the earlier example discussed in this essay. Both examples are Christian but they are different from each other in emphasis and reflect the concerns of the time.

THE ROETTGEN MADONNA

If we move in chronological order to another example of Christian art, the shift that takes place in impact and purpose discloses another feature of Christian sensibilities expressed in a material cultural form.

The *Roettgen Madonna* (Figure 3) is similar in many ways to images that were very popular in the Christian Church of the late Romanesque period. The "pieta" theme was a dominant theme that captured the imagination of the church in the middle ages. It was a cultural form that presented a significant shift away from the vocabulary of hierarchies, rulers, and heavenly powers. The pieta forms emerged from a contemplative set of practices first carried out in the Eastern part of the church, the Byzantine tradition of Christianity that took strong hold in the liturgical life of the churches in the middle ages. The major shift was to a personal piety enriched by empathetic responses to the mother of Jesus holding a mutilated dead son across her lap. The pieta composition enjoyed a vast proliferation across the Christian churches of Eastern Europe and the West and indicate the strong pietistic strain that marked Christianity at that period. Human suffering, deep feelings of sorrow and empathetic responses are reflected back into the medieval Christian community by the evidence of such popular figures.

For instance, the *Roettgen Pieta* is a relatively small sculptural composition that would have been venerated by the faithful in a chapel setting as part of the liturgical life of the church. Note that the narrative moment caught in a "pieta" composition is not scriptural. That is to say that the composition is not a literal moment from the New Testament narrative. It does consist of two important figures of the

Christian tradition that are posed in such a manner as to elicit strong emotional responses to the suffering mother and her dead adult son.

The treatment of the wounds on the body of the Jesus figure are exaggerated and grotesque, as is the stark angularity of the body. At the time in which this sculpture was used in the liturgy, the elements of the Eucharist, the bread and wine were taken from the body of the figure and consumed by the priest on behalf of the mournful worshippers.

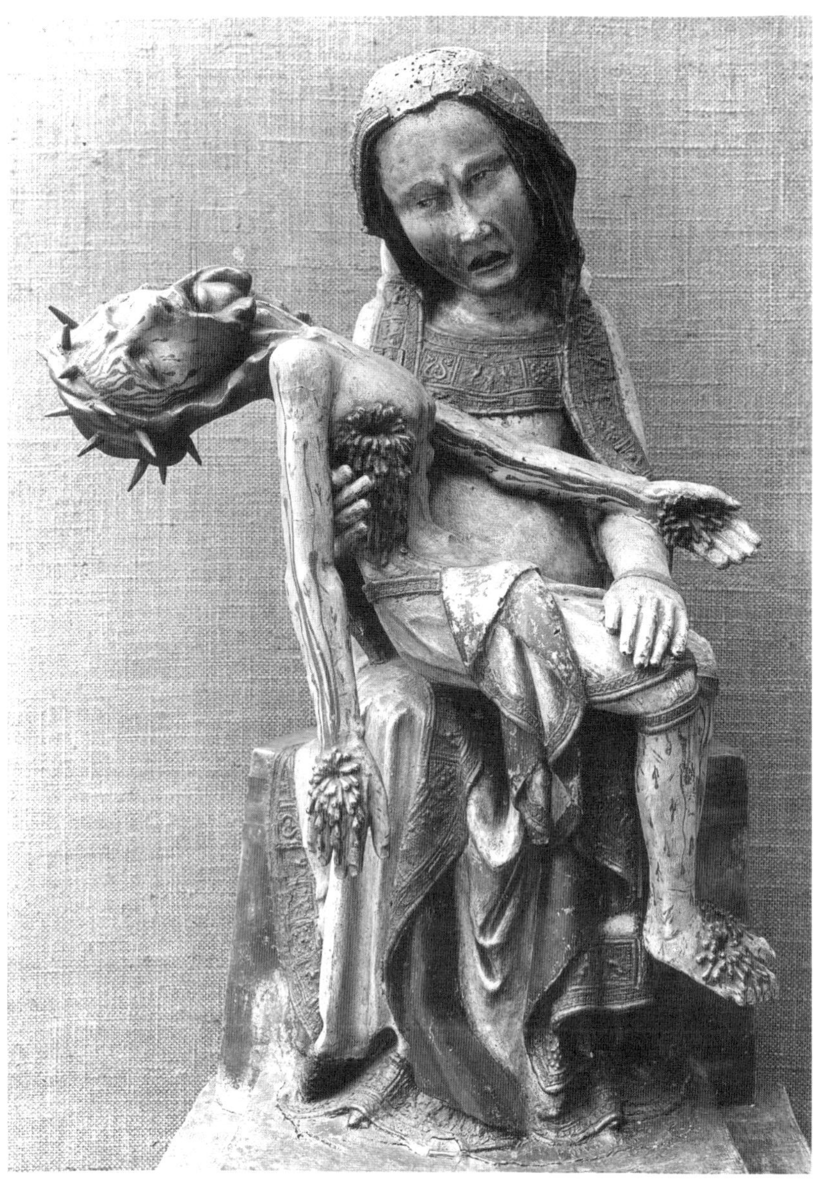

FIG 3.
Wooden Sculpture
The Roettgen Pieta
Reinisches
Landesmuseum
Bonn, Germany,
early 14th Century

  Interpreting Christian Art

The Christian nature and intent of this art is self-explanatory and consistent with the beliefs and actions of the Christian community at the time it was created. Although the art emphasizes an aspect of Christianity that has not been seen in the earlier examples of low-relief sculpture of a sarcophagus or the mosaic program of a Ravenna sanctuary, the Roettgen pieta was authentically Christian.

A BYZANTINE ICON

Perhaps, maybe just perhaps, the Eastern Christian formulation of art forms for worship purposes will prove to be the most Christian of any Christian art ever created. The Byzantine tradition of Christianity is practiced on a worldwide scale today. However, the theology of that tradition has remained steadfast and its art forms have remained true to roots that are deep in Eastern Christian history. A good way to illustrate this intensely Christian form of art is to look carefully at a "Pantocrator" image of Jesus (Figure 4) from the Byzantine tradition.

This panel painting appears on wood, painted in tempera, and follows the compositional guidelines that were established early in the Byzantine tradition. Theologically this is a picture of the consubstantiality of the Father and the Son. The figure type is a portrait presentation from the waist up and always presented in a frontal pose with the right hand lifted in a gesture of benediction and the left hand holding an open book of scripture. Such a figure is found in many media: including ivory, mosaic, sculpture, inlaid stone, metalwork and painting. Since these works are blessed by the clergy and are created by artists who have been commissioned to do this "spiritual" work, it is an intentional art that was believed to be as important as the scripture itself, and it functioned for the faithful as the presence of the image it depicted. Therefore, when an image presents a holy personage, the belief is that the presence of that personage is guaranteed. The veneration of these icons has led uninformed observers to think that the tradition worships art, however it is clear from the teachings of that tradition that every form of veneration of the icons is worship of the one imaged rather than the image itself.

The theology behind the creation of the Pantocrator rests in the Christological debates of the eighth and ninth centuries. The arts were

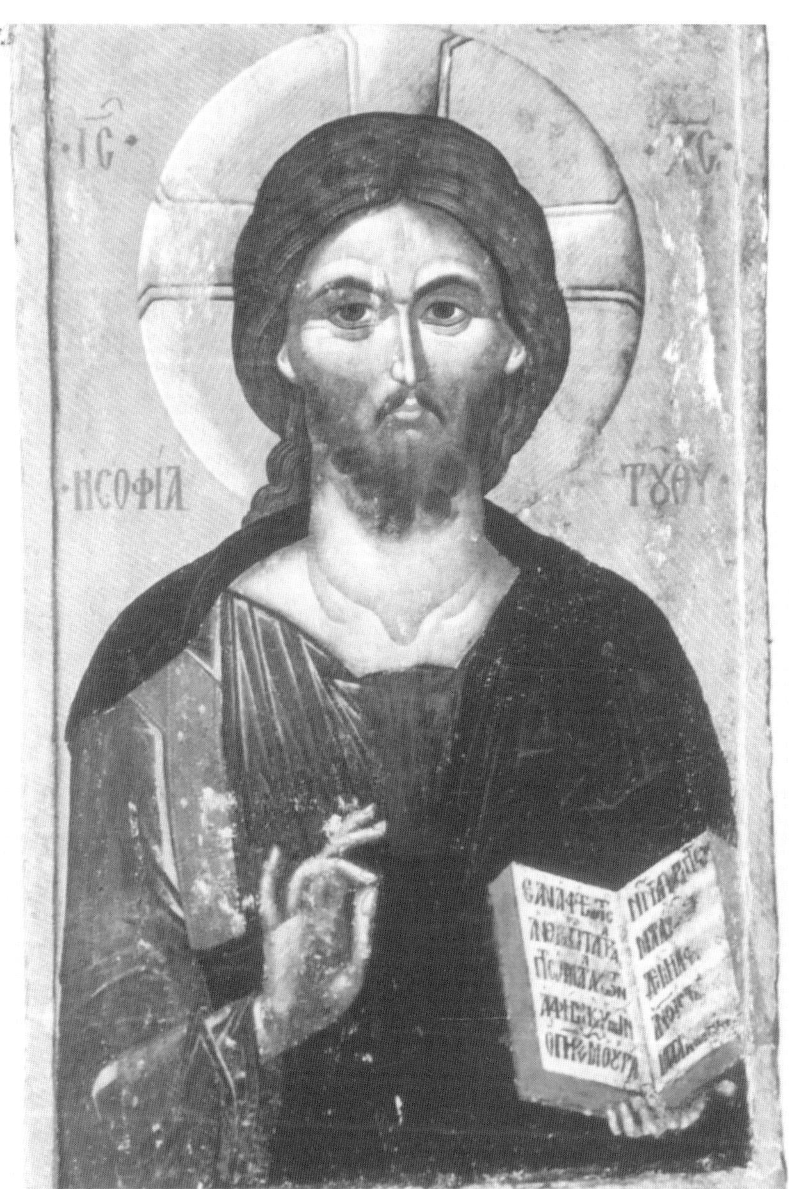

FIG 4.
Panel Painting An Icon of the Pantocrator Athens, Greece, mid-15th Century

raised to the status of scripture, and Jesus was raised to equality with God, the Father. Such a figure was ubiquitous throughout that tradition, even to the present time. Although the compositional demands remain the same, stylistic variations, though subtle, may be discerned in the art. That which remains specifically Christian in this art is the added dimension that believes the real presence of the one imaged accompanies the icon.

The next major shift in Christian art was away from the highly personalized, emotional, and empathetic responses engendered by the proliferation of pieta compositions. The shift was to be in architecture toward a metaphysical, highly symbolic, and abstract spatial concept that gripped the Western world because of its strong appeal to Christian sensibilities. This spatial concept had its roots in the teachings of Augustine and from the early fourth century had evolved by the twelfth century to the point that a theory of proportions became guidelines for architecture. Not until the end of the twelfth century did there appear to be enough conceptual clarity as well as physical know-how (technological sophistication) to achieve a physical space that could be understood to have the status of "the kingdom of God on earth." Three factors had to emerge in concert to achieve the ideal Gothic cathedral. One was the erection and stability of a stone structure that displayed "perfect proportions" in its physical manifestation. The second factor that complimented the structural proportions was the painted glass that accompanied and illuminated the space. Known today as "stained glass" its proliferation was encouraged initially by the belief that it could illuminate the soul of the worshipper in a mystical fashion. The third factor that was necessary for the proportions and illumination to work was the liturgical action that enlivened the entire composition. For approximately 100 years the Christian tradition found in the Gothic concept and technology an artistic material culture that brought God to earth in specific times and places. Although the forms have been popular enough to make the Gothic style a regular feature in every age's artistic expression, it was that period from the latter half of the twelfth to the latter half of the thirteenth centuries that provided specifically Christian art forms. The Gothic achievement was different from everything that had gone before it.

Reims Cathedral (Figure 5) was begun in the early thirteenth century and completed, for the most part in the late thirteenth. It is an excellent example of an architectural form that underwent strong influences from the immediate past. Yet during construction, it kept undergoing refinements and adaptations as the religious intent and technological advances made improvements possible.

Specific features in the construction of Reims Cathedral illustrate the achievements of the age. The ground plan of the nave illustrates the proportional thinking of the planners. The width of the nave is twice that of the side aisles, thereby a ratio of one to two is set. In the elevation the side aisles are the same height as the clerestory that reaches to the springing of the vaulting at the top of the nave. The gallery is one-third the height of the clerestory. Therefore a ratio of one to three is set in the elevation of the nave walls. There are further

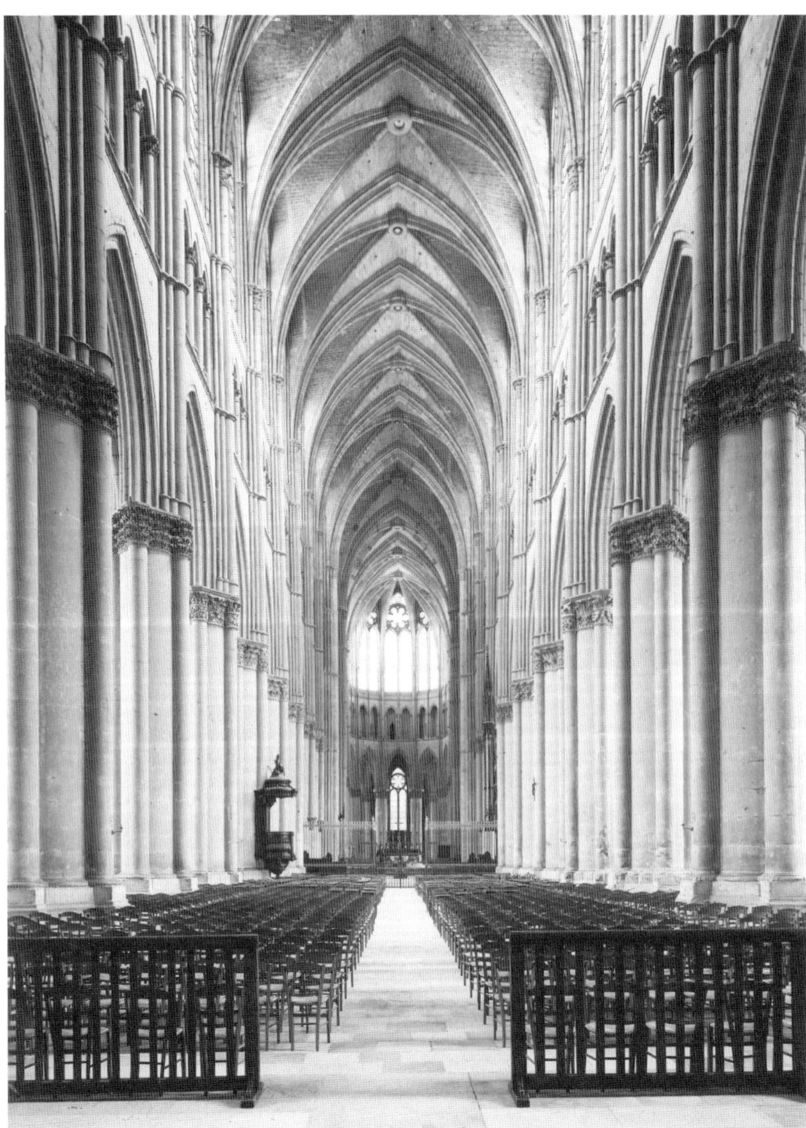

FIG 5.
Interior of Reims
Cathedral Reims,
France, 13th Century

ratios in the details of the structural elements of the building and these were understood to create spatially the perfect harmonies that were suitable for a liturgical activity in which God was made a real presence in the Eucharist. Complimenting these harmonies of proportion were uses of painted glass. Figures in the glass were understood to be illuminated by the sun and thereby shone on the worshippers in ways that illuminated their souls and inspired them. The figures were revivified by the light of God. The mystical illumination revealing the proportions of the structure at the time that God's presence was made real in the Eucharist made the Gothic cathedral the perfect combination of factors that created "the kingdom of God on earth."

But things continued to change. The shift away from the mystical, metaphysical, spatial concept that created the first Gothic cathedral did not signal the death of Christian art. Other priorities emerged that gave yet another perspective that the Christian tradition held in highest esteem.

THE WEIMAR ALTARPIECE

Attention must be paid to the Reformation efforts in the arts to illustrate a theology that emphasized contemporary authority and inspiration. A painting started by Lucas Cranach the Elder and finished by Lucas Cranach the Younger illustrates the point. The Weimar Altarpiece (Figure 6) was completed about 1555. The central panel of the altarpiece is a complex composition that includes imagery from many of the works, engravings, drawings, and paintings that the Cranachs had done previously. They appear here in what looks like a jumble of images representing a number of themes. The composition was easier to understand for Reformation eyes of the sixteenth century because there was such a proliferation of this subject matter at the time.

In sum the painting shows a crucifixion scene where Christ on the cross appears dead. His loincloth billows to the left and right. Blood from his pierced side runs down his torso as well as flows out and down onto the head of the figure of Lucas Cranach the Elder. Such a compositional devise is intended to point out that the artist, in veneration of the crucifixion, is among the valid interpreters of the event.

Cranach stands between the figure of John the Baptist, who points toward the Christ figure, and the figure of Martin Luther who points to an open book in which appear references to scriptures that he preached on in reference to the crucifixion. To the left of the cross is the figure of the resurrected Jesus in a flowing red mantel. He defeats images of death and the devil. At the foot of the cross a lamb stands with a staff on its shoulder. In the middle ground of the painting immediately behind the cross is the figure of Moses presenting the tablets of the law. The elders appear on the right and on the left, while the devil is forcing a male figure toward hellfire. At the back of the painting on the right, an angel in the heavens attracts the shepherds below, and to their right is an encampment of the Hebrew army, in the

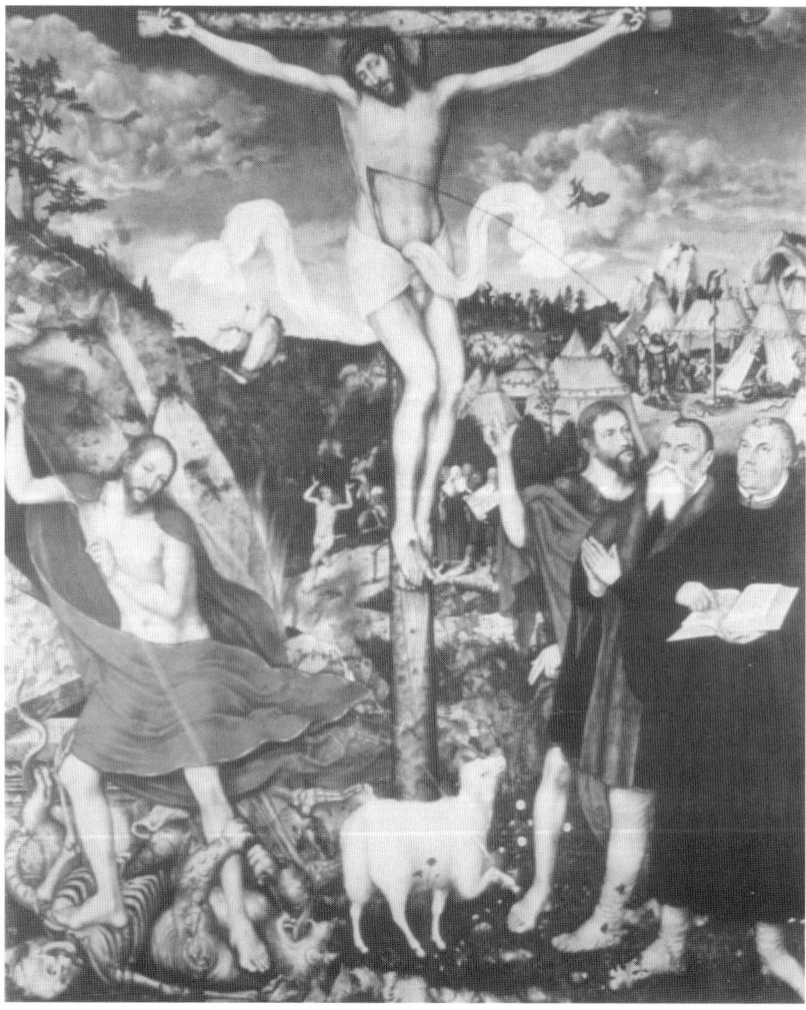

FIG 6.
The Weimar Altarpiece By Lucas Cranach the Elder and Lucas Cranach the Younger Weimar, Germany, C. 1555

midst of which a staff is raised with a serpent on it. All of the images are taken from the Old and New Testaments and refer to the Reformation teaching of Martin Luther concerning the law and the gospel.

That a work of art should make such a theological statement and the role of the artist be so elevated, illustrates a moment in Christian history when the arts and the artist had a strong role to play. Their role was different from that of the icon painter and the icon, but they were, for their time and place, creating a theologically grounded and scripturally specific Christian art.

One of the great counter-Reformation moves was to exploit the possibilities of Baroque and Rococo artistic styles in order to serve the aesthetic purposes of Christian worship. There is a great contrast between the literalism of the Lutheran influence upon the arts and the aestheticism of Baroque and Rococo churches. Eventually both the Roman Catholic and Protestant movements within Western Christianity borrowed from these styles, but one of the most significant achievements of that period is the Wies Church (Figure 7), a Roman Catholic Church built and painted in the middle of the eighteenth century, created by the Zimmermann bothers, Dominicus and Johann Baptist.

Located in Southern Germany, the building is sited in a field away from any urban setting. The interior is a three dimensional environment intended to create, through spatial proportions and decorated surfaces, a world removed from the world. The aesthetic achievement is "out of this world" and appears to be specifically designed as an ethereal environment for a liturgical action that takes place between an earthly and a heavenly realm.

Suspended from a surface of clear windows, white walls, and white columns is a highly gilded treatment of a lectern, a pulpit, near life size statues, and an oval shaped painted ceiling representing a heavenly realm in which the Jesus figure sits on a rainbow. An empty throne appears immediately above the opening in a deep apse in which a gilded high altar with sculpted figures frames a late medieval "Man of Sorrows" image.

Many developments in the arts of the Church influenced the creation of this space. A well-honed liturgical theology lies behind the selection of these art forms. The integration of the elements that went into the assemblage of what we know as the Wies Church was understood at the time to be Christian art and architecture at the height of human capability. What is Christian about this achievement is what its creators understood was their task.

While the Baroque and Rococo styles were serving a large part of the Christian community in one part of the world, there was an

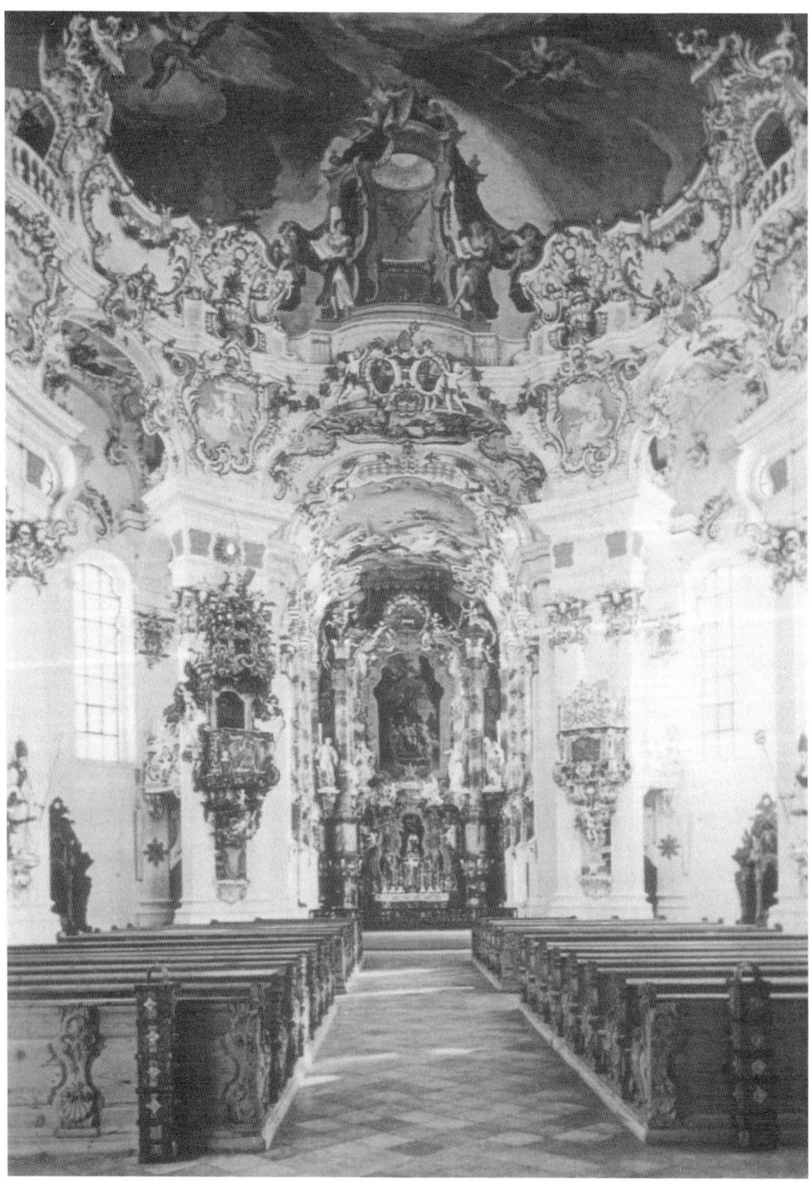

FIG 7.
Interior of the Wies Church South Germany, C. 1750

entirely different Christian art and architecture appearing in the so-called New World.

THE NEW ENGLAND CHURCH

While the United States was evolving into a nation, there was simultaneously an evolution of a building style that was to be one of the most popular forms of church building ever created. Characterized as wooden structures, clad in white siding with a steeple and clear windows, the form of the New England church building reached its

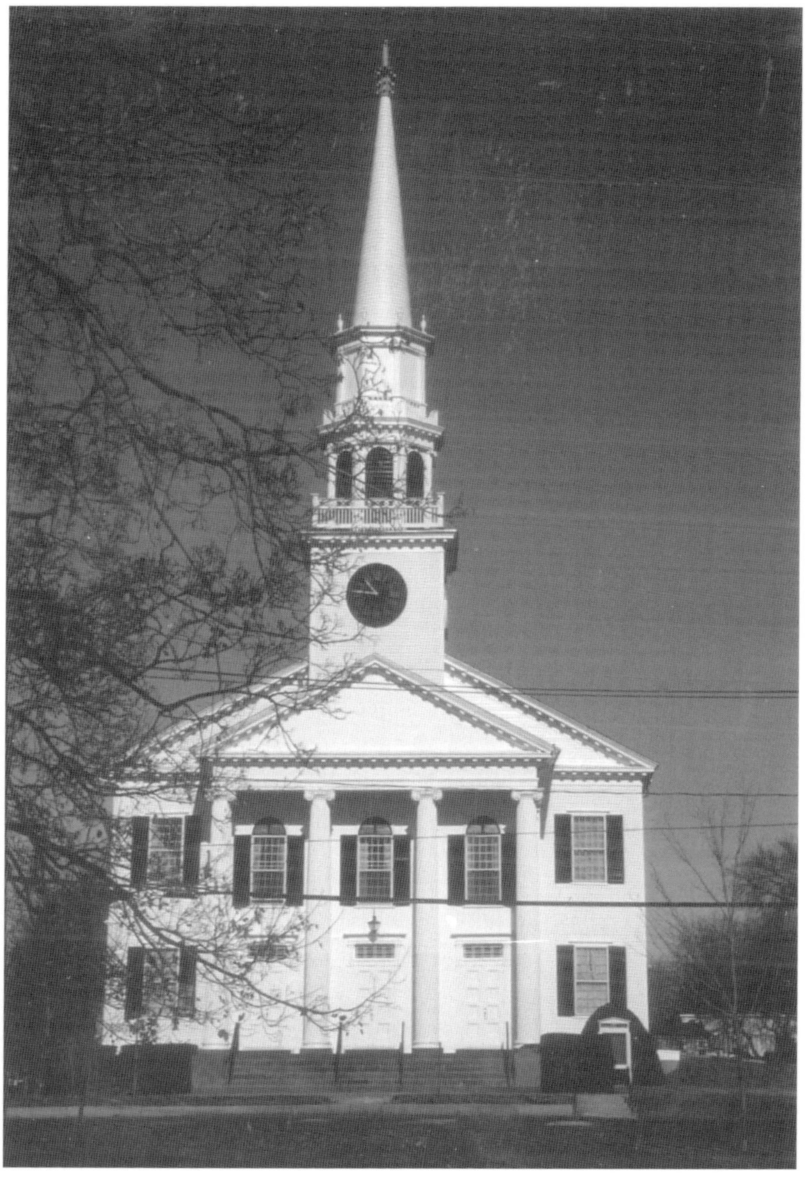

FIG 8.
Exterior of the First
Congregational
Church, Guilford,
Connecticut 1820s

maturity of form by the first third of the nineteenth century. The popularity of that form has subsequently appeared around the world, and a great number of people, when asked to think what a church looks like will mention the New England model.

There are typically three distinct parts to these buildings. First, the house form, expressed on the exterior as a two story white structure, usually houses the congregation. Second, the entrance is usually reached through three doors set within a deep portico created by classical features that recall a temple format. Third, the house and temple façade are capped by the drama of a steeple that is an inverted cone, set on an octagon set upon a square. These three features, variously related in the evolution of this architectural form, establish this style.

Look for instance at the Fist Congregational Church of Guilford, Connecticut (Figure 8). Built in the 1820s, this building combines the architectural features of a house (the nave), a classical temple façade (the entrance), and a tall steeple. Interestingly, the house form borrows heavily from the early New England, secular architecture of the homes that had been built in the "new world" since the seventeenth century. Earlier, the church buildings even had their entrances on the side of these house forms similar to the private houses. The classical motifs were added as the influence of the classical world shaped the studies of history and the Baroque styles were better known. The spires appeared first as attachments to church buildings, and then, later, were integrated into the whole massing of the buildings. Here again, the influence of Baroque forms can be seen as New England spires took on a mature shape.

A two-story elevation on the exterior served an interior that provided for a seated congregation on the floor level, and a balcony on three sides at the second story level. At one end of the interior was an elevated pulpit that provided the focal point of the entire architectural arrangement. The architectural aesthetic on the exterior reflected an integration of forms that respected the early American home architecture, the classical roots of the tradition, plus a European Baroque motif. The interior architectural aesthetic served a liturgy focused on listening to proclamation as its primary value. The New England church building was primarily a listening hall. The elimination of gilded surfaces, elaborate sculptural and painted programs of iconography, stained-glass windows, and fanciful liturgical furnishings left the New England church as a place to hear and to decide how to act. It was, therefore, intended to provide intellectual engagement with religious principles without the distraction of aesthetic elements.

The proliferation of these forms to such a vast extent and the long life of these forms in the history of Christianity and elsewhere witness to their profound impact as religious elements in society. They evolved over a long period of time to become what we now say is an authentic church form. What is Christian about them is their rootedness in culture as a place to hear the word of God.

THE WILLEM DE KOONING ALTARPIECE

The striking shift that has taken place in the Christian tradition in the twentieth century is how directly the authority of the Church and its scripture has been internalized. What I mean by that is the pervasive claim that one's own feeling and knowledge establish an authority that has not been a part of the Christian tradition to such an extent

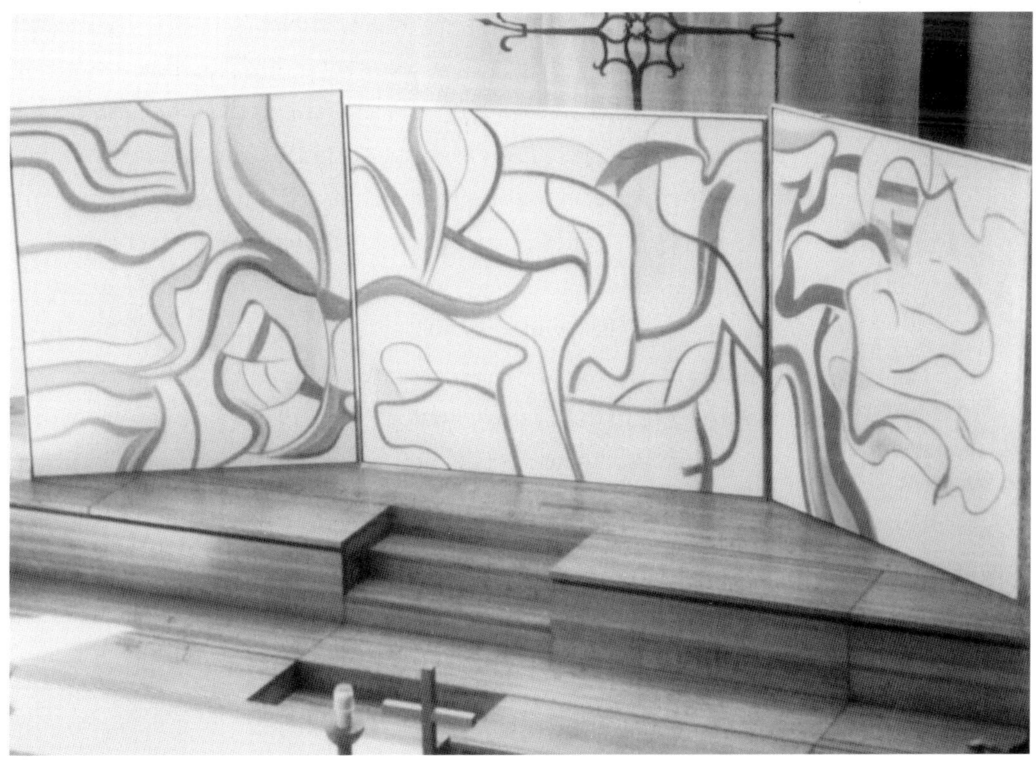

FIG 9.
Willem de Kooning Altarpiece Designed for the St. Peter Lutheran Church, New York, New York 1980

until now. The examples in this paper that illustrate what is Christian about Christian art have, up until this point, been selected because they played a broad, significant role in the age in which they were created. Now, in the twentieth century, there is an individualism to be dealt with that transcends cultural and religious patterns of behavior.

Therefore, I have chosen to conclude with a work of art that illustrates, not where a cultural form of the Christian tradition shaped a people's sensibilities, but, on the contrary, a work of art that was commissioned by a church community but ended up dividing and alienating church members. I refer to a Willem de Kooning altarpiece (Figure 9) that was one Christian's work of art, but the community for which it was intended found itself divided by it.

On the basis of an interview in the New York Times and the church's interest in the contemporary arts, de Kooning was commissioned by a committee of the St. Peters Lutheran Church in New York City to paint an altarpiece. After visiting the building and studying the space, the artist proceeded, in his Long Island studio, to create a triptych. While the three-part composition was a typical form taken directly from Christian precedents, the content was abstract and consistent with de Kooning's style of painting. Associated with the art movement called "abstract expressionism" the artist has created a painting of lines and colors that, according to the artist, celebrate what he wanted to say in art about Christianity. It is a highly personal painting intended for community worship.

When the altarpiece was delivered to the church reactions were varied and strong. Some reactions were positive, many were negative. The negative voices seemed genuinely confused about whether there was meaning in a work that appeared to be made of swirling primary color lines. In the final analysis the supporters of the work seemed to accept the piece because it was by a world-renowned artist. Neither side in the arguments that ensued took the artwork itself seriously.

If looked at from the point of view of the artist (and I was able to confirm the reading of the symbolism of the piece with the artist), it is a symbolic work relying upon the action and interaction of red, blue, and yellow. The composition is to be read from left to right. All colors in the left panel enter the space as a thrust of power, forcefully integrating onto the white plane. Red refers to life, blood, and the earth. Yellow refers to light, and blue seems to be an ethereal, spiritual element. An embryonic core seems to form as the elements integrate. The central panel is more like a dance of interlocking colors that form the focal point of the entire piece. According to the artist the lines of color refer to the essential elements of life moving rhythmically, yet in harmony with one another. The right panel shows a burst of energy in the elements themselves until they dramatically fade away and the wispy blue remains at the end tentatively turning back as though resisting the bare emptiness at the end.

After the death of the artist, the painting was returned to the estate and claimed by the artist's daughter. It remains in the estate and was shown recently in an exhibition of de Kooning's late work at the Museum of Modern Art in New York. It seemed comfortably at home within the context of the artist's late work and in a museum setting. More appropriate than it ever seemed in the sanctuary of the St. Peters Church.

What is Christian about the de Kooning altarpiece lies in the memory and reflection of the artist and became a puzzle, sometimes an alienating puzzle for a congregation. Among other things, this work of art illustrates how radical individuality becomes in itself an art form: a private vision that may or may not be accepted by the public. There are many examples in twentieth-century art of attempts to make the internal visions of the artists acceptable to a community. Within modern Christian traditions there is a basic contradiction between the arts of radical individuality and the corporate realities of worshipping communities. Therefore, this age seems bereft of those broadly accepted Christian art forms that shaped belief and behavior.

CONCLUSION

What is Christian about Christian art is a question that seems to have been answered directly in different ages of the history of the Church. There is no one answer. There is no easy sound bite that displays certitude and unanimity. The arts have always been an irrepressible aspect of Christian belief and practice. Each age has its own material cultural answer to the question. As we enter the twenty-first century, it is inevitable that Christian art making on a global scale will be practiced, and the resolutions of radical individuality will find a way to speak through the arts to believing communities.